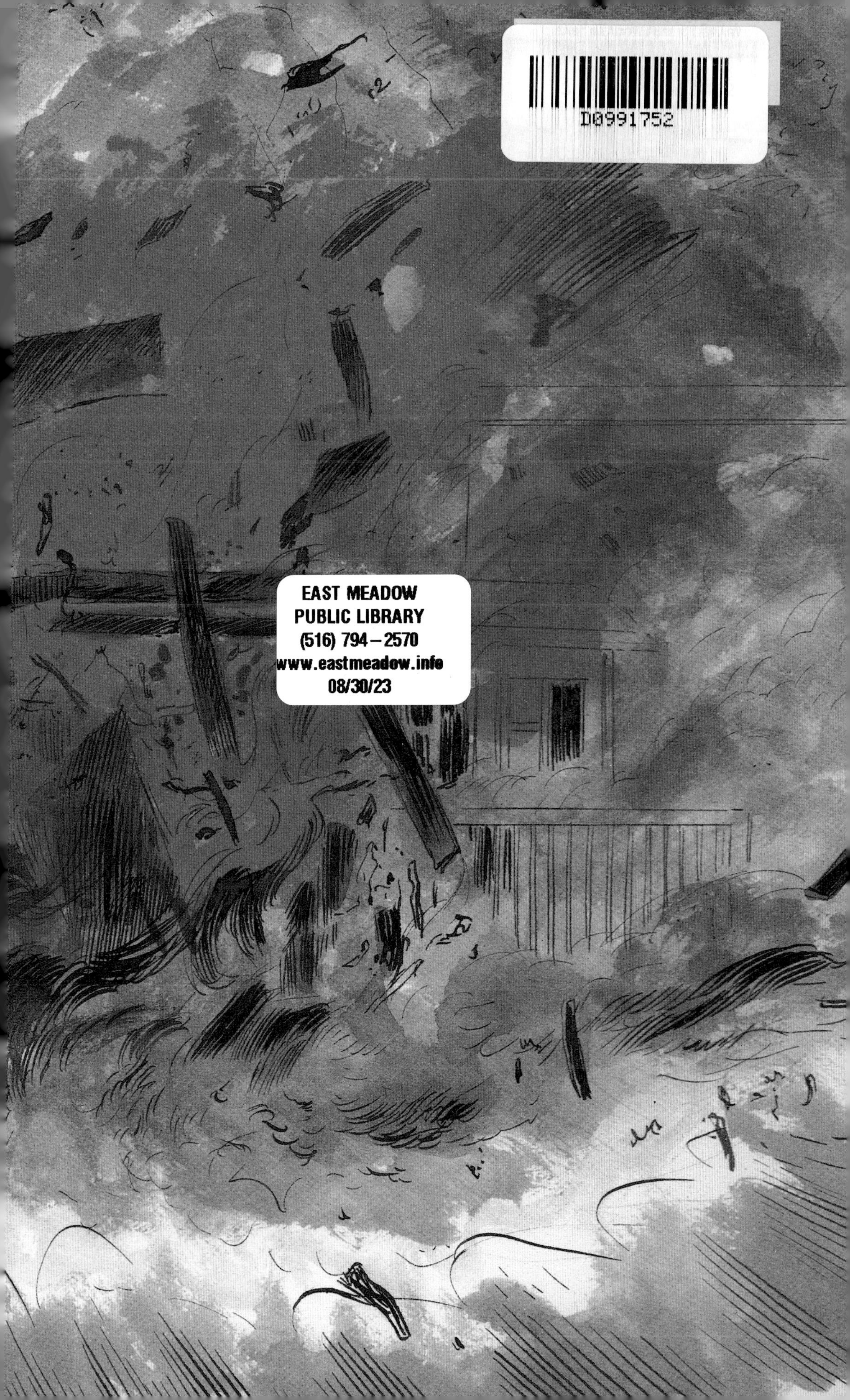

MOTHER NATURE

JAMIE LEE CURTIS
RUSSELL GOLDMAN
KARL STEVENS

GROUP EDITOR
JAKE DEVINE

DESIGNER
DONNA ASKEM

TITAN COMICS

EDITORIAL ASSISTANT
IBRAHEEM KAZI

PUBLICITY & SALES COORDINATOR
ALEXANDRA ICIEK

ASSISTANT EDITOR
CALUM COLLINS

PUBLICITY MANAGER
WILL O'MULLANE

EDITOR
PHOEBE HEDGES

DIGITAL & MARKETING MANAGER
JO TEATHER

SENIOR CREATIVE EDITOR
DAVID LEACH

HEAD OF RIGHTS
JENNY BOYCE

ART DIRECTOR
OZ BROWNE

HEAD OF CREATIVE & BUSINESS DEVELOPMENT
DUNCAN BAIZLEY

PRODUCTION CONTROLLERS
CATERINA FALQUI & KELLY FENLON

PUBLISHING DIRECTORS
RICKY CLAYDON & JOHN DZIEWIATKOWSKI

PRODUCTION MANAGER
JACKIE FLOOK

GROUP OPERATIONS DIRECTOR
ALEX RUTHEN

SALES & CIRCULATION MANAGER
STEVE TOTHILL

EXECUTIVE VICE PRESIDENT
ANDREW SUMNER

MARKETING COORDINATOR
LAUREN NODING

PUBLISHERS
VIVIAN CHEUNG & NICK LANDAU

MOTHER NATURE
Standard Edition: 9781787739130
Direct Market Edition: 9781787741188
Signed Edition: 9781787741607

Published by Titan Comics
A division of Titan Publishing Group Ltd. 144 Southwark St., London. SE1 0UP
Titan Comics is a registered trademark of Titan Publishing Group, Ltd. All rights reserved.

Changing Woman design by Dale Deforest
Diné Bahane by Paul Zolbrod. Copyright © 1984 University of New Mexico Press.
Mother Nature © Blumhouse Productions, LLC

A CIP catalogue record for this title is available from the British Library.
First edition: July 2023

10 9 8 7 6 5 4 3 2 1

Printed in China.

MOTHER NATURE

SCRIPT BY
JAMIE LEE CURTIS &
RUSSELL GOLDMAN

ADAPTED AND ILLUSTRATED BY
KARL STEVENS

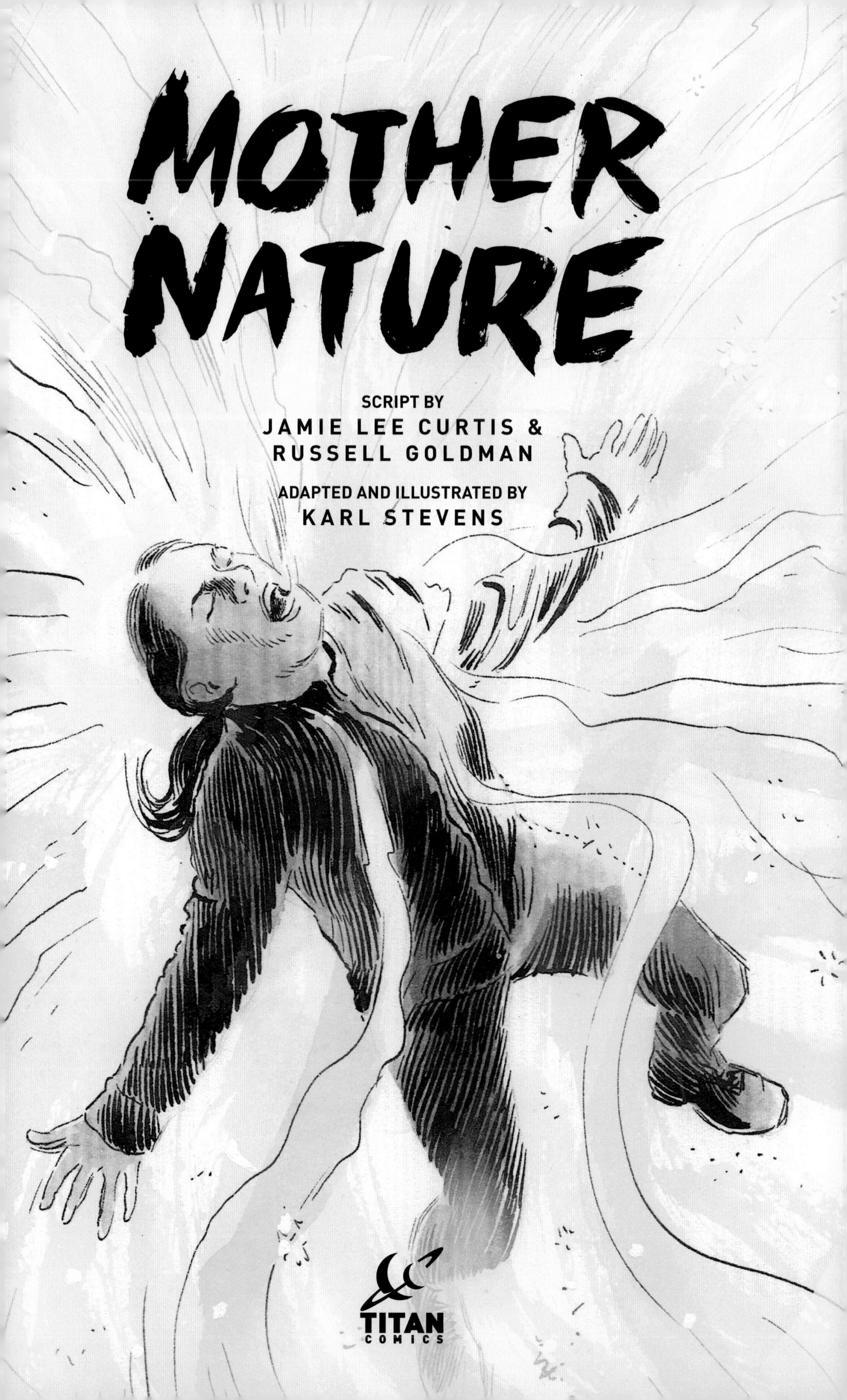

TITAN COMICS

"To every writer, scientist and activist who contributed to or inspired this story. Including: Greta Thunberg, Kendra Pinto, Marc Reisner, Julia Beral, Tom Wagner, Judi Brewer, Rebecca Sobel, Mark Pearson, Aaluk Edwardson, Jeremiah Watchman, and Brian Lee Young."

-Jamie Lee Curtis & Russell Goldman

"Thank you to Alex for her love, patience, and understanding throughout the production of this book."

-Karl Stevens

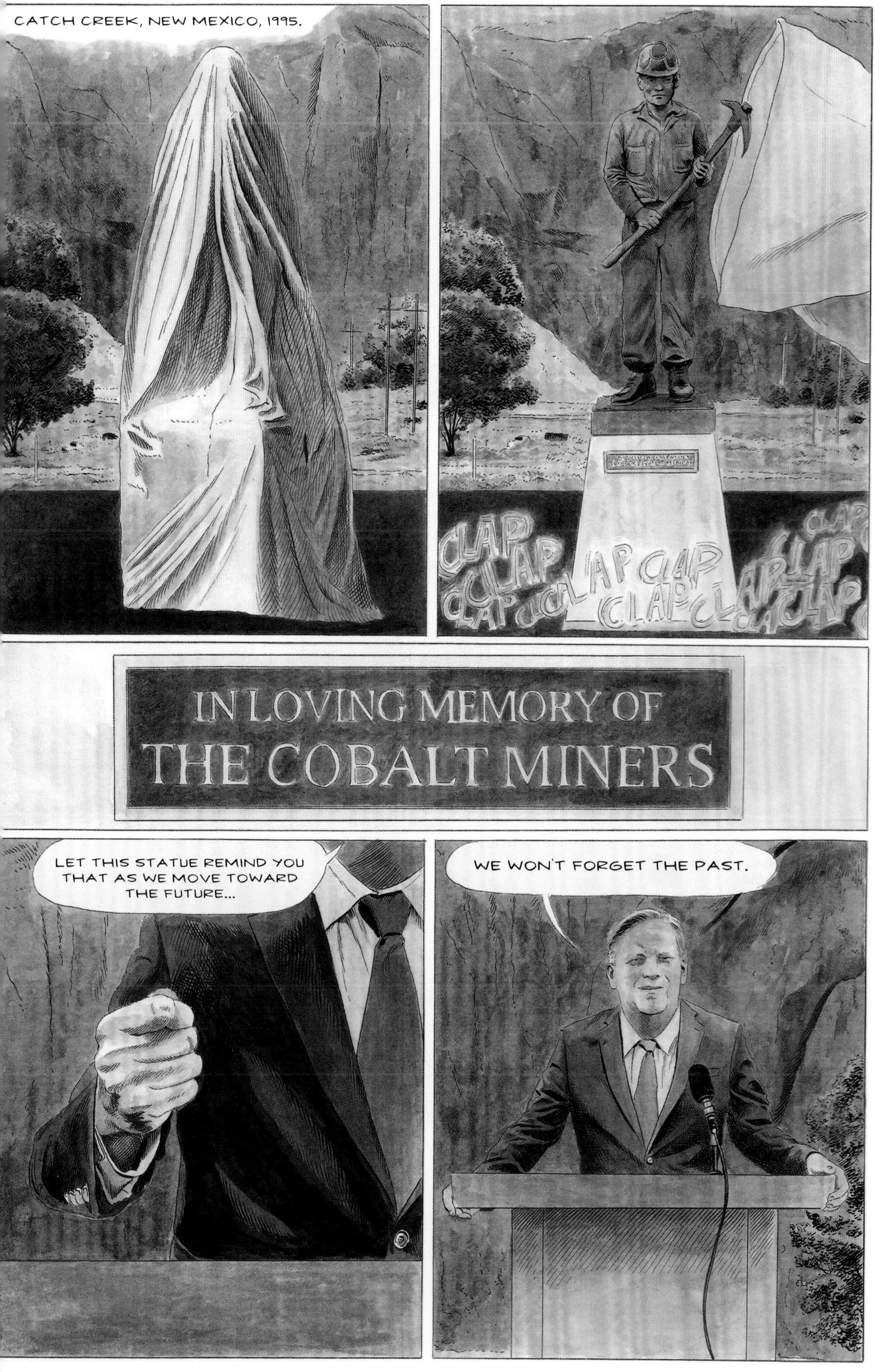
CATCH CREEK, NEW MEXICO, 1995.
CLAP CLAP CLAP CLAP CLAP CLAP CLAP CLAP CLAP CLAP CLAP
IN LOVING MEMORY OF
THE COBALT MINERS
LET THIS STATUE REMIND YOU THAT AS WE MOVE TOWARD THE FUTURE...
WE WON'T FORGET THE PAST.

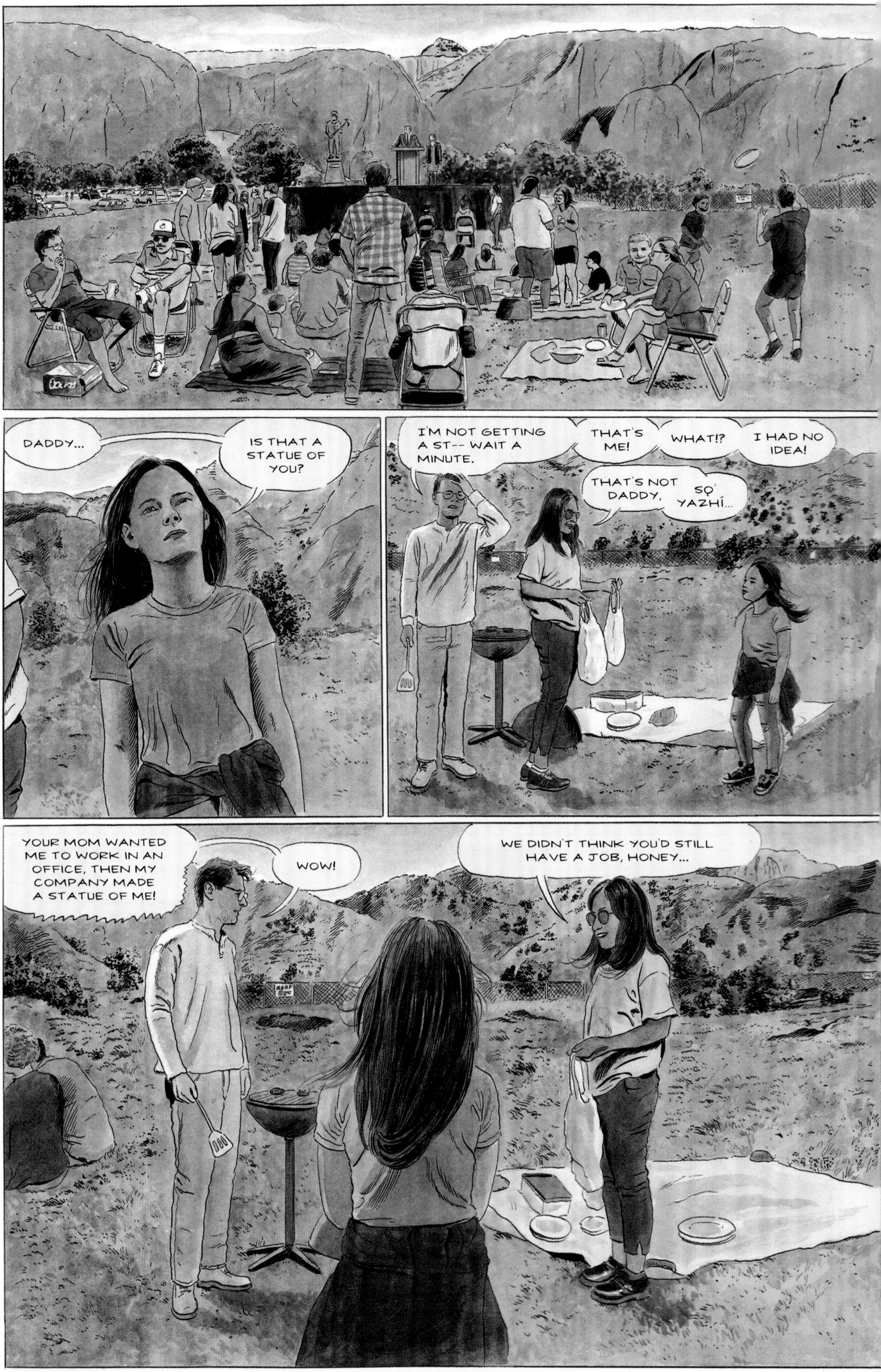
DADDY...
IS THAT A STATUE OF YOU?
I'M NOT GETTING A ST-- WAIT A MINUTE.
THAT'S ME!
WHAT!?
I HAD NO IDEA!
THAT'S NOT DADDY,
SǪ' YAZHÍ...
YOUR MOM WANTED ME TO WORK IN AN OFFICE, THEN MY COMPANY MADE A STATUE OF ME!
WOW!
WE DIDN'T THINK YOU'D STILL HAVE A JOB, HONEY...

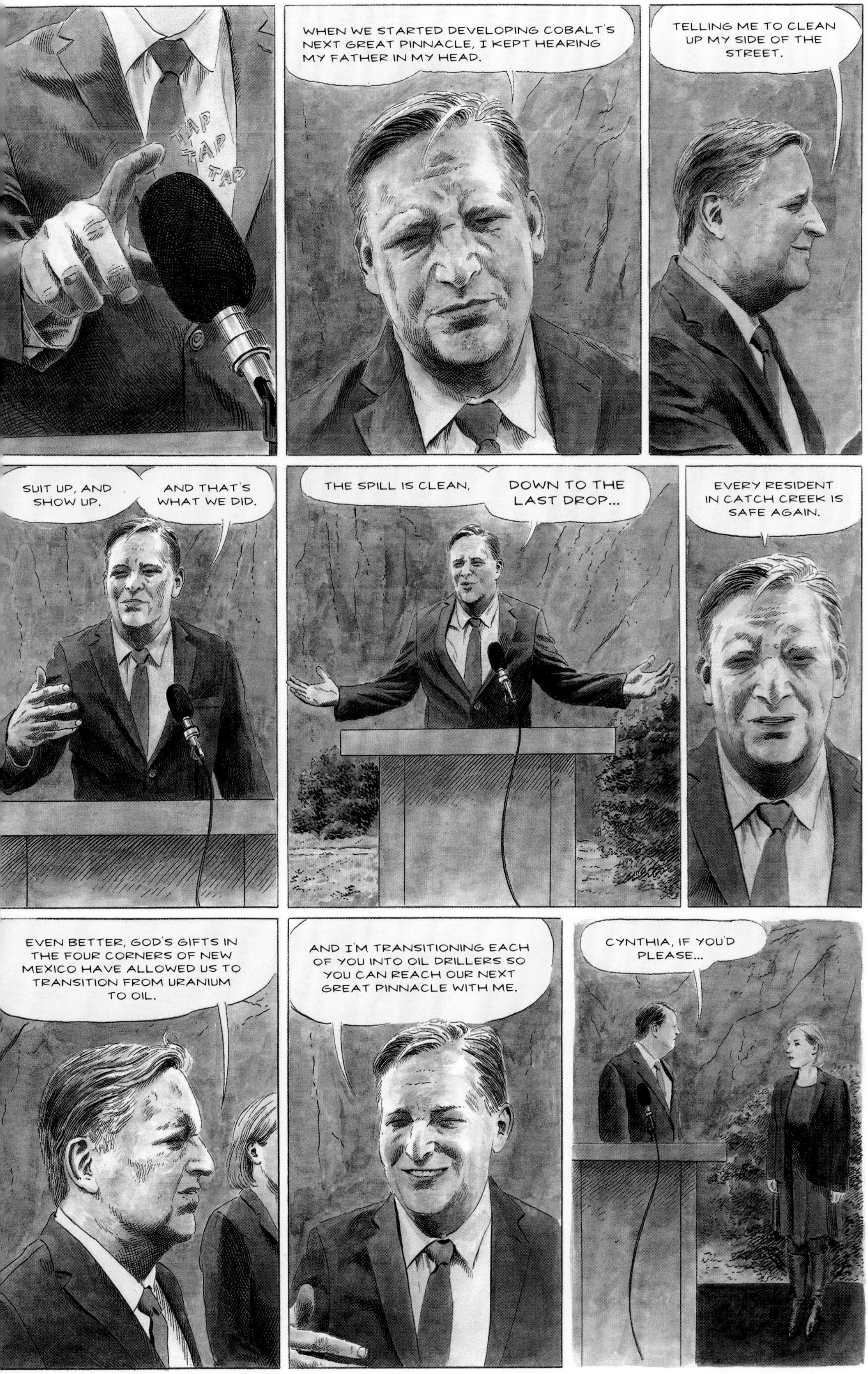
TAP
TAP
TAP
WHEN WE STARTED DEVELOPING COBALT'S NEXT GREAT PINNACLE, I KEPT HEARING MY FATHER IN MY HEAD.
TELLING ME TO CLEAN UP MY SIDE OF THE STREET.
SUIT UP, AND SHOW UP.
AND THAT'S WHAT WE DID.
THE SPILL IS CLEAN,
DOWN TO THE LAST DROP...
EVERY RESIDENT IN CATCH CREEK IS SAFE AGAIN.
EVEN BETTER, GOD'S GIFTS IN THE FOUR CORNERS OF NEW MEXICO HAVE ALLOWED US TO TRANSITION FROM URANIUM TO OIL.
AND I'M TRANSITIONING EACH OF YOU INTO OIL DRILLERS SO YOU CAN REACH OUR NEXT GREAT PINNACLE WITH ME.
CYNTHIA, IF YOU'D PLEASE...

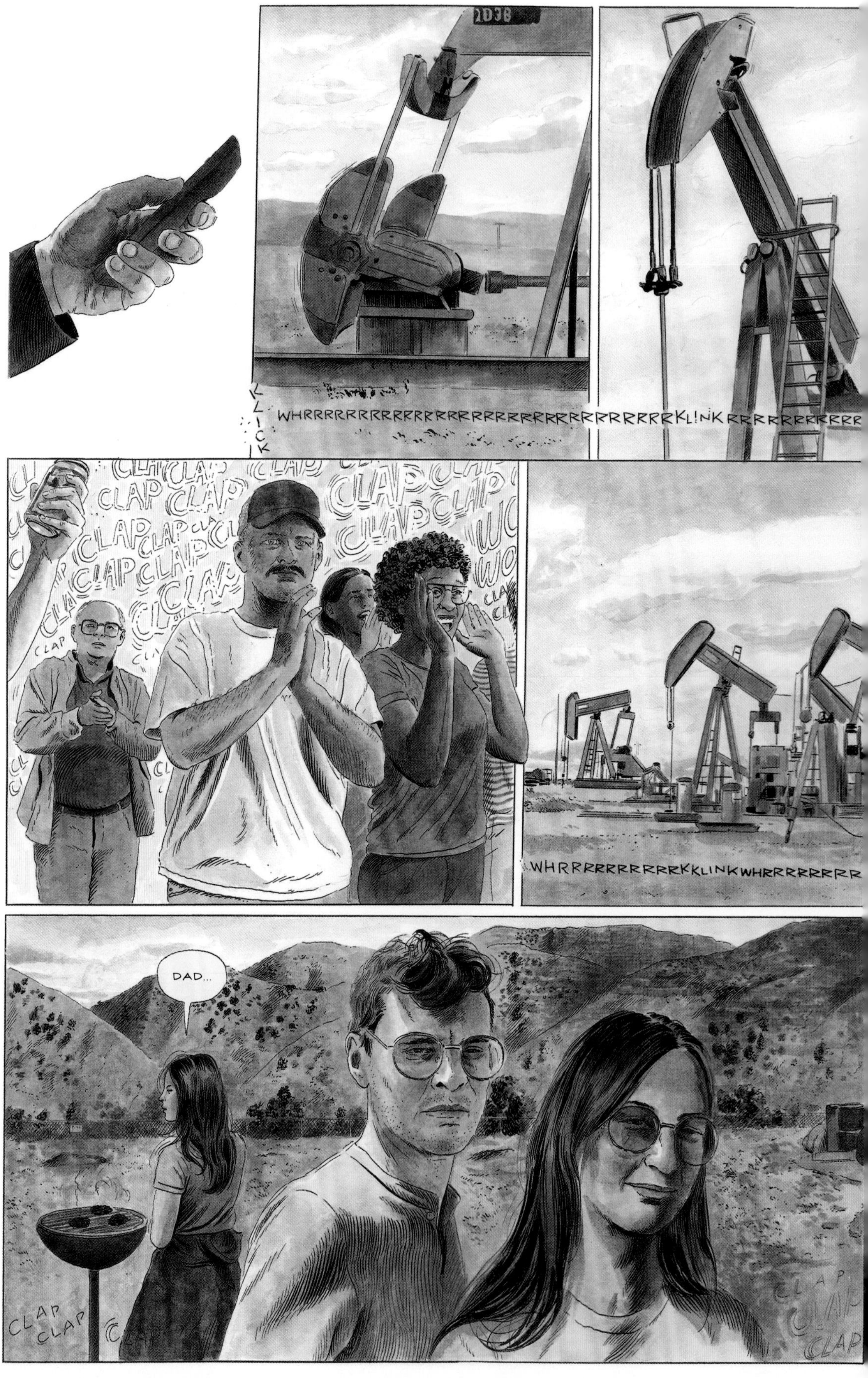

KLICK
WHRRRRRRRRRRRRRRRRRRRRRRRRRRRRRRRRKLINKRRRRRRRRRRR
CLAP CLAP CLAP CLAP CLAP CLAP CLAP CLAP
WHRRRRRRRRRRKLINKWHRRRRRRRRR
DAD...
CLAP CLAP
CLAP CLAP CLAP

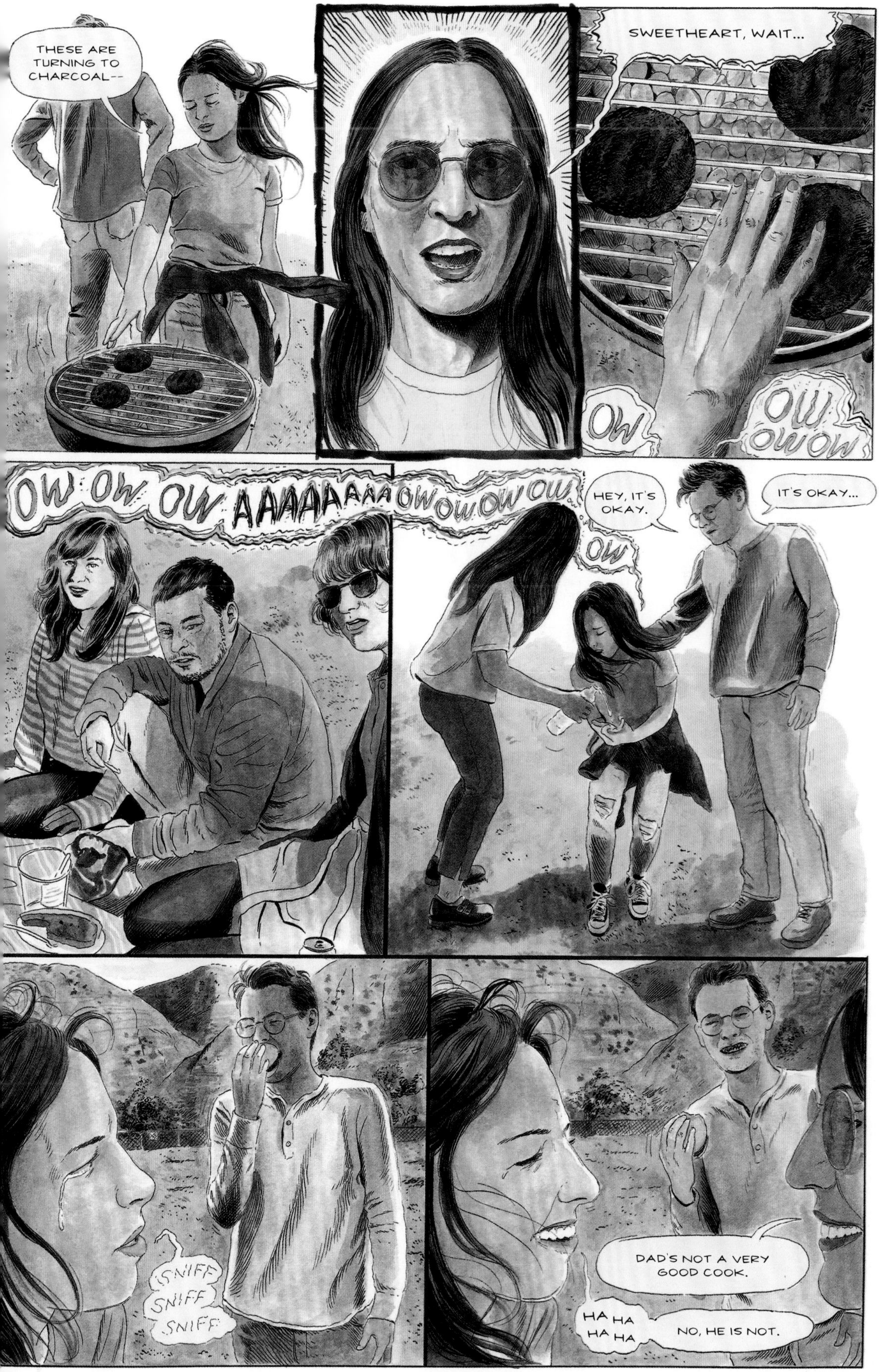
THESE ARE TURNING TO CHARCOAL--
SWEETHEART, WAIT...
OW
OW OW OW
OW OW OW AAAAAAAA OW OW OW OW
HEY, IT'S OKAY.
IT'S OKAY...
OW
SNIFF
SNIFF
SNIFF
DAD'S NOT A VERY GOOD COOK.
HA HA
HA HA
NO, HE IS NOT.

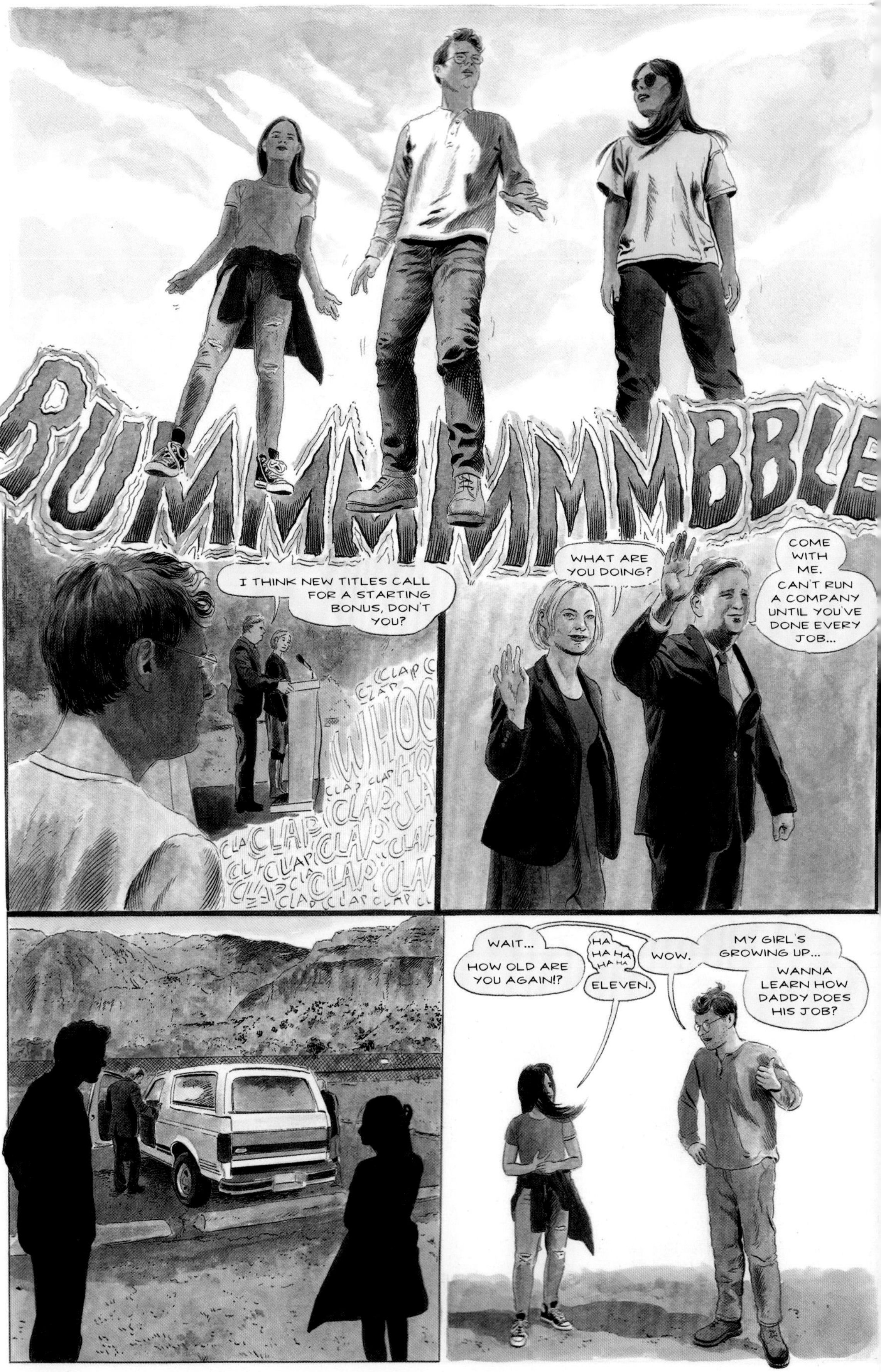
RUMMMMMMMBBLE
I THINK NEW TITLES CALL FOR A STARTING BONUS, DON'T YOU?
CLAP CLAP
WHAT ARE YOU DOING?
COME WITH ME. CAN'T RUN A COMPANY UNTIL YOU'VE DONE EVERY JOB...
WAIT... HOW OLD ARE YOU AGAIN!?
HA HA HA HA HA
ELEVEN.
WOW.
MY GIRL'S GROWING UP... WANNA LEARN HOW DADDY DOES HIS JOB?

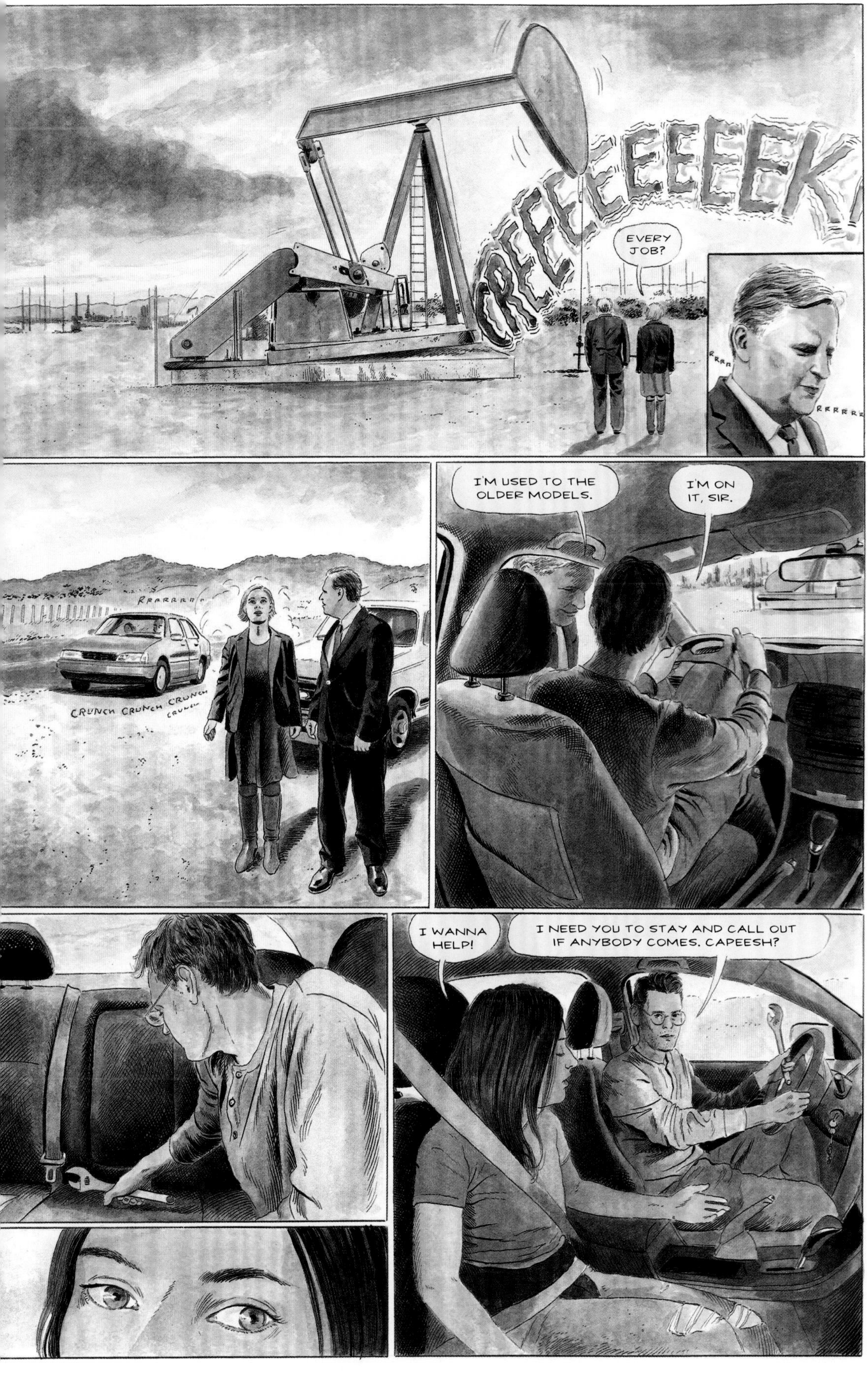
GREEEEEEEK!
EVERY JOB?
RRRR
RRRRRR
RRRRRRR
CRUNCH CRUNCH CRUNCH CRUNCH
I'M USED TO THE OLDER MODELS.
I'M ON IT, SIR.
I WANNA HELP!
I NEED YOU TO STAY AND CALL OUT IF ANYBODY COMES. CAPEESH?

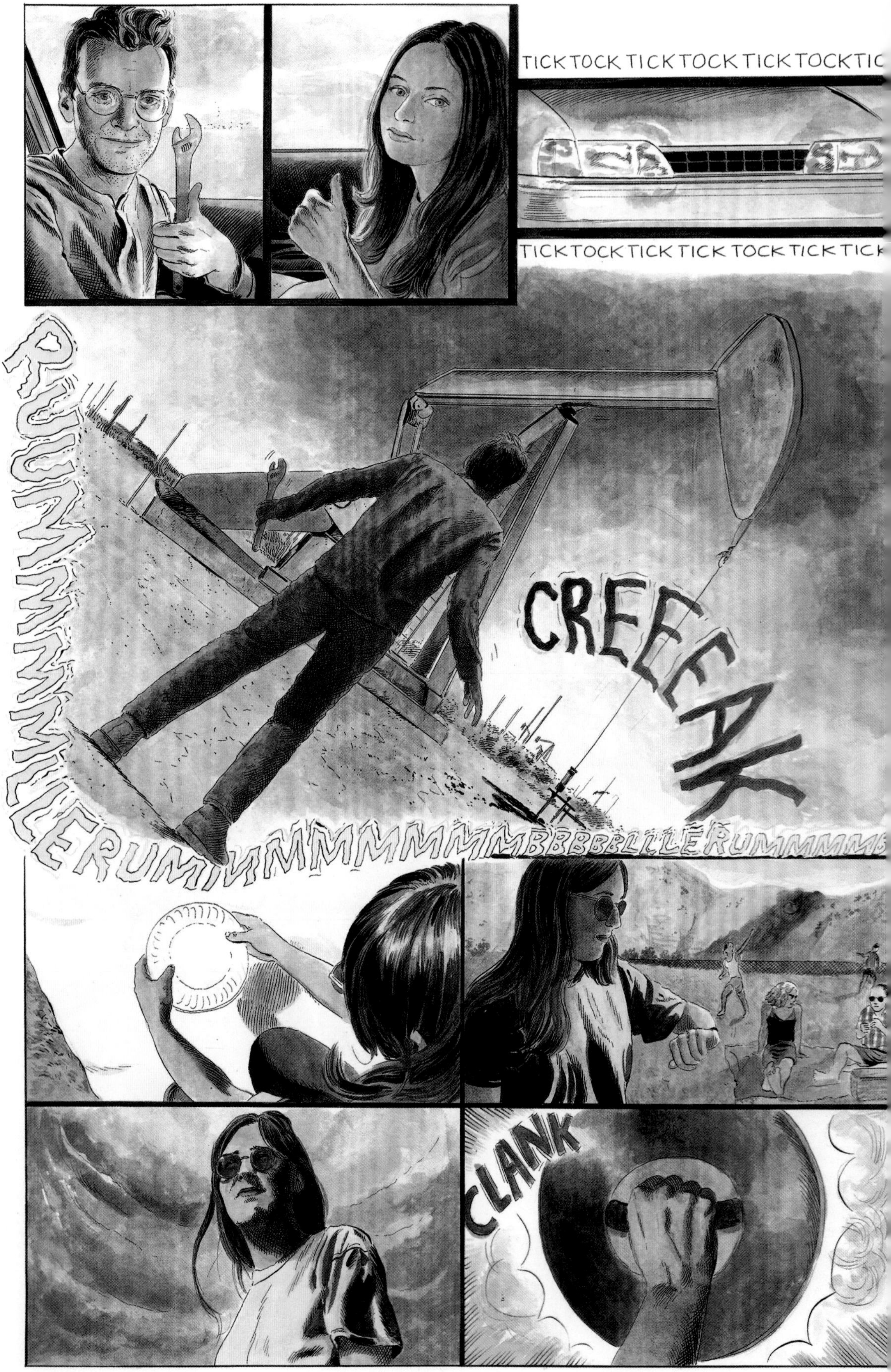
TICKTOCK TICKTOCK TICKTOCKTIC
TICKTOCKTICK TICK TOCK TICK TICK
RUMMMMLERUMMMMMMMMMMBBBBBLLLERUMMMMM
CREEEAK
CLANK

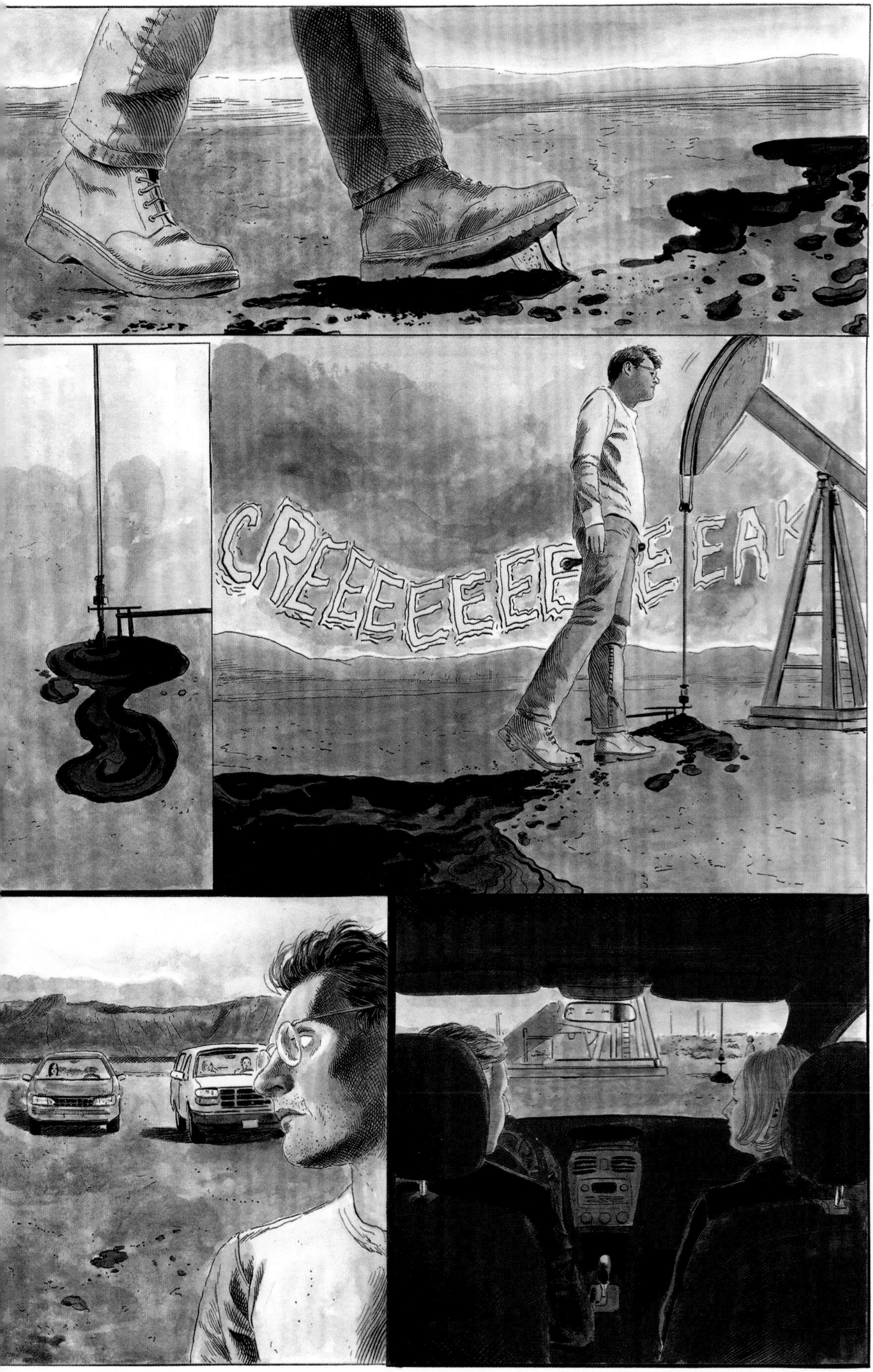
CREEEEEEEEEAK

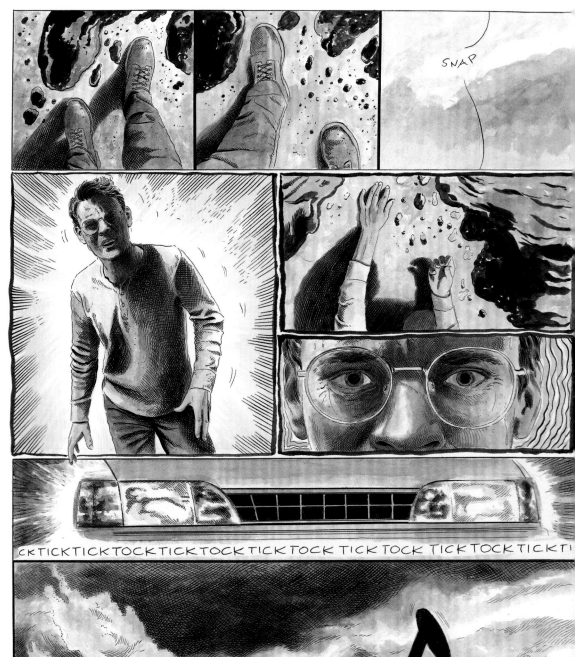

SNAP

CKTICKTICK TOCK TICK TOCK TICK TOCK TICK TOCK TICK TOCK TICKTI

RUMMMBBBBBBLLLE

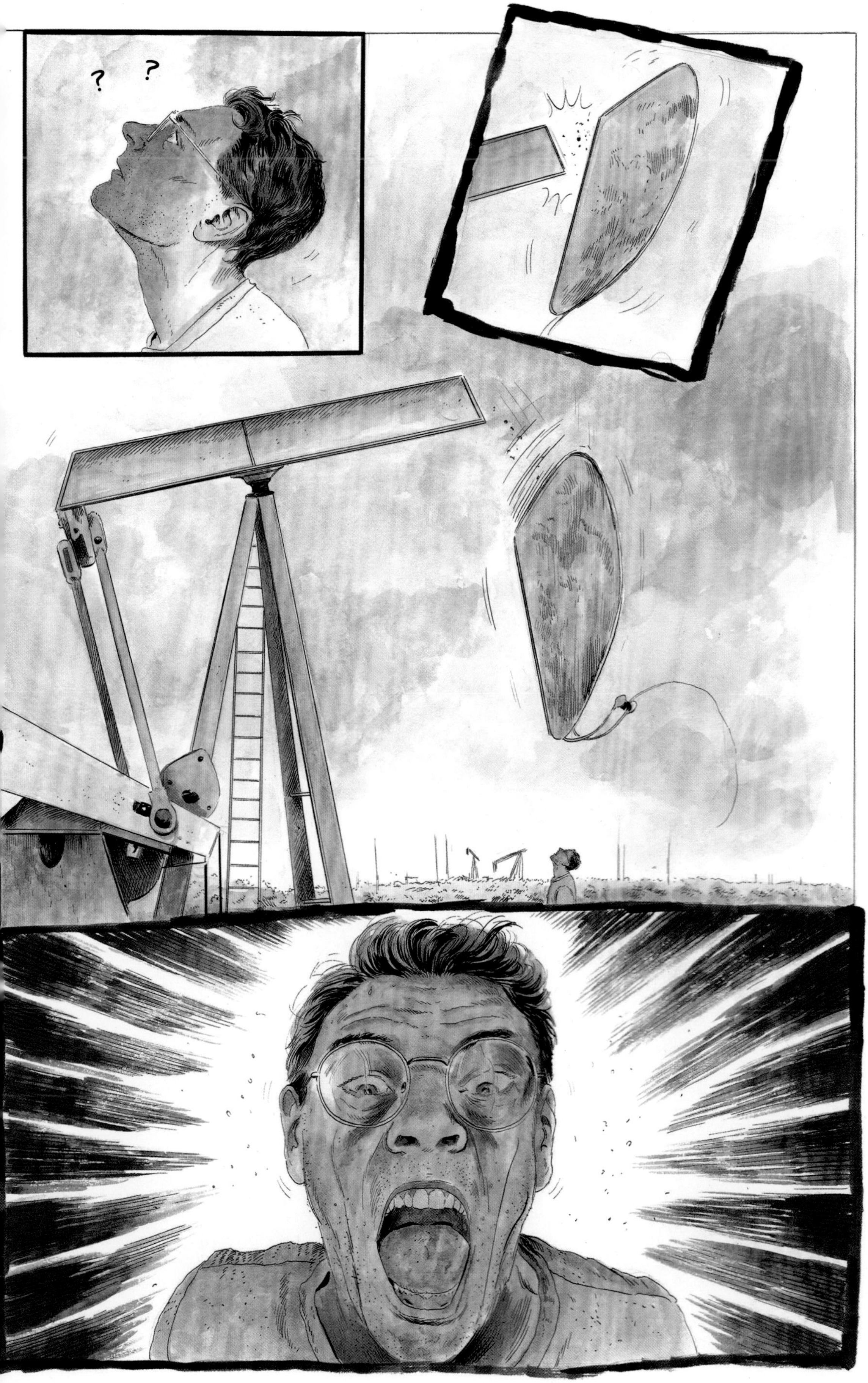
? ?

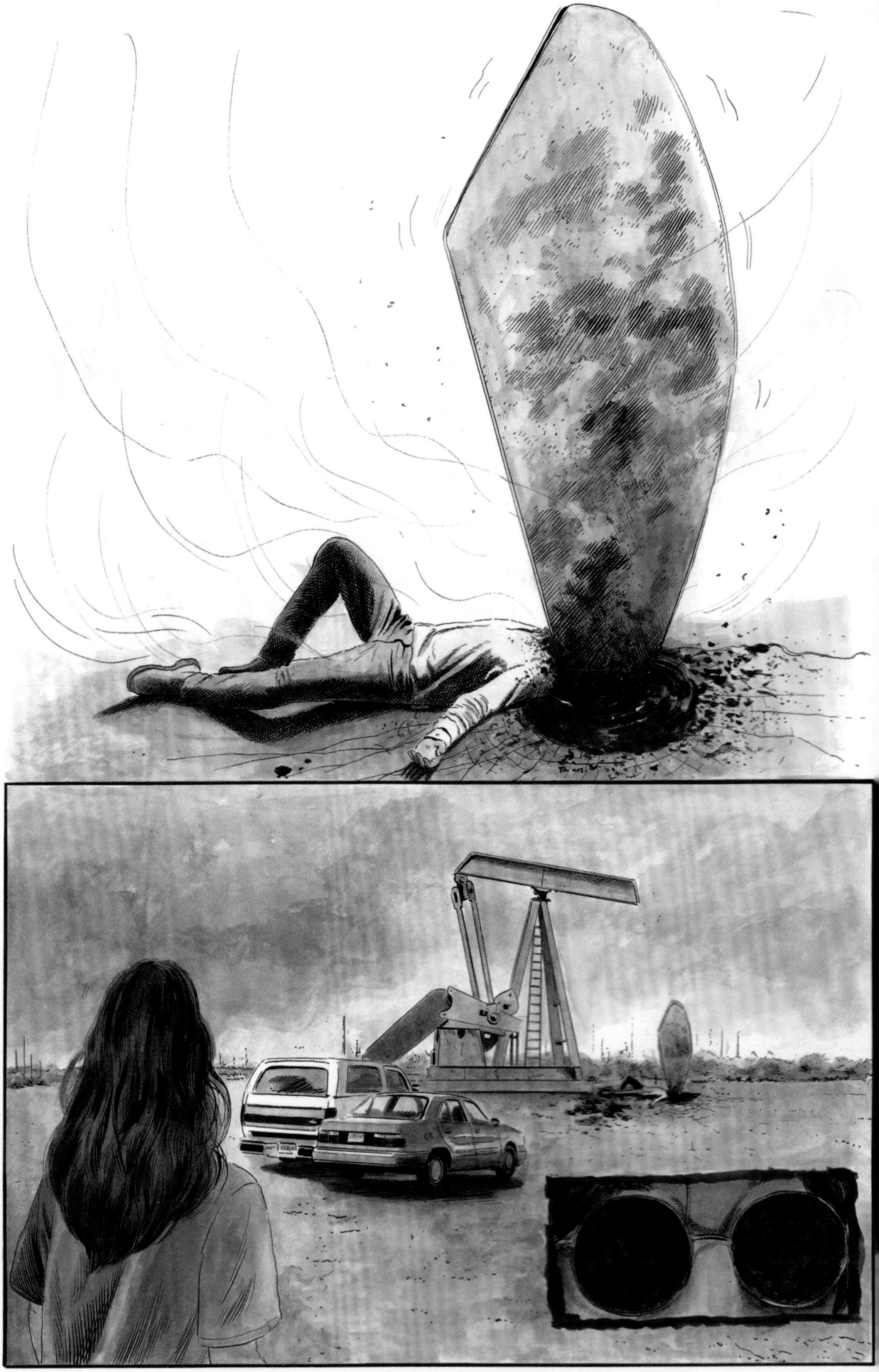

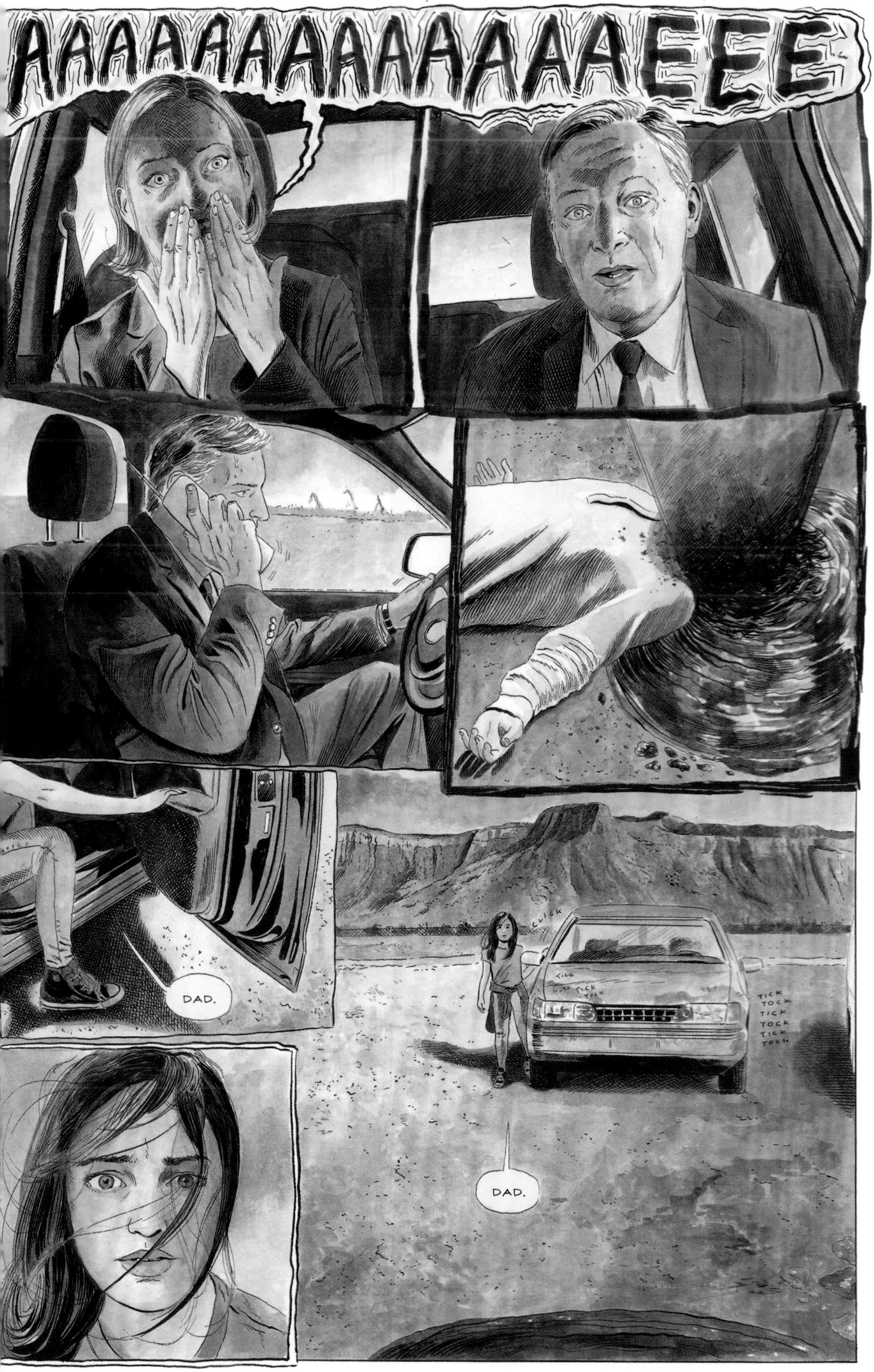
AAAAAAAAAAAAEEE
DAD.
CLICK
TICK TOCK TICK TOCK
TICK TOCK TICK TOCK TICK TOCK
DAD.

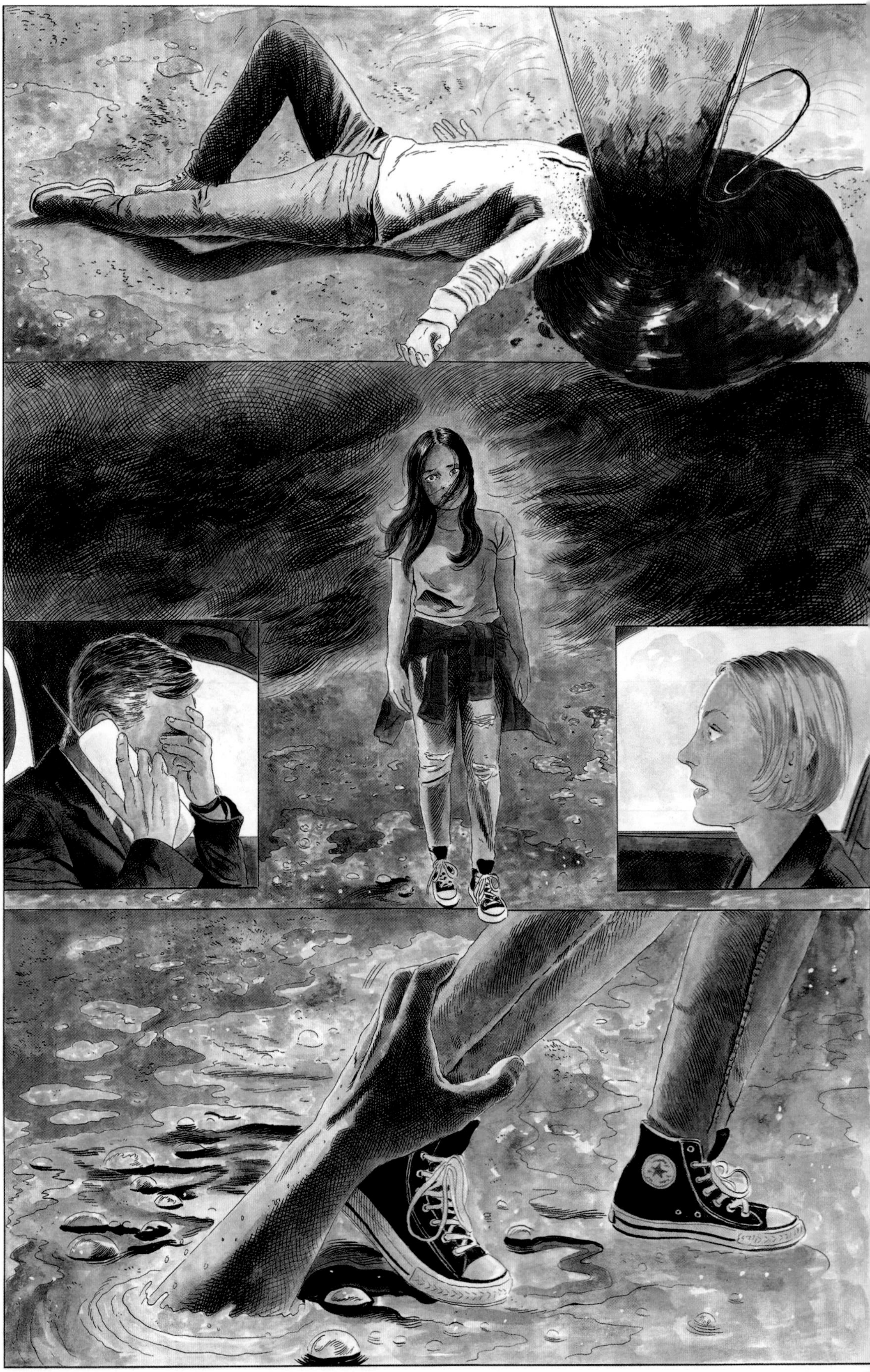

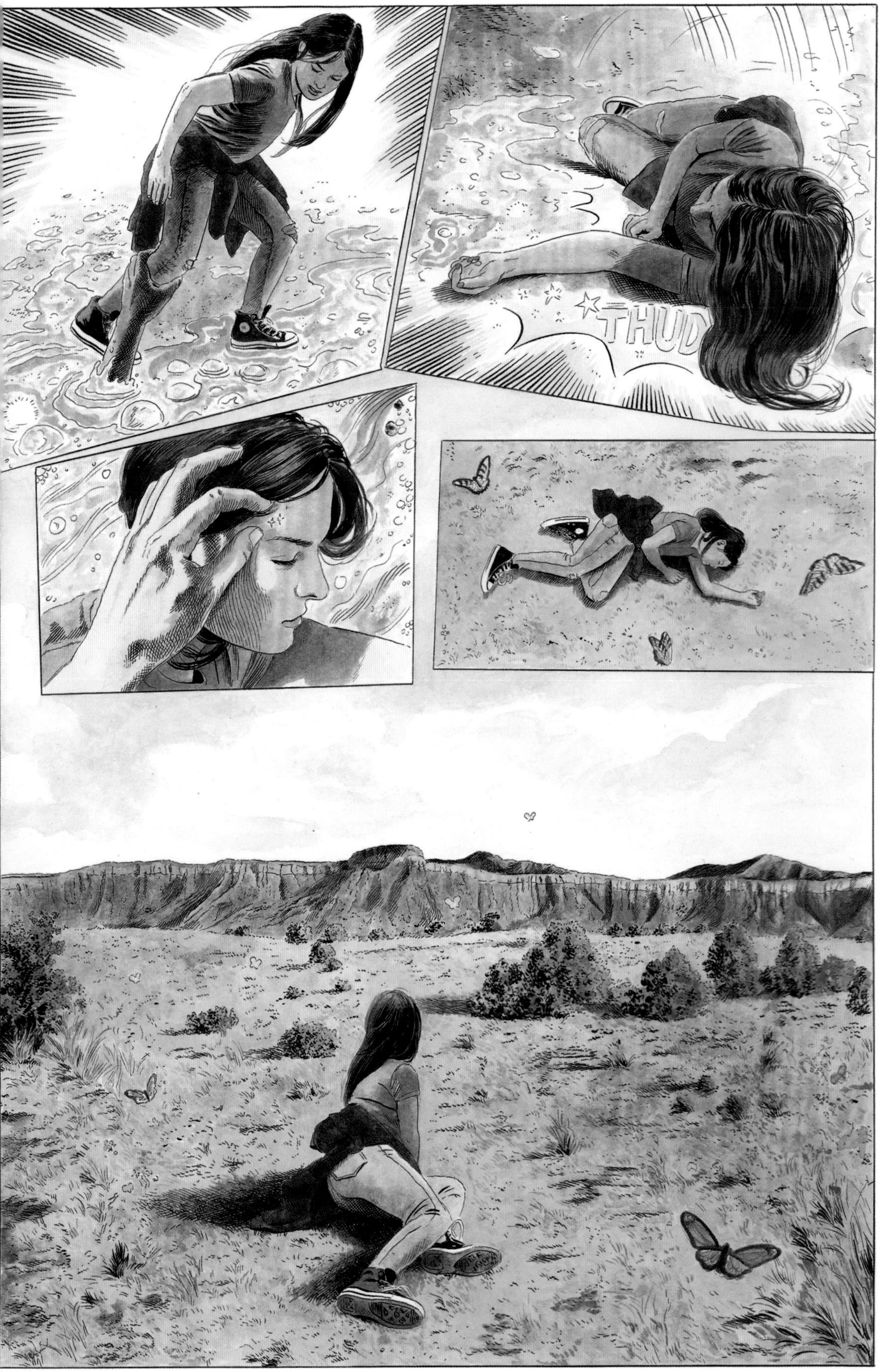
THUD

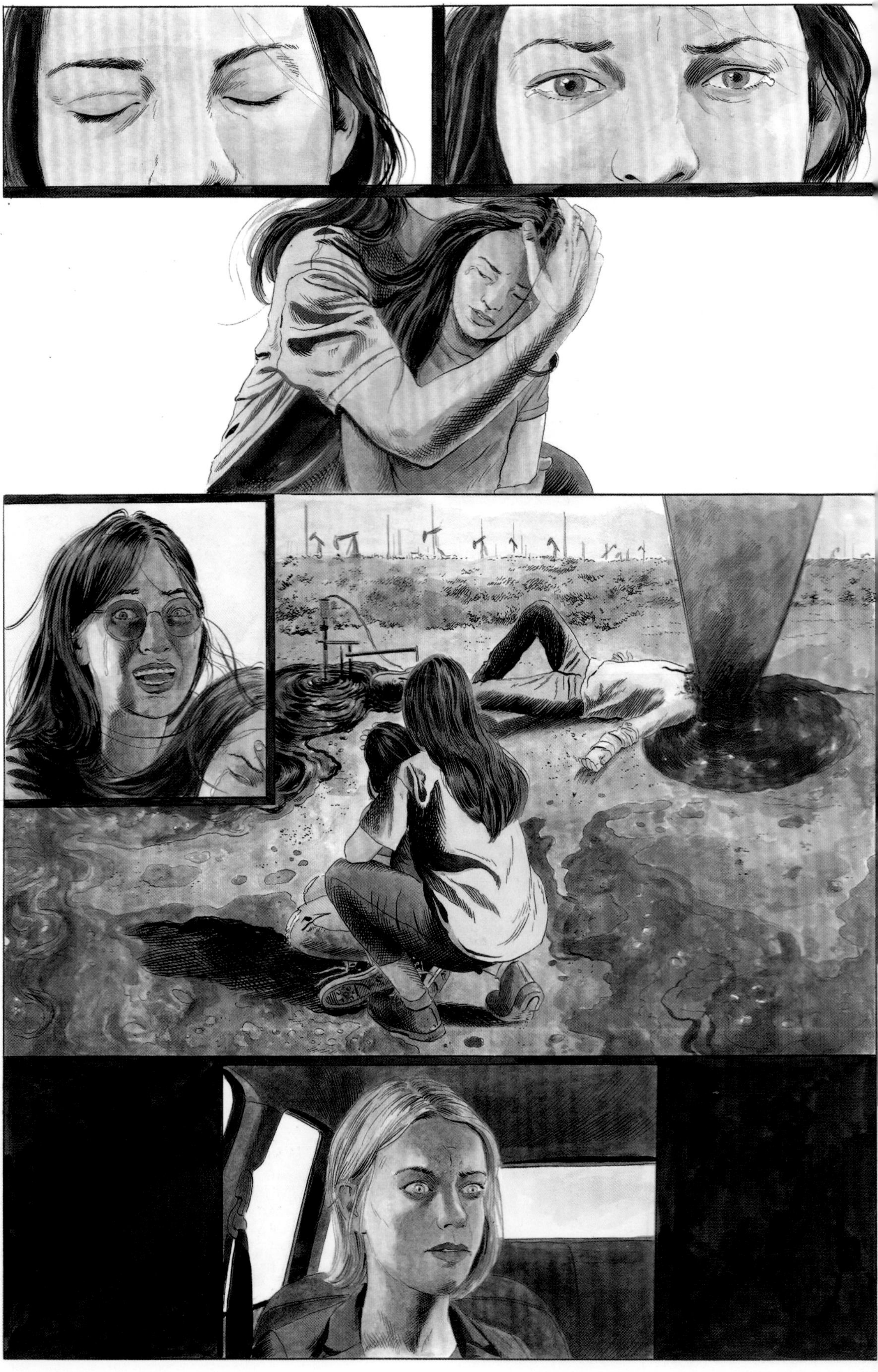

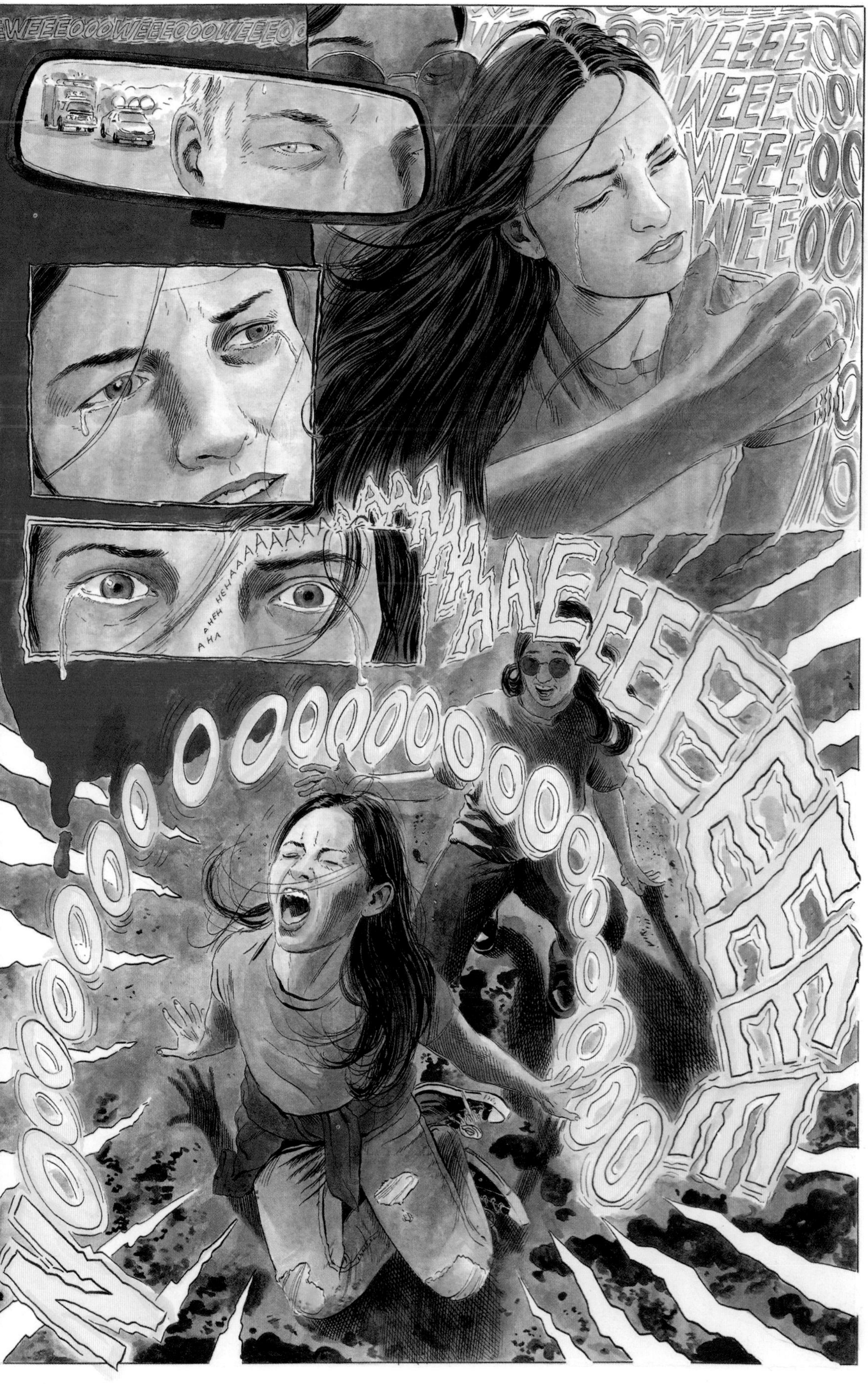

WEEEOOOWEEEOOOWEEEO
AHA AHEH HEHAAAAAAAA

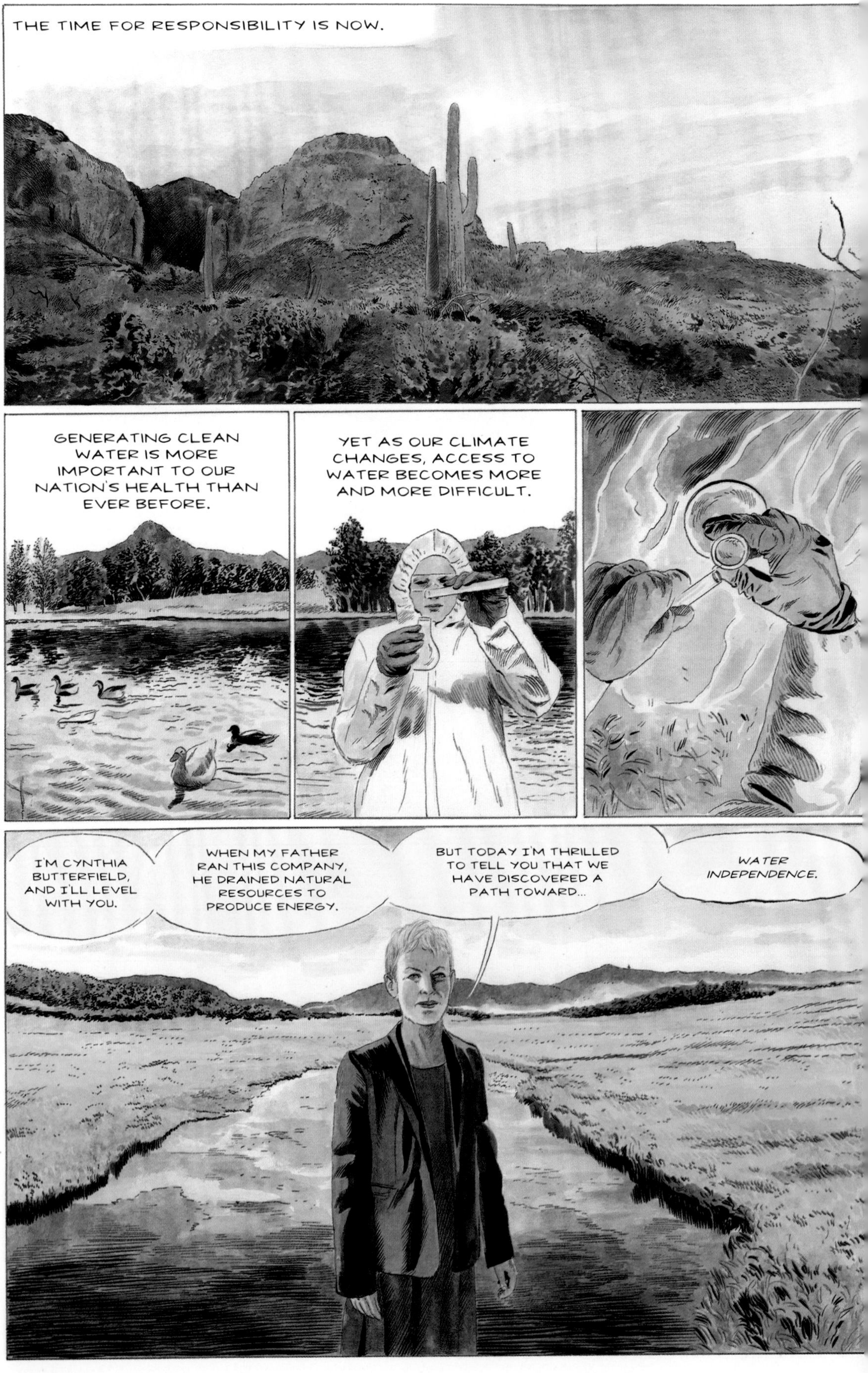
THE TIME FOR RESPONSIBILITY IS NOW.
GENERATING CLEAN WATER IS MORE IMPORTANT TO OUR NATION'S HEALTH THAN EVER BEFORE.
YET AS OUR CLIMATE CHANGES, ACCESS TO WATER BECOMES MORE AND MORE DIFFICULT.
I'M CYNTHIA BUTTERFIELD, AND I'LL LEVEL WITH YOU.
WHEN MY FATHER RAN THIS COMPANY, HE DRAINED NATURAL RESOURCES TO PRODUCE ENERGY.
BUT TODAY I'M THRILLED TO TELL YOU THAT WE HAVE DISCOVERED A PATH TOWARD...
WATER INDEPENDENCE.

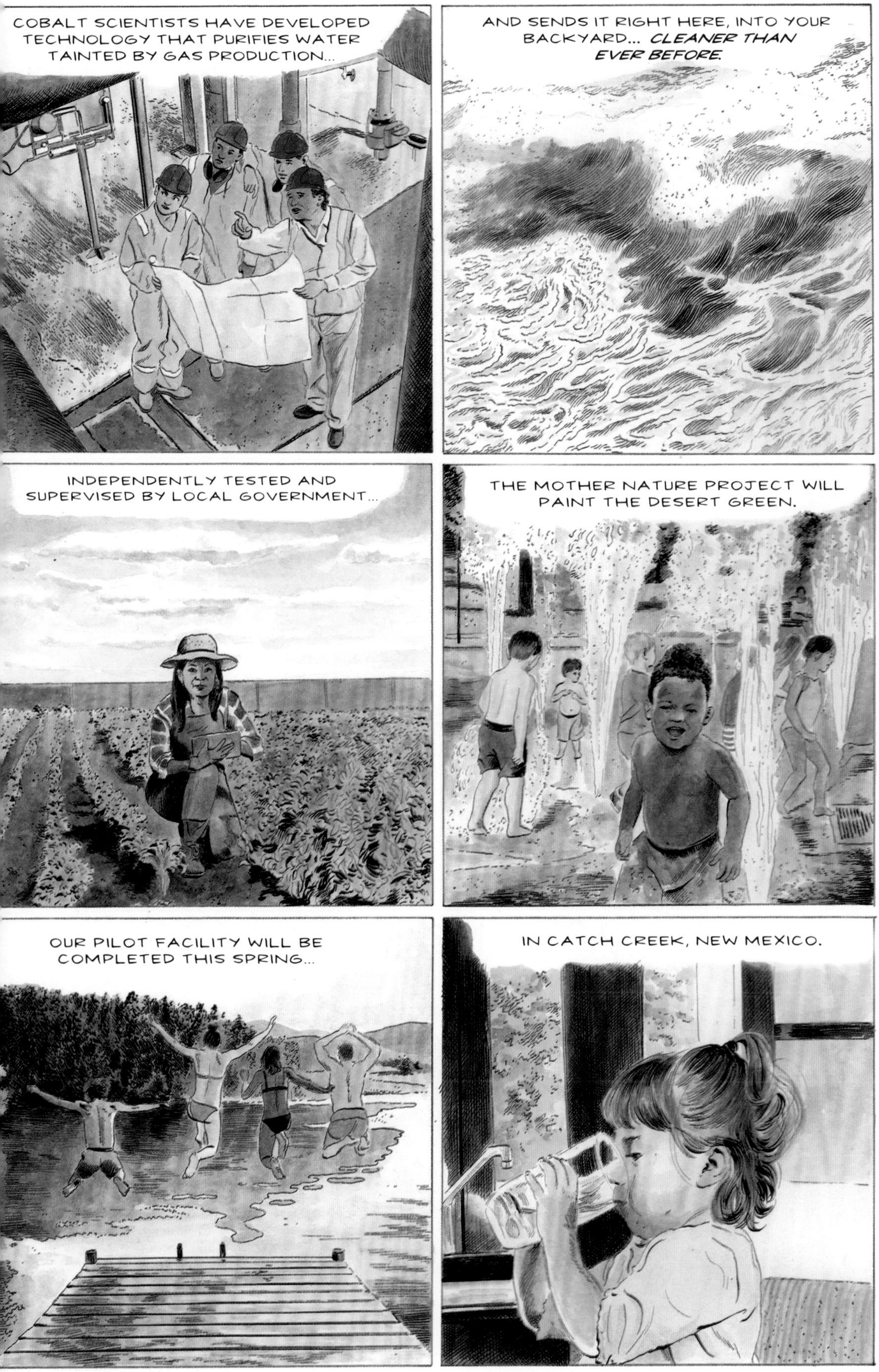
COBALT SCIENTISTS HAVE DEVELOPED TECHNOLOGY THAT PURIFIES WATER TAINTED BY GAS PRODUCTION...
AND SENDS IT RIGHT HERE, INTO YOUR BACKYARD... *CLEANER THAN EVER BEFORE.*
INDEPENDENTLY TESTED AND SUPERVISED BY LOCAL GOVERNMENT...
THE MOTHER NATURE PROJECT WILL PAINT THE DESERT GREEN.
OUR PILOT FACILITY WILL BE COMPLETED THIS SPRING...
IN CATCH CREEK, NEW MEXICO.

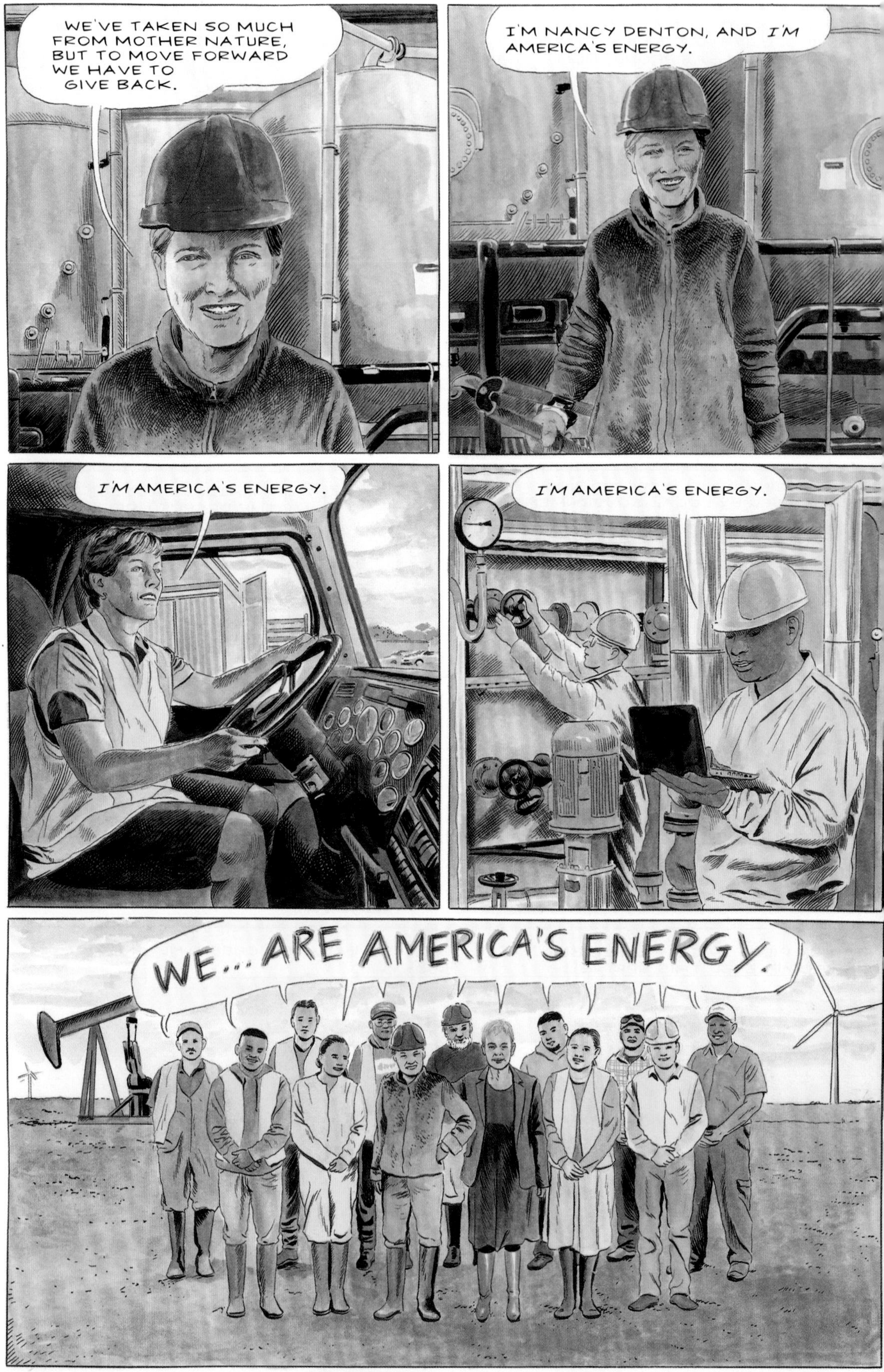
WE'VE TAKEN SO MUCH FROM MOTHER NATURE, BUT TO MOVE FORWARD WE HAVE TO GIVE BACK.
I'M NANCY DENTON, AND I'M AMERICA'S ENERGY.
I'M AMERICA'S ENERGY.
I'M AMERICA'S ENERGY.
WE... ARE AMERICA'S ENERGY.

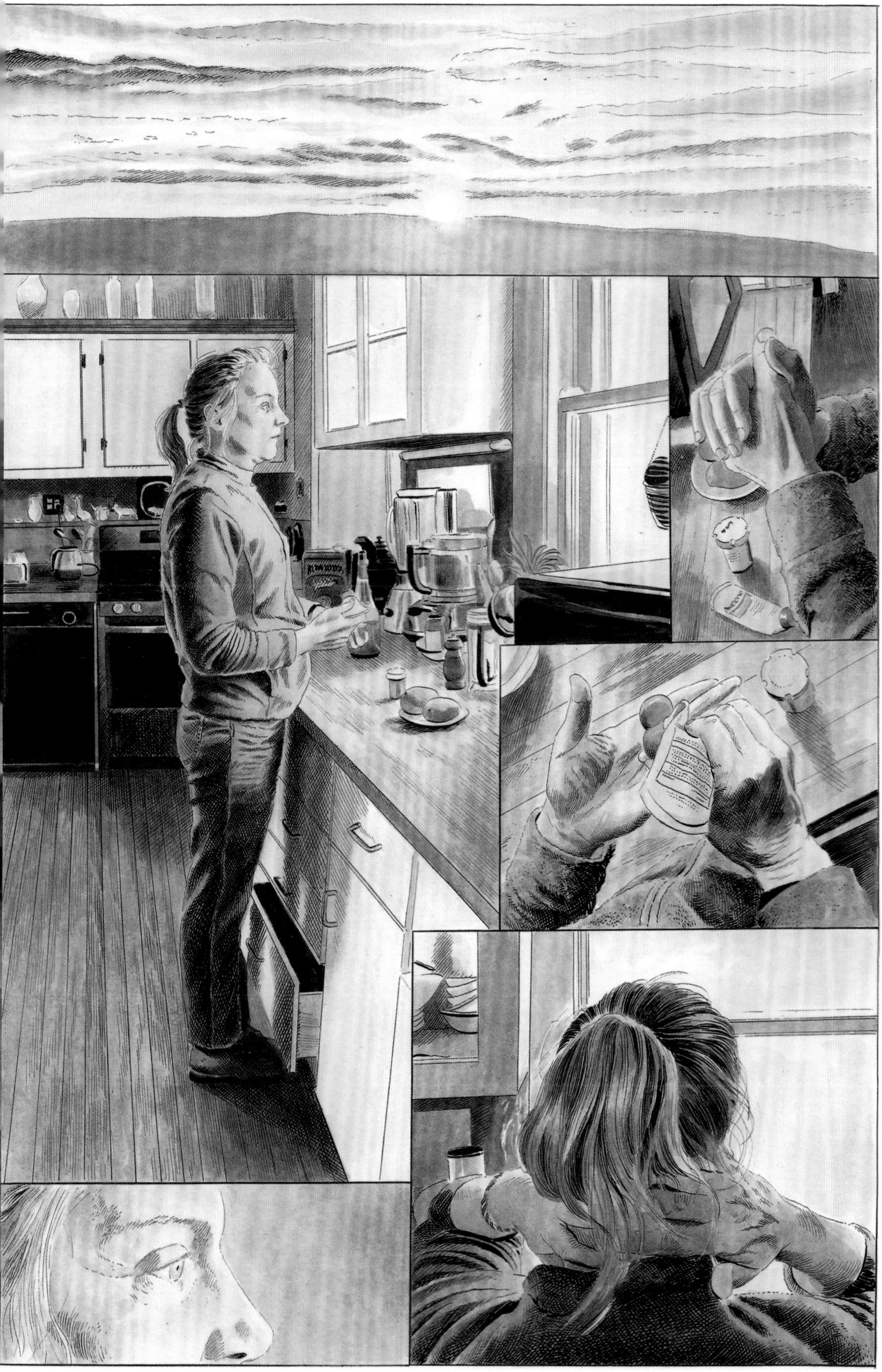

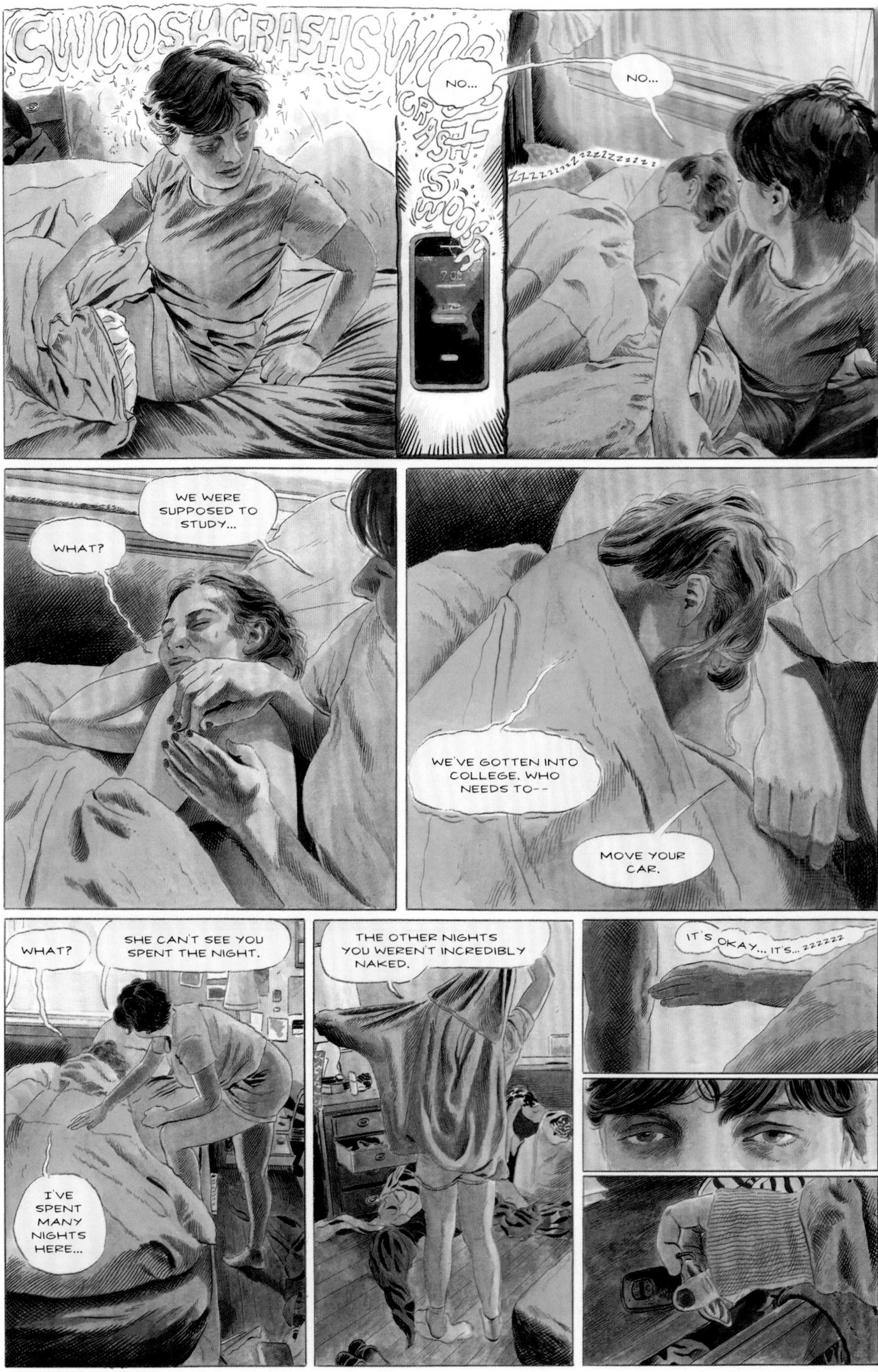
SWOOSH CRASH SWOO
CRASH
SWOOSH
NO...
NO...
ZZZZZZZZZZZZZZZZZZZZ
WE WERE SUPPOSED TO STUDY...
WHAT?
WE'VE GOTTEN INTO COLLEGE. WHO NEEDS TO--
MOVE YOUR CAR.
WHAT?
SHE CAN'T SEE YOU SPENT THE NIGHT.
I'VE SPENT MANY NIGHTS HERE...
THE OTHER NIGHTS YOU WEREN'T INCREDIBLY NAKED.
IT'S OKAY... IT'S... ZZZZZZ

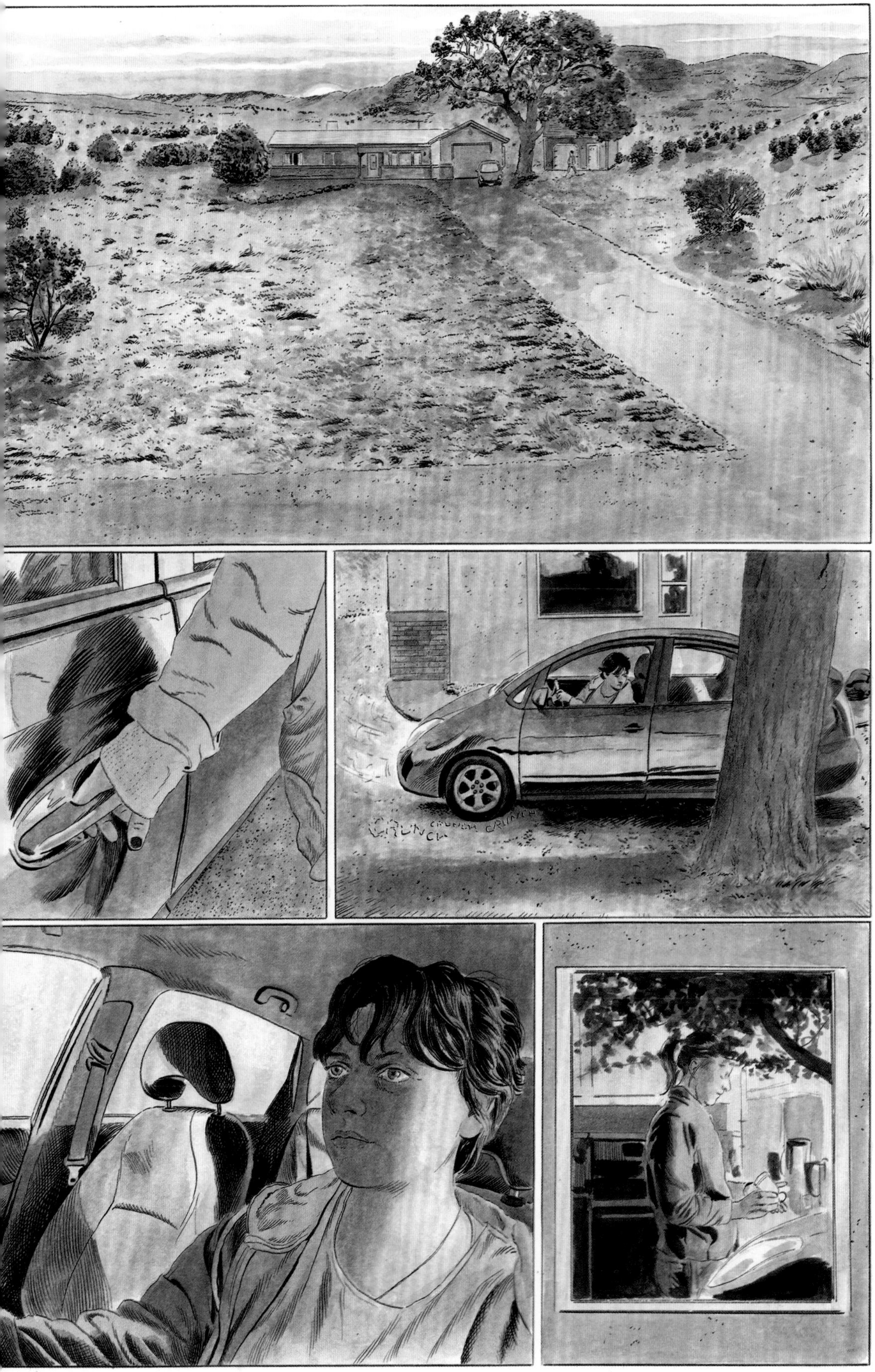
CRUNCH
CRUNCH
CRUNCH

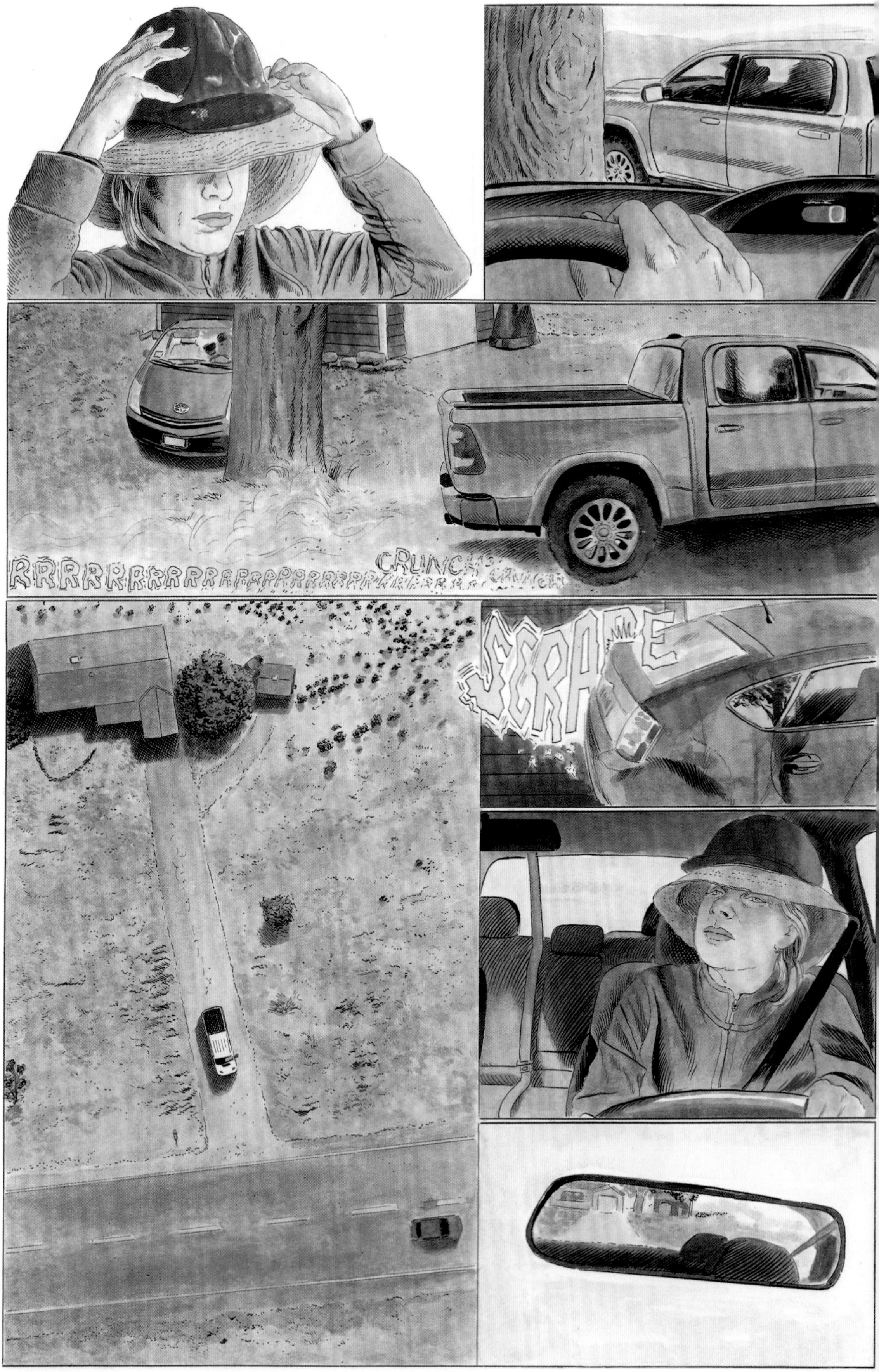
RRRRRRRRRRRRRRRRRRRRRRRRRRR
CRUNCH
CRUNCH
SCRAPE

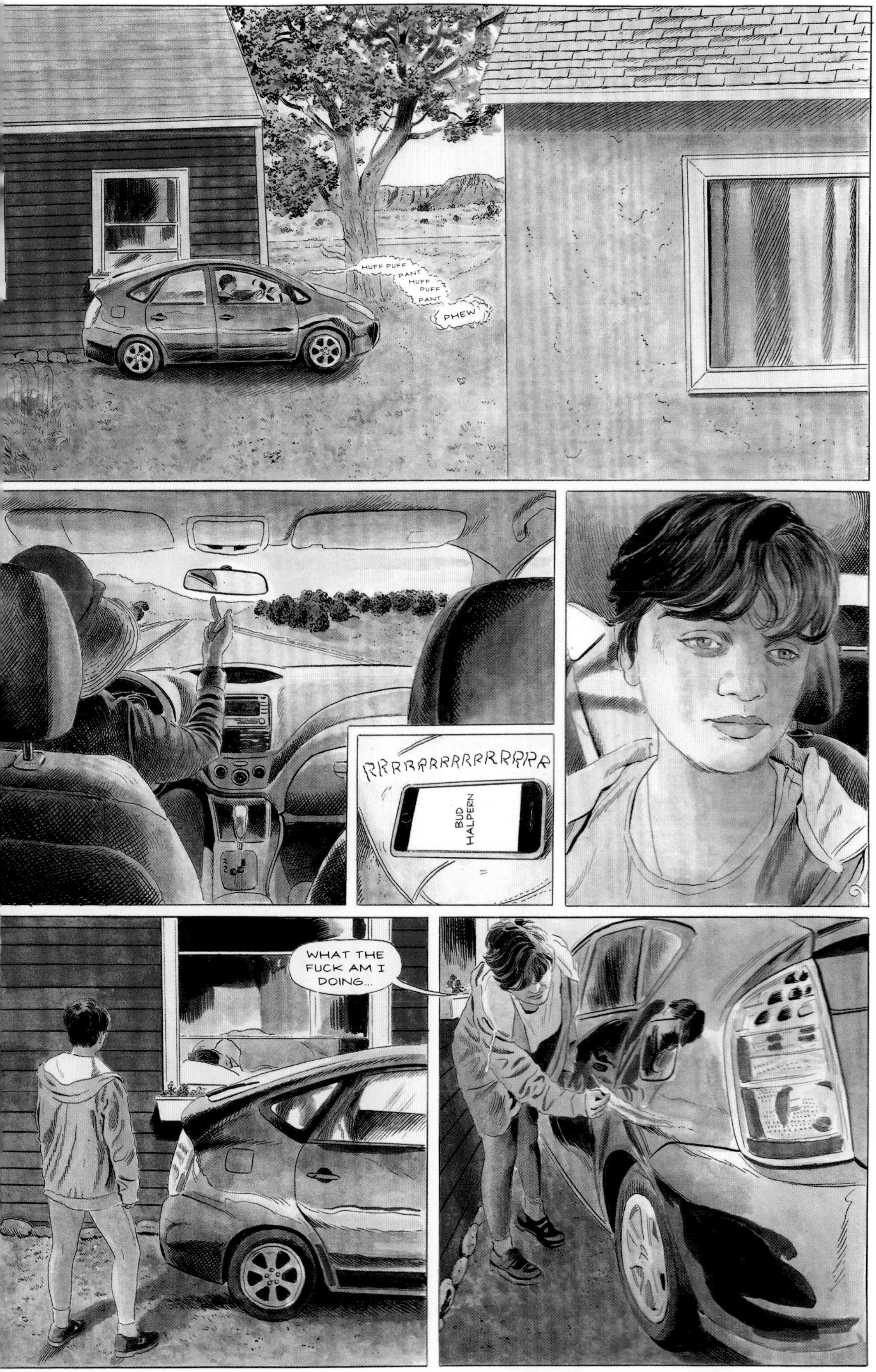
HUFF PUFF
PANT
HUFF
PUFF
PANT
PHEW
RRRRRRRRRRRRRRRRR
BUD HALPERN
WHAT THE FUCK AM I DOING...

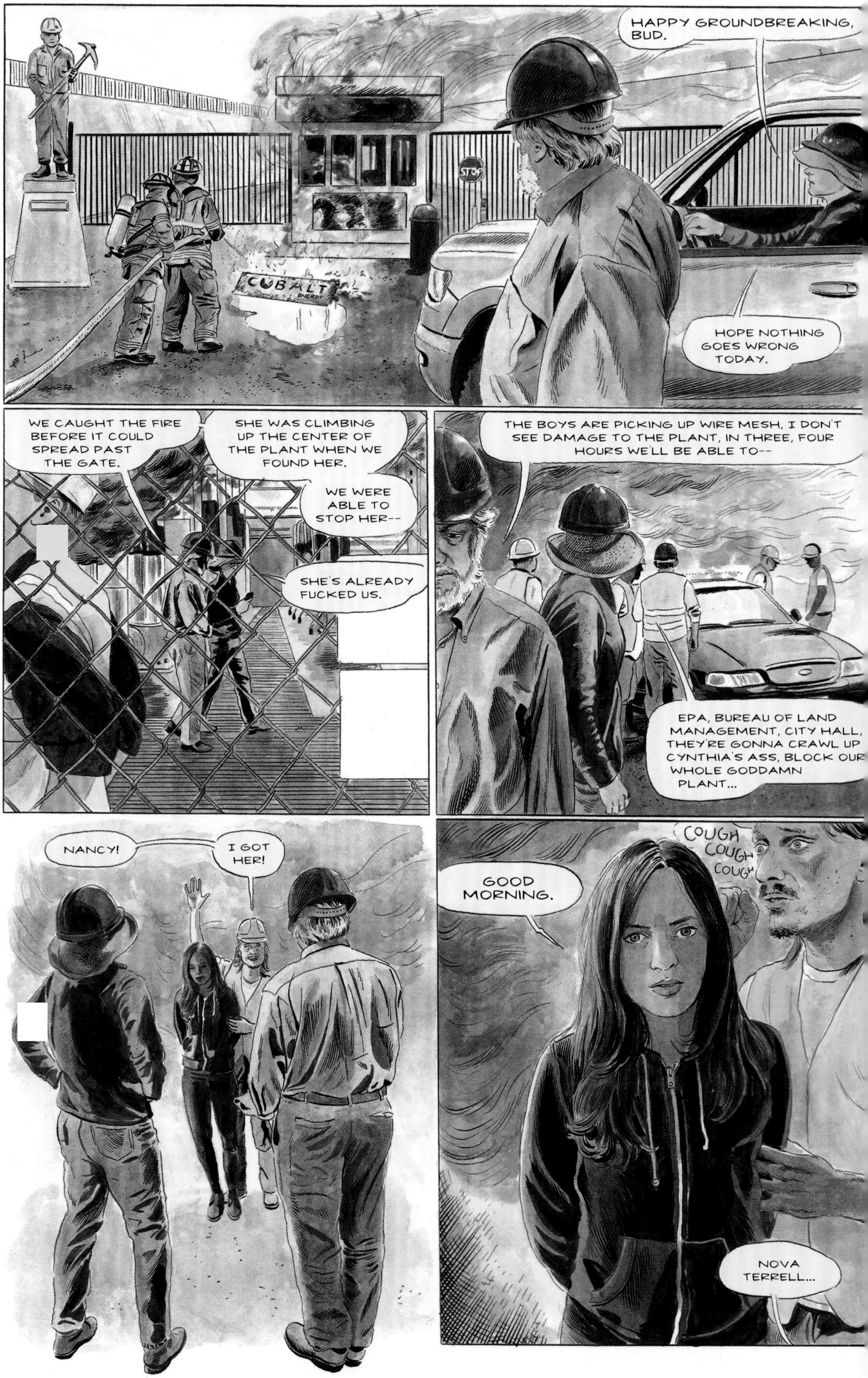
HAPPY GROUNDBREAKING, BUD.
COBALT
STOP
HOPE NOTHING GOES WRONG TODAY.
WE CAUGHT THE FIRE BEFORE IT COULD SPREAD PAST THE GATE.
SHE WAS CLIMBING UP THE CENTER OF THE PLANT WHEN WE FOUND HER.
WE WERE ABLE TO STOP HER--
SHE'S ALREADY FUCKED US.
THE BOYS ARE PICKING UP WIRE MESH, I DON'T SEE DAMAGE TO THE PLANT, IN THREE, FOUR HOURS WE'LL BE ABLE TO--
EPA, BUREAU OF LAND MANAGEMENT, CITY HALL, THEY'RE GONNA CRAWL UP CYNTHIA'S ASS, BLOCK OUR WHOLE GODDAMN PLANT...
NANCY!
I GOT HER!
COUGH COUGH COUGH
GOOD MORNING.
NOVA TERRELL...

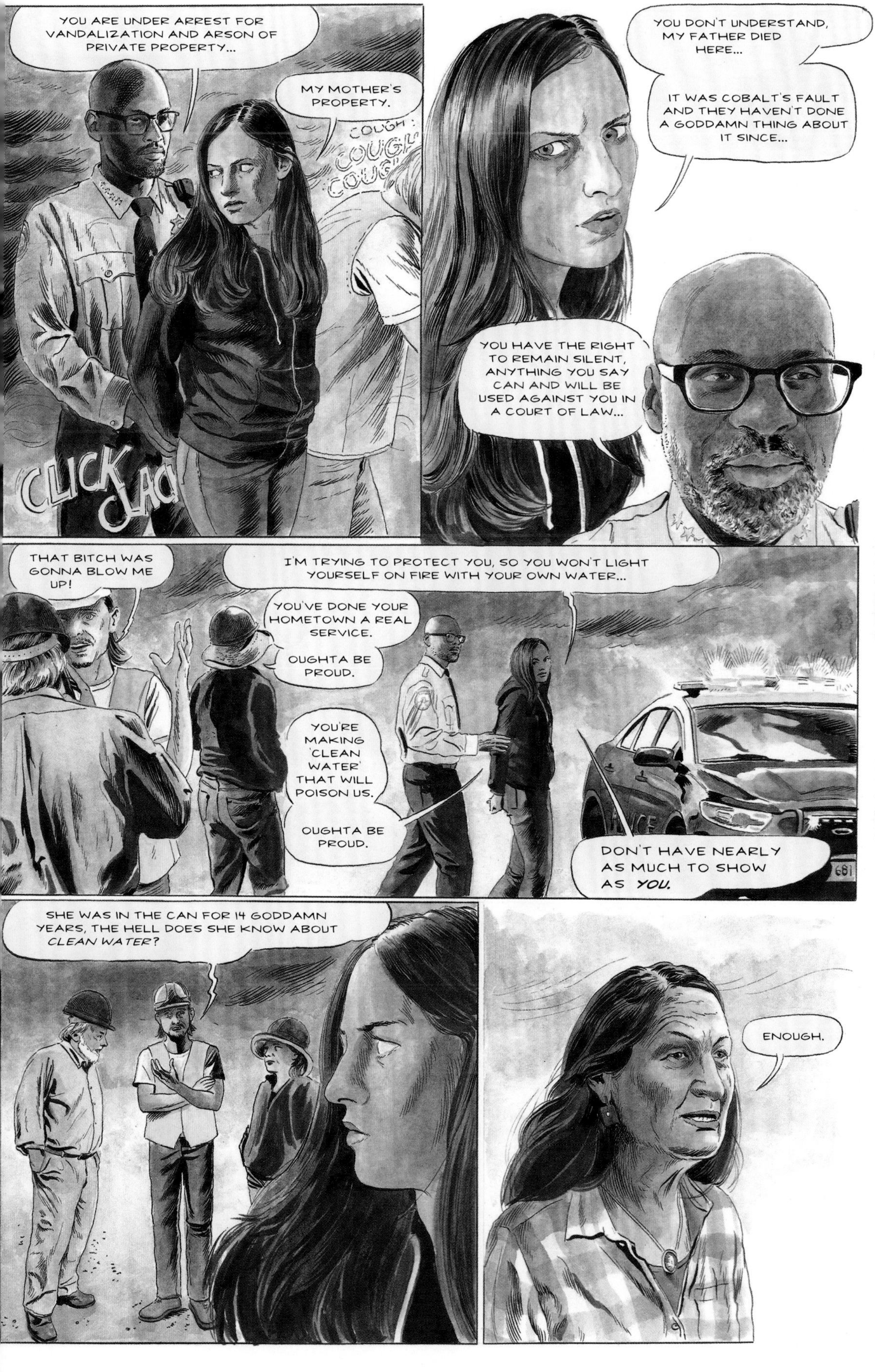

YOU ARE UNDER ARREST FOR VANDALIZATION AND ARSON OF PRIVATE PROPERTY...
MY MOTHER'S PROPERTY.
COUGH
CLICK
YOU DON'T UNDERSTAND, MY FATHER DIED HERE...
IT WAS COBALT'S FAULT AND THEY HAVEN'T DONE A GODDAMN THING ABOUT IT SINCE...
YOU HAVE THE RIGHT TO REMAIN SILENT, ANYTHING YOU SAY CAN AND WILL BE USED AGAINST YOU IN A COURT OF LAW...
THAT BITCH WAS GONNA BLOW ME UP!
I'M TRYING TO PROTECT YOU, SO YOU WON'T LIGHT YOURSELF ON FIRE WITH YOUR OWN WATER...
YOU'VE DONE YOUR HOMETOWN A REAL SERVICE.
OUGHTA BE PROUD.
YOU'RE MAKING 'CLEAN WATER' THAT WILL POISON US.
OUGHTA BE PROUD.
DON'T HAVE NEARLY AS MUCH TO SHOW AS *YOU.*
SHE WAS IN THE CAN FOR 14 GODDAMN YEARS, THE HELL DOES SHE KNOW ABOUT *CLEAN WATER*?
ENOUGH.

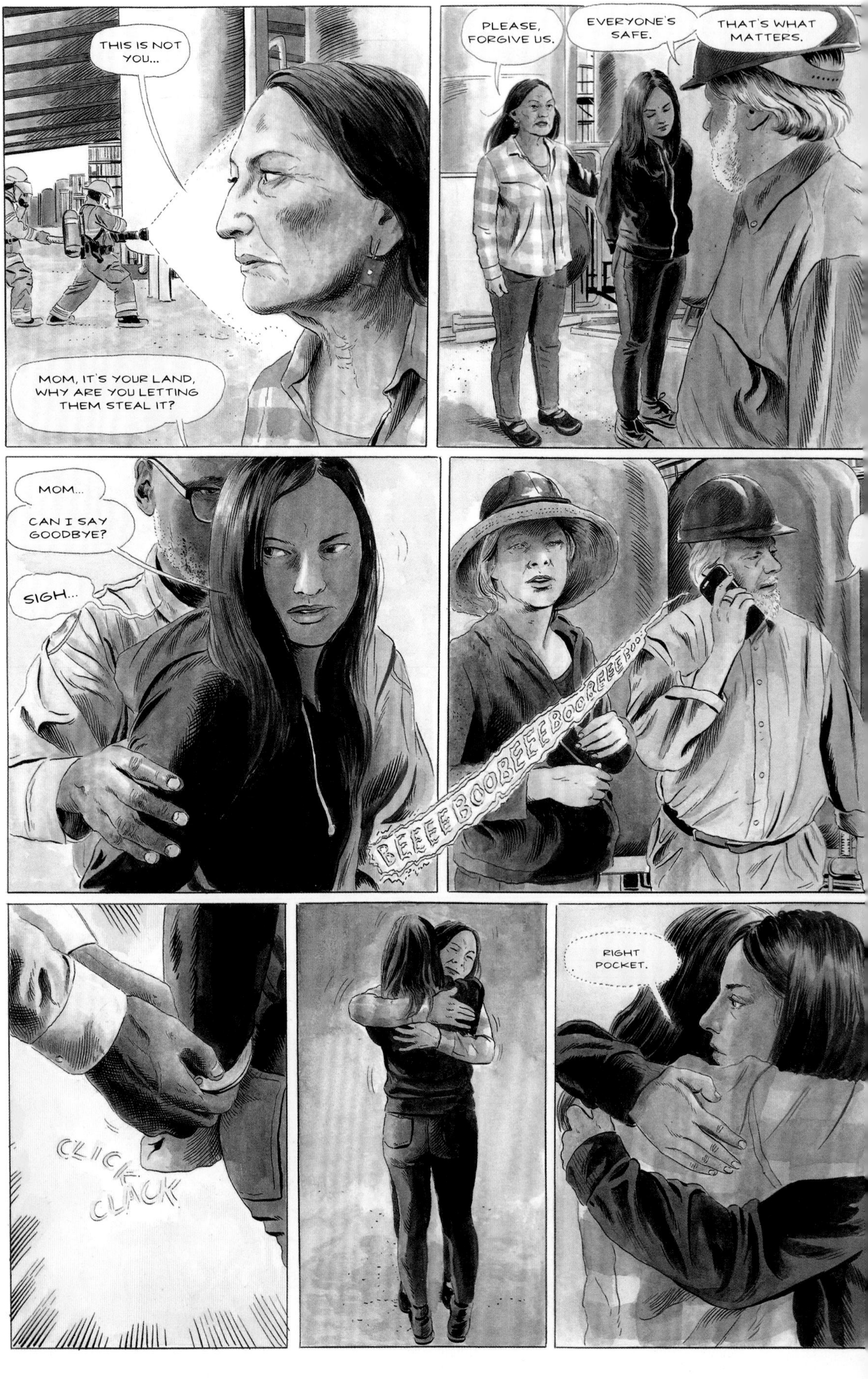
THIS IS NOT YOU...
MOM, IT'S YOUR LAND, WHY ARE YOU LETTING THEM STEAL IT?
PLEASE, FORGIVE US.
EVERYONE'S SAFE.
THAT'S WHAT MATTERS.
MOM...
CAN I SAY GOODBYE?
SIGH...
BEEEEBOOBEEEBOOBEEEBOO
CLICK
CLACK
RIGHT POCKET.

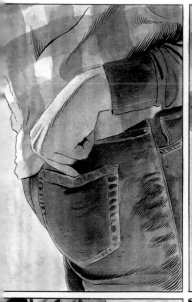

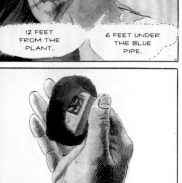

12 FEET FROM THE PLANT.

6 FEET UNDER THE BLUE PIPE.

SHE'S ASKING IF THERE'S A HOLDUP.

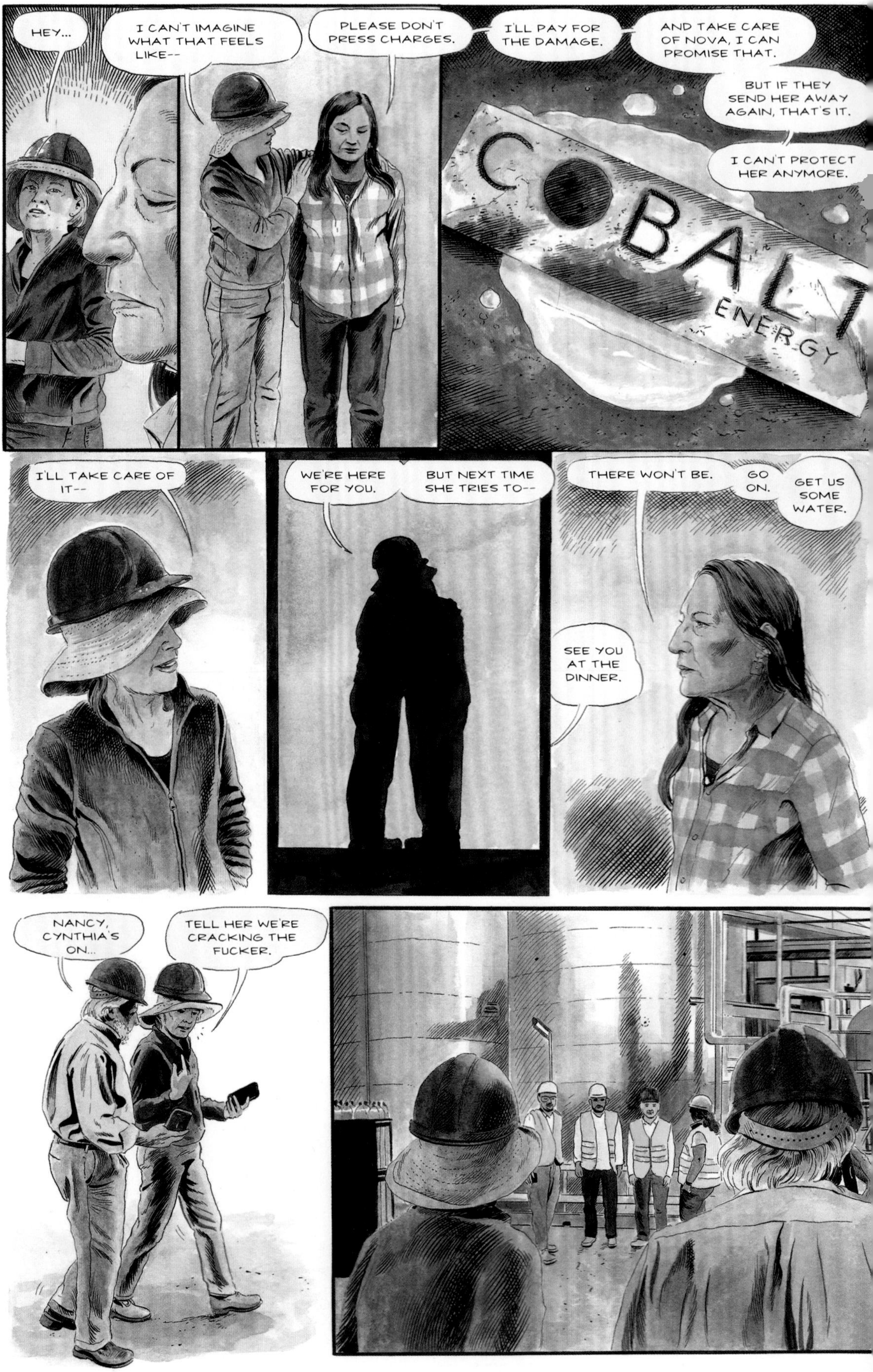
HEY...
I CAN'T IMAGINE WHAT THAT FEELS LIKE--
PLEASE DON'T PRESS CHARGES.
I'LL PAY FOR THE DAMAGE.
AND TAKE CARE OF NOVA, I CAN PROMISE THAT.
BUT IF THEY SEND HER AWAY AGAIN, THAT'S IT.
I CAN'T PROTECT HER ANYMORE.
COBALT
ENERGY
I'LL TAKE CARE OF IT--
WE'RE HERE FOR YOU.
BUT NEXT TIME SHE TRIES TO--
THERE WON'T BE.
GO ON.
GET US SOME WATER.
SEE YOU AT THE DINNER.
NANCY, CYNTHIA'S ON...
TELL HER WE'RE CRACKING THE FUCKER.

CHUGGACHUGG
CLICK CLICKCLICK CLIC
CHUGGACHUG
CLICK CL

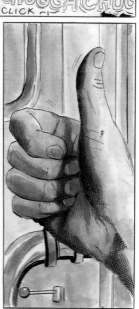

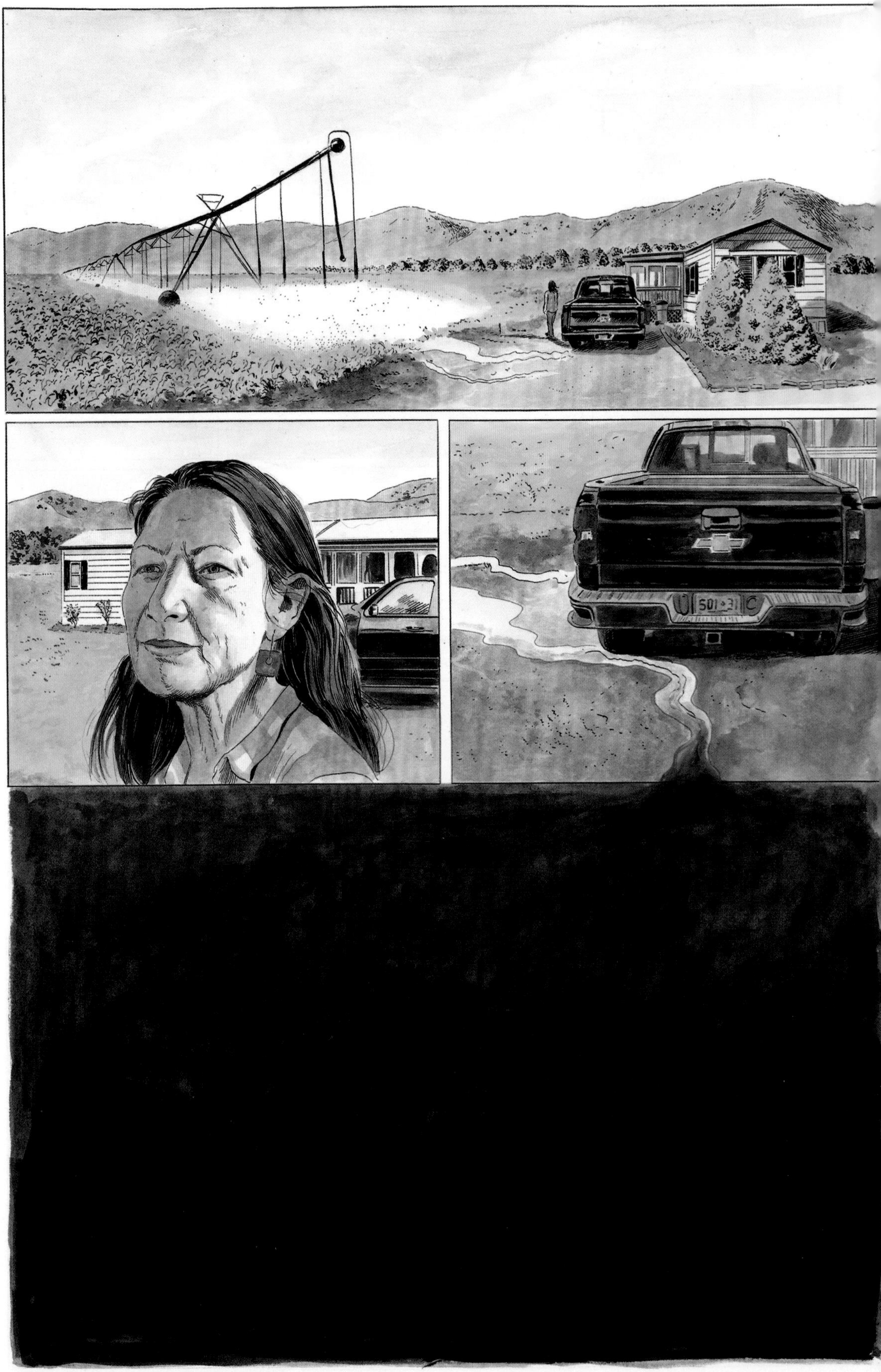

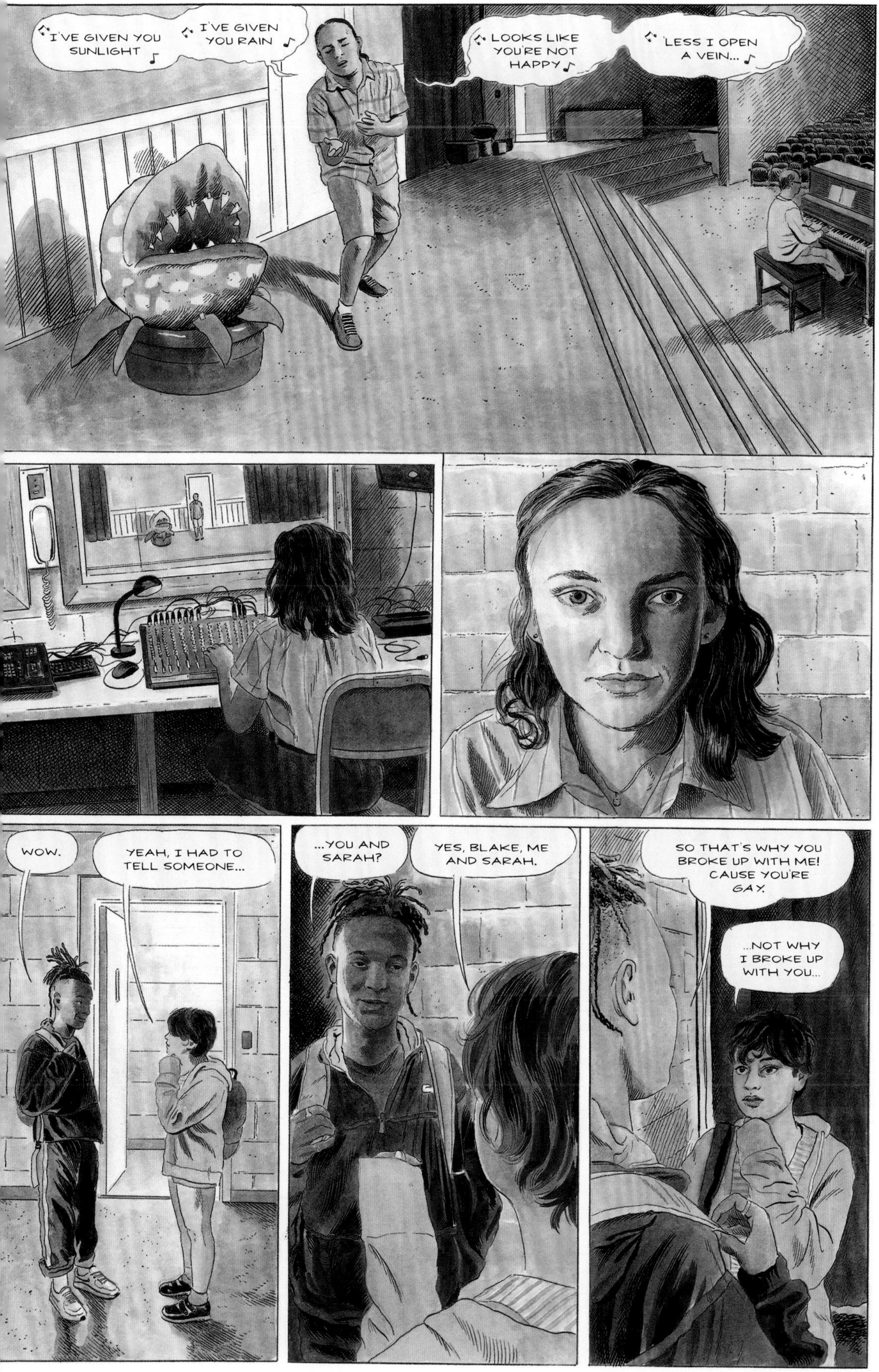
I'VE GIVEN YOU SUNLIGHT
I'VE GIVEN YOU RAIN
LOOKS LIKE YOU'RE NOT HAPPY
'LESS I OPEN A VEIN...
WOW.
YEAH, I HAD TO TELL SOMEONE...
...YOU AND SARAH?
YES, BLAKE, ME AND SARAH.
SO THAT'S WHY YOU BROKE UP WITH ME! CAUSE YOU'RE GAY.
...NOT WHY I BROKE UP WITH YOU...

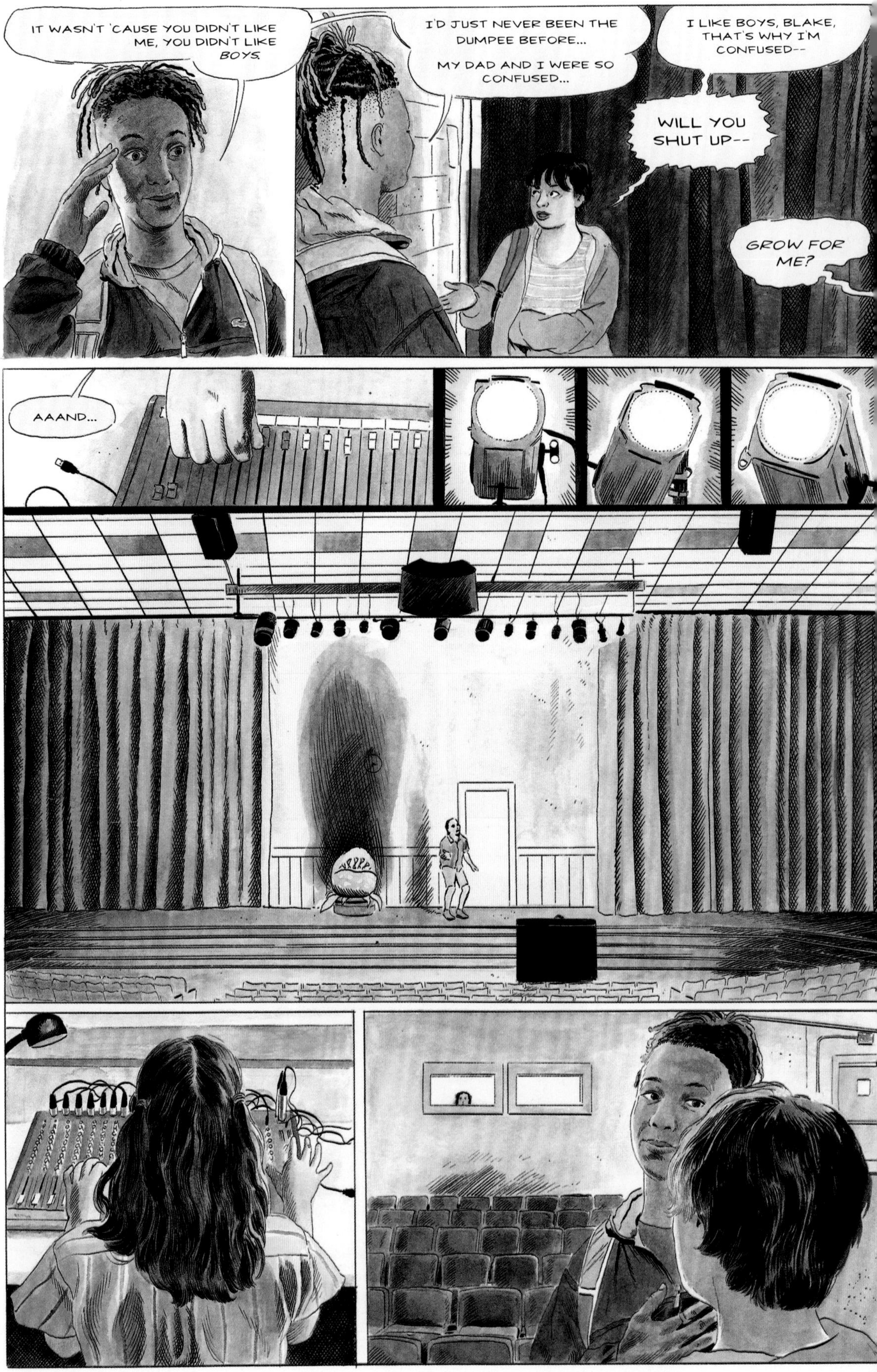
IT WASN'T 'CAUSE YOU DIDN'T LIKE ME, YOU DIDN'T LIKE *BOYS*.
I'D JUST NEVER BEEN THE DUMPEE BEFORE...
MY DAD AND I WERE SO CONFUSED...
I LIKE BOYS, BLAKE, THAT'S WHY I'M CONFUSED--
WILL YOU SHUT UP--
GROW FOR ME?
AAAND...

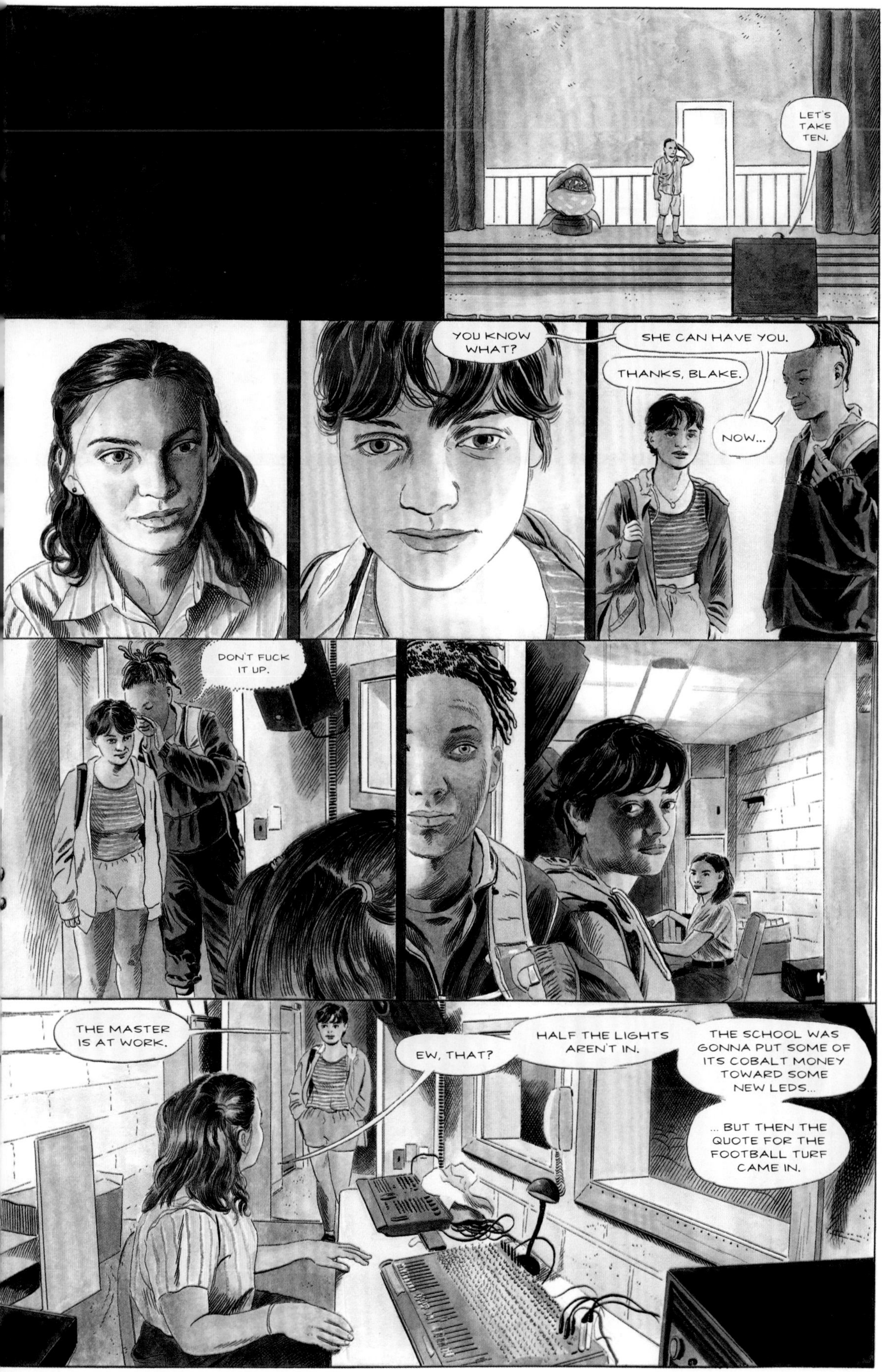
LET'S TAKE TEN.
YOU KNOW WHAT?
SHE CAN HAVE YOU.
THANKS, BLAKE.
NOW...
DON'T FUCK IT UP.
THE MASTER IS AT WORK.
EW, THAT?
HALF THE LIGHTS AREN'T IN.
THE SCHOOL WAS GONNA PUT SOME OF ITS COBALT MONEY TOWARD SOME NEW LEDS...
... BUT THEN THE QUOTE FOR THE FOOTBALL TURF CAME IN.

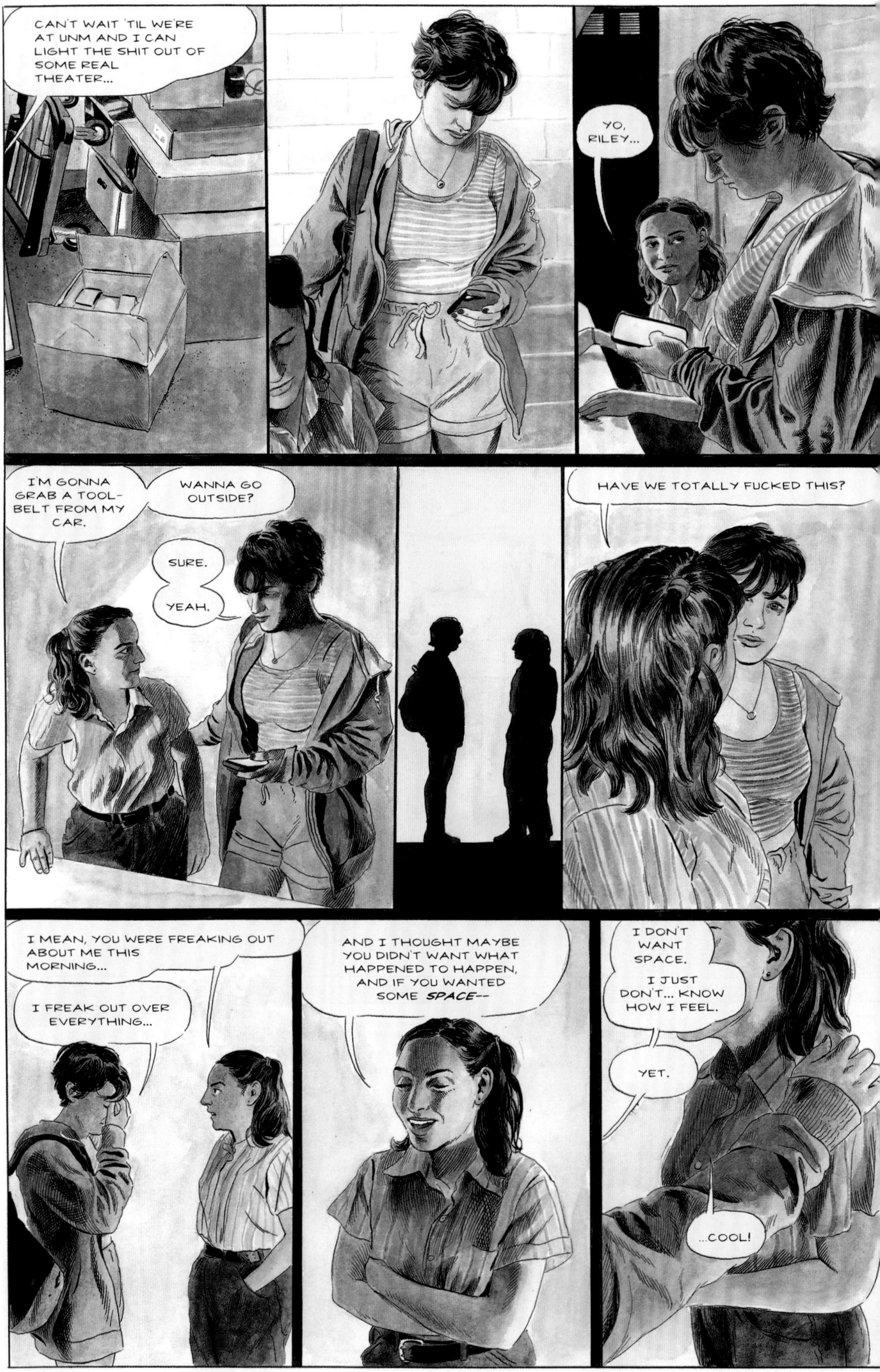
CAN'T WAIT 'TIL WE'RE AT UNM AND I CAN LIGHT THE SHIT OUT OF SOME REAL THEATER...
YO, RILEY...
I'M GONNA GRAB A TOOL-BELT FROM MY CAR.
WANNA GO OUTSIDE?
SURE.
YEAH.
HAVE WE TOTALLY FUCKED THIS?
I MEAN, YOU WERE FREAKING OUT ABOUT ME THIS MORNING...
I FREAK OUT OVER EVERYTHING...
AND I THOUGHT MAYBE YOU DIDN'T WANT WHAT HAPPENED TO HAPPEN, AND IF YOU WANTED SOME SPACE--
I DON'T WANT SPACE.
I JUST DON'T... KNOW HOW I FEEL.
YET.
...COOL!

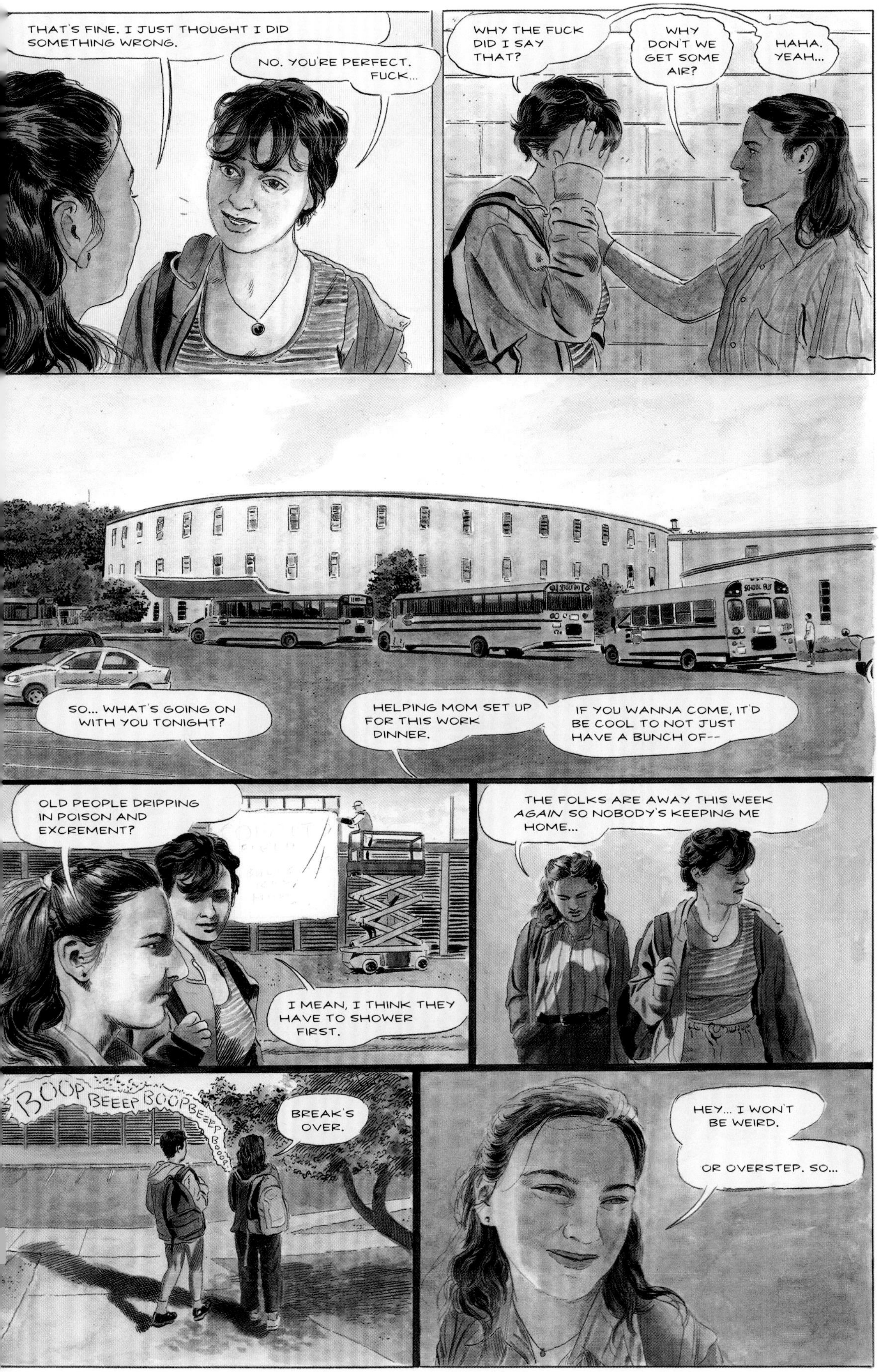
THAT'S FINE. I JUST THOUGHT I DID SOMETHING WRONG.
NO. YOU'RE PERFECT. FUCK...
WHY THE FUCK DID I SAY THAT?
WHY DON'T WE GET SOME AIR?
HAHA. YEAH...
SO... WHAT'S GOING ON WITH YOU TONIGHT?
HELPING MOM SET UP FOR THIS WORK DINNER.
IF YOU WANNA COME, IT'D BE COOL TO NOT JUST HAVE A BUNCH OF--
OLD PEOPLE DRIPPING IN POISON AND EXCREMENT?
I MEAN, I THINK THEY HAVE TO SHOWER FIRST.
THE FOLKS ARE AWAY THIS WEEK *AGAIN* SO NOBODY'S KEEPING ME HOME...
BOOP BEEEP BOOP BEEEP BOOOP
BREAK'S OVER.
HEY... I WON'T BE WEIRD.
OR OVERSTEP. SO...

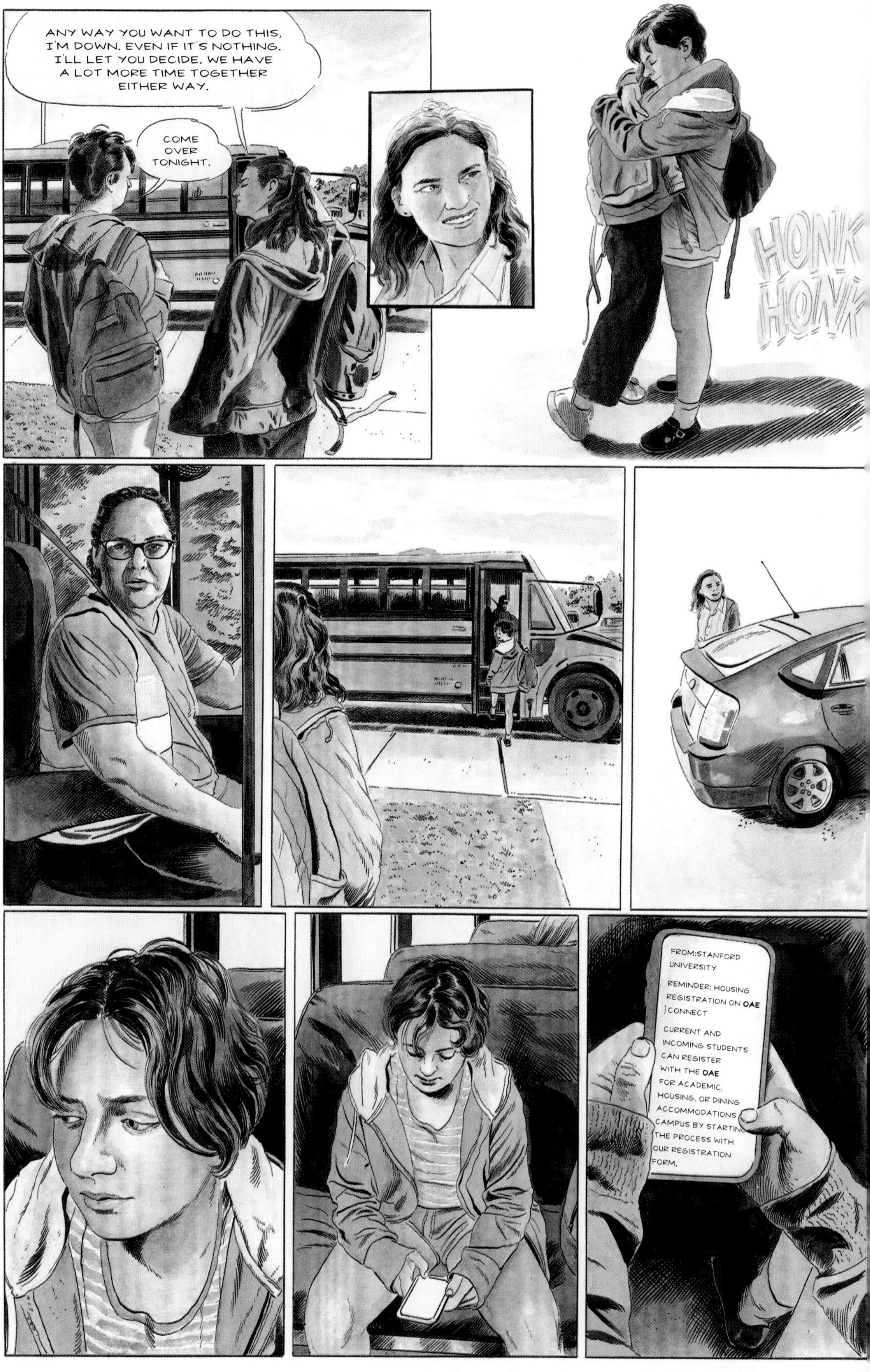
ANY WAY YOU WANT TO DO THIS, I'M DOWN. EVEN IF IT'S NOTHING. I'LL LET YOU DECIDE. WE HAVE A LOT MORE TIME TOGETHER EITHER WAY.
COME OVER TONIGHT.
HONK HONK
FROM:STANFORD UNIVERSITY
REMINDER: HOUSING REGISTRATION ON OAE CONNECT
CURRENT AND INCOMING STUDENTS CAN REGISTER WITH THE OAE FOR ACADEMIC, HOUSING, OR DINING ACCOMMODATIONS CAMPUS BY STARTING THE PROCESS WITH OUR REGISTRATION FORM.

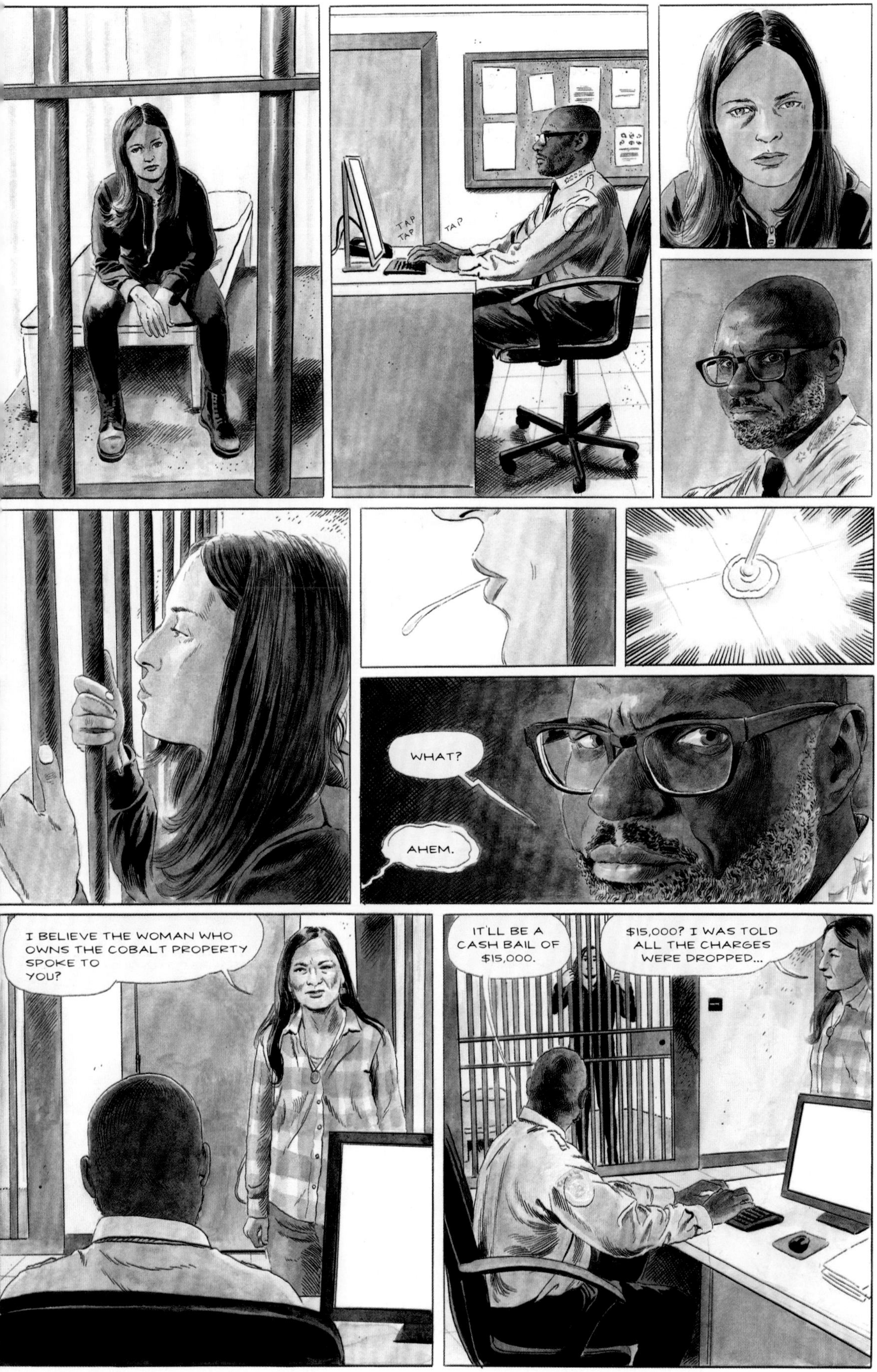
TAP
TAP
TAP
WHAT?
AHEM.
I BELIEVE THE WOMAN WHO OWNS THE COBALT PROPERTY SPOKE TO YOU?
IT'LL BE A CASH BAIL OF $15,000.
$15,000? I WAS TOLD ALL THE CHARGES WERE DROPPED...

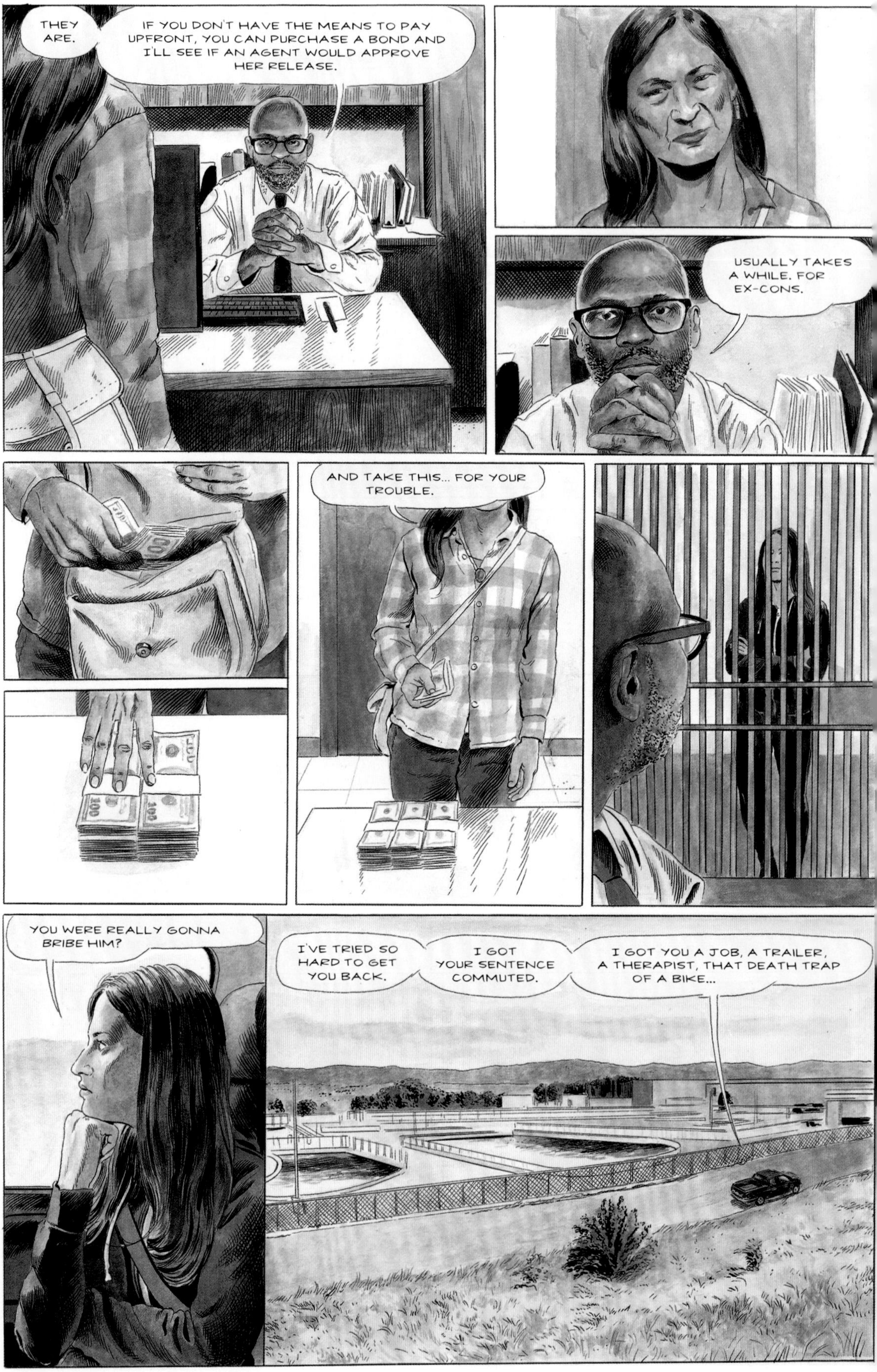
THEY ARE.
IF YOU DON'T HAVE THE MEANS TO PAY UPFRONT, YOU CAN PURCHASE A BOND AND I'LL SEE IF AN AGENT WOULD APPROVE HER RELEASE.
USUALLY TAKES A WHILE. FOR EX-CONS.
AND TAKE THIS... FOR YOUR TROUBLE.
YOU WERE REALLY GONNA BRIBE HIM?
I'VE TRIED SO HARD TO GET YOU BACK.
I GOT YOUR SENTENCE COMMUTED.
I GOT YOU A JOB, A TRAILER, A THERAPIST, THAT DEATH TRAP OF A BIKE...

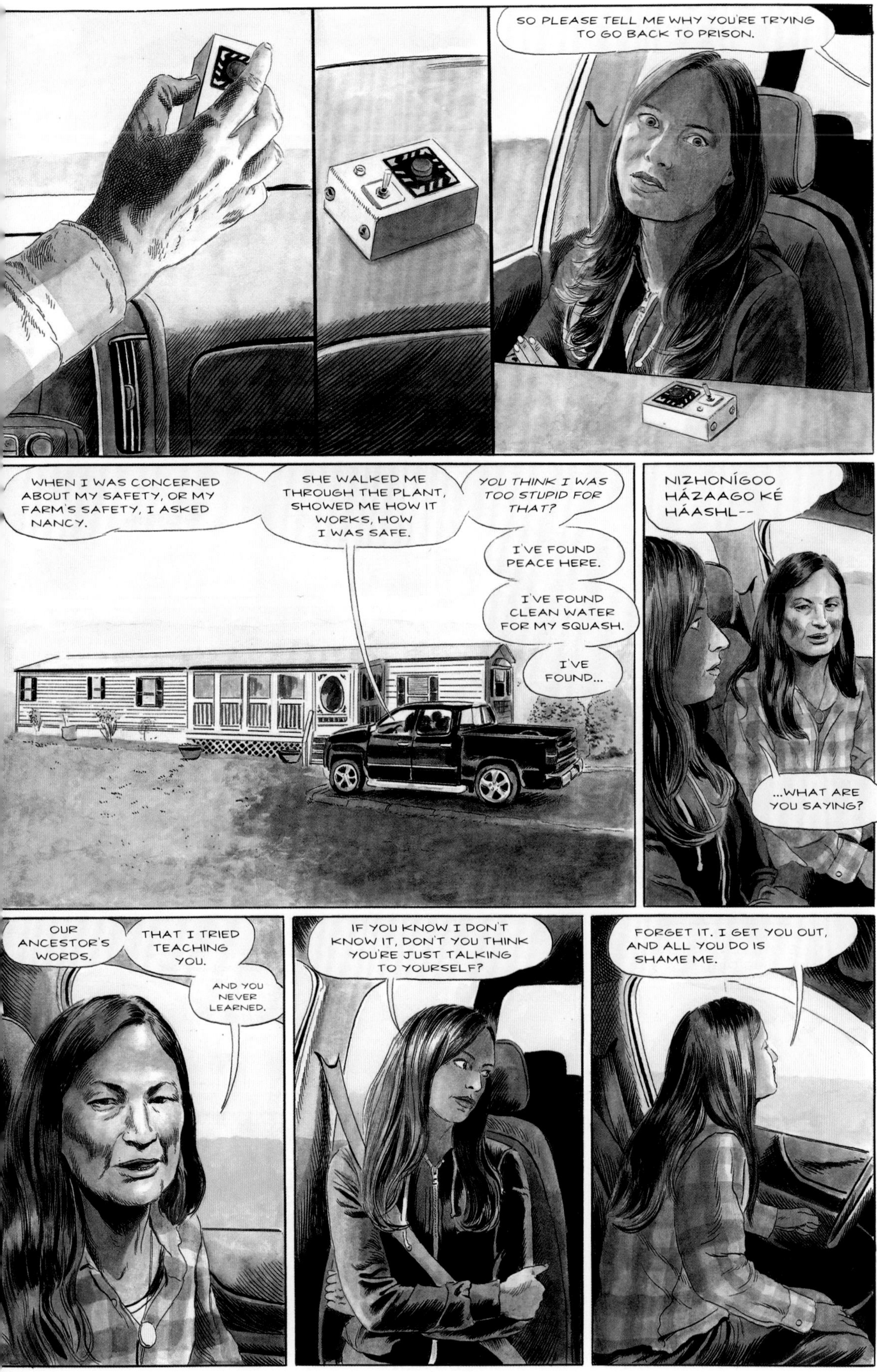
SO PLEASE TELL ME WHY YOU'RE TRYING TO GO BACK TO PRISON.
WHEN I WAS CONCERNED ABOUT MY SAFETY, OR MY FARM'S SAFETY, I ASKED NANCY.
SHE WALKED ME THROUGH THE PLANT, SHOWED ME HOW IT WORKS, HOW I WAS SAFE.
YOU THINK I WAS TOO STUPID FOR THAT?
I'VE FOUND PEACE HERE.
I'VE FOUND CLEAN WATER FOR MY SQUASH.
I'VE FOUND...
NIZHONÍGOO HÁZAAGO KÉ HÁASHL--
...WHAT ARE YOU SAYING?
OUR ANCESTOR'S WORDS.
THAT I TRIED TEACHING YOU.
AND YOU NEVER LEARNED.
IF YOU KNOW I DON'T KNOW IT, DON'T YOU THINK YOU'RE JUST TALKING TO YOURSELF?
FORGET IT. I GET YOU OUT, AND ALL YOU DO IS SHAME ME.

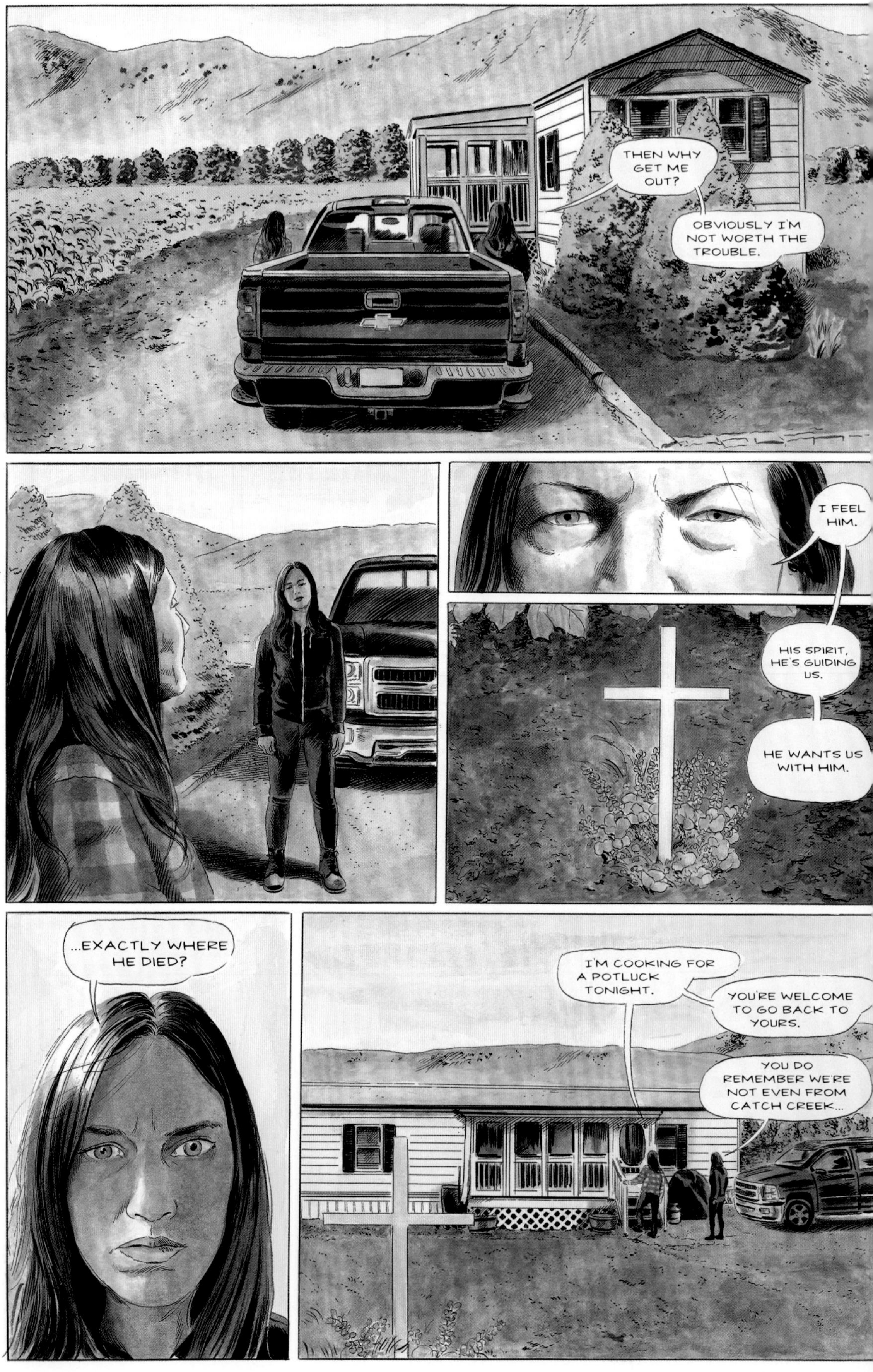
THEN WHY GET ME OUT?
OBVIOUSLY I'M NOT WORTH THE TROUBLE.
I FEEL HIM.
HIS SPIRIT, HE'S GUIDING US.
HE WANTS US WITH HIM.
...EXACTLY WHERE HE DIED?
I'M COOKING FOR A POTLUCK TONIGHT.
YOU'RE WELCOME TO GO BACK TO YOURS.
YOU DO REMEMBER WE'RE NOT EVEN FROM CATCH CREEK...

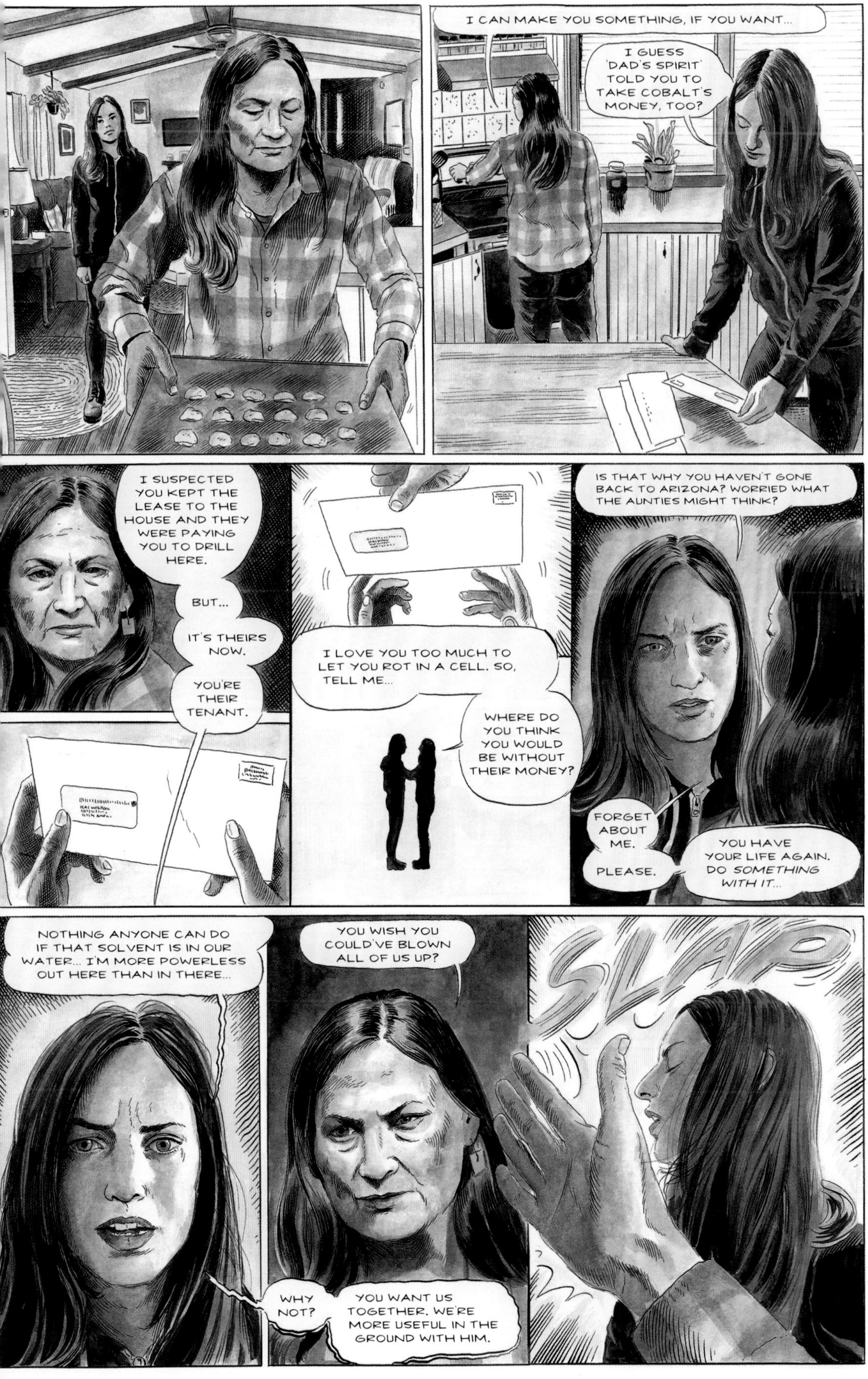
I CAN MAKE YOU SOMETHING, IF YOU WANT...
I GUESS 'DAD'S SPIRIT' TOLD YOU TO TAKE COBALT'S MONEY, TOO?
I SUSPECTED YOU KEPT THE LEASE TO THE HOUSE AND THEY WERE PAYING YOU TO DRILL HERE.
BUT...
IT'S THEIRS NOW.
YOU'RE THEIR TENANT.
I LOVE YOU TOO MUCH TO LET YOU ROT IN A CELL. SO, TELL ME...
WHERE DO YOU THINK YOU WOULD BE WITHOUT THEIR MONEY?
IS THAT WHY YOU HAVEN'T GONE BACK TO ARIZONA? WORRIED WHAT THE AUNTIES MIGHT THINK?
FORGET ABOUT ME.
PLEASE.
YOU HAVE YOUR LIFE AGAIN. DO *SOMETHING* WITH IT...
NOTHING ANYONE CAN DO IF THAT SOLVENT IS IN OUR WATER... I'M MORE POWERLESS OUT HERE THAN IN THERE...
YOU WISH YOU COULD'VE BLOWN ALL OF US UP?
WHY NOT?
YOU WANT US TOGETHER. WE'RE MORE USEFUL IN THE GROUND WITH HIM.
SLAP

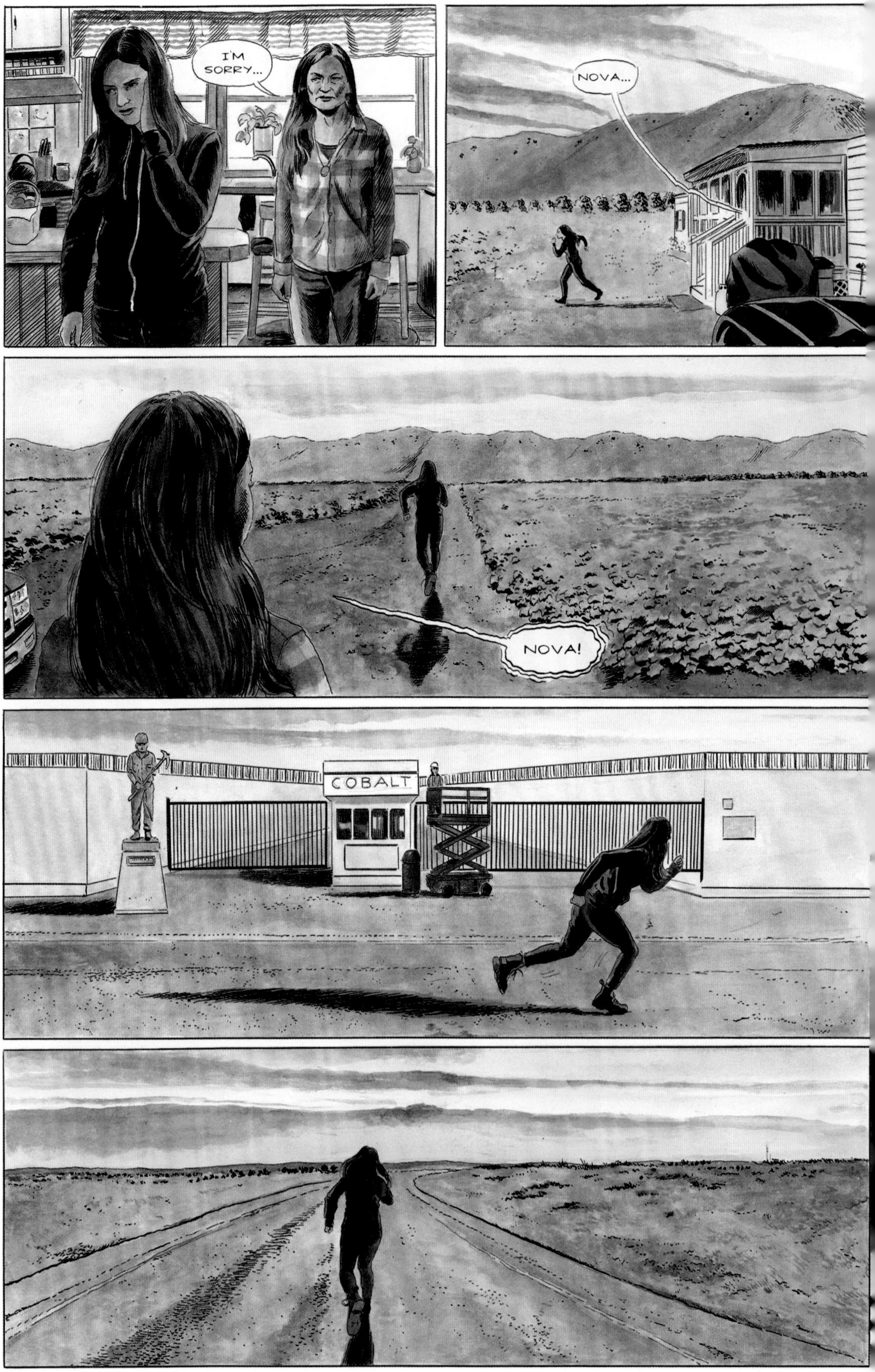
I'M SORRY...
NOVA...
NOVA!
COBALT

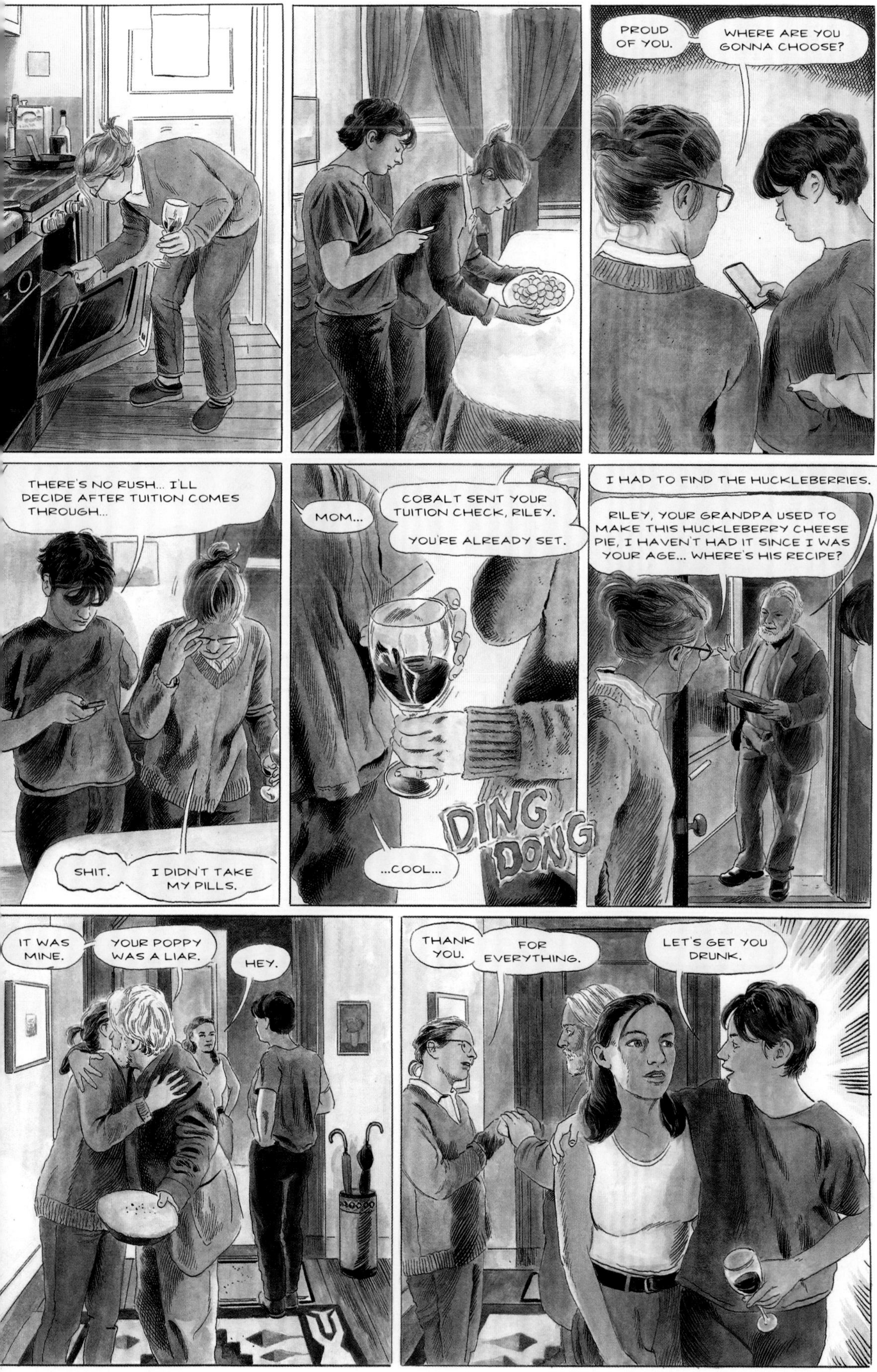
PROUD OF YOU.
WHERE ARE YOU GONNA CHOOSE?
THERE'S NO RUSH... I'LL DECIDE AFTER TUITION COMES THROUGH...
SHIT.
I DIDN'T TAKE MY PILLS.
MOM...
COBALT SENT YOUR TUITION CHECK, RILEY.
YOU'RE ALREADY SET.
...COOL...
DING DONG
I HAD TO FIND THE HUCKLEBERRIES.
RILEY, YOUR GRANDPA USED TO MAKE THIS HUCKLEBERRY CHEESE PIE, I HAVEN'T HAD IT SINCE I WAS YOUR AGE... WHERE'S HIS RECIPE?
IT WAS MINE.
YOUR POPPY WAS A LIAR.
HEY.
THANK YOU.
FOR EVERYTHING.
LET'S GET YOU DRUNK.

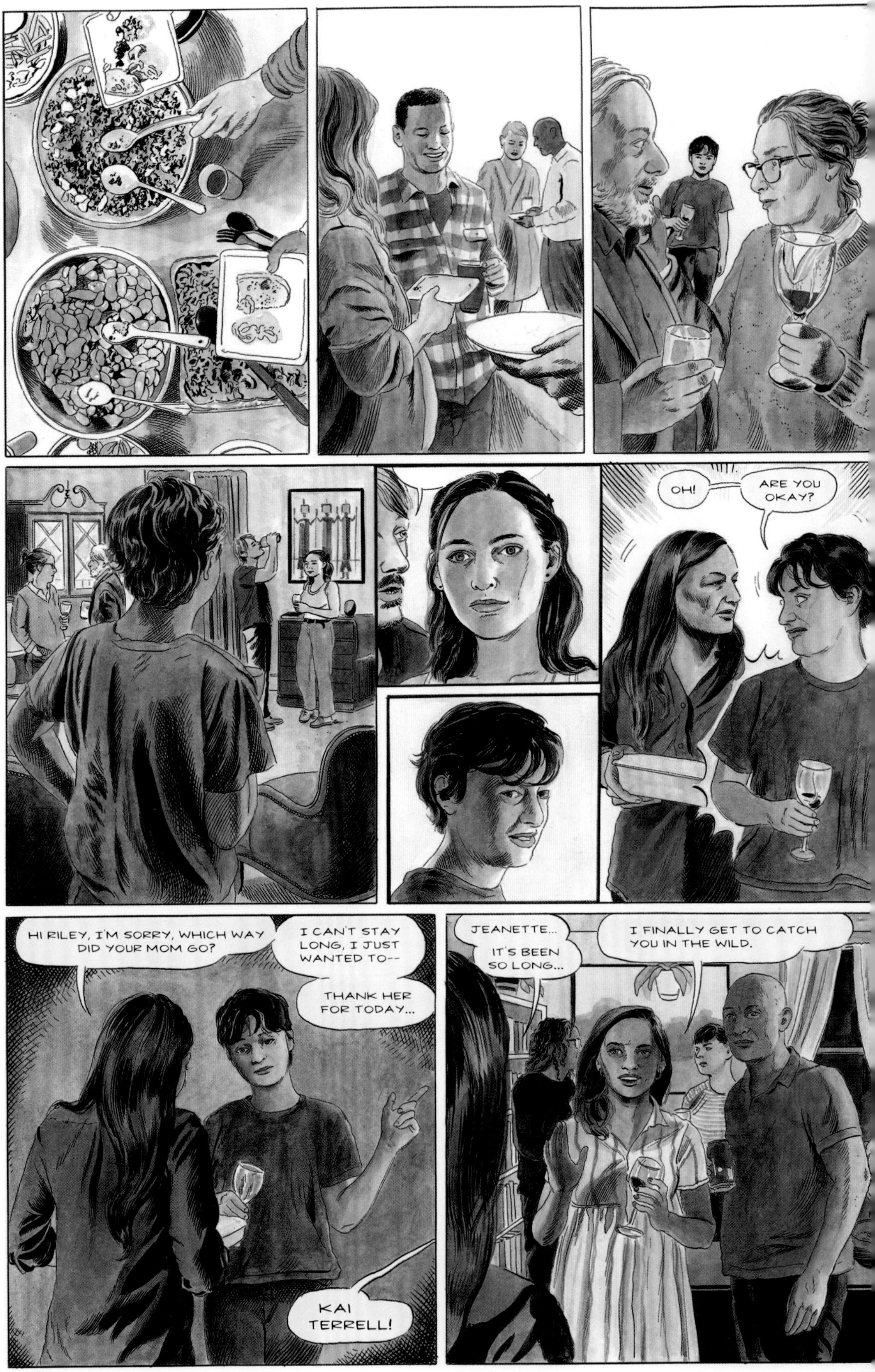
OH!
ARE YOU OKAY?
HI RILEY, I'M SORRY, WHICH WAY DID YOUR MOM GO?
I CAN'T STAY LONG, I JUST WANTED TO--
THANK HER FOR TODAY...
KAI TERRELL!
JEANETTE...
IT'S BEEN SO LONG...
I FINALLY GET TO CATCH YOU IN THE WILD.

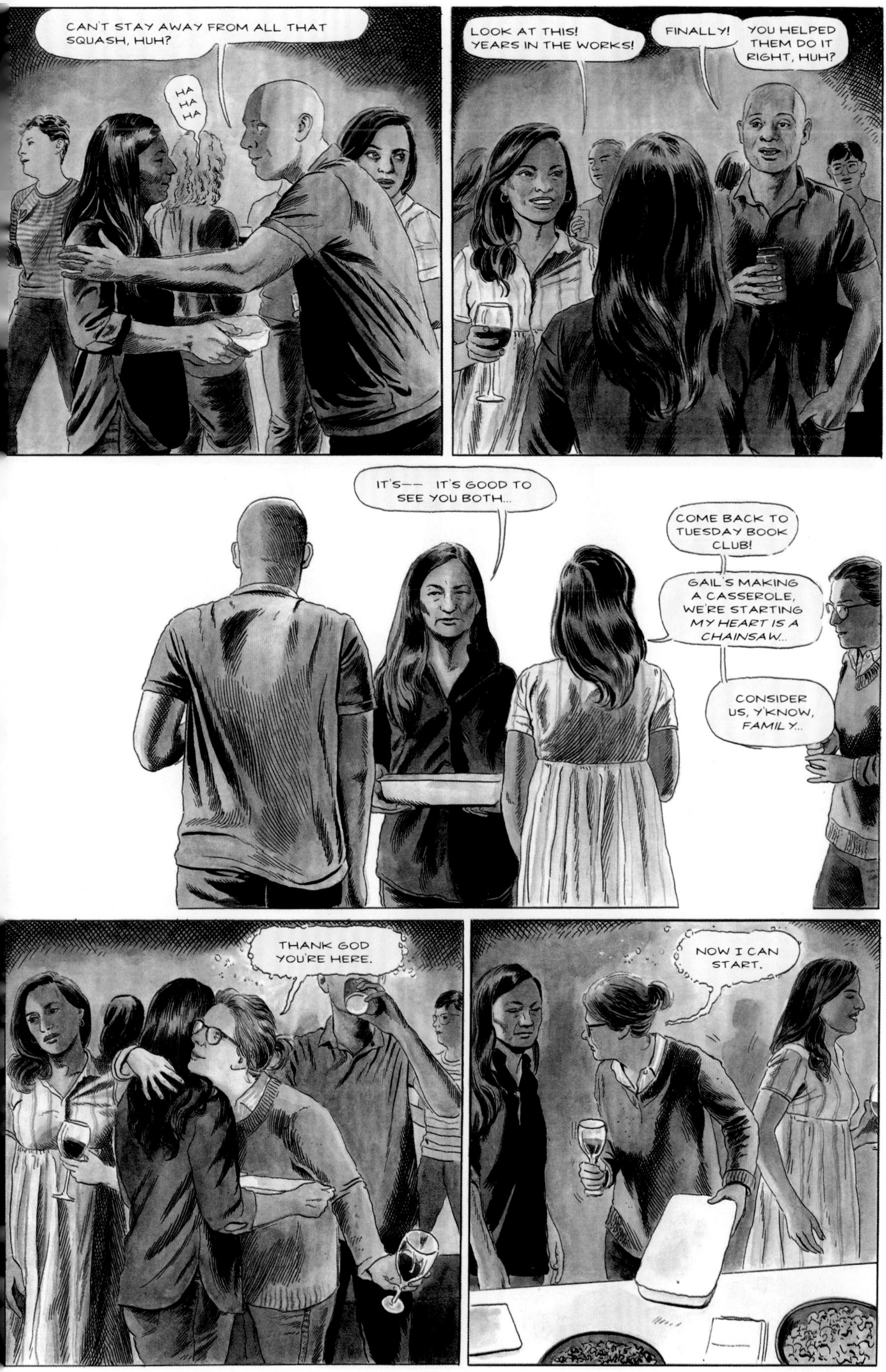
CAN'T STAY AWAY FROM ALL THAT SQUASH, HUH?
HA HA HA
LOOK AT THIS! YEARS IN THE WORKS!
FINALLY!
YOU HELPED THEM DO IT RIGHT, HUH?
IT'S-- IT'S GOOD TO SEE YOU BOTH...
COME BACK TO TUESDAY BOOK CLUB!
GAIL'S MAKING A CASSEROLE, WE'RE STARTING *MY HEART IS A CHAINSAW*...
CONSIDER US, Y'KNOW, *FAMILY*...
THANK GOD YOU'RE HERE.
NOW I CAN START.

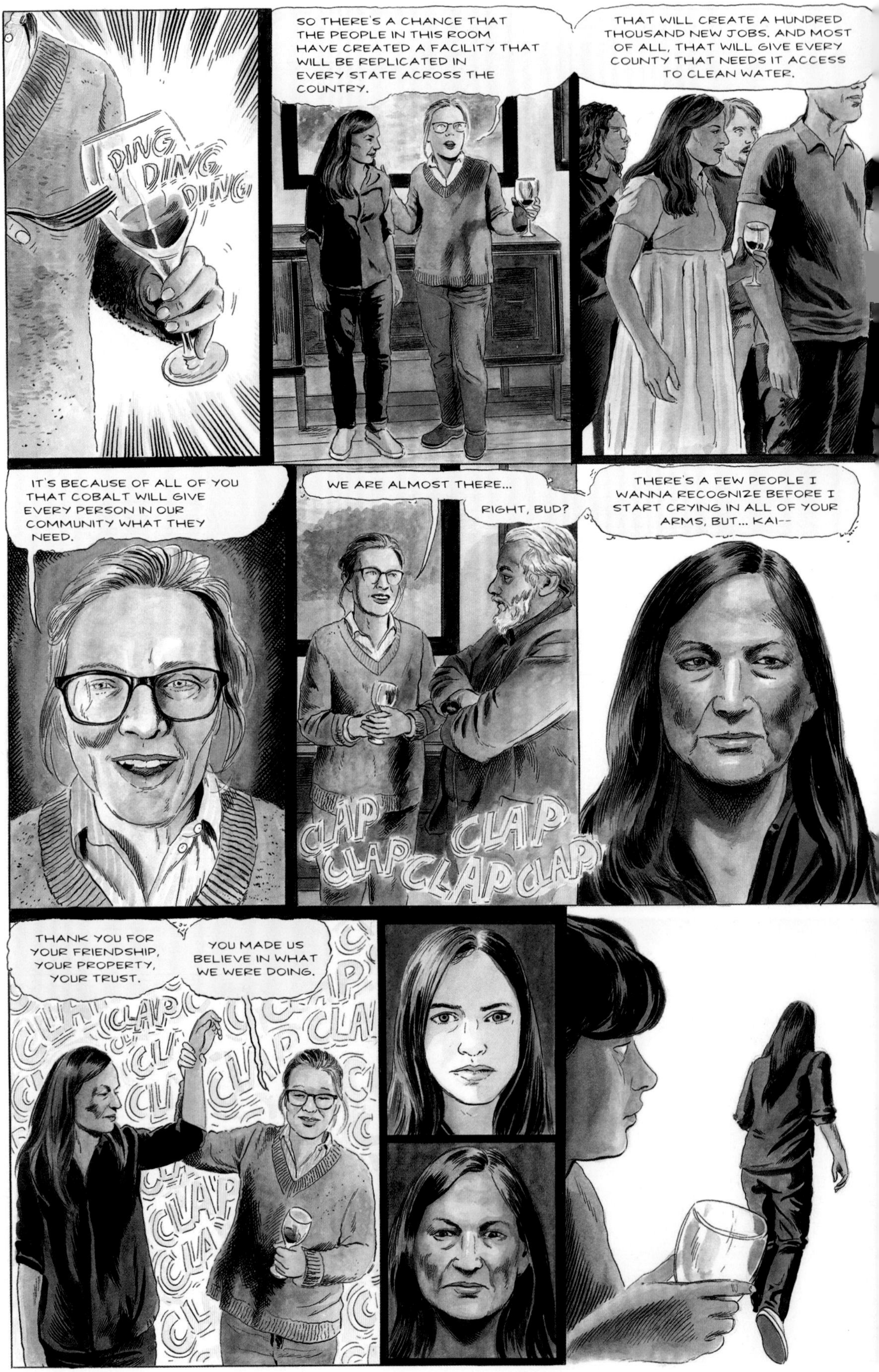
DING
DING
DING
SO THERE'S A CHANCE THAT THE PEOPLE IN THIS ROOM HAVE CREATED A FACILITY THAT WILL BE REPLICATED IN EVERY STATE ACROSS THE COUNTRY.
THAT WILL CREATE A HUNDRED THOUSAND NEW JOBS. AND MOST OF ALL, THAT WILL GIVE EVERY COUNTY THAT NEEDS IT ACCESS TO CLEAN WATER.
IT'S BECAUSE OF ALL OF YOU THAT COBALT WILL GIVE EVERY PERSON IN OUR COMMUNITY WHAT THEY NEED.
WE ARE ALMOST THERE...
RIGHT, BUD?
CLAP CLAP CLAP CLAP CLAP CLAP
THERE'S A FEW PEOPLE I WANNA RECOGNIZE BEFORE I START CRYING IN ALL OF YOUR ARMS, BUT... KAI--
THANK YOU FOR YOUR FRIENDSHIP, YOUR PROPERTY, YOUR TRUST.
YOU MADE US BELIEVE IN WHAT WE WERE DOING.
CLAP CLAP CLAP

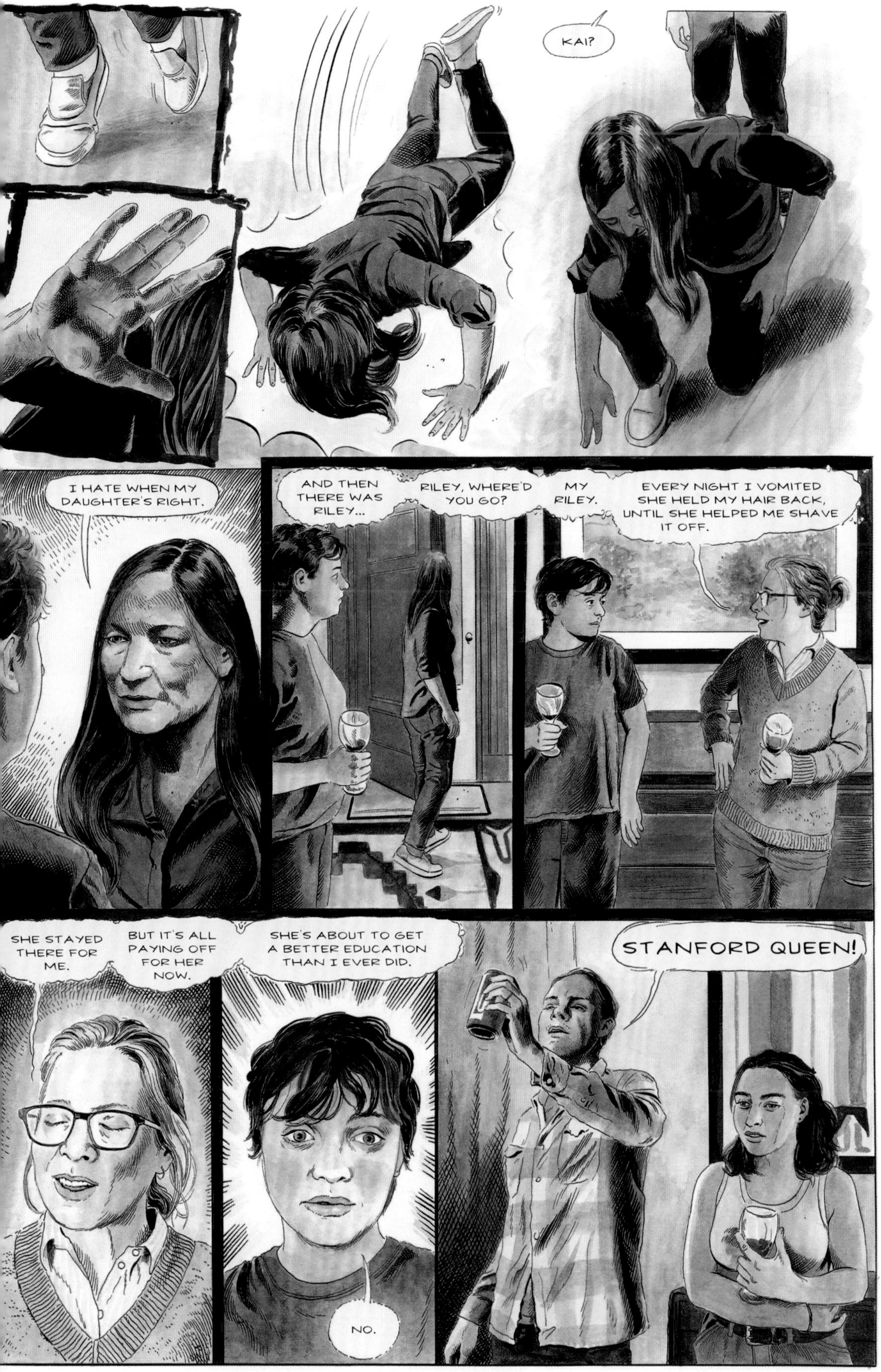
KAI?
I HATE WHEN MY DAUGHTER'S RIGHT.
AND THEN THERE WAS RILEY...
RILEY, WHERE'D YOU GO?
MY RILEY.
EVERY NIGHT I VOMITED SHE HELD MY HAIR BACK, UNTIL SHE HELPED ME SHAVE IT OFF.
SHE STAYED THERE FOR ME.
BUT IT'S ALL PAYING OFF FOR HER NOW.
SHE'S ABOUT TO GET A BETTER EDUCATION THAN I EVER DID.
NO.
STANFORD QUEEN!

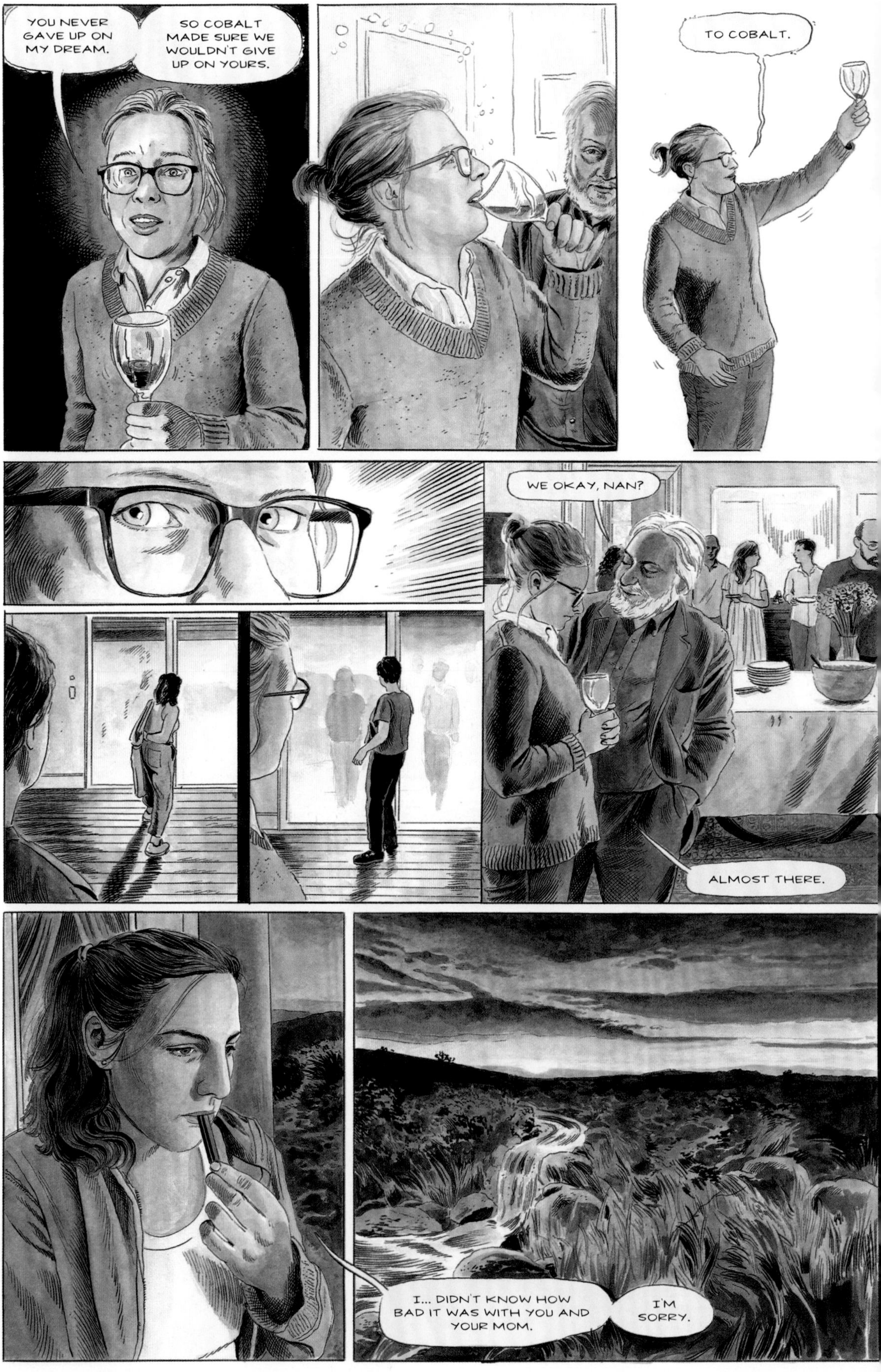
YOU NEVER GAVE UP ON MY DREAM.
SO COBALT MADE SURE WE WOULDN'T GIVE UP ON YOURS.
TO COBALT.
WE OKAY, NAN?
ALMOST THERE.
I... DIDN'T KNOW HOW BAD IT WAS WITH YOU AND YOUR MOM.
I'M SORRY.

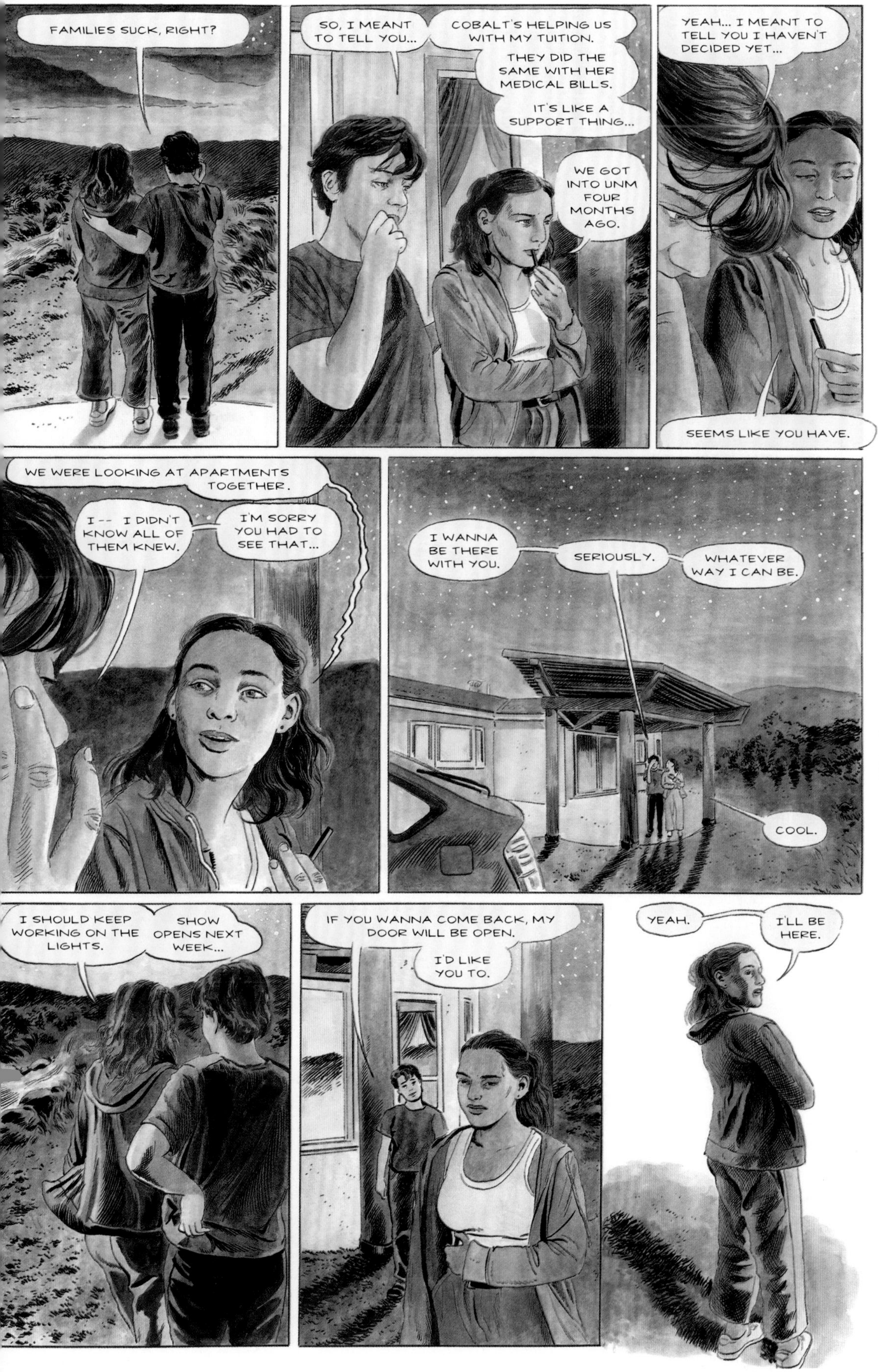

FAMILIES SUCK, RIGHT?
SO, I MEANT TO TELL YOU...
COBALT'S HELPING US WITH MY TUITION.
THEY DID THE SAME WITH HER MEDICAL BILLS.
IT'S LIKE A SUPPORT THING...
WE GOT INTO UNM FOUR MONTHS AGO.
YEAH... I MEANT TO TELL YOU I HAVEN'T DECIDED YET...
SEEMS LIKE YOU HAVE.
WE WERE LOOKING AT APARTMENTS TOGETHER.
I -- I DIDN'T KNOW ALL OF THEM KNEW.
I'M SORRY YOU HAD TO SEE THAT...
I WANNA BE THERE WITH YOU.
SERIOUSLY.
WHATEVER WAY I CAN BE.
COOL.
I SHOULD KEEP WORKING ON THE LIGHTS.
SHOW OPENS NEXT WEEK...
IF YOU WANNA COME BACK, MY DOOR WILL BE OPEN.
I'D LIKE YOU TO.
YEAH.
I'LL BE HERE.

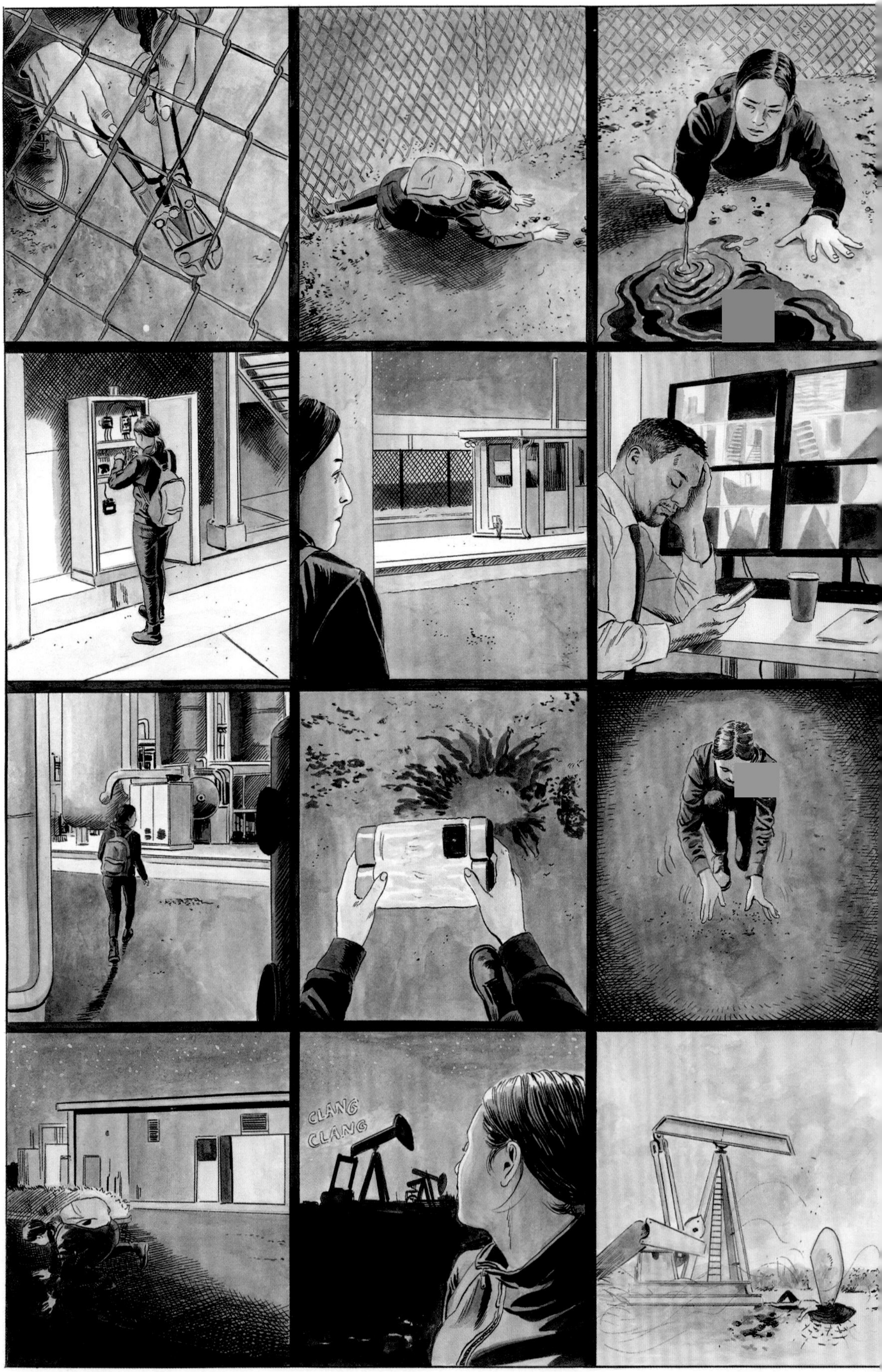
CLANG
CLANG

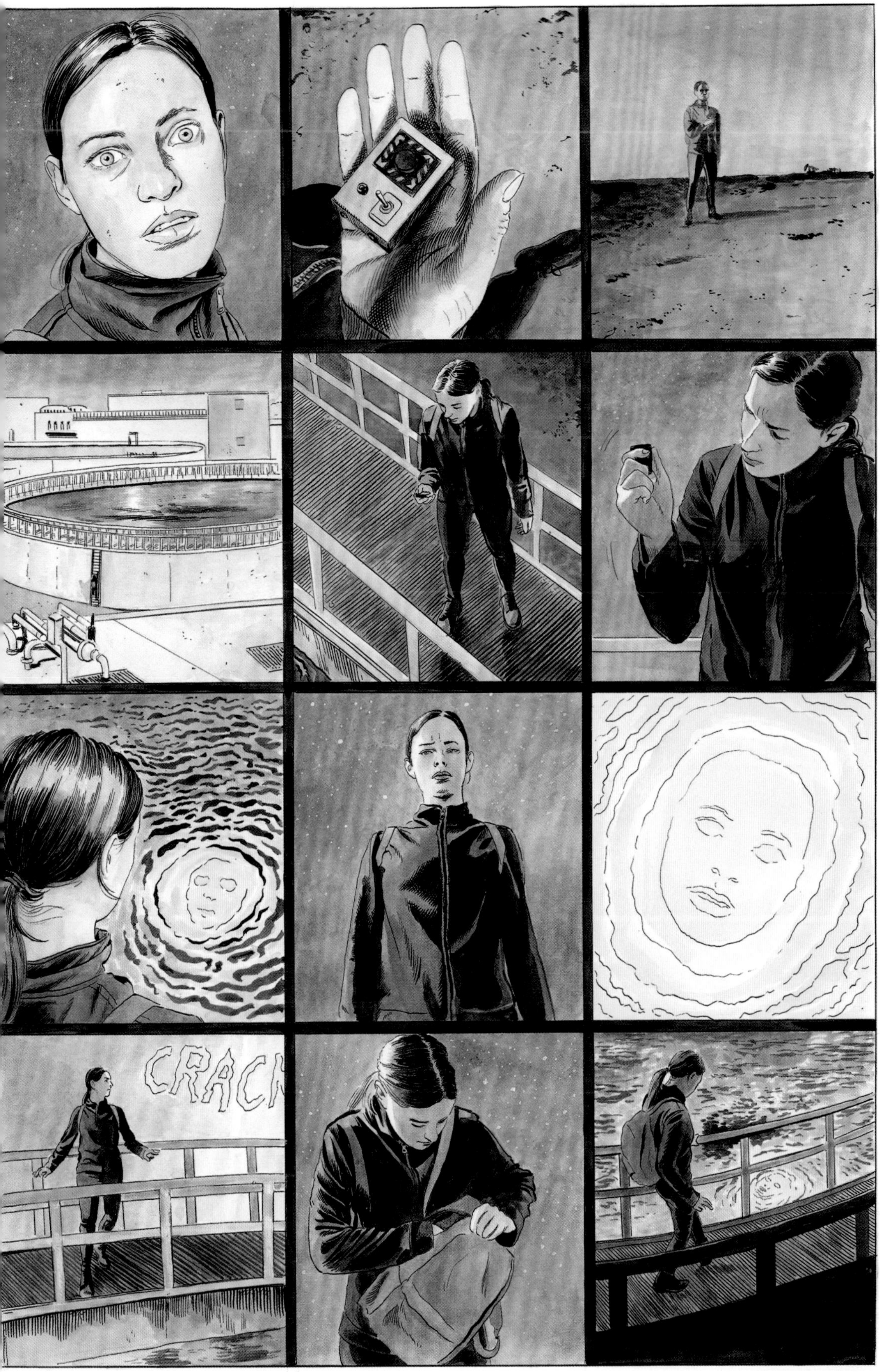
CRAC

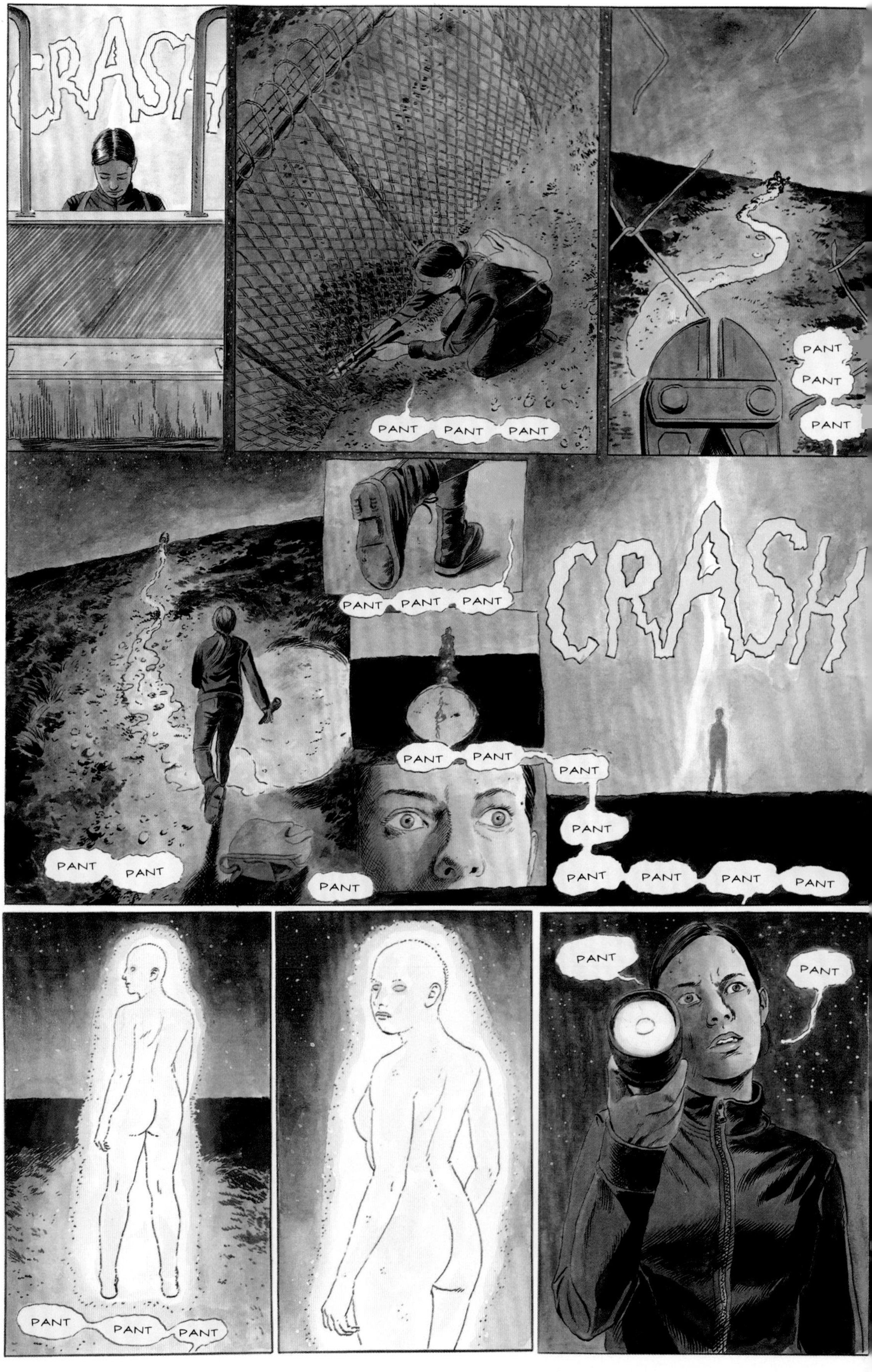
CRASH
PANT PANT PANT
PANT
PANT
PANT
PANT PANT PANT
CRASH
PANT PANT
PANT PANT
PANT
PANT
PANT
PANT PANT PANT PANT
PANT PANT PANT
PANT
PANT

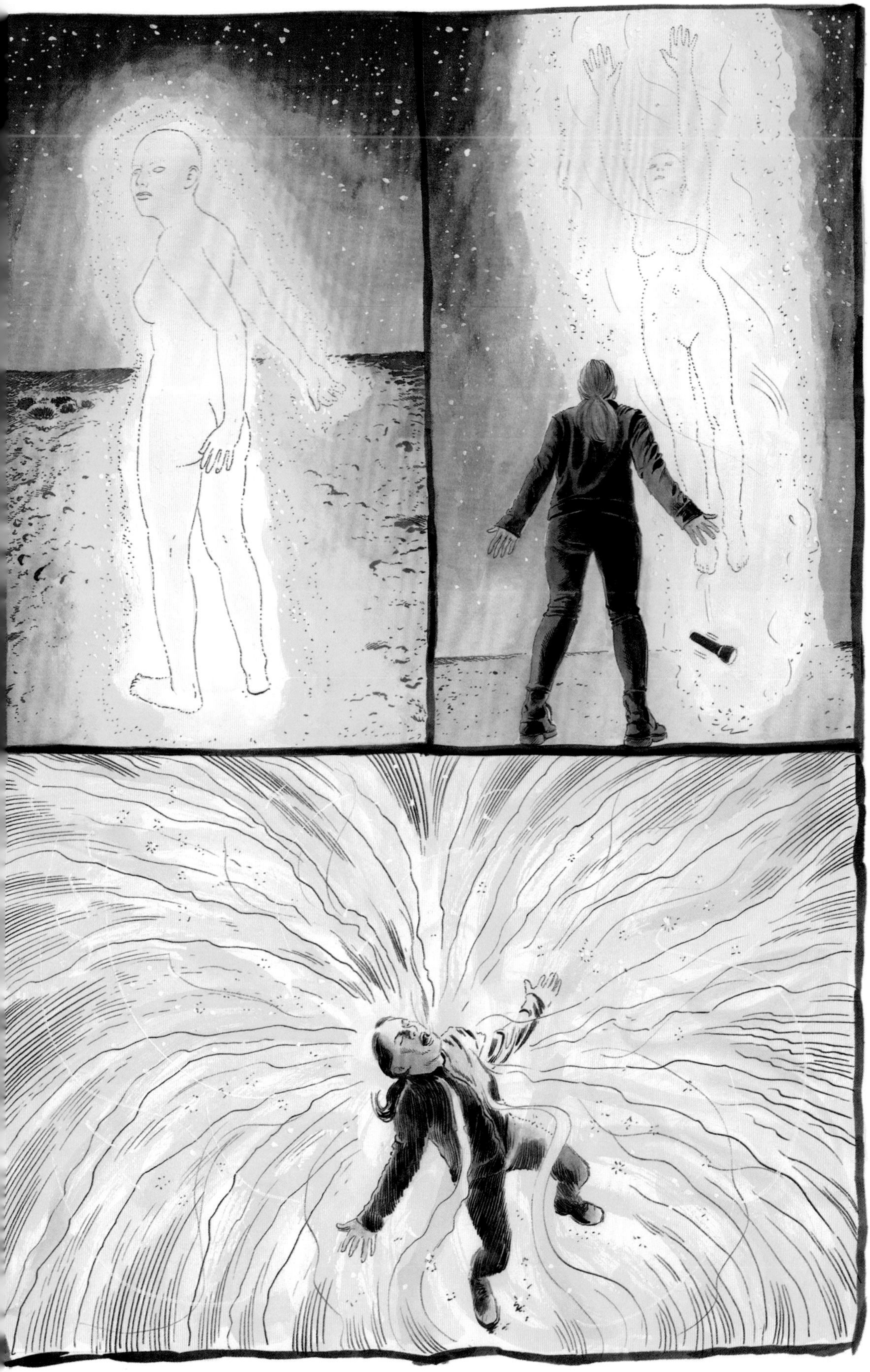

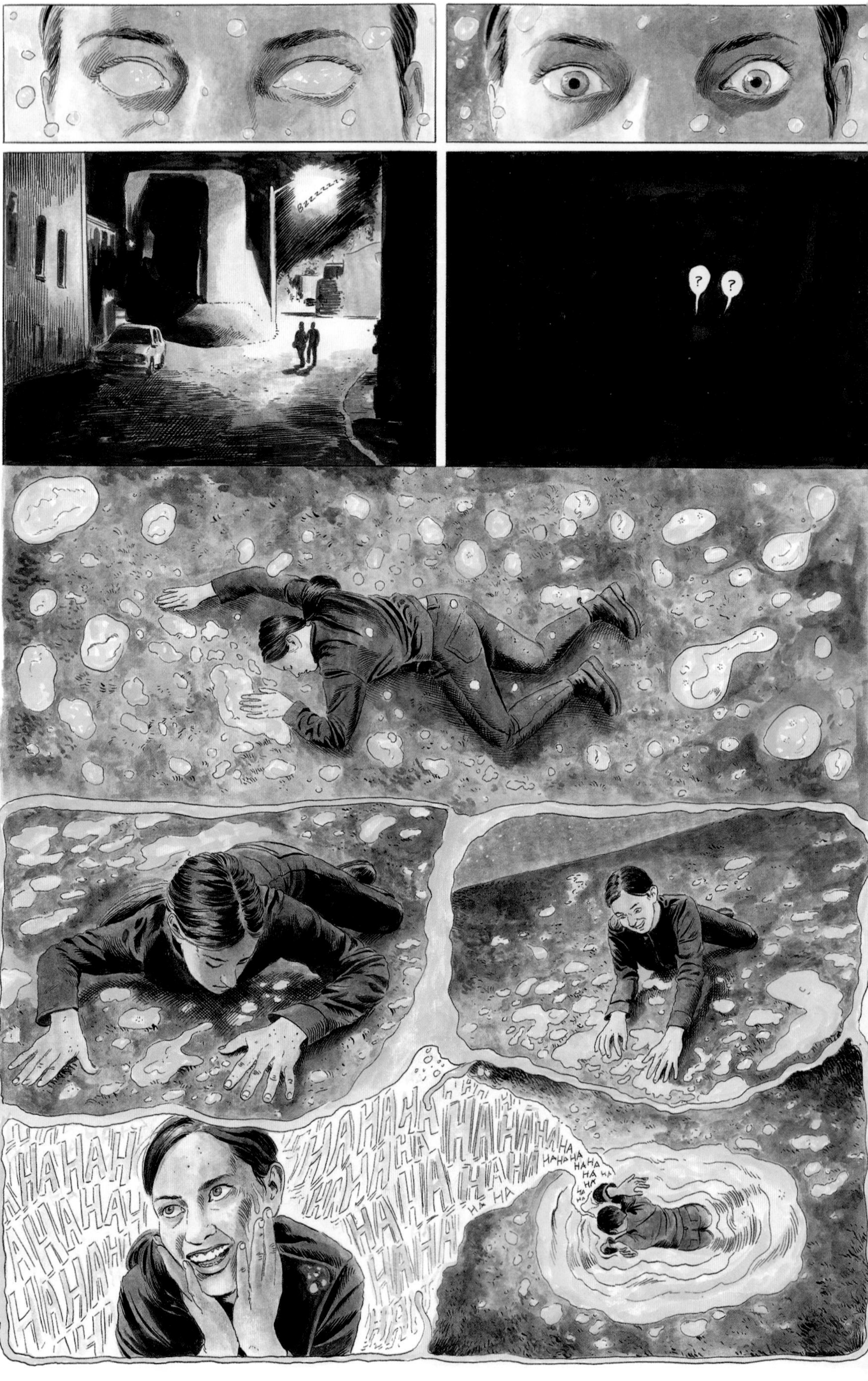
Bzzzzzzz
?
?
HA HA HA HA

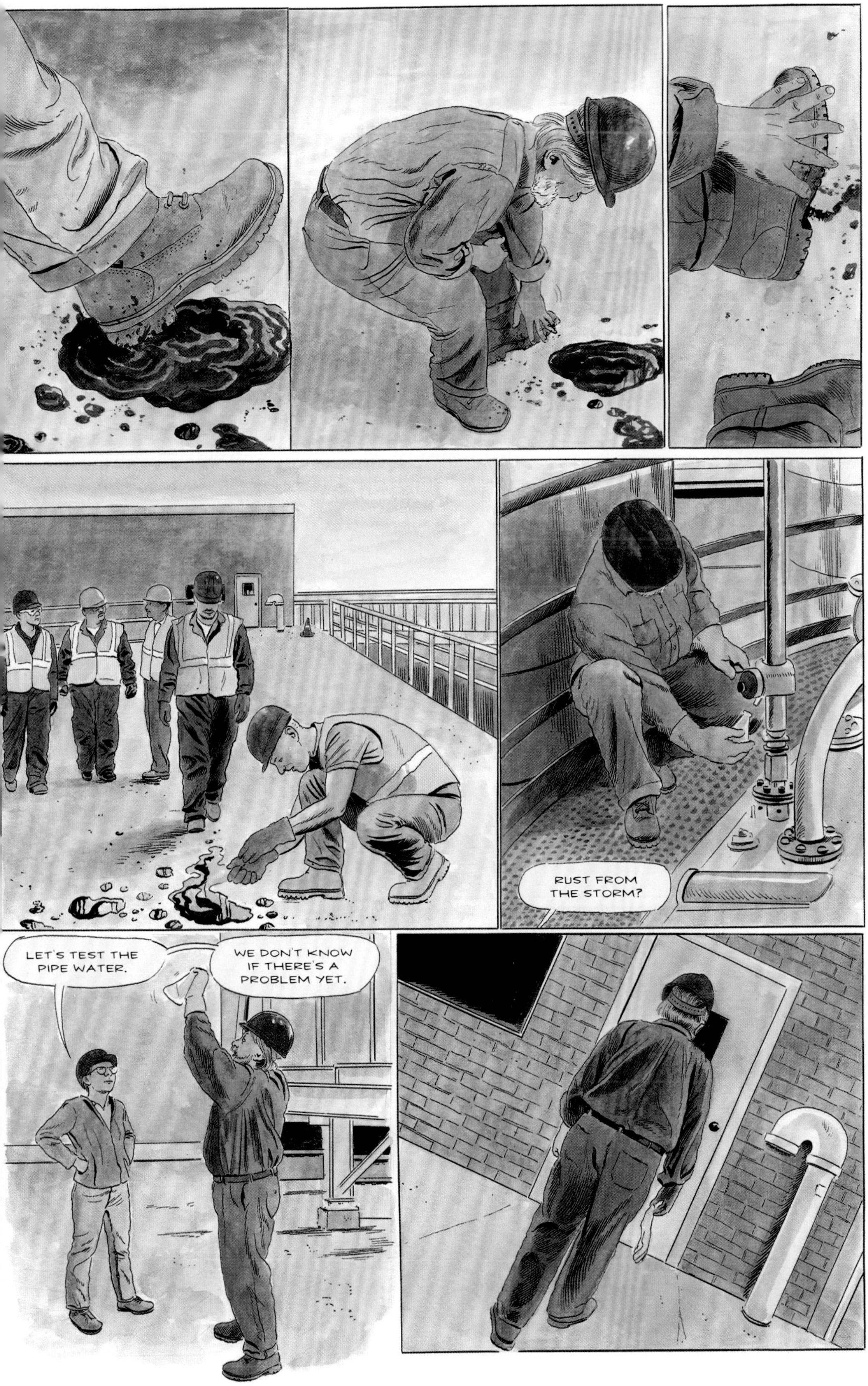
RUST FROM THE STORM?
LET'S TEST THE PIPE WATER.
WE DON'T KNOW IF THERE'S A PROBLEM YET.

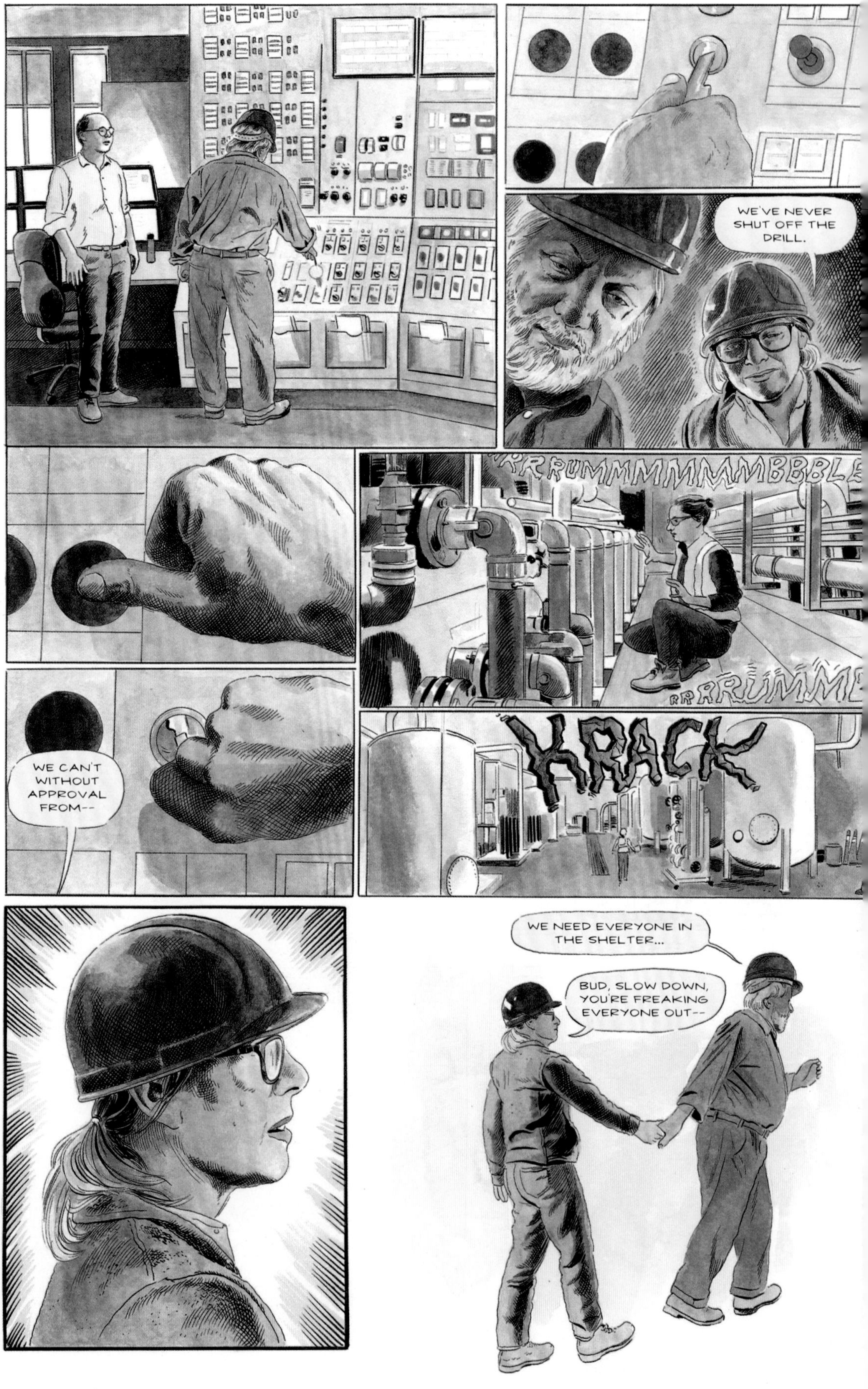
WE'VE NEVER SHUT OFF THE DRILL.
RRRUMMMMMMMMBBBLE
RRRRUMMM
WE CAN'T WITHOUT APPROVAL FROM--
KRACK
WE NEED EVERYONE IN THE SHELTER...
BUD, SLOW DOWN, YOU'RE FREAKING EVERYONE OUT--

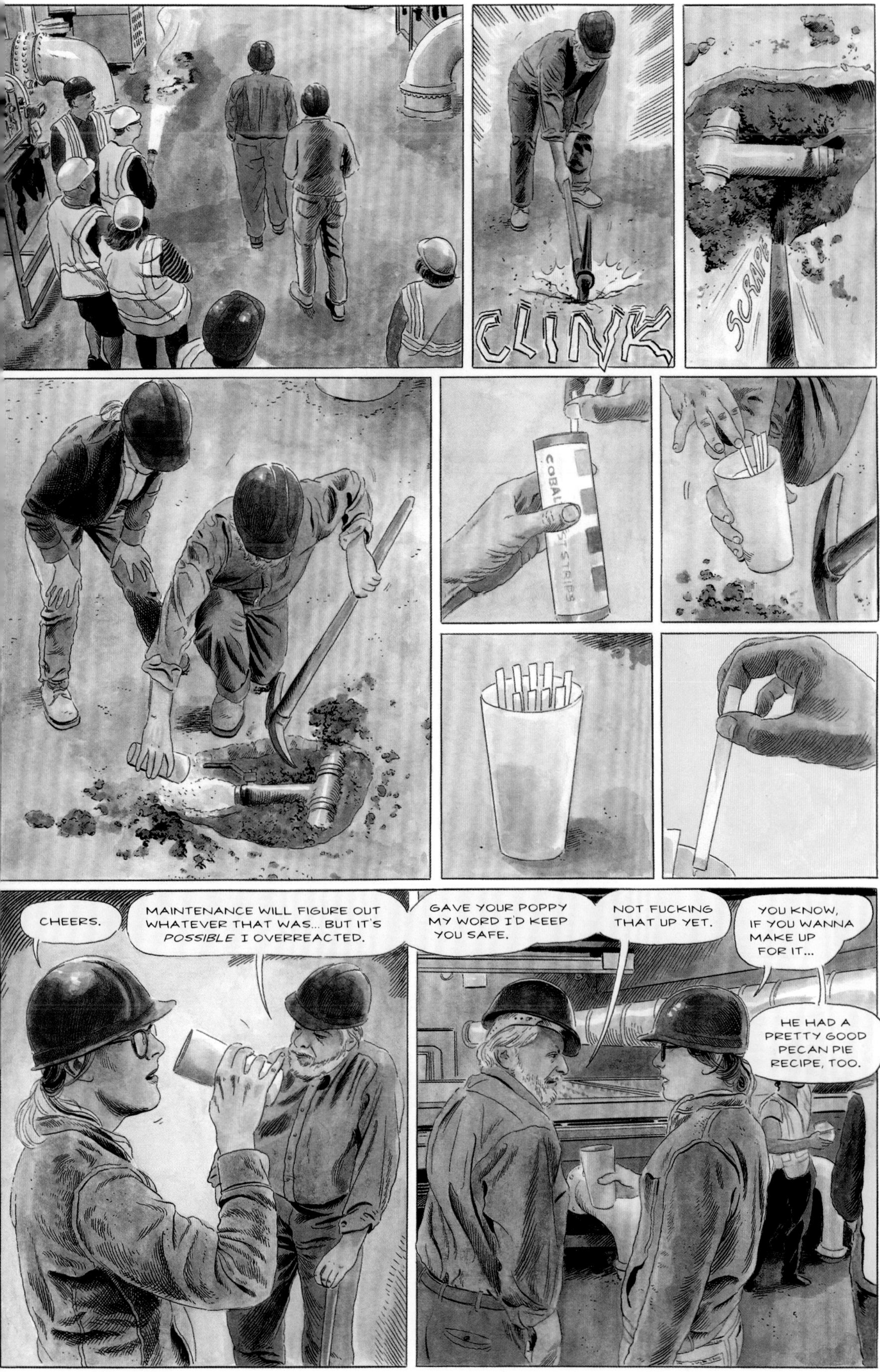
CLINK
SCRAPE
CHEERS.
MAINTENANCE WILL FIGURE OUT WHATEVER THAT WAS... BUT IT'S *POSSIBLE* I OVERREACTED.
GAVE YOUR POPPY MY WORD I'D KEEP YOU SAFE.
NOT FUCKING THAT UP YET.
YOU KNOW, IF YOU WANNA MAKE UP FOR IT...
HE HAD A PRETTY GOOD PECAN PIE RECIPE, TOO.

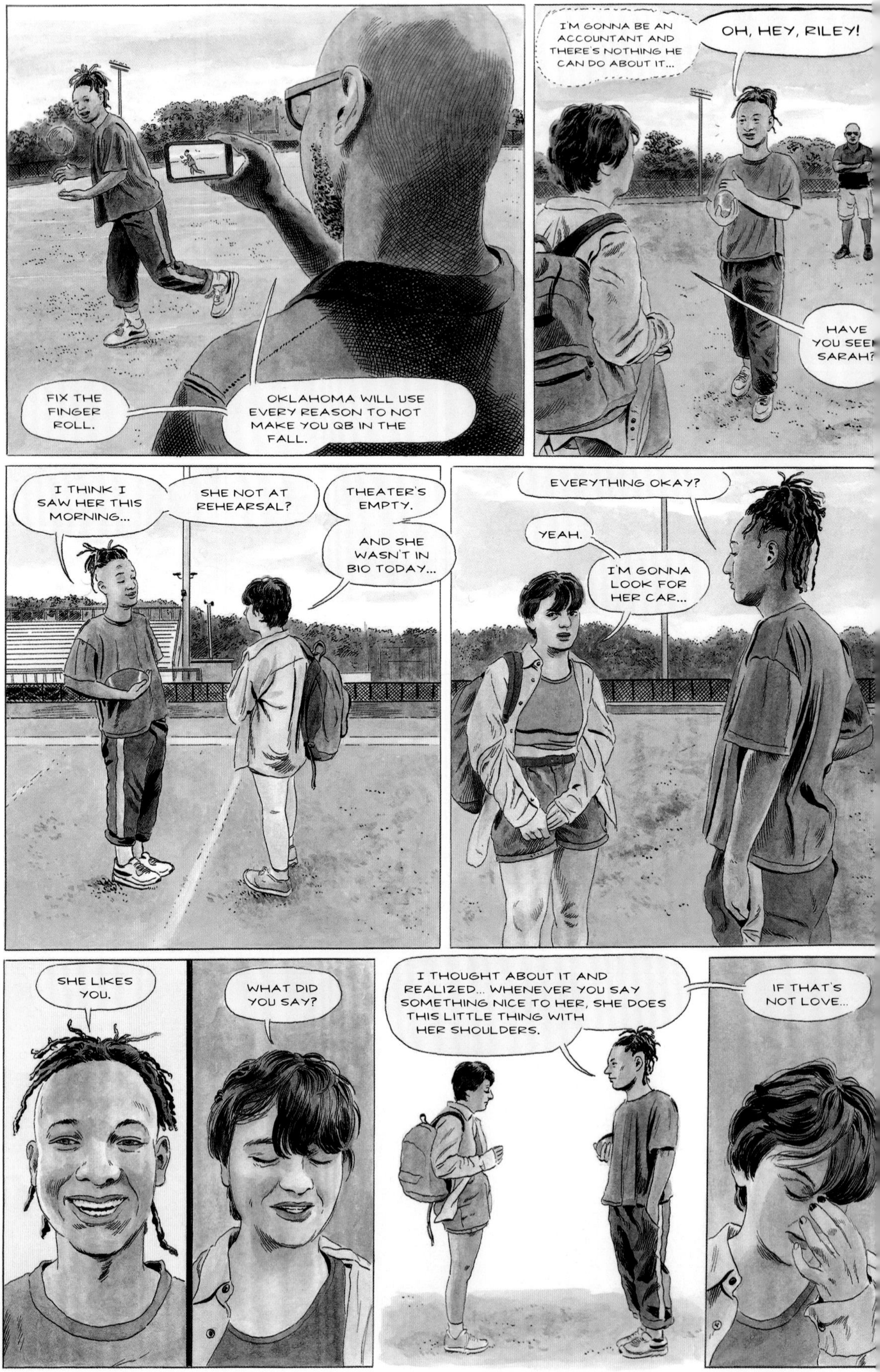
FIX THE FINGER ROLL.
OKLAHOMA WILL USE EVERY REASON TO NOT MAKE YOU QB IN THE FALL.
I'M GONNA BE AN ACCOUNTANT AND THERE'S NOTHING HE CAN DO ABOUT IT...
OH, HEY, RILEY!
HAVE YOU SEEN SARAH?
I THINK I SAW HER THIS MORNING...
SHE NOT AT REHEARSAL?
THEATER'S EMPTY.
AND SHE WASN'T IN BIO TODAY...
EVERYTHING OKAY?
YEAH.
I'M GONNA LOOK FOR HER CAR...
SHE LIKES YOU.
WHAT DID YOU SAY?
I THOUGHT ABOUT IT AND REALIZED... WHENEVER YOU SAY SOMETHING NICE TO HER, SHE DOES THIS LITTLE THING WITH HER SHOULDERS.
IF THAT'S NOT LOVE...

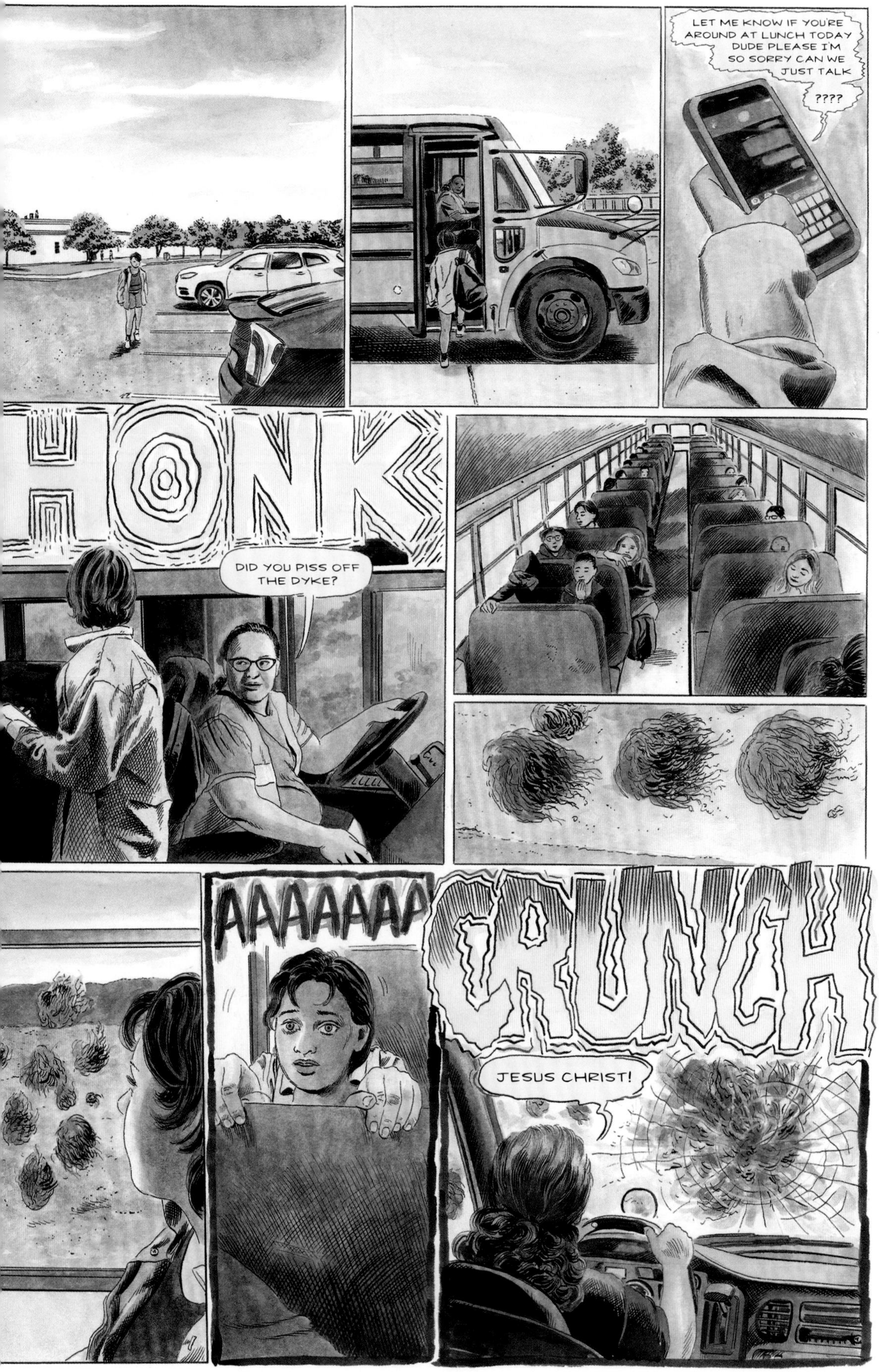
LET ME KNOW IF YOU'RE AROUND AT LUNCH TODAY
DUDE PLEASE I'M SO SORRY CAN WE JUST TALK
????
HONK
DID YOU PISS OFF THE DYKE?
AAAAAAA
CRUNCH
JESUS CHRIST!

SCREEEEEEEEEECH!

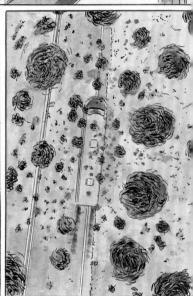

SHUT THE FUCK UP ON MY BUS!

SAN JUAN COUNTY, WHAT'S YOUR EMERGENCY?

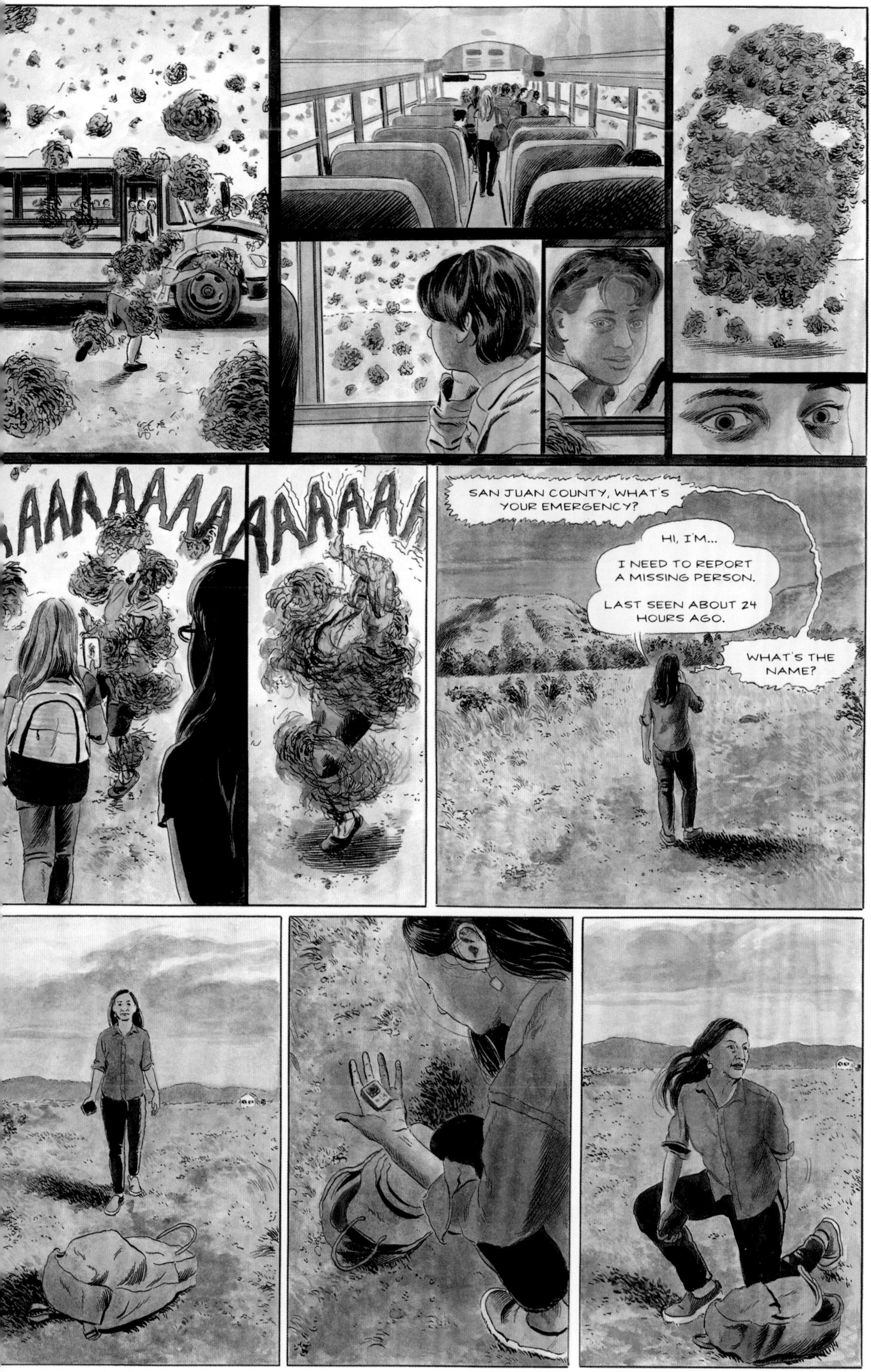
AAAAAAAAA
AAAAAA
SAN JUAN COUNTY, WHAT'S YOUR EMERGENCY?
HI, I'M...
I NEED TO REPORT A MISSING PERSON.
LAST SEEN ABOUT 24 HOURS AGO.
WHAT'S THE NAME?

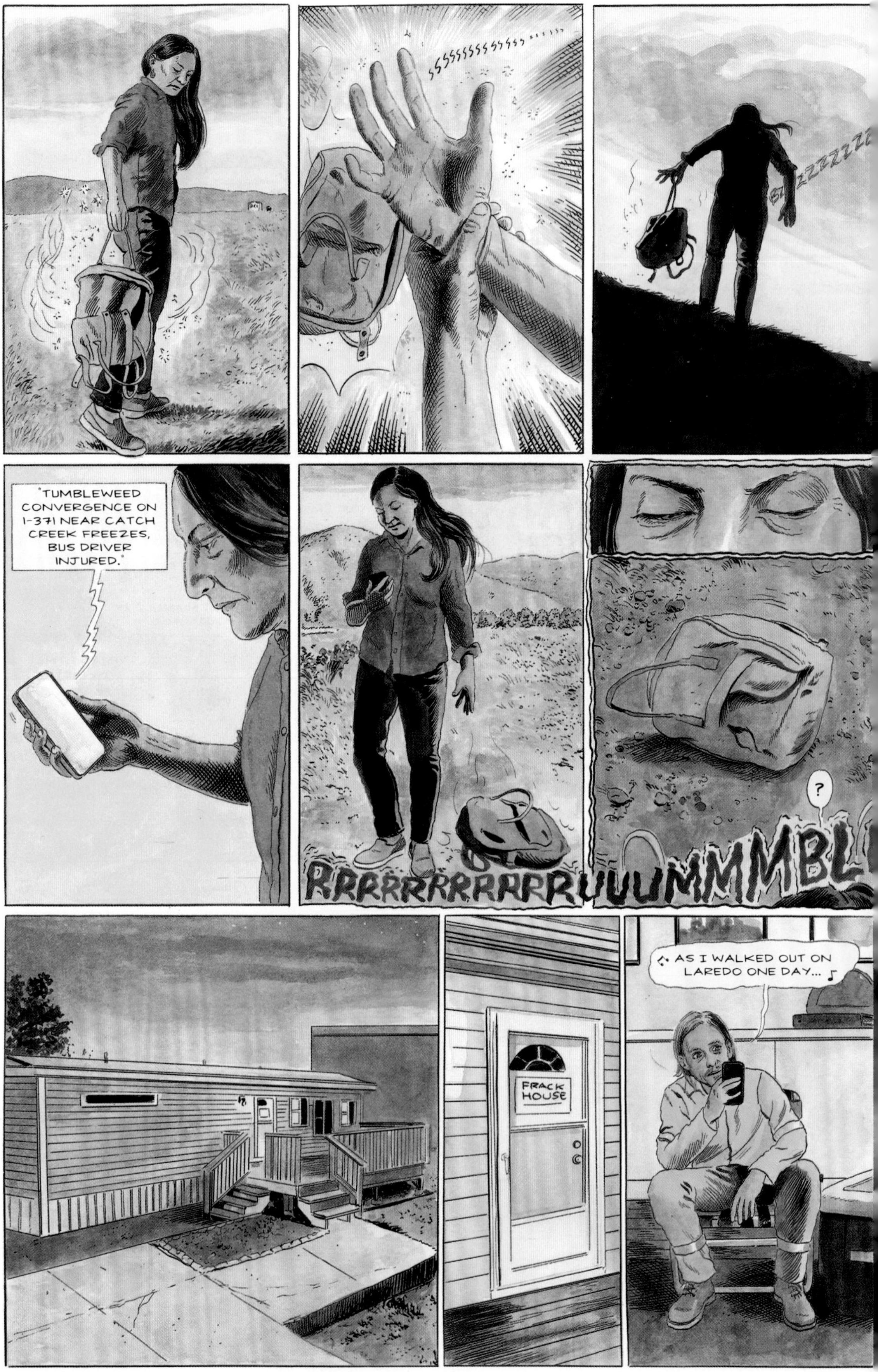
sssssssssssss
BZZZZZZZZ
"TUMBLEWEED CONVERGENCE ON I-371 NEAR CATCH CREEK FREEZES, BUS DRIVER INJURED."
RRRRRRRRRRRRUUUMMMBL
?
FRACK HOUSE
AS I WALKED OUT ON LAREDO ONE DAY...

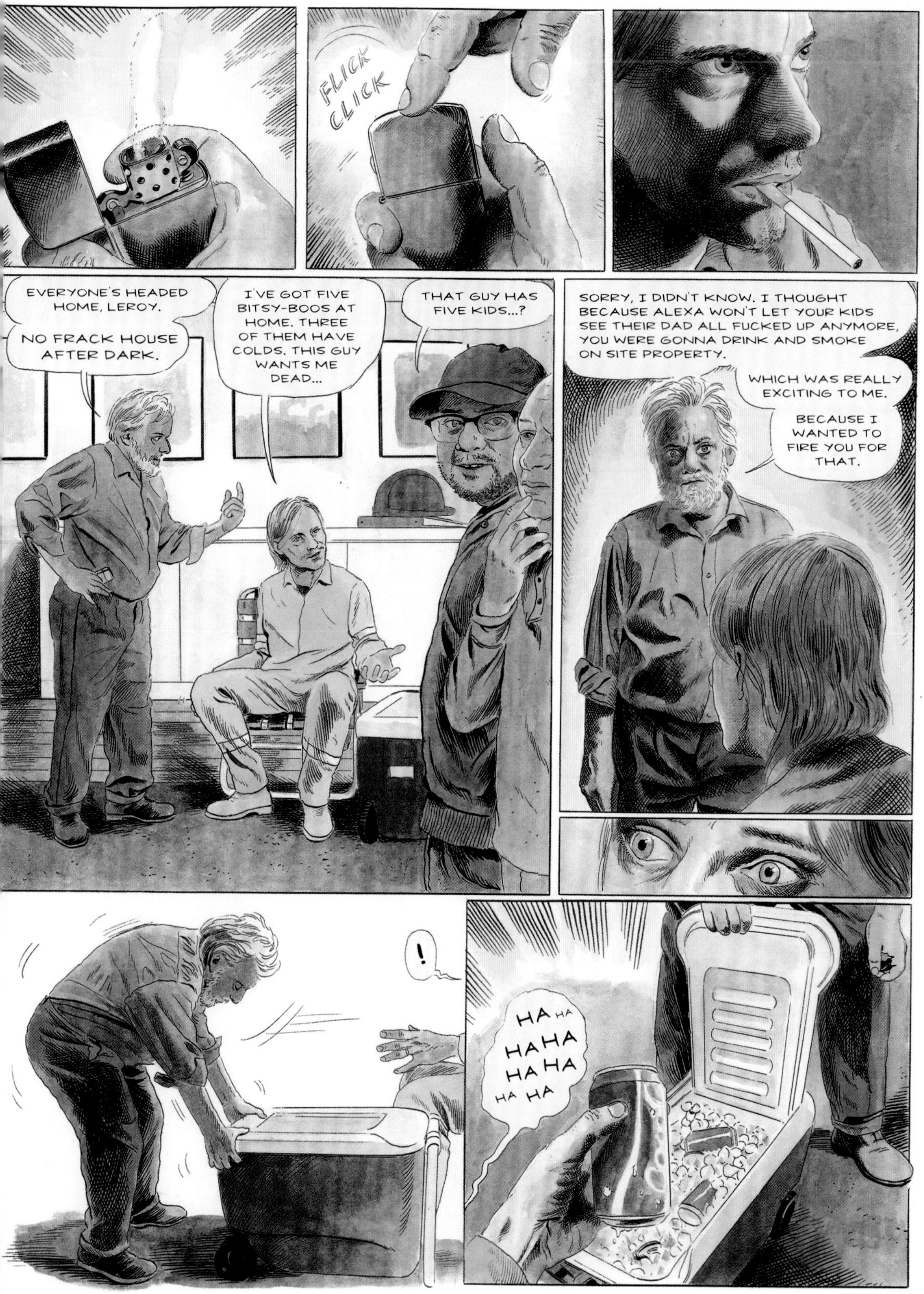
FLICK CLICK
EVERYONE'S HEADED HOME, LEROY.
NO FRACK HOUSE AFTER DARK.
I'VE GOT FIVE BITSY-BOOS AT HOME. THREE OF THEM HAVE COLDS. THIS GUY WANTS ME DEAD...
THAT GUY HAS FIVE KIDS...?
SORRY, I DIDN'T KNOW. I THOUGHT BECAUSE ALEXA WON'T LET YOUR KIDS SEE THEIR DAD ALL FUCKED UP ANYMORE, YOU WERE GONNA DRINK AND SMOKE ON SITE PROPERTY.
WHICH WAS REALLY EXCITING TO ME.
BECAUSE I WANTED TO FIRE YOU FOR THAT.
!
HA HA HA HA HA HA HA HA

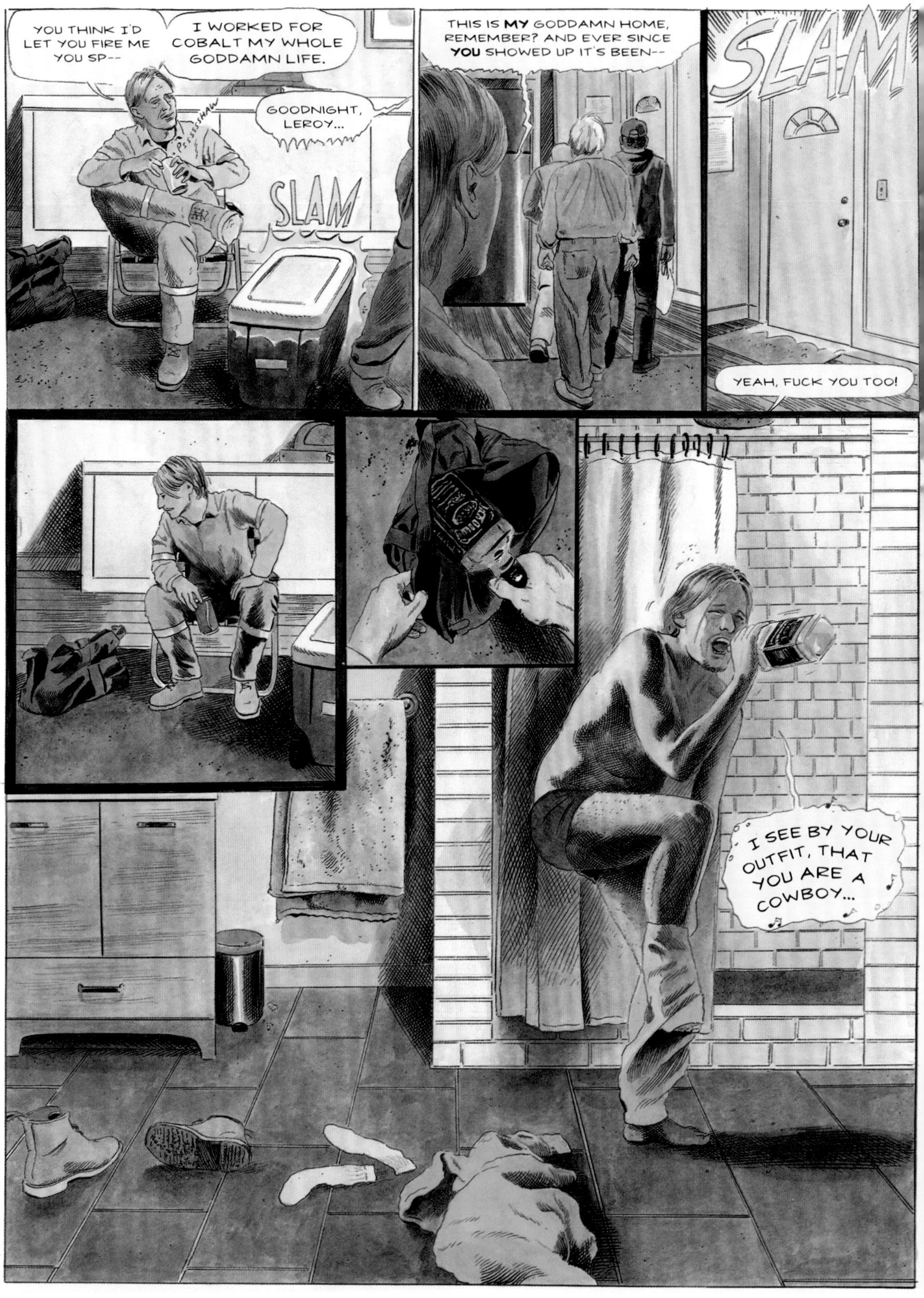
YOU THINK I'D LET YOU FIRE ME YOU SP--
I WORKED FOR COBALT MY WHOLE GODDAMN LIFE.
GOODNIGHT, LEROY...
SLAM
THIS IS MY GODDAMN HOME, REMEMBER? AND EVER SINCE YOU SHOWED UP IT'S BEEN--
SLAM
YEAH, FUCK YOU TOO!
I SEE BY YOUR OUTFIT, THAT YOU ARE A COWBOY...

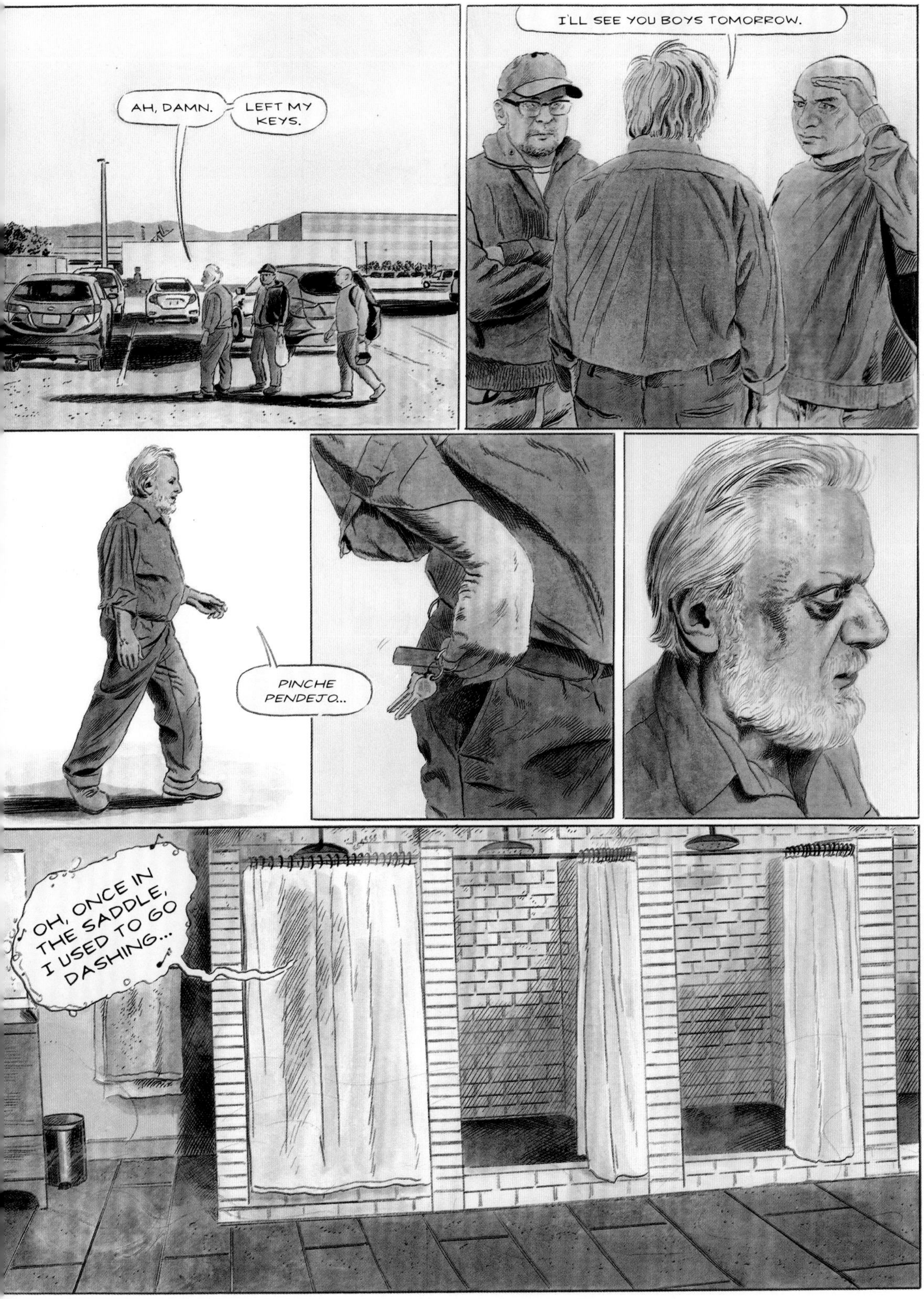
AH, DAMN.
LEFT MY KEYS.
I'LL SEE YOU BOYS TOMORROW.
PINCHE PENDEJO...
OH, ONCE IN THE SADDLE, I USED TO GO DASHING...

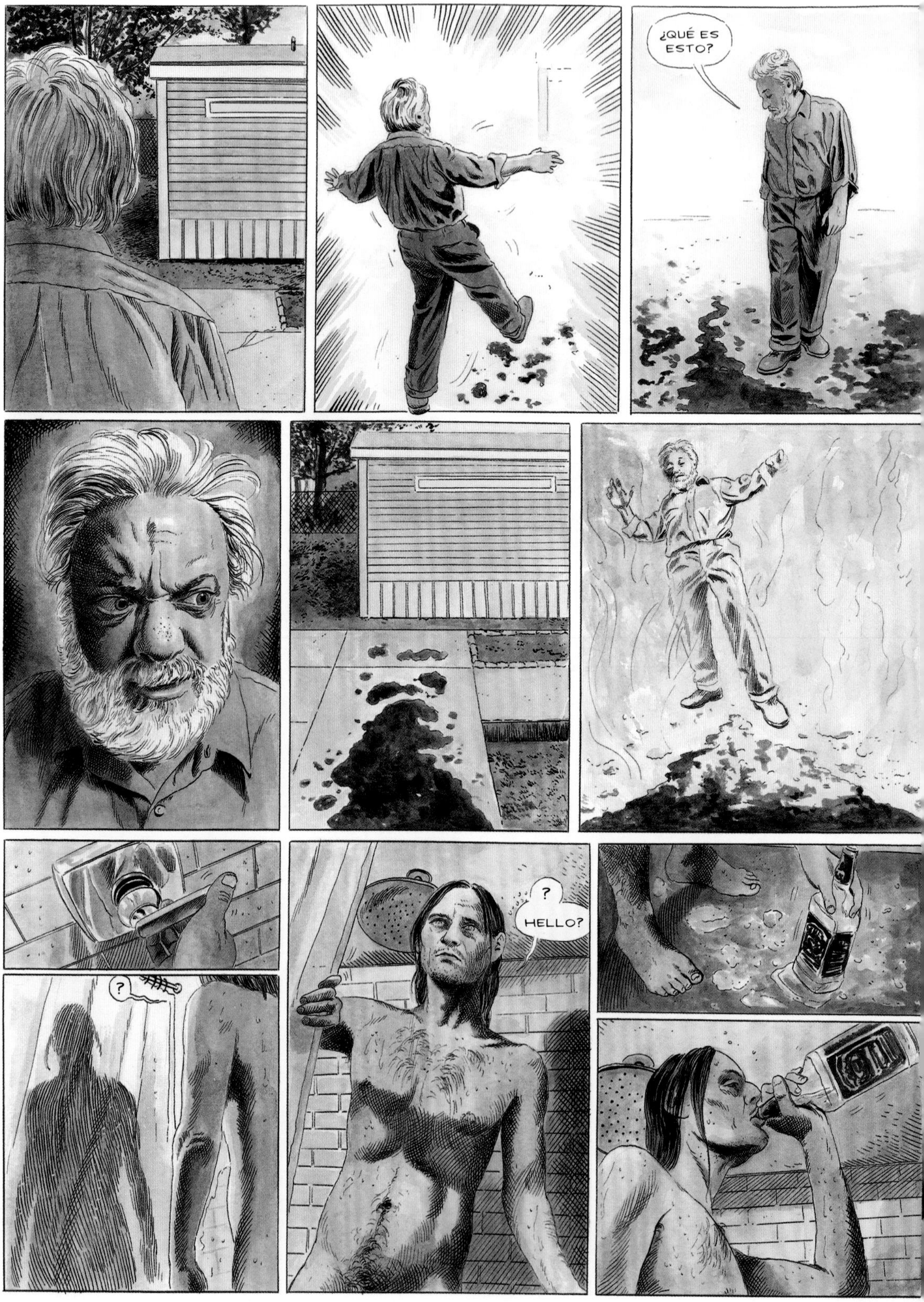
¿QUÉ ES ESTO?
?
?
HELLO?

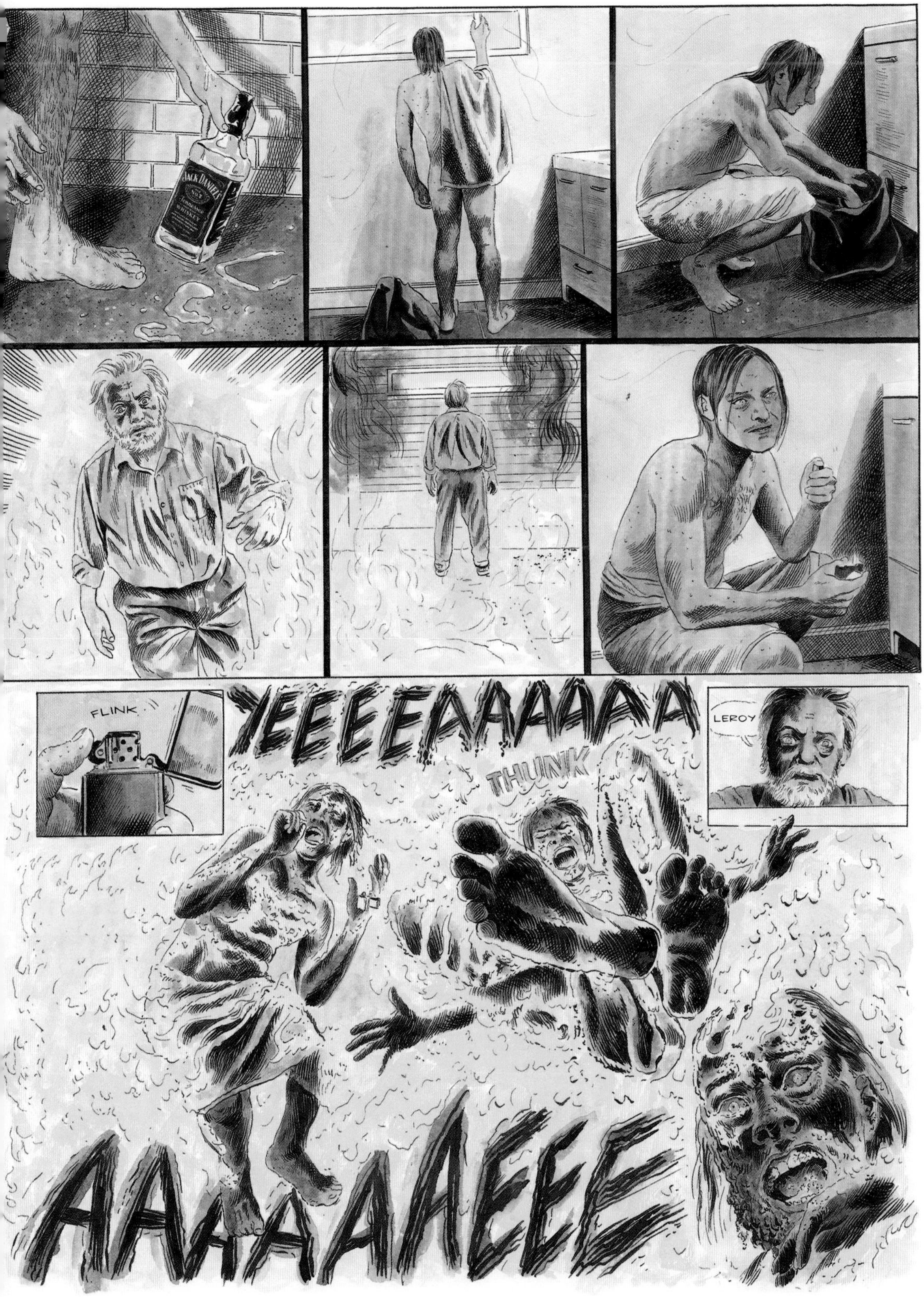
FLINK
YEEEEAAAAAA
THUNK
LEROY
AAAAAEEE

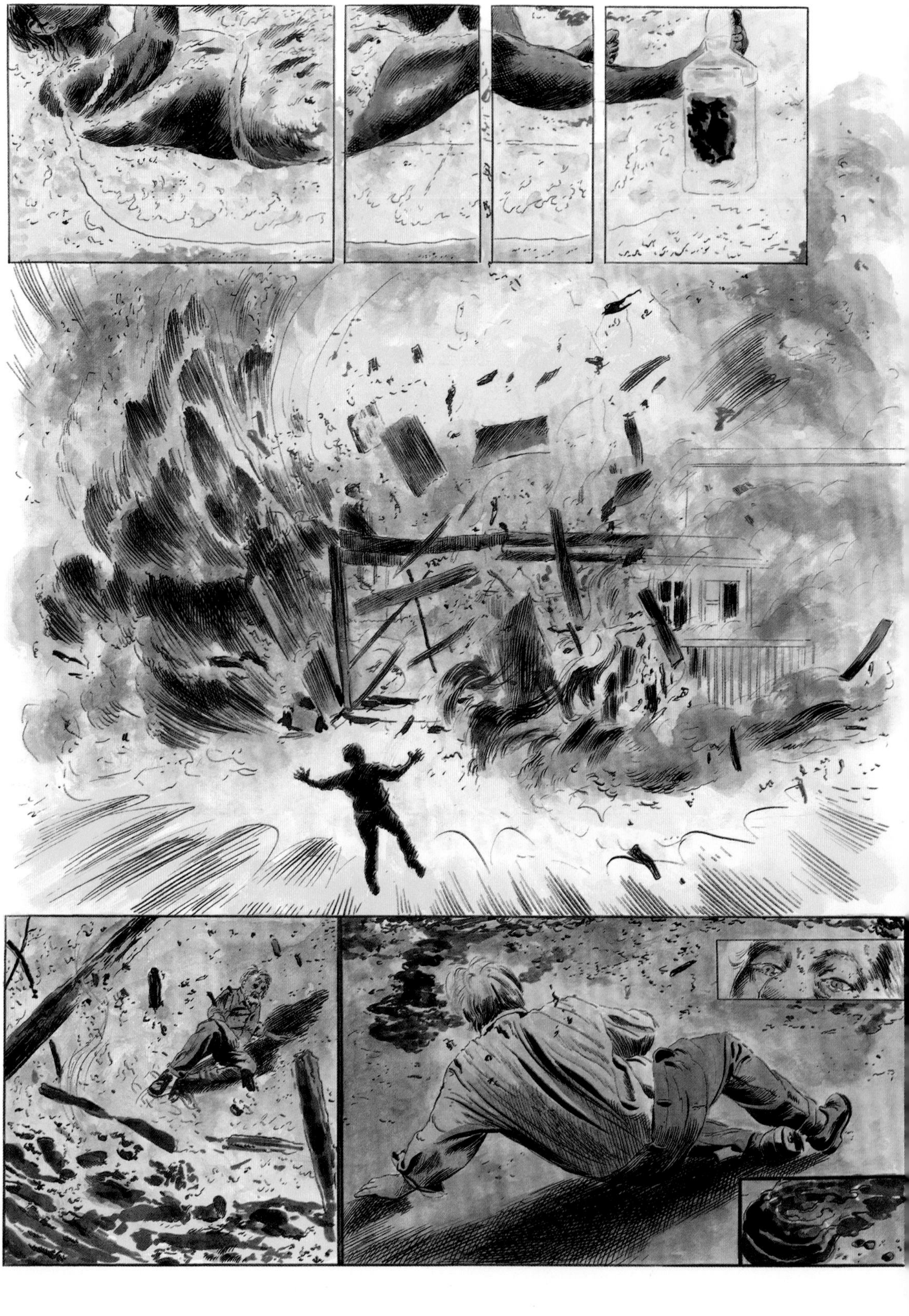

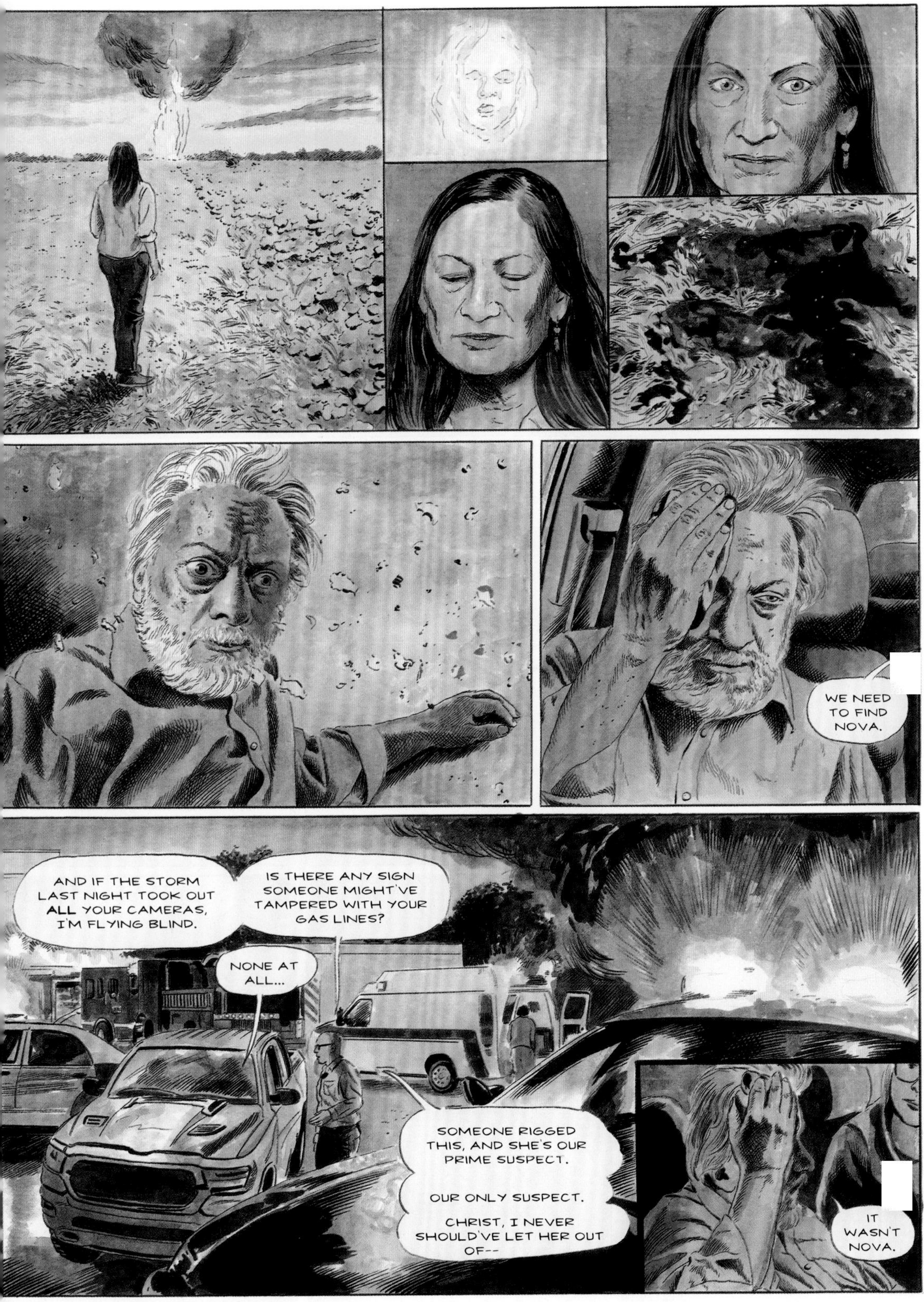
WE NEED TO FIND NOVA.
AND IF THE STORM LAST NIGHT TOOK OUT **ALL** YOUR CAMERAS, I'M FLYING BLIND.
IS THERE ANY SIGN SOMEONE MIGHT'VE TAMPERED WITH YOUR GAS LINES?
NONE AT ALL...
SOMEONE RIGGED THIS, AND SHE'S OUR PRIME SUSPECT.
OUR ONLY SUSPECT.
CHRIST, I NEVER SHOULD'VE LET HER OUT OF--
IT WASN'T NOVA.

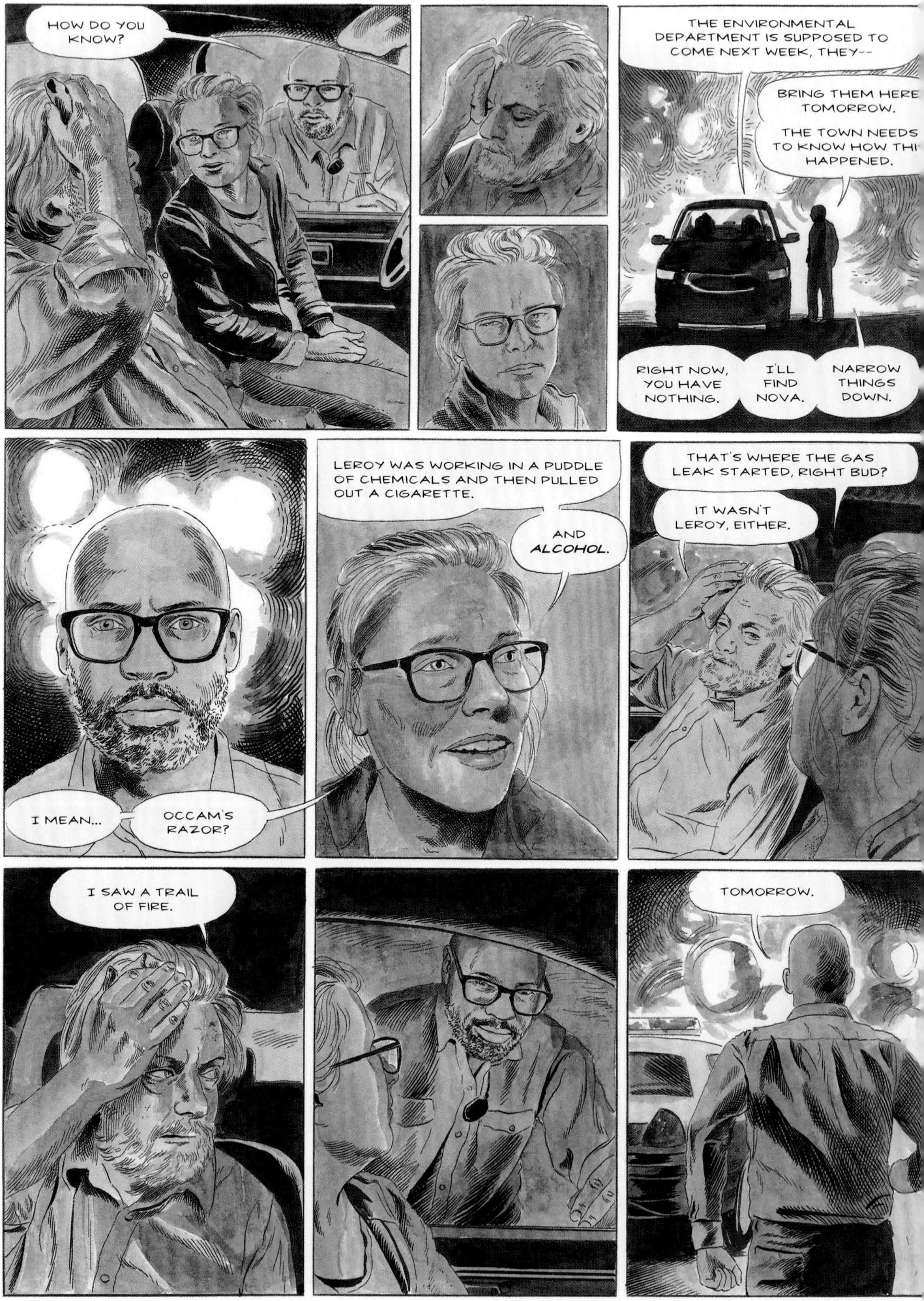
HOW DO YOU KNOW?
THE ENVIRONMENTAL DEPARTMENT IS SUPPOSED TO COME NEXT WEEK, THEY--
BRING THEM HERE TOMORROW.
THE TOWN NEEDS TO KNOW HOW THI HAPPENED.
RIGHT NOW, YOU HAVE NOTHING.
I'LL FIND NOVA.
NARROW THINGS DOWN.
I MEAN...
OCCAM'S RAZOR?
LEROY WAS WORKING IN A PUDDLE OF CHEMICALS AND THEN PULLED OUT A CIGARETTE.
AND *ALCOHOL*.
THAT'S WHERE THE GAS LEAK STARTED, RIGHT BUD?
IT WASN'T LEROY, EITHER.
I SAW A TRAIL OF FIRE.
TOMORROW.

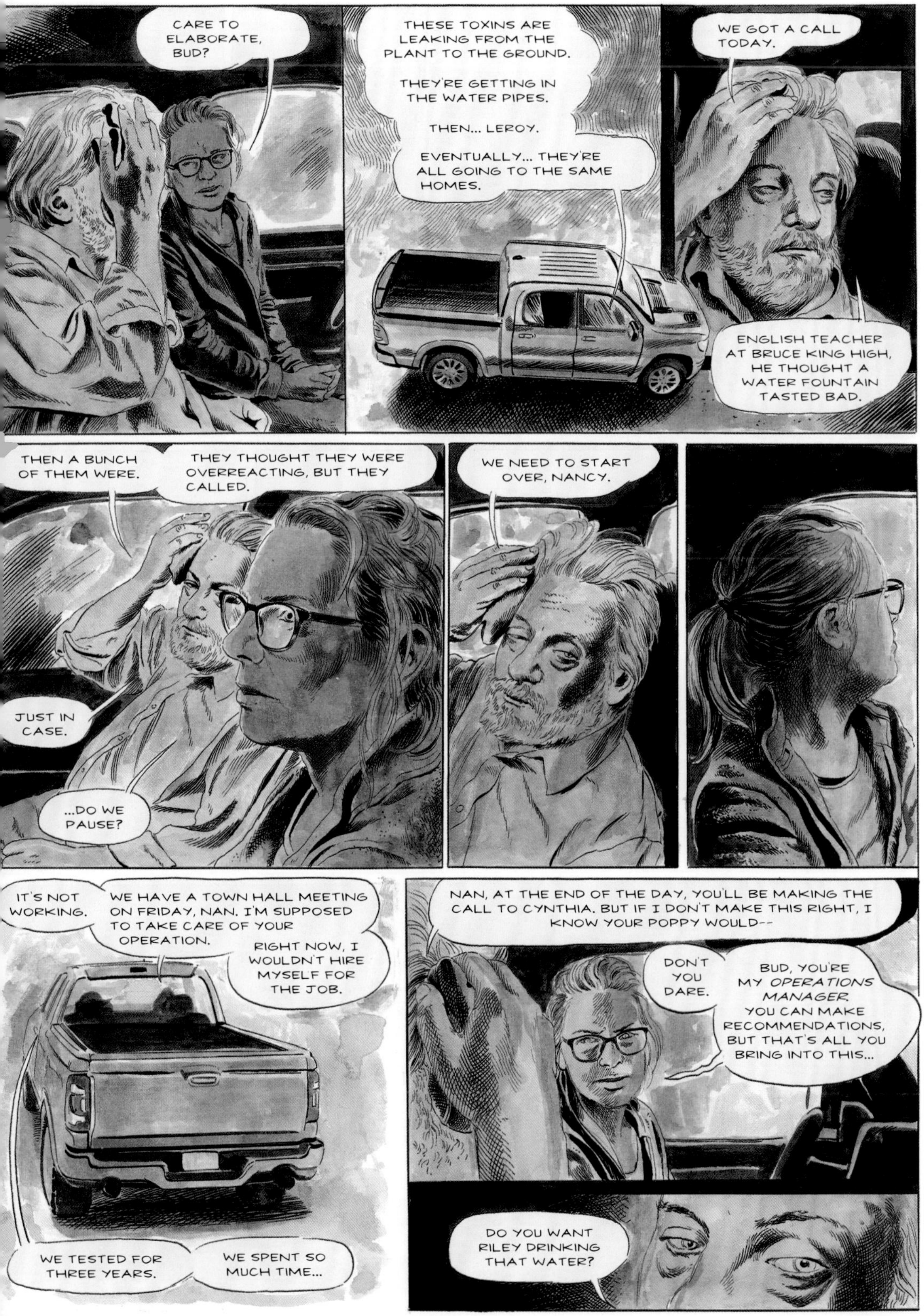
CARE TO ELABORATE, BUD?
THESE TOXINS ARE LEAKING FROM THE PLANT TO THE GROUND.
THEY'RE GETTING IN THE WATER PIPES.
THEN... LEROY.
EVENTUALLY... THEY'RE ALL GOING TO THE SAME HOMES.
WE GOT A CALL TODAY.
ENGLISH TEACHER AT BRUCE KING HIGH, HE THOUGHT A WATER FOUNTAIN TASTED BAD.
THEN A BUNCH OF THEM WERE.
THEY THOUGHT THEY WERE OVERREACTING, BUT THEY CALLED.
JUST IN CASE.
...DO WE PAUSE?
WE NEED TO START OVER, NANCY.
IT'S NOT WORKING.
WE HAVE A TOWN HALL MEETING ON FRIDAY, NAN. I'M SUPPOSED TO TAKE CARE OF YOUR OPERATION.
RIGHT NOW, I WOULDN'T HIRE MYSELF FOR THE JOB.
WE TESTED FOR THREE YEARS.
WE SPENT SO MUCH TIME...
NAN, AT THE END OF THE DAY, YOU'LL BE MAKING THE CALL TO CYNTHIA. BUT IF I DON'T MAKE THIS RIGHT, I KNOW YOUR POPPY WOULD--
DON'T YOU DARE.
BUD, YOU'RE MY *OPERATIONS MANAGER*. YOU CAN MAKE RECOMMENDATIONS, BUT THAT'S ALL YOU BRING INTO THIS...
DO YOU WANT RILEY DRINKING THAT WATER?

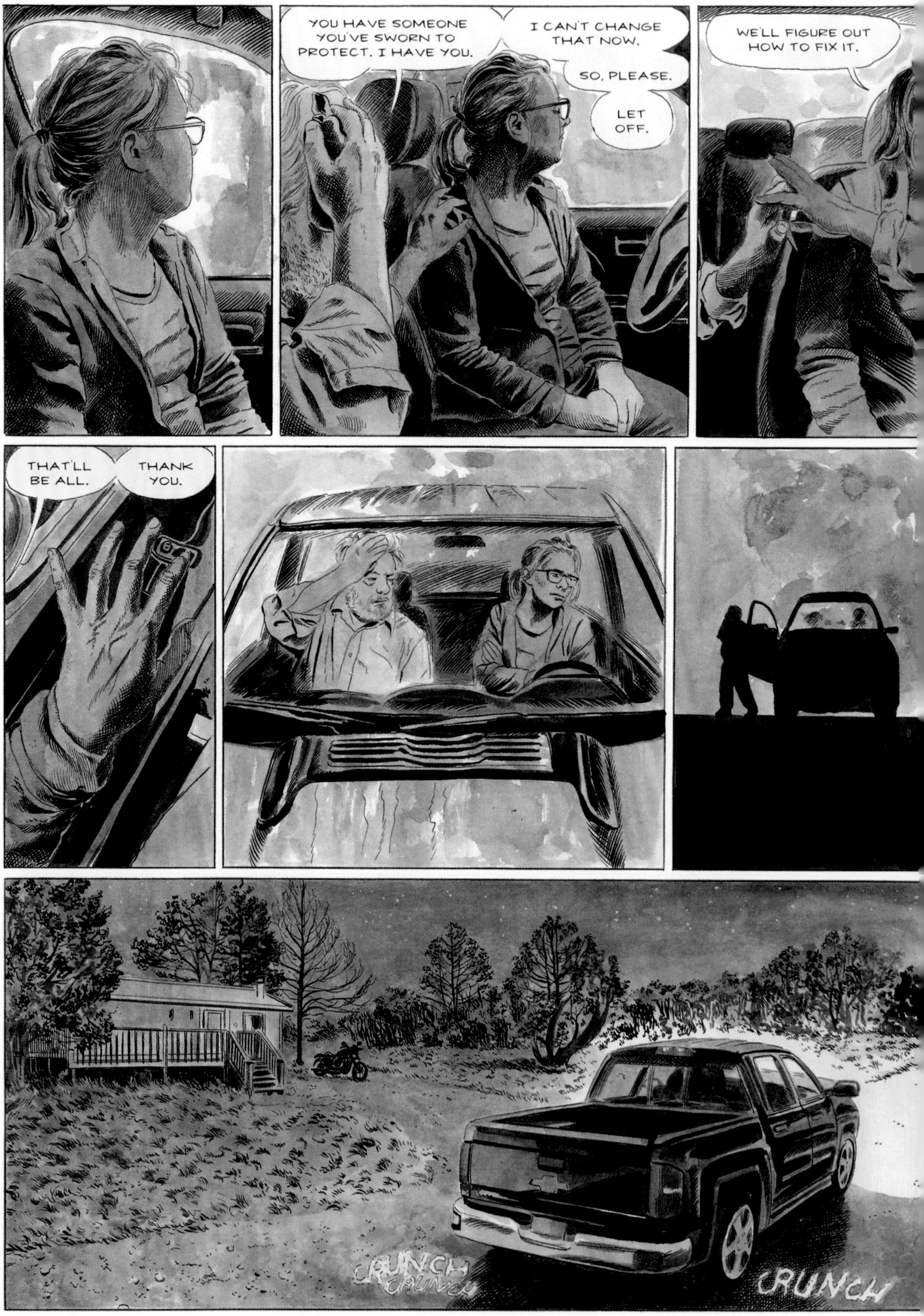
YOU HAVE SOMEONE YOU'VE SWORN TO PROTECT. I HAVE YOU.
I CAN'T CHANGE THAT NOW.
SO, PLEASE.
LET OFF.
WE'LL FIGURE OUT HOW TO FIX IT.
THAT'LL BE ALL.
THANK YOU.
CRUNCH
CRUNCH
CRUNCH

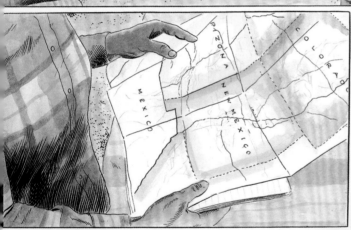

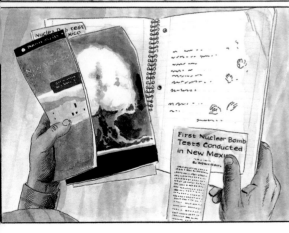

First Nuclear Bomb Tests Conducted in New Mexico

naayéé

How do you sleep?

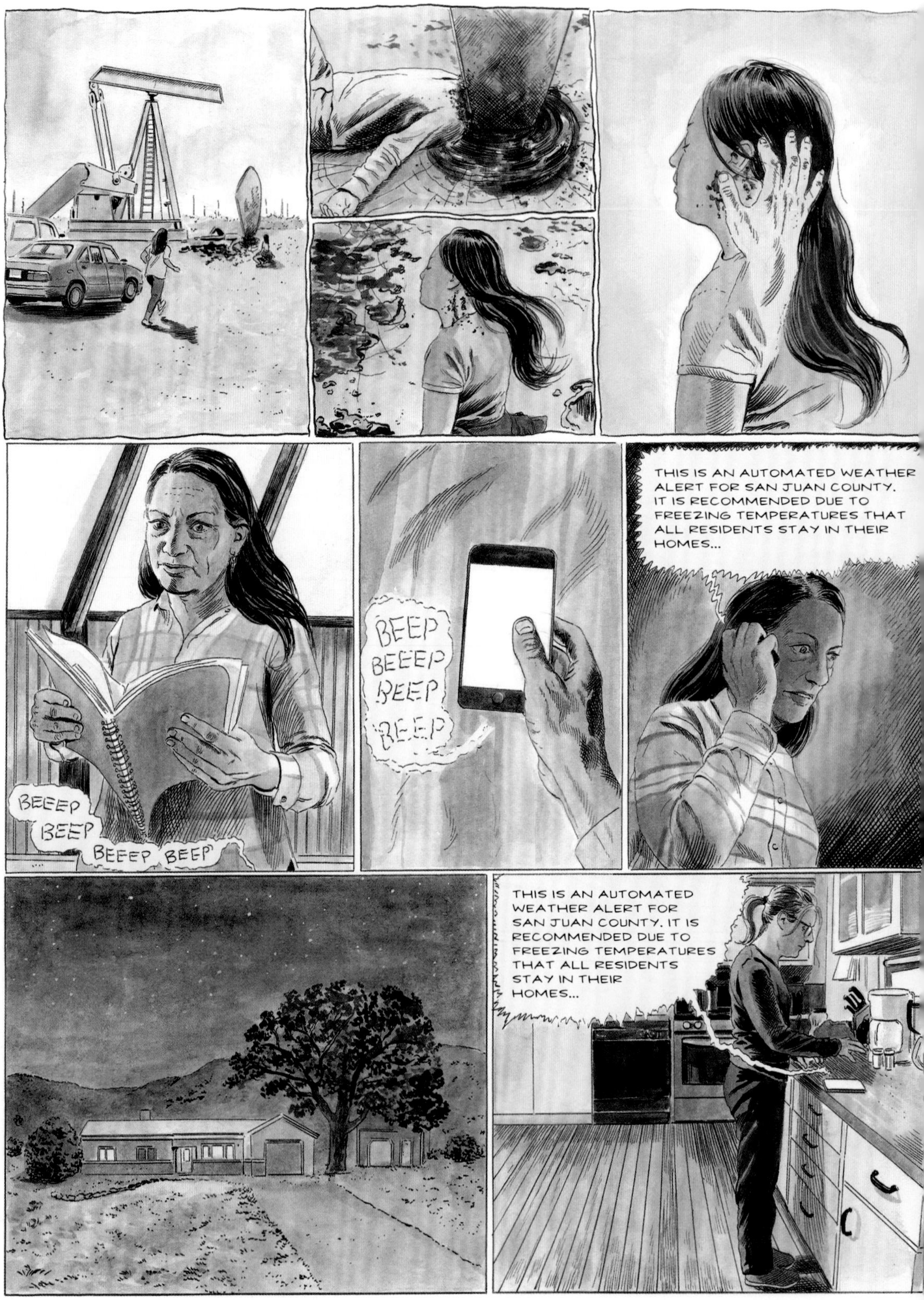
BEEEP
BEEP
BEEEP BEEP
BEEP
BEEEP
BEEP
BEEP
THIS IS AN AUTOMATED WEATHER ALERT FOR SAN JUAN COUNTY. IT IS RECOMMENDED DUE TO FREEZING TEMPERATURES THAT ALL RESIDENTS STAY IN THEIR HOMES...
THIS IS AN AUTOMATED WEATHER ALERT FOR SAN JUAN COUNTY. IT IS RECOMMENDED DUE TO FREEZING TEMPERATURES THAT ALL RESIDENTS STAY IN THEIR HOMES...

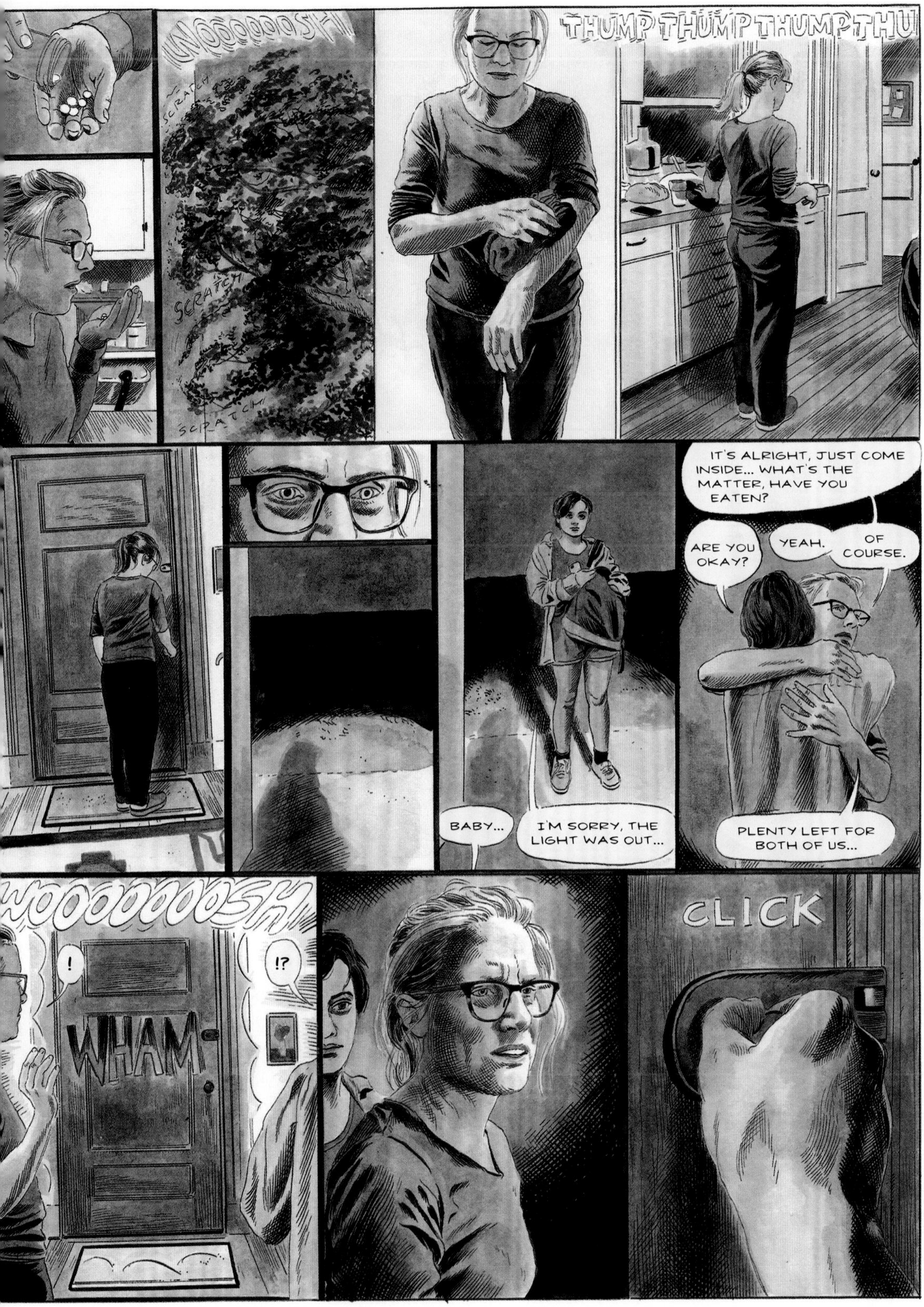
WOOOOOOSH!
SCRATCH
SCRATCH
SCRATCH
SCRATCH
THUMP THUMP THUMP THU
BABY...
I'M SORRY, THE LIGHT WAS OUT...
IT'S ALRIGHT, JUST COME INSIDE... WHAT'S THE MATTER, HAVE YOU EATEN?
ARE YOU OKAY?
YEAH.
OF COURSE.
PLENTY LEFT FOR BOTH OF US...
WOOOOOOOOSH!
!
!?
WHAM
CLICK

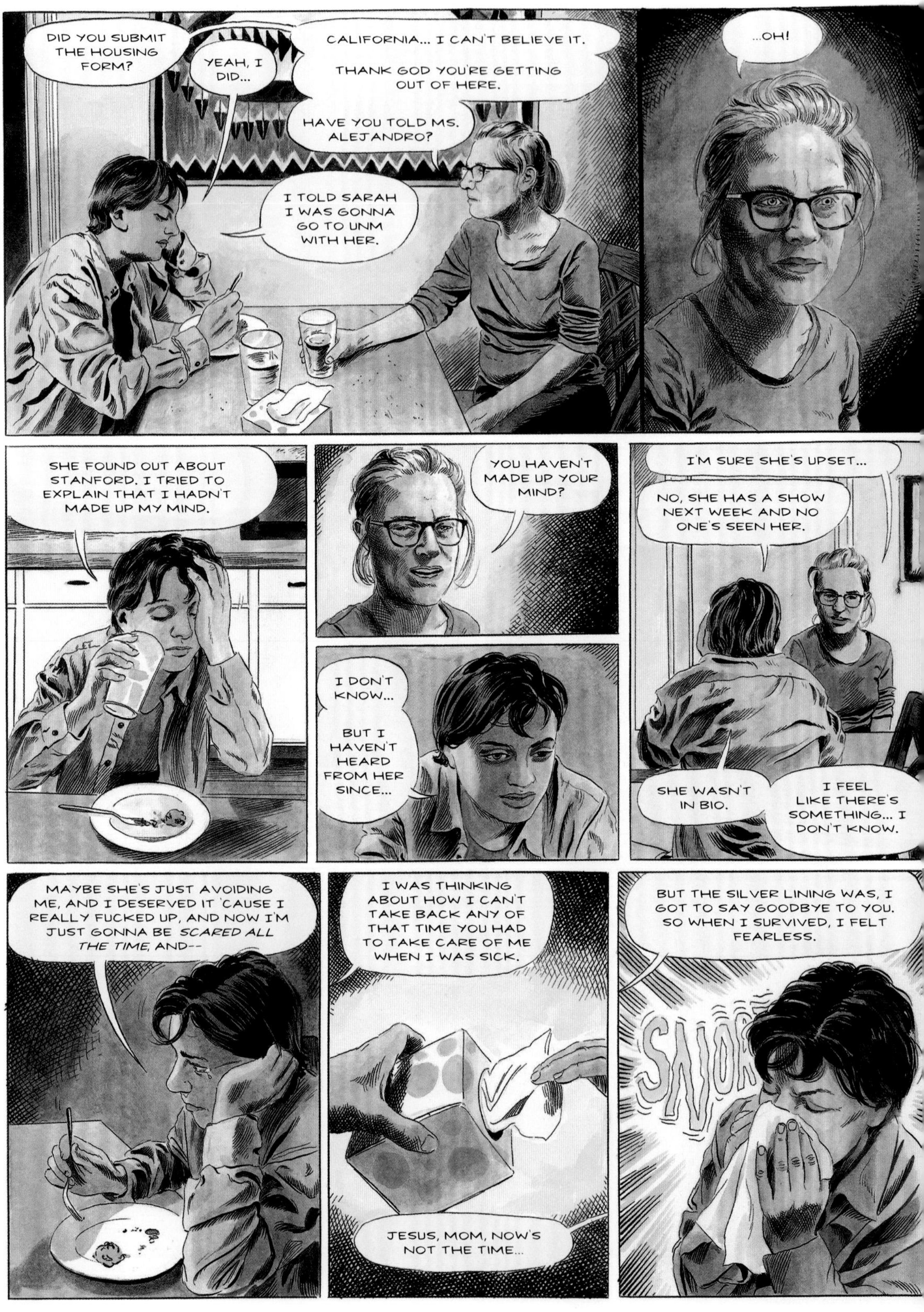
DID YOU SUBMIT THE HOUSING FORM?
YEAH, I DID...
CALIFORNIA... I CAN'T BELIEVE IT.
THANK GOD YOU'RE GETTING OUT OF HERE.
HAVE YOU TOLD MS. ALEJANDRO?
I TOLD SARAH I WAS GONNA GO TO UNM WITH HER.
...OH!
SHE FOUND OUT ABOUT STANFORD. I TRIED TO EXPLAIN THAT I HADN'T MADE UP MY MIND.
YOU HAVEN'T MADE UP YOUR MIND?
I DON'T KNOW...
BUT I HAVEN'T HEARD FROM HER SINCE...
I'M SURE SHE'S UPSET...
NO, SHE HAS A SHOW NEXT WEEK AND NO ONE'S SEEN HER.
SHE WASN'T IN BIO.
I FEEL LIKE THERE'S SOMETHING... I DON'T KNOW.
MAYBE SHE'S JUST AVOIDING ME, AND I DESERVED IT 'CAUSE I REALLY FUCKED UP, AND NOW I'M JUST GONNA BE *SCARED ALL THE TIME,* AND--
I WAS THINKING ABOUT HOW I CAN'T TAKE BACK ANY OF THAT TIME YOU HAD TO TAKE CARE OF ME WHEN I WAS SICK.
JESUS, MOM, NOW'S NOT THE TIME...
BUT THE SILVER LINING WAS, I GOT TO SAY GOODBYE TO YOU. SO WHEN I SURVIVED, I FELT FEARLESS.
SNORT

TIME TO GET BACK TO WORK. BREAK GROUND, WORK MY ASS OFF. GIVE YOU A FUTURE. WHAT ELSE DID I HAVE TO LOSE?

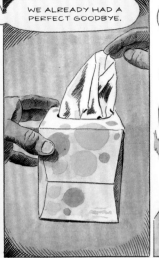

WE ALREADY HAD A PERFECT GOODBYE.

GIVE SARAH TIME. SHE'LL UNDERSTAND. THEN, GO TO PALO ALTO AND FOLLOW YOUR DREAM.

WHAT IF I'M WRONG ABOUT THAT TOO?

SNORT

YOU HAVE SO MUCH TIME, RI. I JUST WANNA GIVE YOU THAT TIME. 'CAUSE YOU'RE GONNA GET MUCH MORE FEARLESS FROM HERE.

PFFFFFFTT

OKAY, SURE...

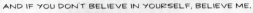

AND IF YOU DON'T BELIEVE IN YOURSELF, BELIEVE ME.

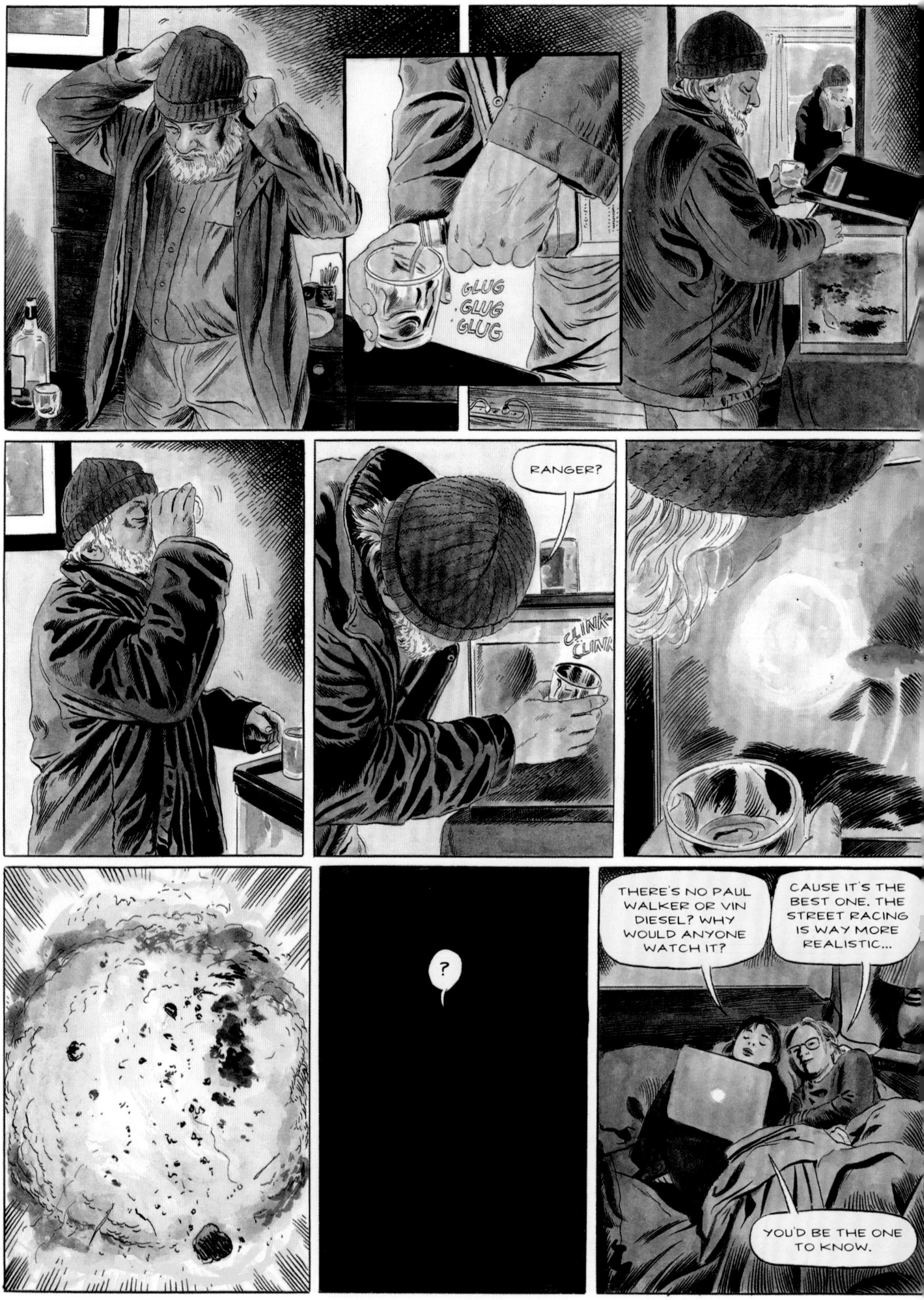
GLUG
GLUG
GLUG
RANGER?
CLINK-
CLINK
?
THERE'S NO PAUL WALKER OR VIN DIESEL? WHY WOULD ANYONE WATCH IT?
CAUSE IT'S THE BEST ONE. THE STREET RACING IS WAY MORE REALISTIC...
YOU'D BE THE ONE TO KNOW.

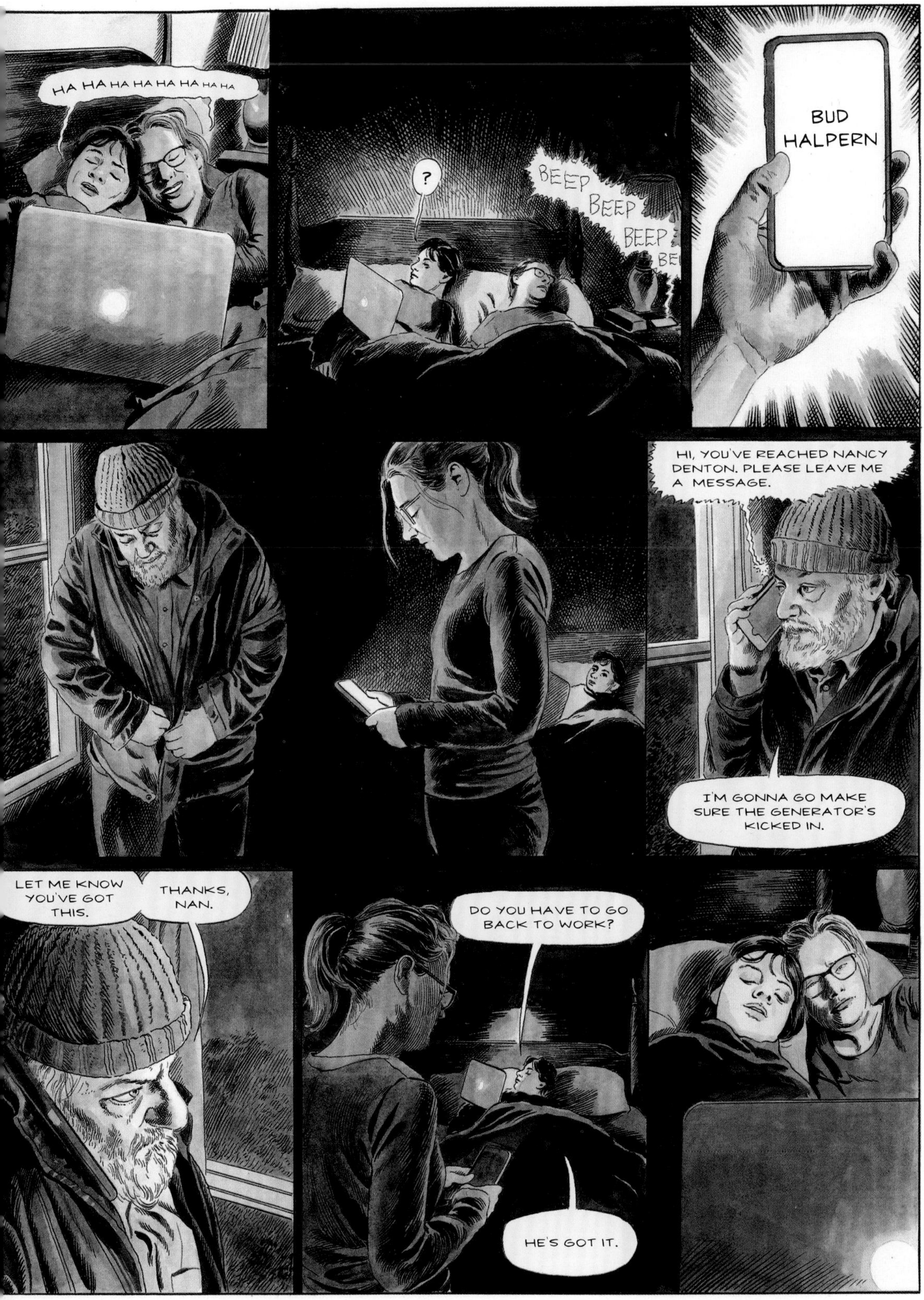
HA HA HA HA HA HA HA HA HA HA
?
BEEP
BEEP
BEEP
BE
BUD HALPERN
HI, YOU'VE REACHED NANCY DENTON. PLEASE LEAVE ME A MESSAGE.
I'M GONNA GO MAKE SURE THE GENERATOR'S KICKED IN.
LET ME KNOW YOU'VE GOT THIS.
THANKS, NAN.
DO YOU HAVE TO GO BACK TO WORK?
HE'S GOT IT.

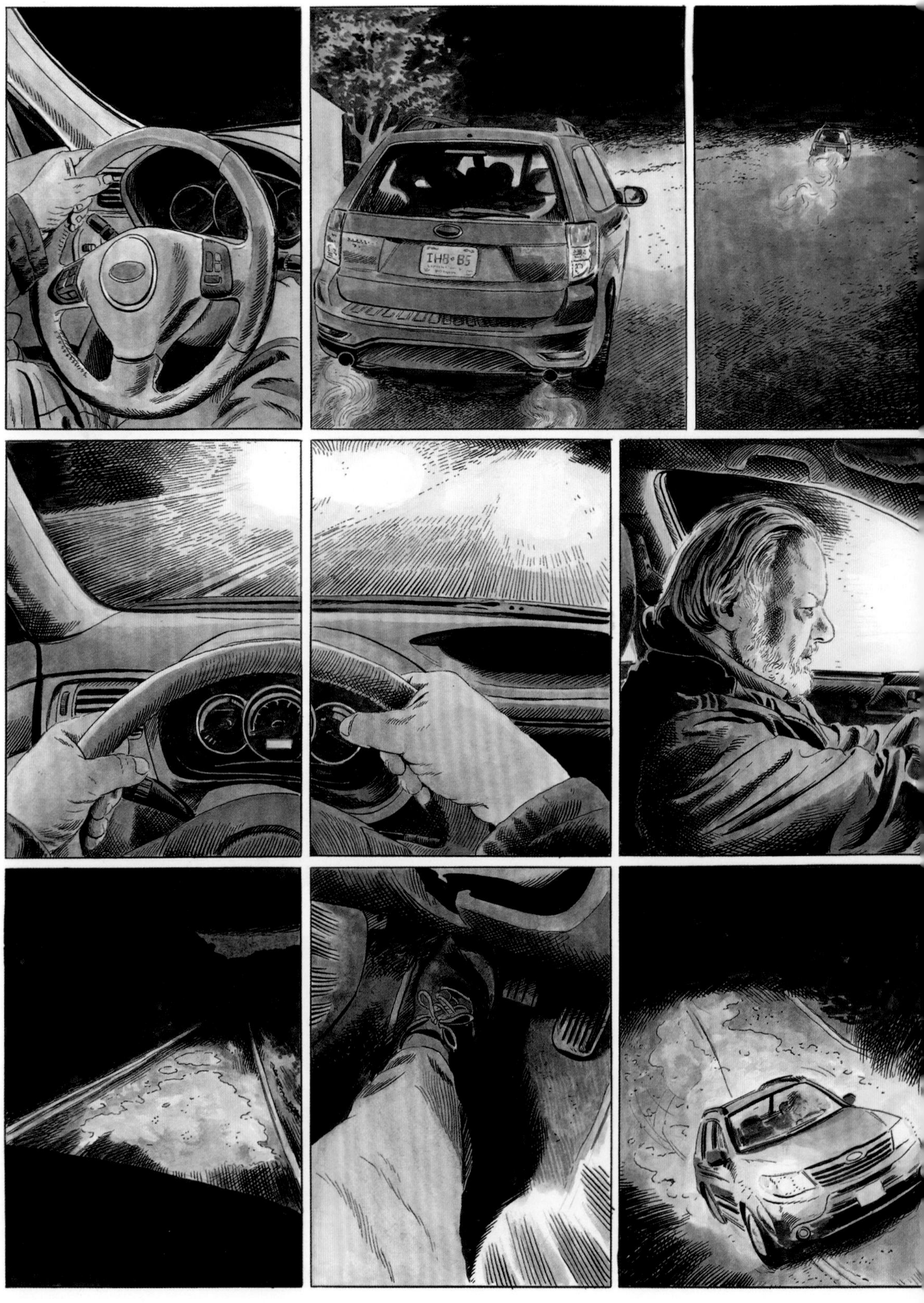
IH8•B5

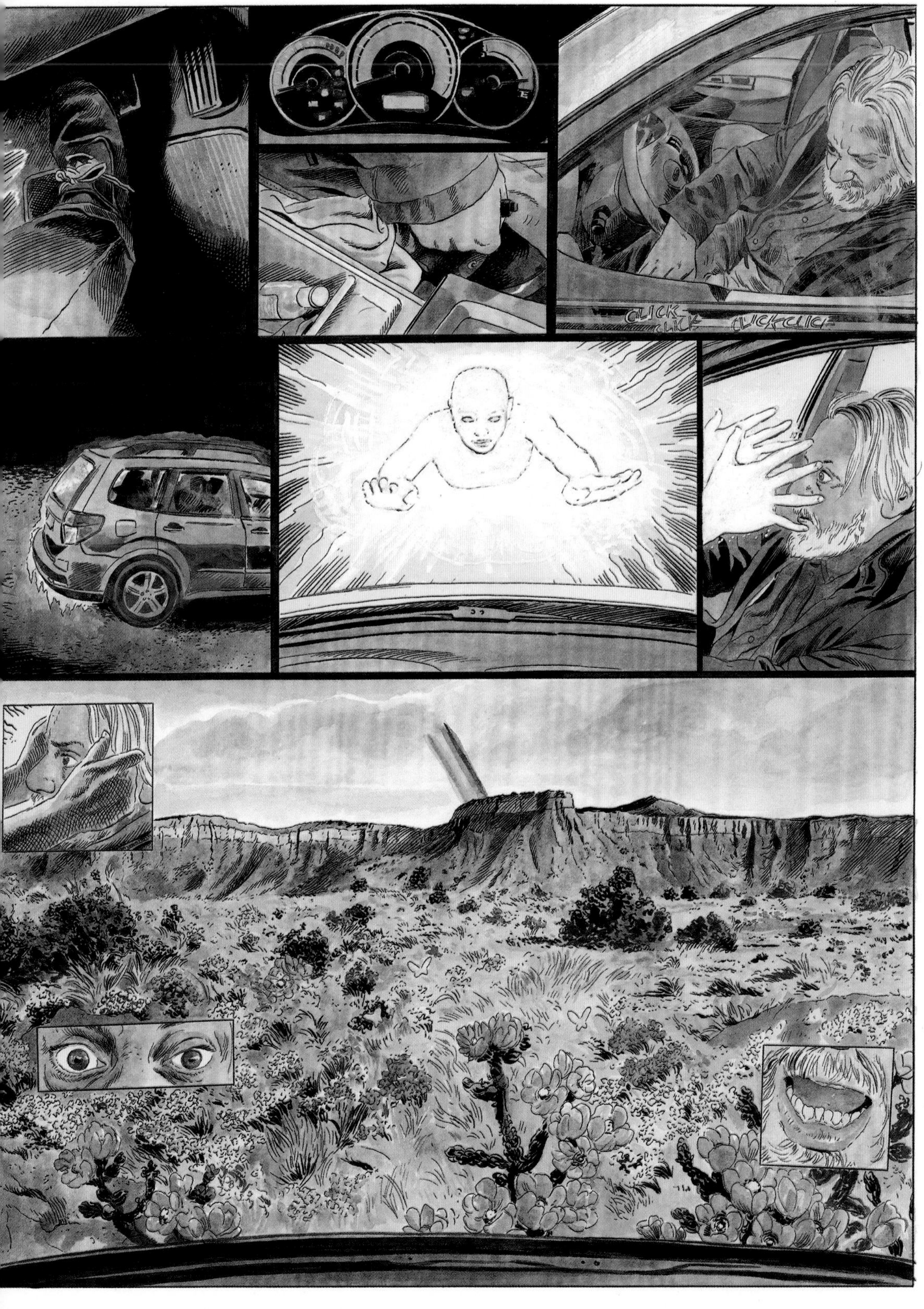
CLICK

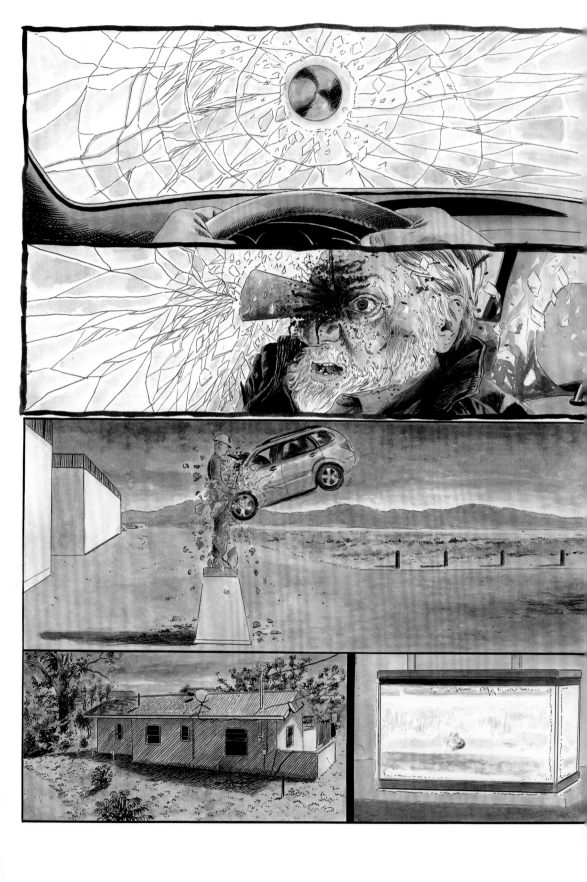

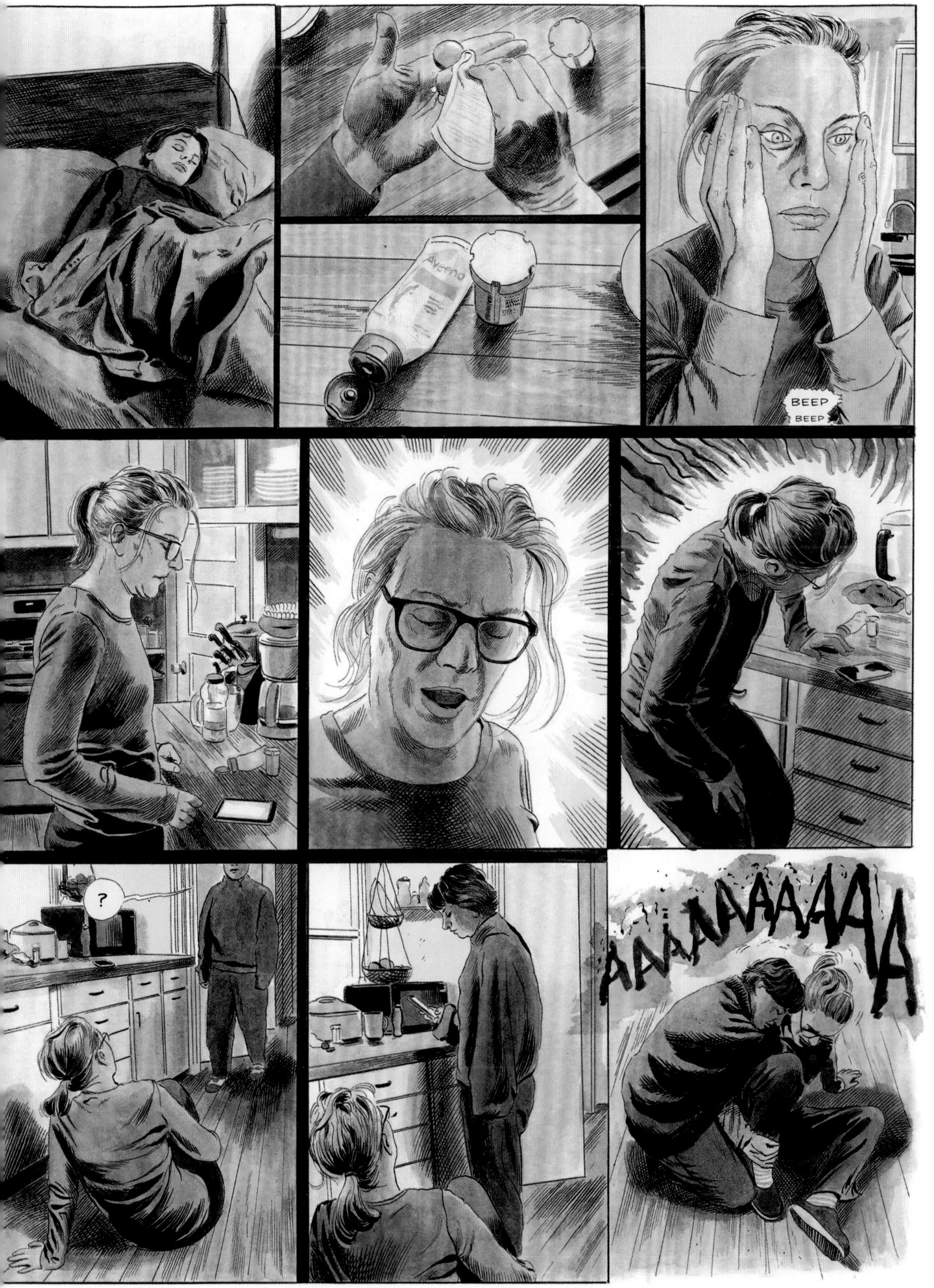
Aveeno
BEEP
BEEP
?
AAAAAAAAAA

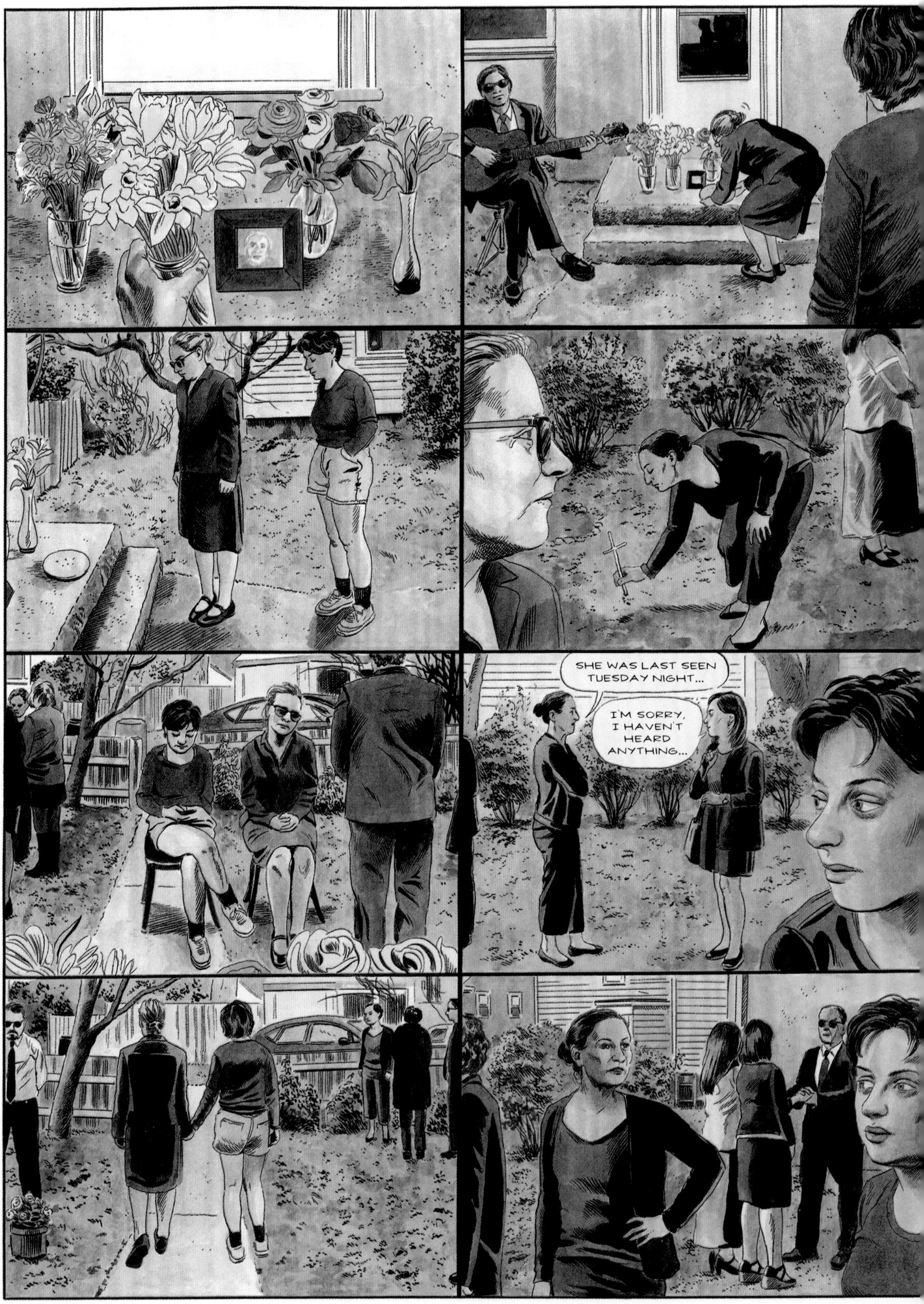
SHE WAS LAST SEEN TUESDAY NIGHT...
I'M SORRY, I HAVEN'T HEARD ANYTHING...

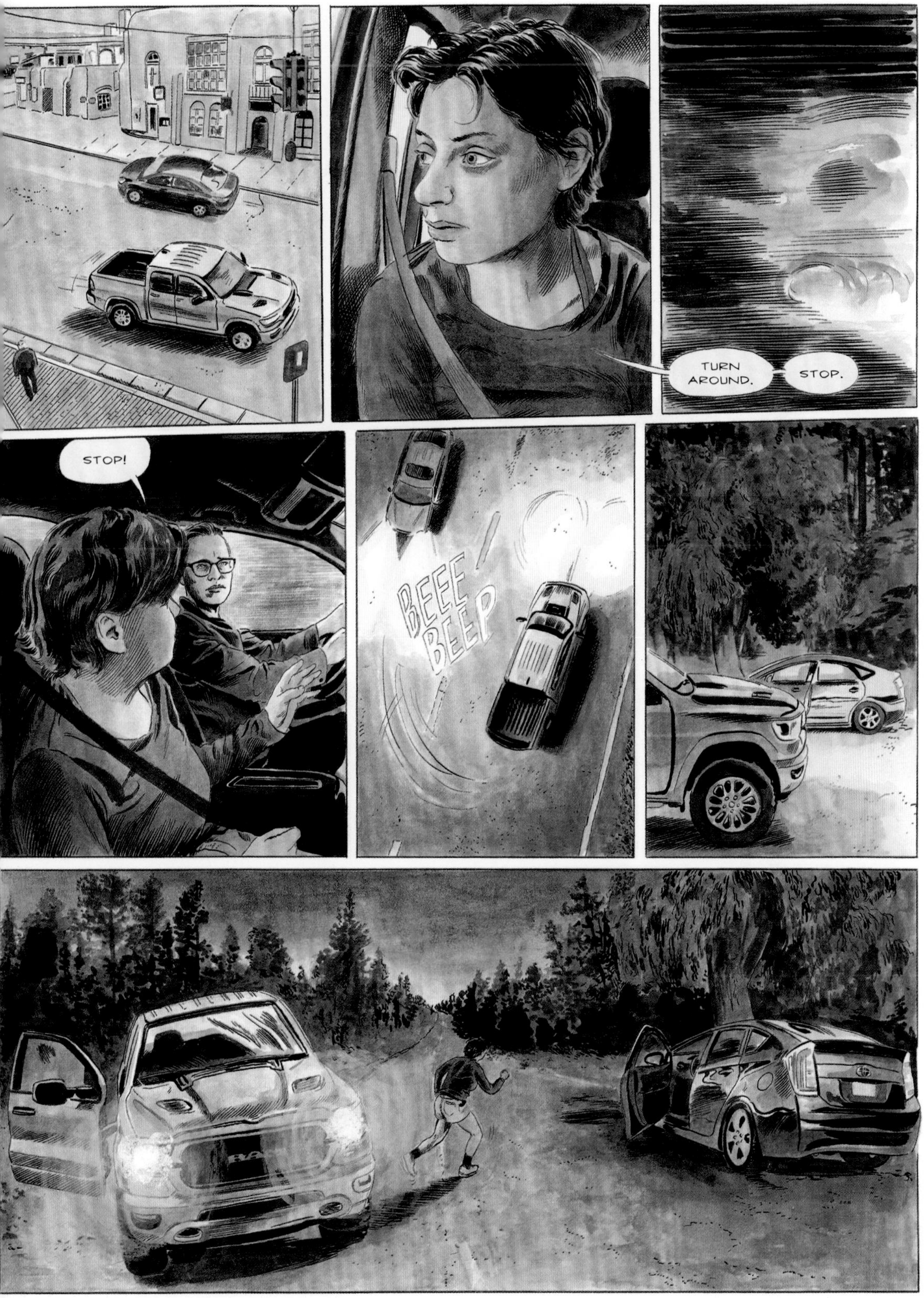
TURN AROUND.
STOP.
STOP!
BEEE BEEP

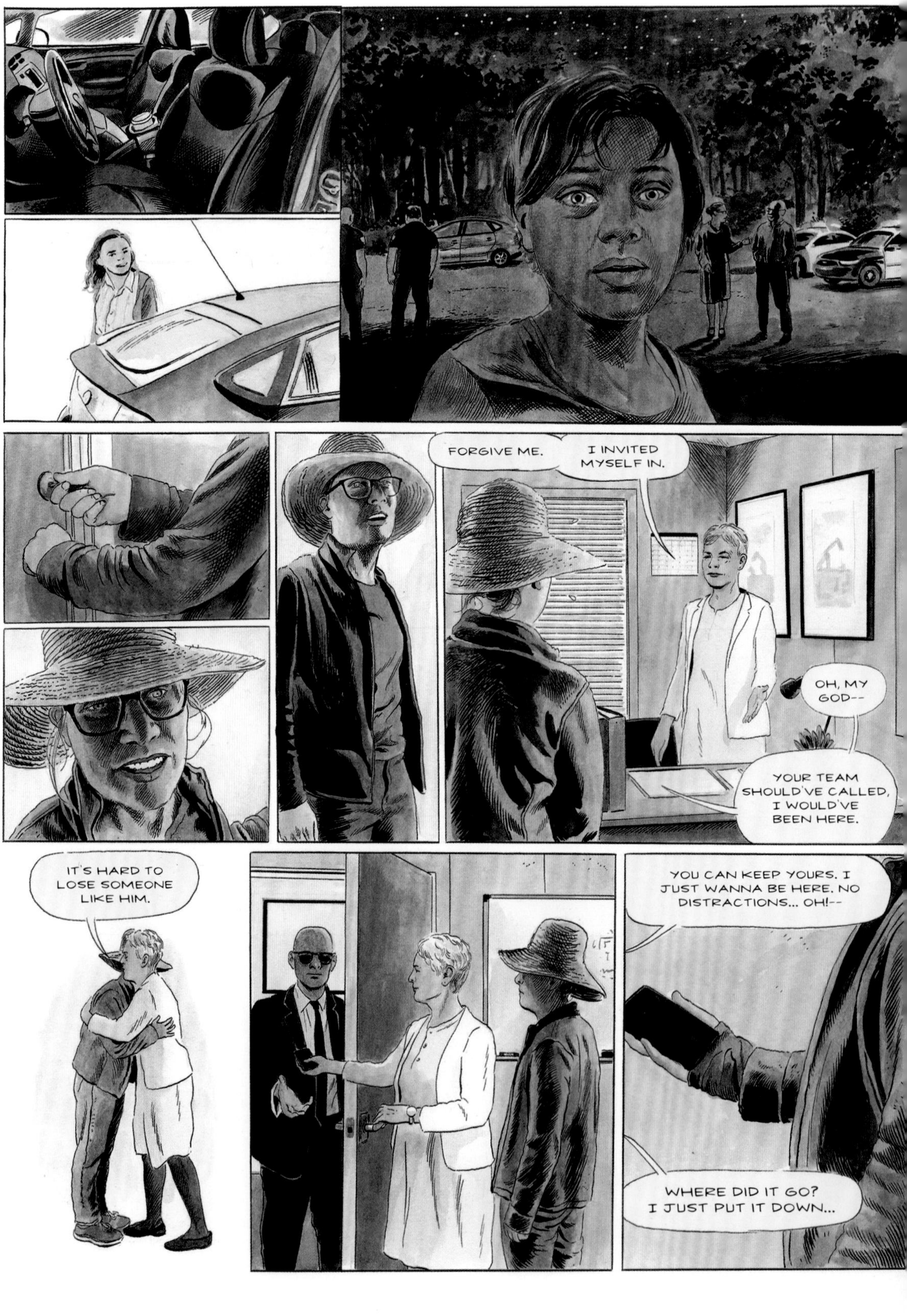
FORGIVE ME.
I INVITED MYSELF IN.
OH, MY GOD--
YOUR TEAM SHOULD'VE CALLED, I WOULD'VE BEEN HERE.
IT'S HARD TO LOSE SOMEONE LIKE HIM.
YOU CAN KEEP YOURS. I JUST WANNA BE HERE. NO DISTRACTIONS... OH!--
WHERE DID IT GO? I JUST PUT IT DOWN...

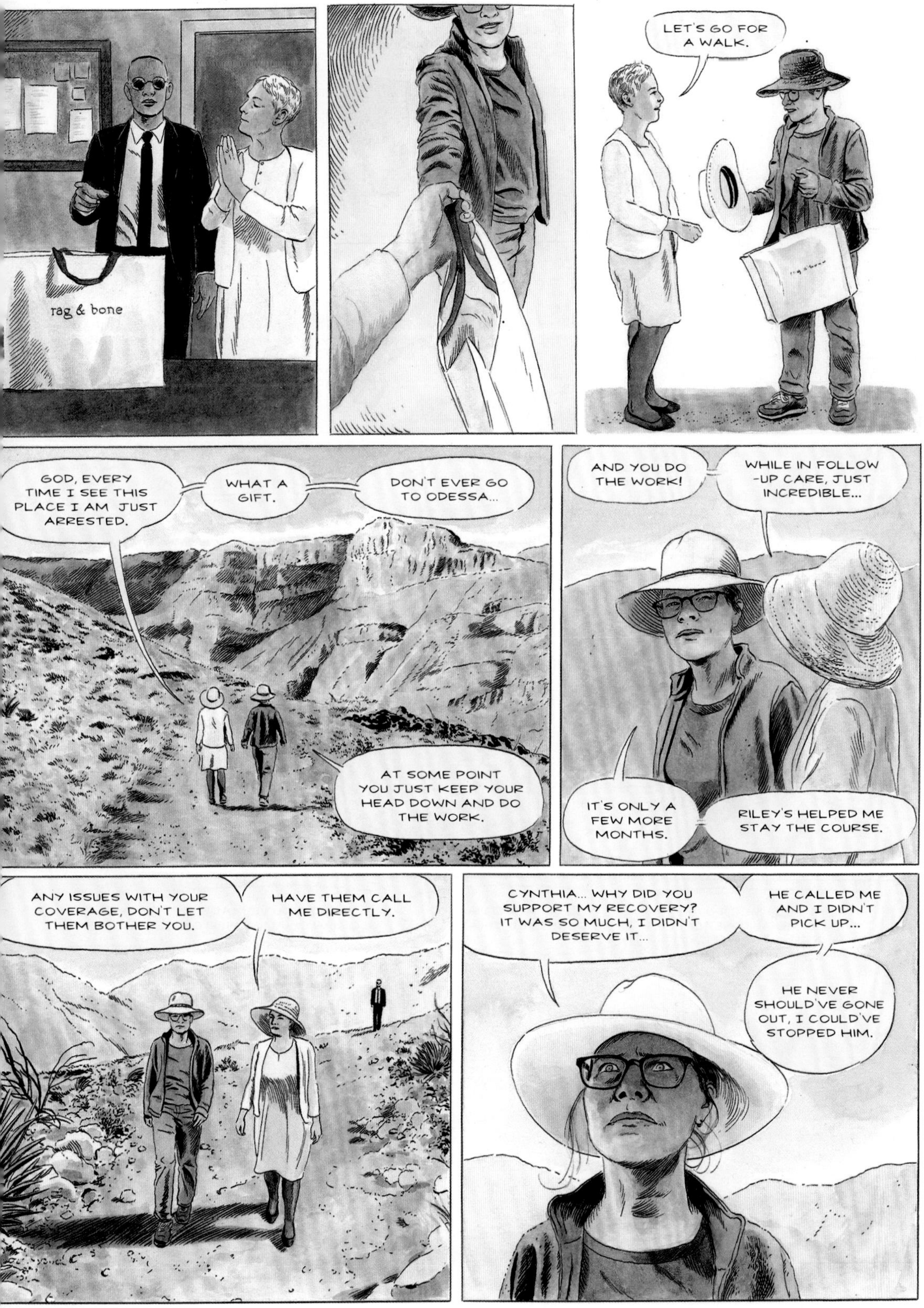
rag & bone
LET'S GO FOR A WALK.
GOD, EVERY TIME I SEE THIS PLACE I AM JUST ARRESTED.
WHAT A GIFT.
DON'T EVER GO TO ODESSA...
AT SOME POINT YOU JUST KEEP YOUR HEAD DOWN AND DO THE WORK.
AND YOU DO THE WORK!
WHILE IN FOLLOW-UP CARE, JUST INCREDIBLE...
IT'S ONLY A FEW MORE MONTHS.
RILEY'S HELPED ME STAY THE COURSE.
ANY ISSUES WITH YOUR COVERAGE, DON'T LET THEM BOTHER YOU.
HAVE THEM CALL ME DIRECTLY.
CYNTHIA... WHY DID YOU SUPPORT MY RECOVERY? IT WAS SO MUCH, I DIDN'T DESERVE IT...
HE CALLED ME AND I DIDN'T PICK UP...
HE NEVER SHOULD'VE GONE OUT, I COULD'VE STOPPED HIM.

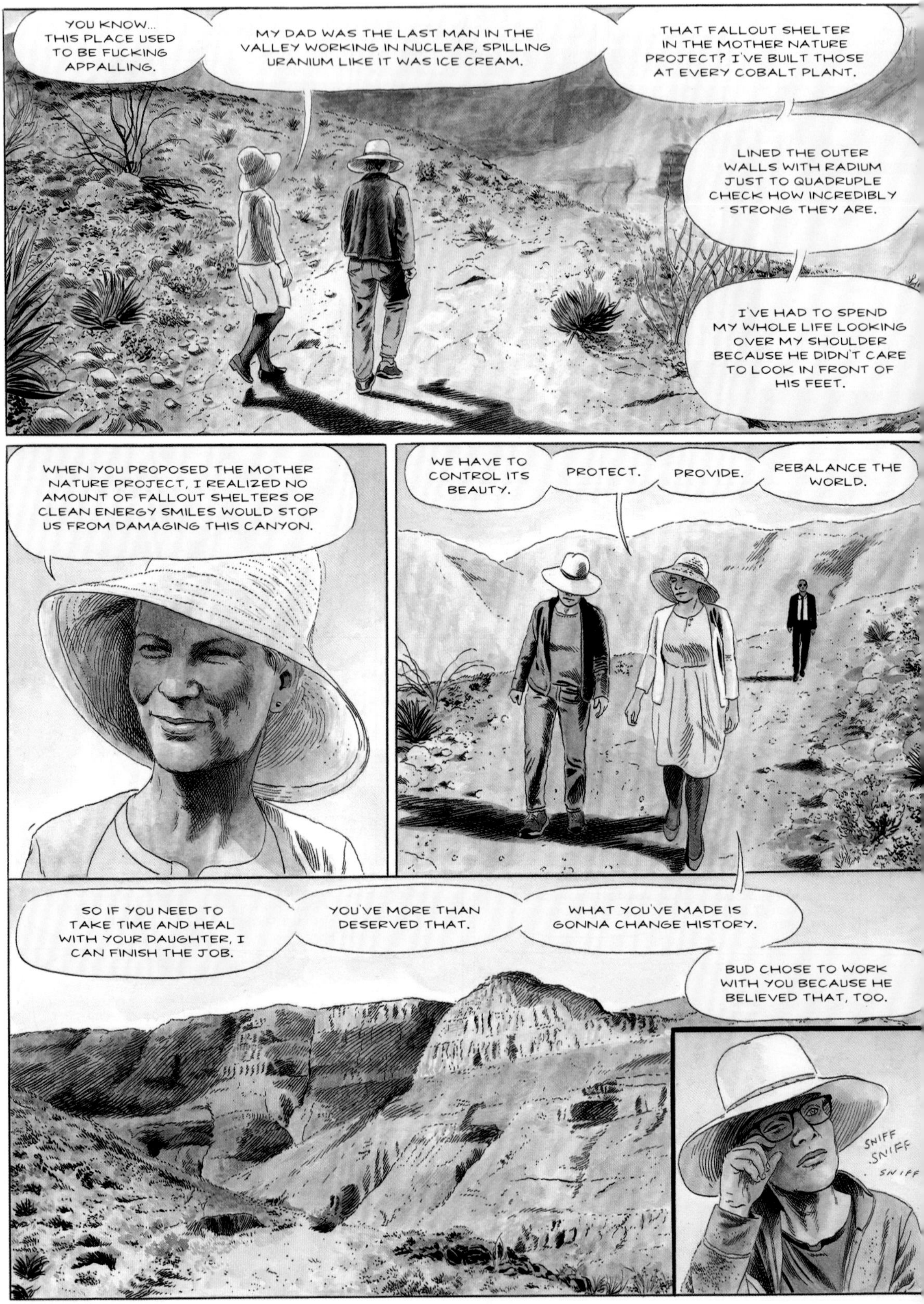

YOU KNOW... THIS PLACE USED TO BE FUCKING APPALLING.
MY DAD WAS THE LAST MAN IN THE VALLEY WORKING IN NUCLEAR, SPILLING URANIUM LIKE IT WAS ICE CREAM.
THAT FALLOUT SHELTER IN THE MOTHER NATURE PROJECT? I'VE BUILT THOSE AT EVERY COBALT PLANT.
LINED THE OUTER WALLS WITH RADIUM JUST TO QUADRUPLE CHECK HOW INCREDIBLY STRONG THEY ARE.
I'VE HAD TO SPEND MY WHOLE LIFE LOOKING OVER MY SHOULDER BECAUSE HE DIDN'T CARE TO LOOK IN FRONT OF HIS FEET.
WHEN YOU PROPOSED THE MOTHER NATURE PROJECT, I REALIZED NO AMOUNT OF FALLOUT SHELTERS OR CLEAN ENERGY SMILES WOULD STOP US FROM DAMAGING THIS CANYON.
WE HAVE TO CONTROL ITS BEAUTY.
PROTECT.
PROVIDE.
REBALANCE THE WORLD.
SO IF YOU NEED TO TAKE TIME AND HEAL WITH YOUR DAUGHTER, I CAN FINISH THE JOB.
YOU'VE MORE THAN DESERVED THAT.
WHAT YOU'VE MADE IS GONNA CHANGE HISTORY.
BUD CHOSE TO WORK WITH YOU BECAUSE HE BELIEVED THAT, TOO.
SNIFF SNIFF SNIFF

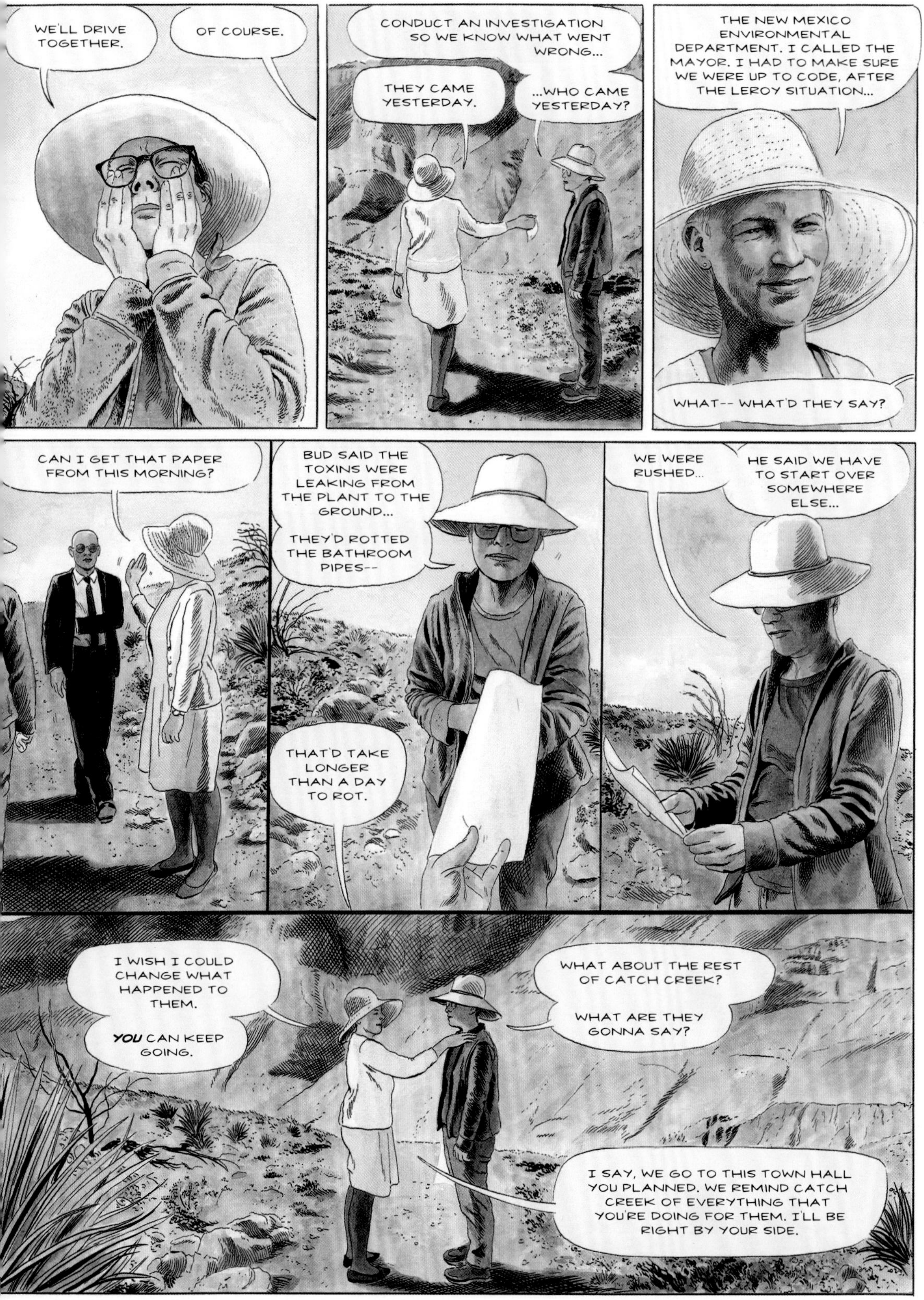
WE'LL DRIVE TOGETHER.
OF COURSE.
CONDUCT AN INVESTIGATION SO WE KNOW WHAT WENT WRONG...
THEY CAME YESTERDAY.
...WHO CAME YESTERDAY?
THE NEW MEXICO ENVIRONMENTAL DEPARTMENT. I CALLED THE MAYOR. I HAD TO MAKE SURE WE WERE UP TO CODE, AFTER THE LEROY SITUATION...
WHAT-- WHAT'D THEY SAY?
CAN I GET THAT PAPER FROM THIS MORNING?
BUD SAID THE TOXINS WERE LEAKING FROM THE PLANT TO THE GROUND...
THEY'D ROTTED THE BATHROOM PIPES--
THAT'D TAKE LONGER THAN A DAY TO ROT.
WE WERE RUSHED...
HE SAID WE HAVE TO START OVER SOMEWHERE ELSE...
I WISH I COULD CHANGE WHAT HAPPENED TO THEM.
YOU CAN KEEP GOING.
WHAT ABOUT THE REST OF CATCH CREEK?
WHAT ARE THEY GONNA SAY?
I SAY, WE GO TO THIS TOWN HALL YOU PLANNED. WE REMIND CATCH CREEK OF EVERYTHING THAT YOU'RE DOING FOR THEM. I'LL BE RIGHT BY YOUR SIDE.

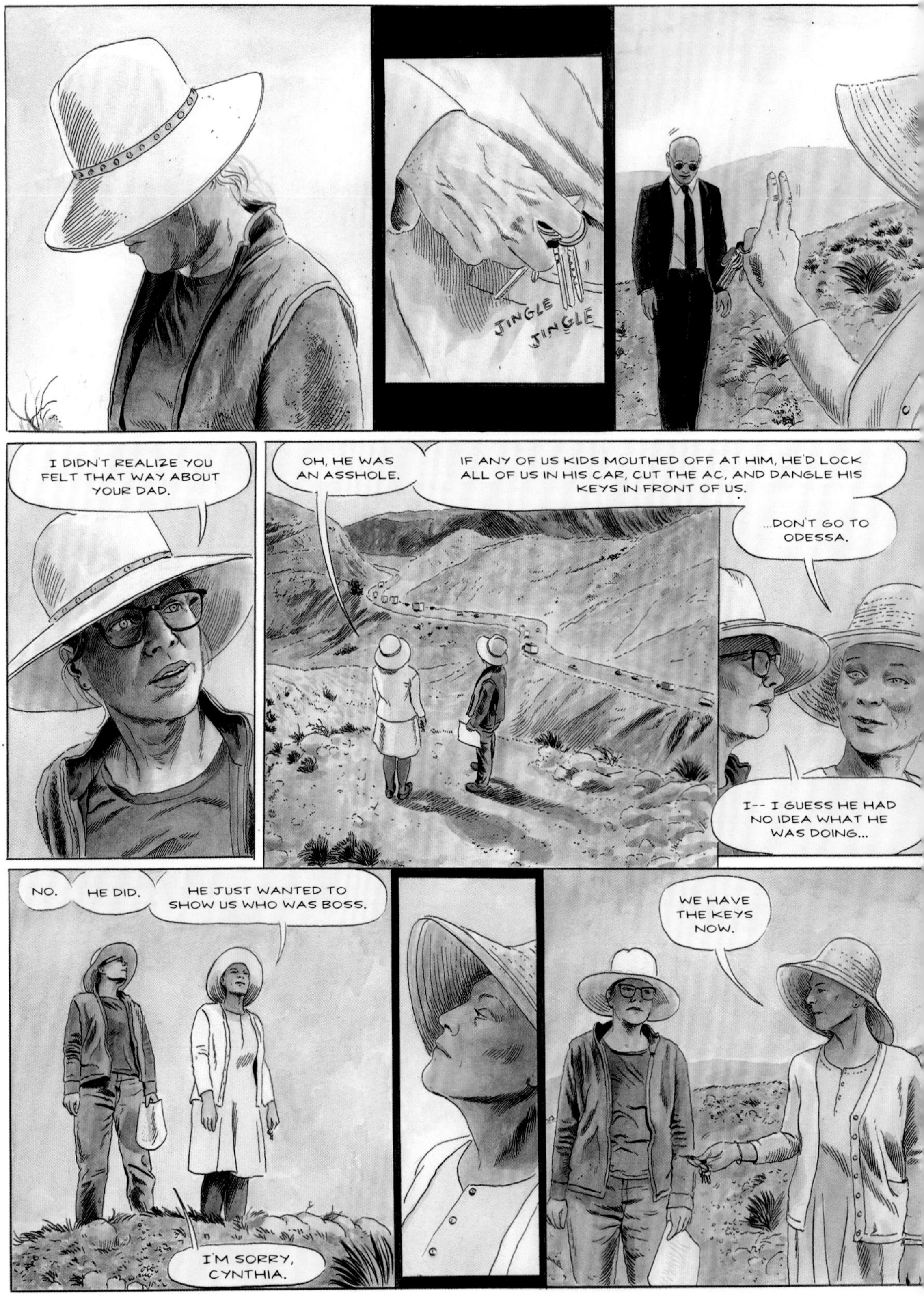
JINGLE
JINGLE
I DIDN'T REALIZE YOU FELT THAT WAY ABOUT YOUR DAD.
OH, HE WAS AN ASSHOLE.
IF ANY OF US KIDS MOUTHED OFF AT HIM, HE'D LOCK ALL OF US IN HIS CAR, CUT THE AC, AND DANGLE HIS KEYS IN FRONT OF US.
...DON'T GO TO ODESSA.
I-- I GUESS HE HAD NO IDEA WHAT HE WAS DOING...
NO.
HE DID.
HE JUST WANTED TO SHOW US WHO WAS BOSS.
I'M SORRY, CYNTHIA.
WE HAVE THE KEYS NOW.

KNOCK KNOCK

HI, I'M SORRY TO BOTHER YOU--

HOW'S YOUR MOM?

...SHE'S ALRIGHT.

THANKS.

I KNOW YOUR DAUGHTER'S MISSING.

MY FRIEND IS, TOO.

WE FOUND HER CAR OFF THE SIDE OF HIGHWAY 12.

SHE WENT MISSING THE SAME NIGHT THAT NOVA...

...WHY DON'T YOU COME INSIDE?

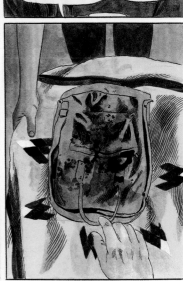

THEN I FOUND THIS OUT ON THE FIELD, COVERED IN OIL.

I TRIED HER HOUSE BUT ALL I SAW WERE THESE PHOTOS.

THAT'S NOT OIL...

OW!

SSSSS!!

DO YOU HAVE A RADIOACTIVE CONTAINER, OR WASTE BIN?

...NO?

RIGHT.

SORRY...

WHAT ABOUT, LIKE, TUPPERWARE? SEALABLE TUPPERWARE...

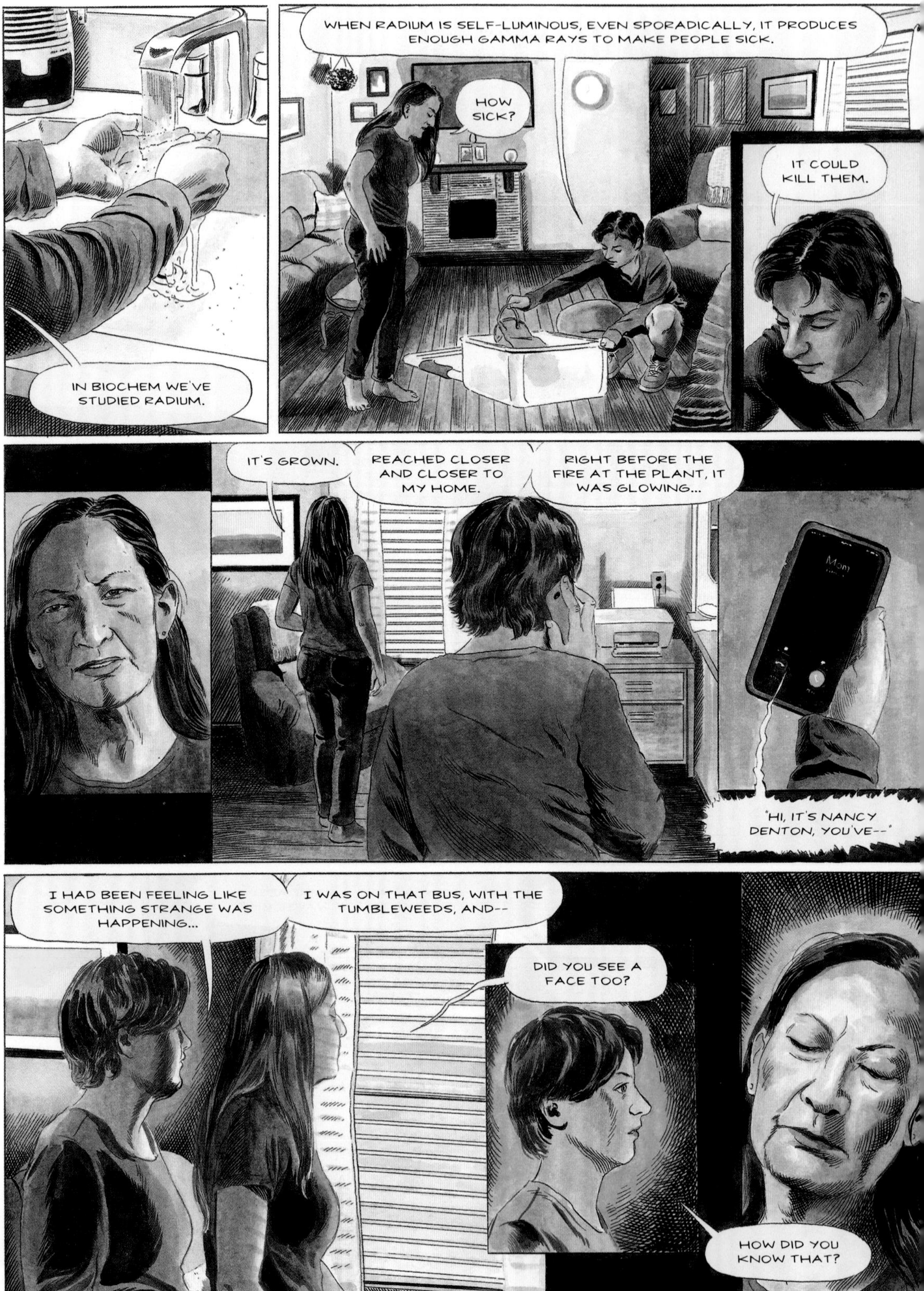
IN BIOCHEM WE'VE STUDIED RADIUM.
WHEN RADIUM IS SELF-LUMINOUS, EVEN SPORADICALLY, IT PRODUCES ENOUGH GAMMA RAYS TO MAKE PEOPLE SICK.
HOW SICK?
IT COULD KILL THEM.
IT'S GROWN.
REACHED CLOSER AND CLOSER TO MY HOME.
RIGHT BEFORE THE FIRE AT THE PLANT, IT WAS GLOWING...
Mom
"HI, IT'S NANCY DENTON, YOU'VE--"
I HAD BEEN FEELING LIKE SOMETHING STRANGE WAS HAPPENING...
I WAS ON THAT BUS, WITH THE TUMBLEWEEDS, AND--
DID YOU SEE A FACE TOO?
HOW DID YOU KNOW THAT?

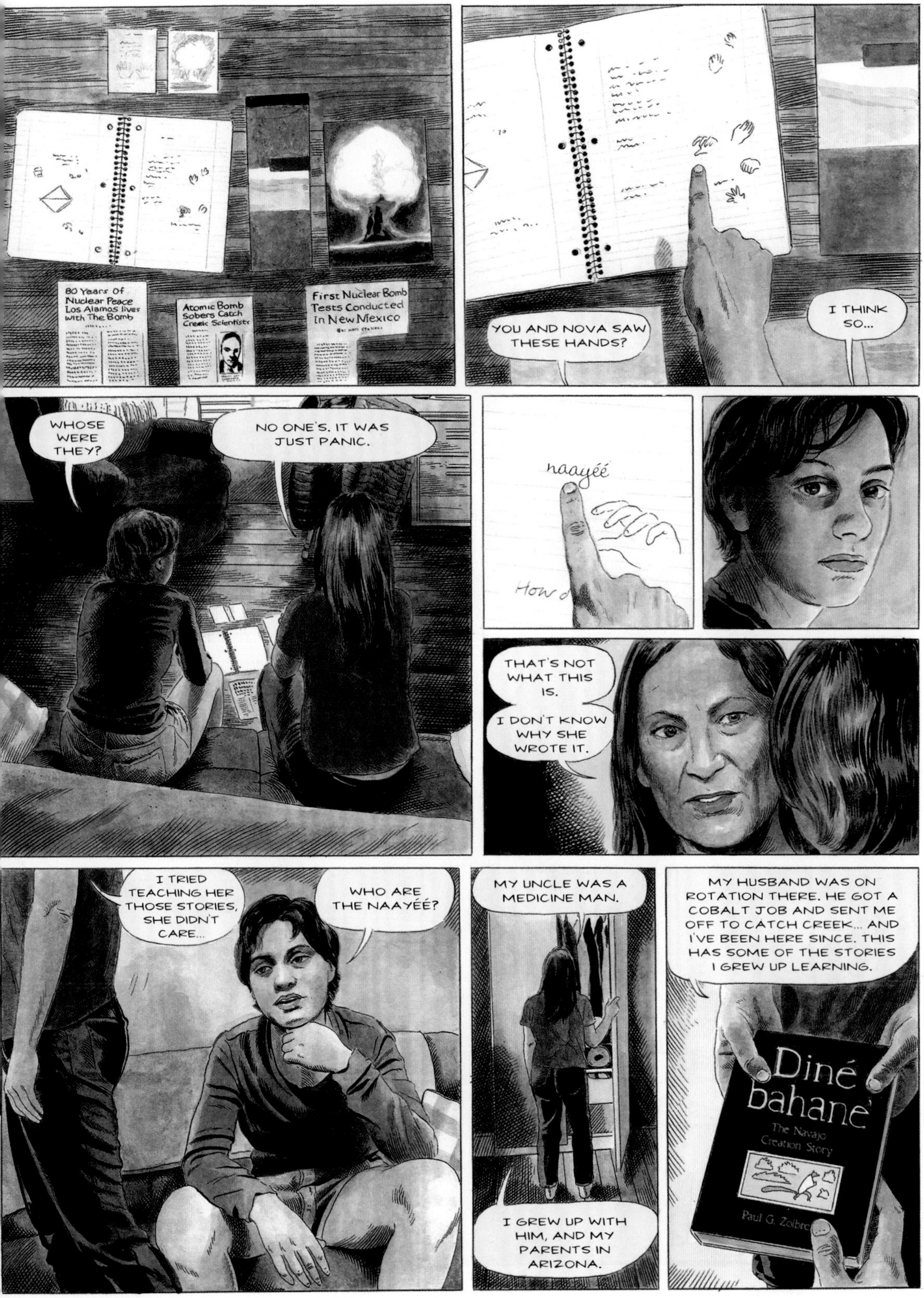
80 Years Of Nuclear Peace Los Alamos lives with The Bomb
Atomic Bomb Sobers Catch Creek Scientists
First Nuclear Bomb Tests Conducted In New Mexico
YOU AND NOVA SAW THESE HANDS?
I THINK SO...
WHOSE WERE THEY?
NO ONE'S. IT WAS JUST PANIC.
naayéé
THAT'S NOT WHAT THIS IS.
I DON'T KNOW WHY SHE WROTE IT.
I TRIED TEACHING HER THOSE STORIES, SHE DIDN'T CARE...
WHO ARE THE NAAYÉÉ?
MY UNCLE WAS A MEDICINE MAN.
I GREW UP WITH HIM, AND MY PARENTS IN ARIZONA.
MY HUSBAND WAS ON ROTATION THERE. HE GOT A COBALT JOB AND SENT ME OFF TO CATCH CREEK... AND I'VE BEEN HERE SINCE. THIS HAS SOME OF THE STORIES I GREW UP LEARNING.
Diné bahane'
The Navajo Creation Story

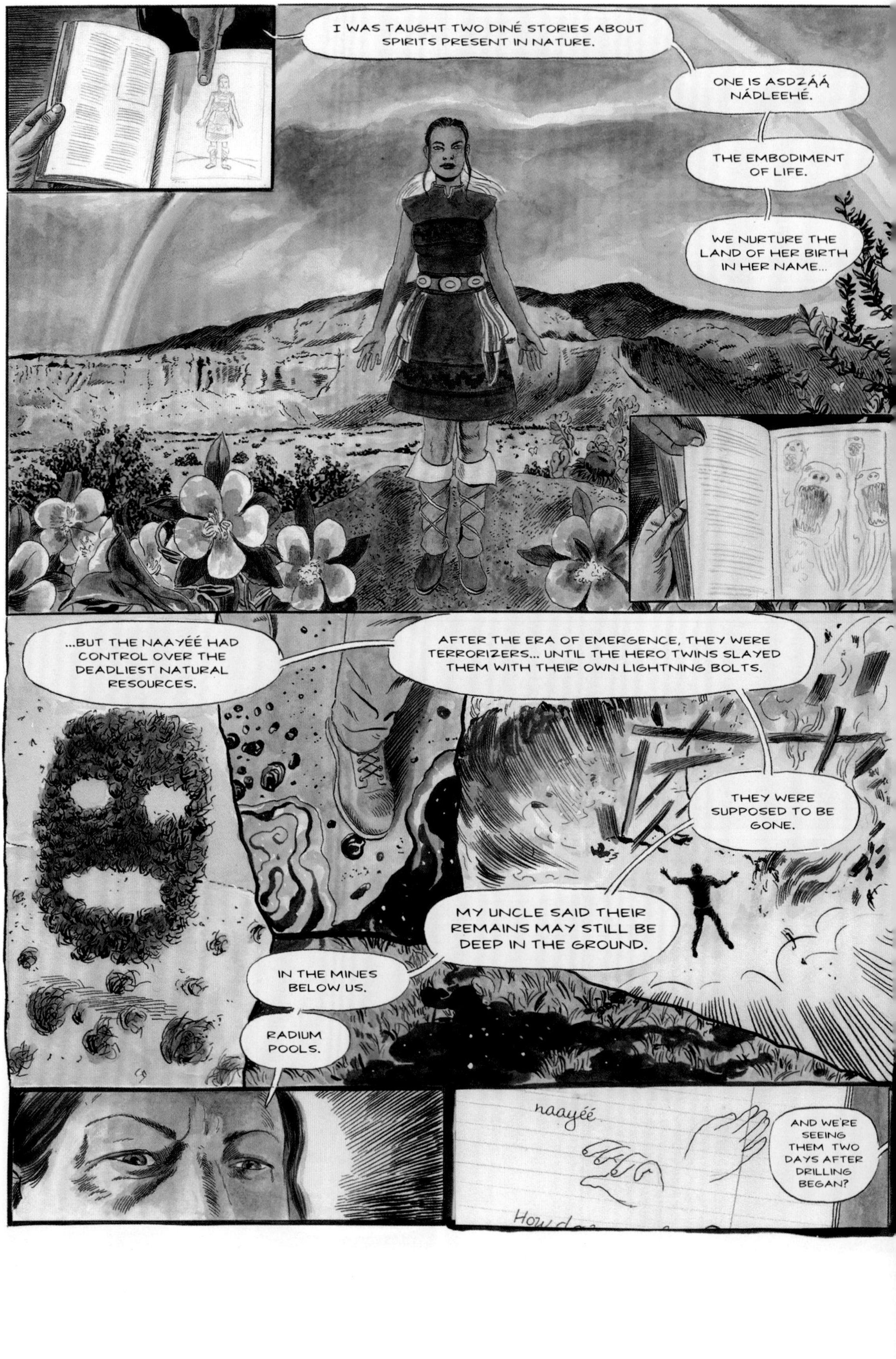

I WAS TAUGHT TWO DINÉ STORIES ABOUT SPIRITS PRESENT IN NATURE.
ONE IS ASDZÁÁ NÁDLEEHÉ.
THE EMBODIMENT OF LIFE.
WE NURTURE THE LAND OF HER BIRTH IN HER NAME...
...BUT THE NAAYÉÉ HAD CONTROL OVER THE DEADLIEST NATURAL RESOURCES.
AFTER THE ERA OF EMERGENCE, THEY WERE TERRORIZERS... UNTIL THE HERO TWINS SLAYED THEM WITH THEIR OWN LIGHTNING BOLTS.
THEY WERE SUPPOSED TO BE GONE.
MY UNCLE SAID THEIR REMAINS MAY STILL BE DEEP IN THE GROUND.
IN THE MINES BELOW US.
RADIUM POOLS.
naayéé.
AND WE'RE SEEING THEM TWO DAYS AFTER DRILLING BEGAN?

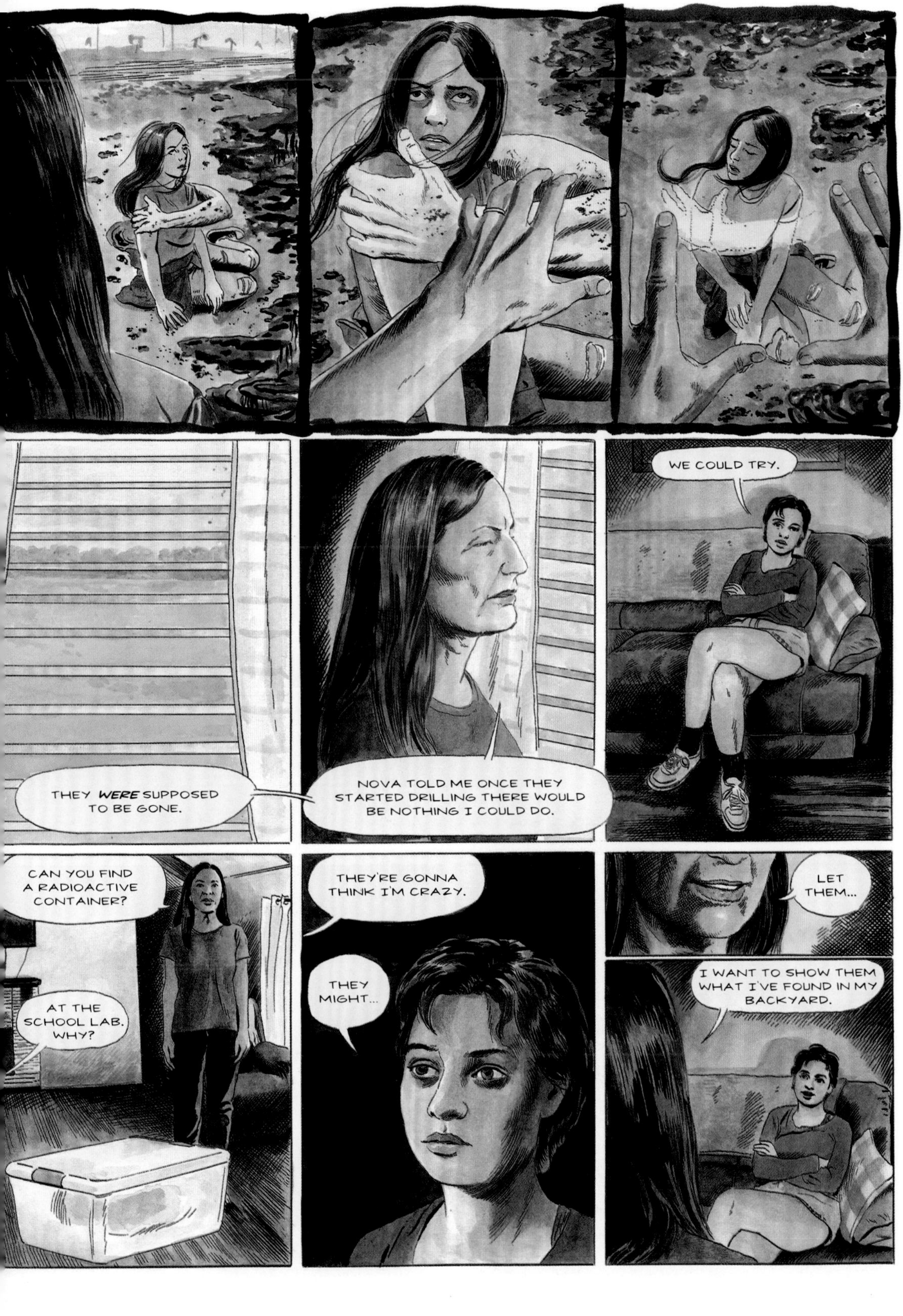
THEY WERE SUPPOSED TO BE GONE.
NOVA TOLD ME ONCE THEY STARTED DRILLING THERE WOULD BE NOTHING I COULD DO.
WE COULD TRY.
CAN YOU FIND A RADIOACTIVE CONTAINER?
AT THE SCHOOL LAB. WHY?
THEY'RE GONNA THINK I'M CRAZY.
THEY MIGHT...
LET THEM...
I WANT TO SHOW THEM WHAT I'VE FOUND IN MY BACKYARD.

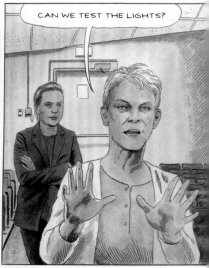

CAN WE TEST THE LIGHTS?

BE THERE IN A MINUTE.

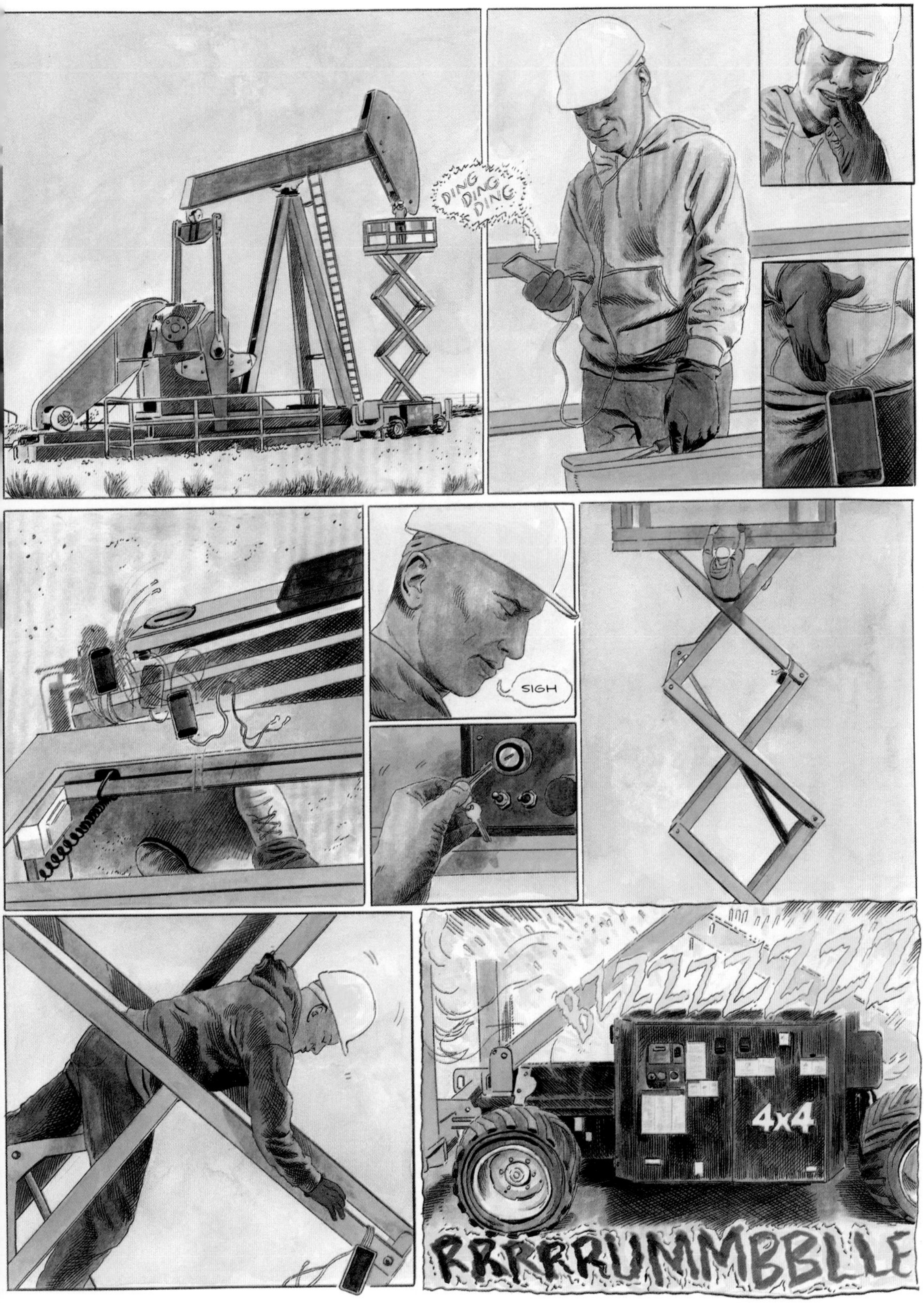
DING DING DING
SIGH
BZZZZZZZZZ
4x4
RRRRRUMMBBLLE

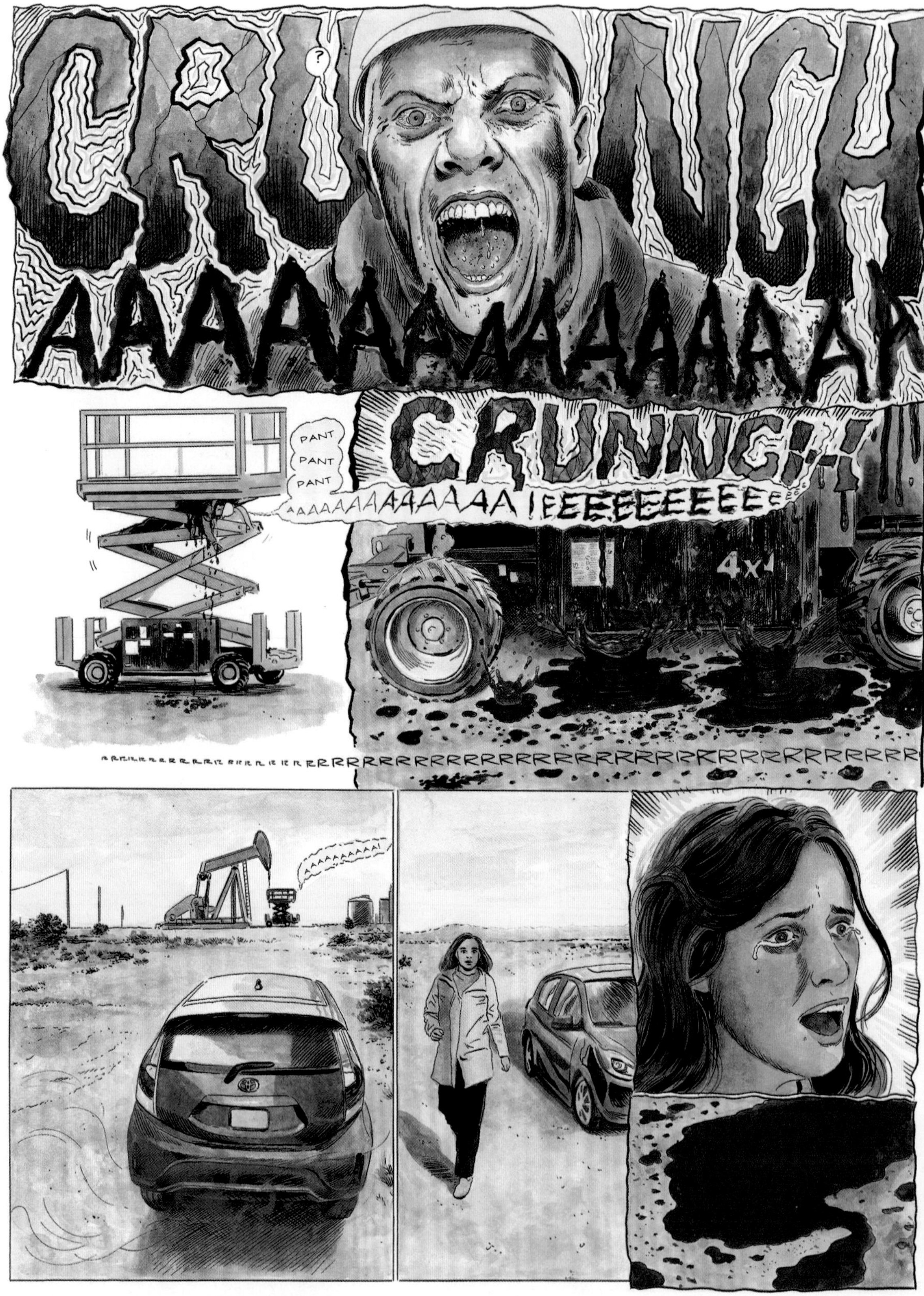
CRUNCH
?
AAAAAAAAAAAAAK
PANT
PANT
PANT
AAAAAAAAAAAAAAIEEEEEEEEEEE
CRUNNCH
4x4
RRRRRRRRRRRRRRRRRRRRRRRRRRRRRRRRRRRRRRRRRRRRRRRRRRRRRRRRRRRRRR
AAAAAAAAAA!

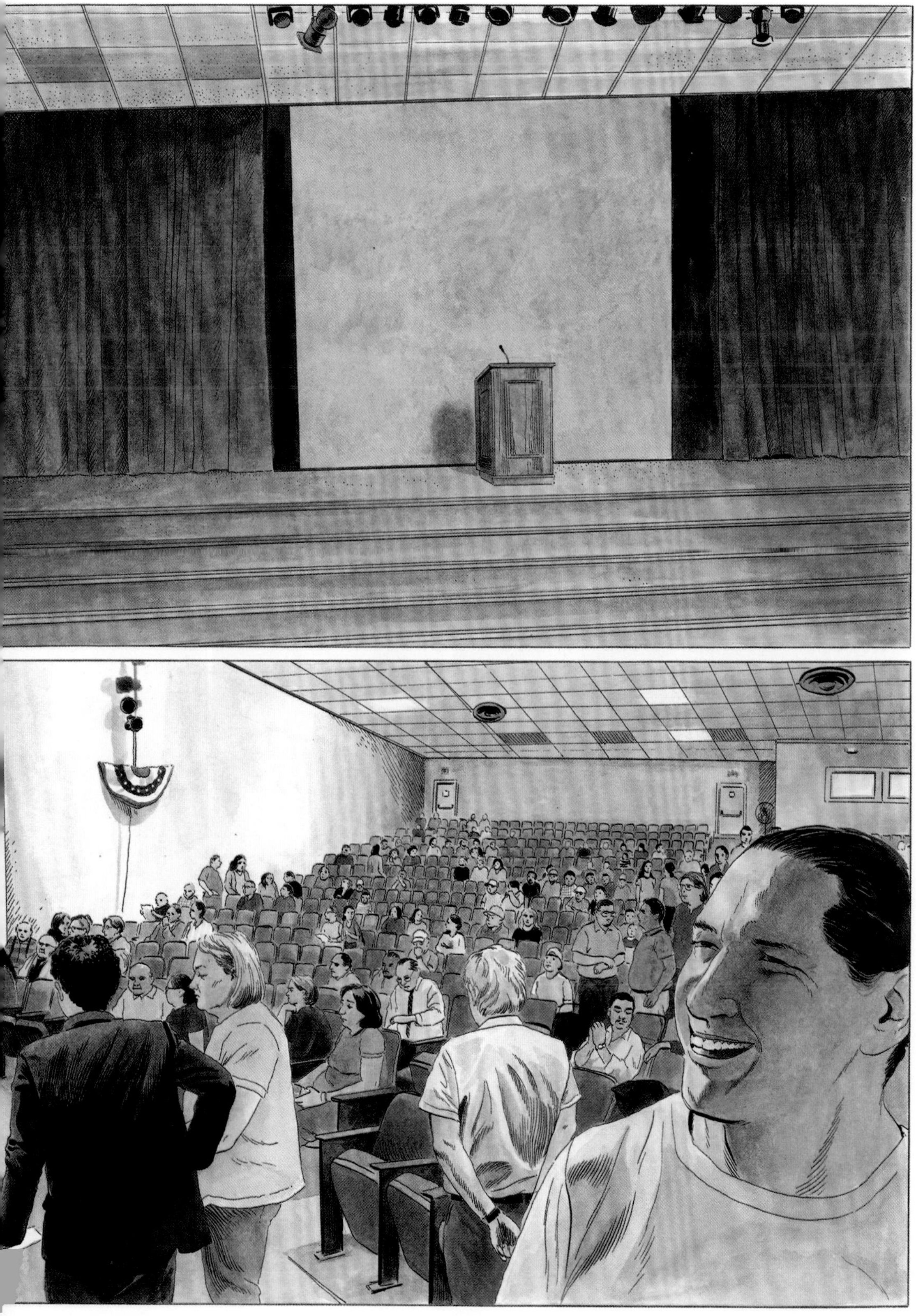

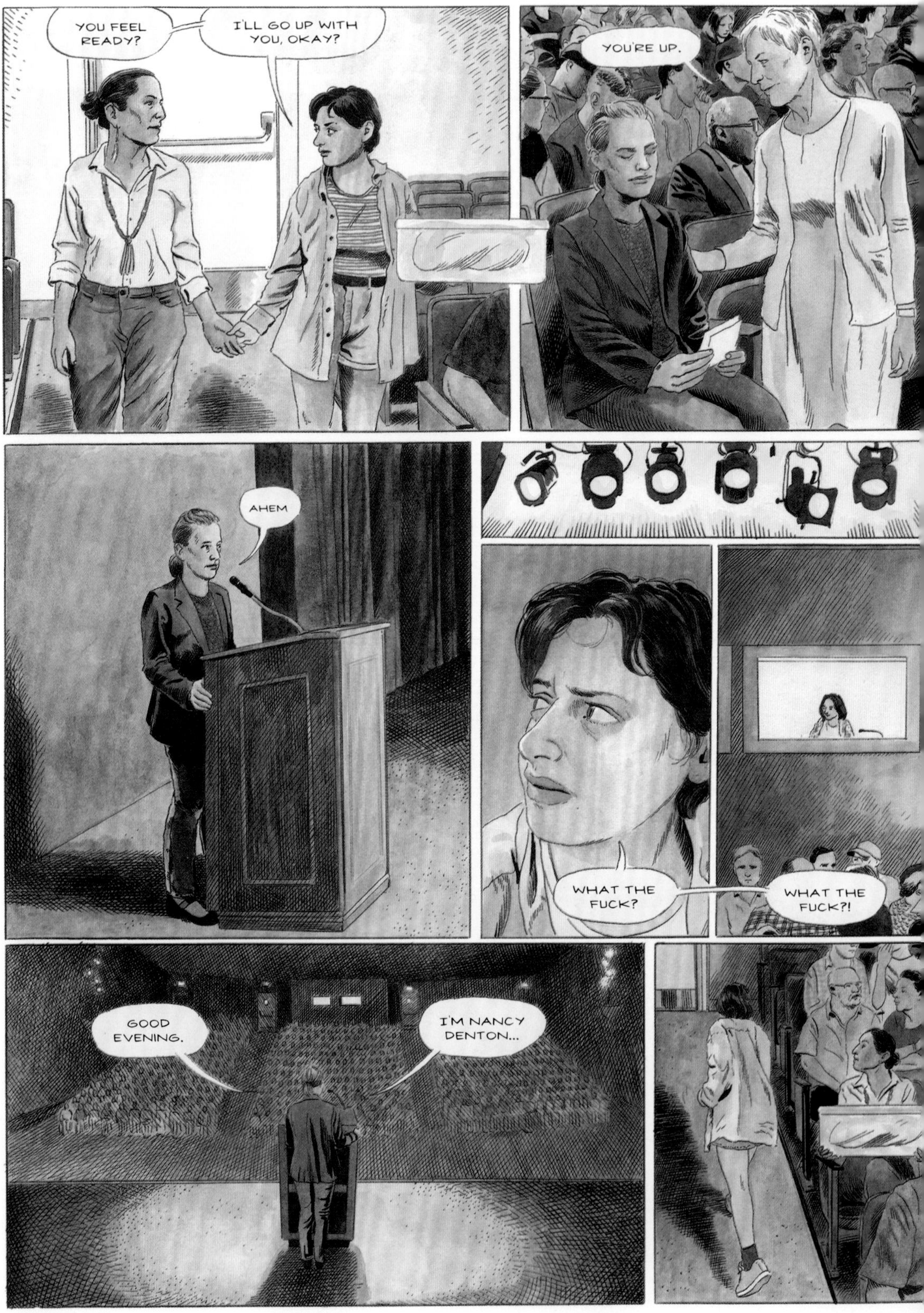
YOU FEEL READY?
I'LL GO UP WITH YOU, OKAY?
YOU'RE UP.
AHEM
WHAT THE FUCK?
WHAT THE FUCK?!
GOOD EVENING.
I'M NANCY DENTON...

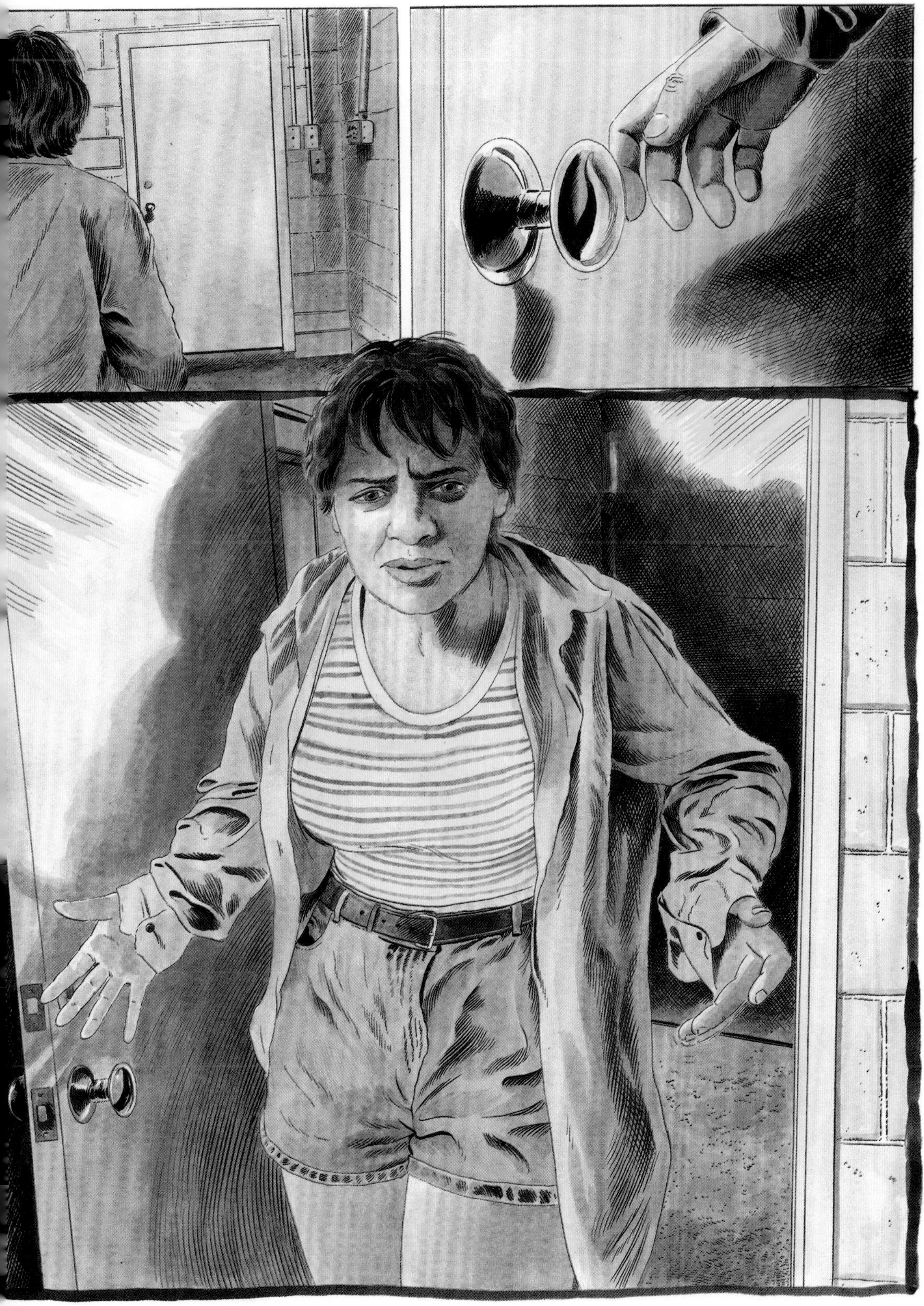

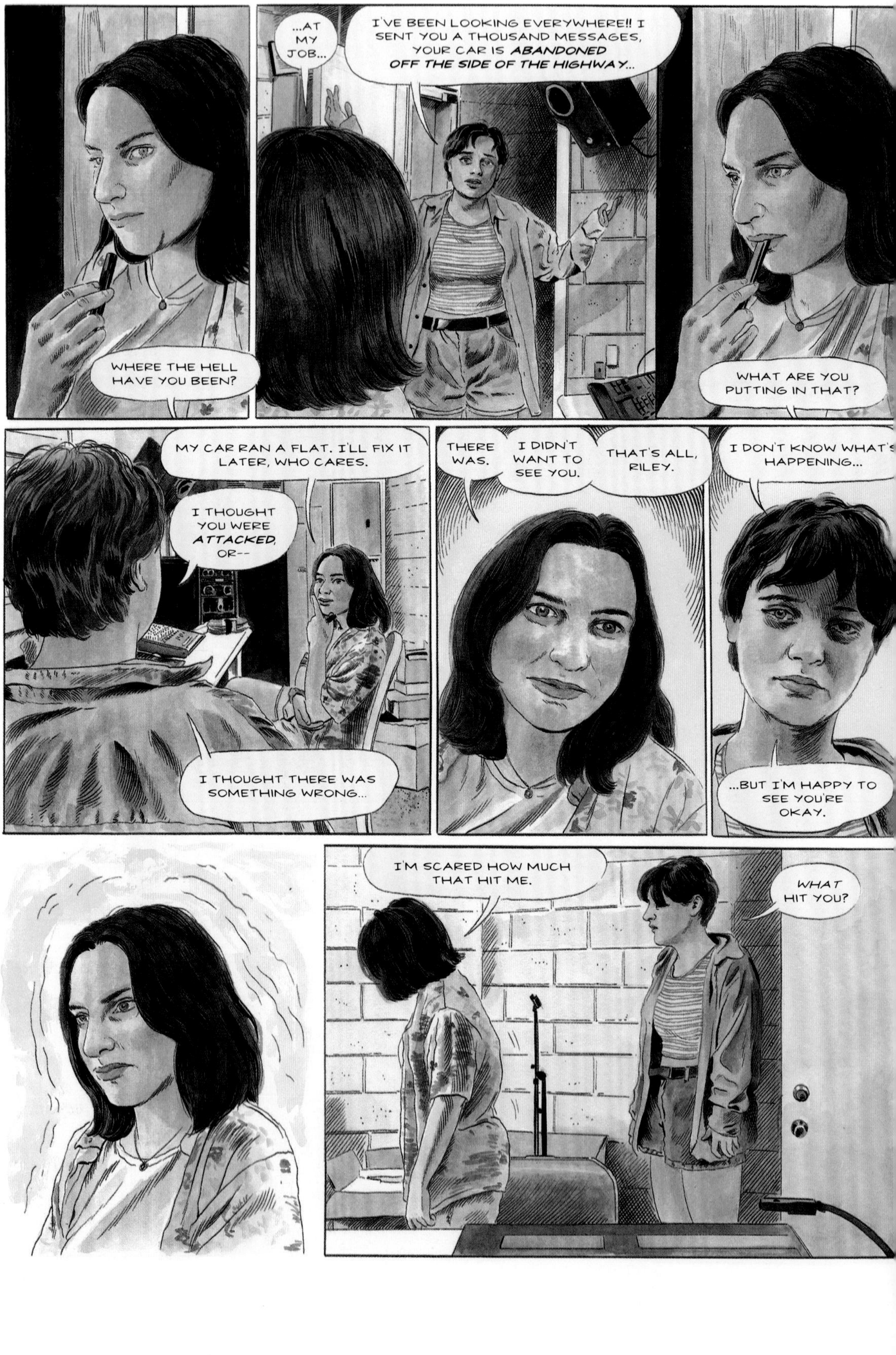
WHERE THE HELL HAVE YOU BEEN?
...AT MY JOB...
I'VE BEEN LOOKING EVERYWHERE!! I SENT YOU A THOUSAND MESSAGES, YOUR CAR IS ABANDONED OFF THE SIDE OF THE HIGHWAY...
WHAT ARE YOU PUTTING IN THAT?
MY CAR RAN A FLAT. I'LL FIX IT LATER, WHO CARES.
I THOUGHT YOU WERE ATTACKED, OR--
I THOUGHT THERE WAS SOMETHING WRONG...
THERE WAS.
I DIDN'T WANT TO SEE YOU.
THAT'S ALL, RILEY.
I DON'T KNOW WHAT'S HAPPENING...
...BUT I'M HAPPY TO SEE YOU'RE OKAY.
I'M SCARED HOW MUCH THAT HIT ME.
WHAT HIT YOU?

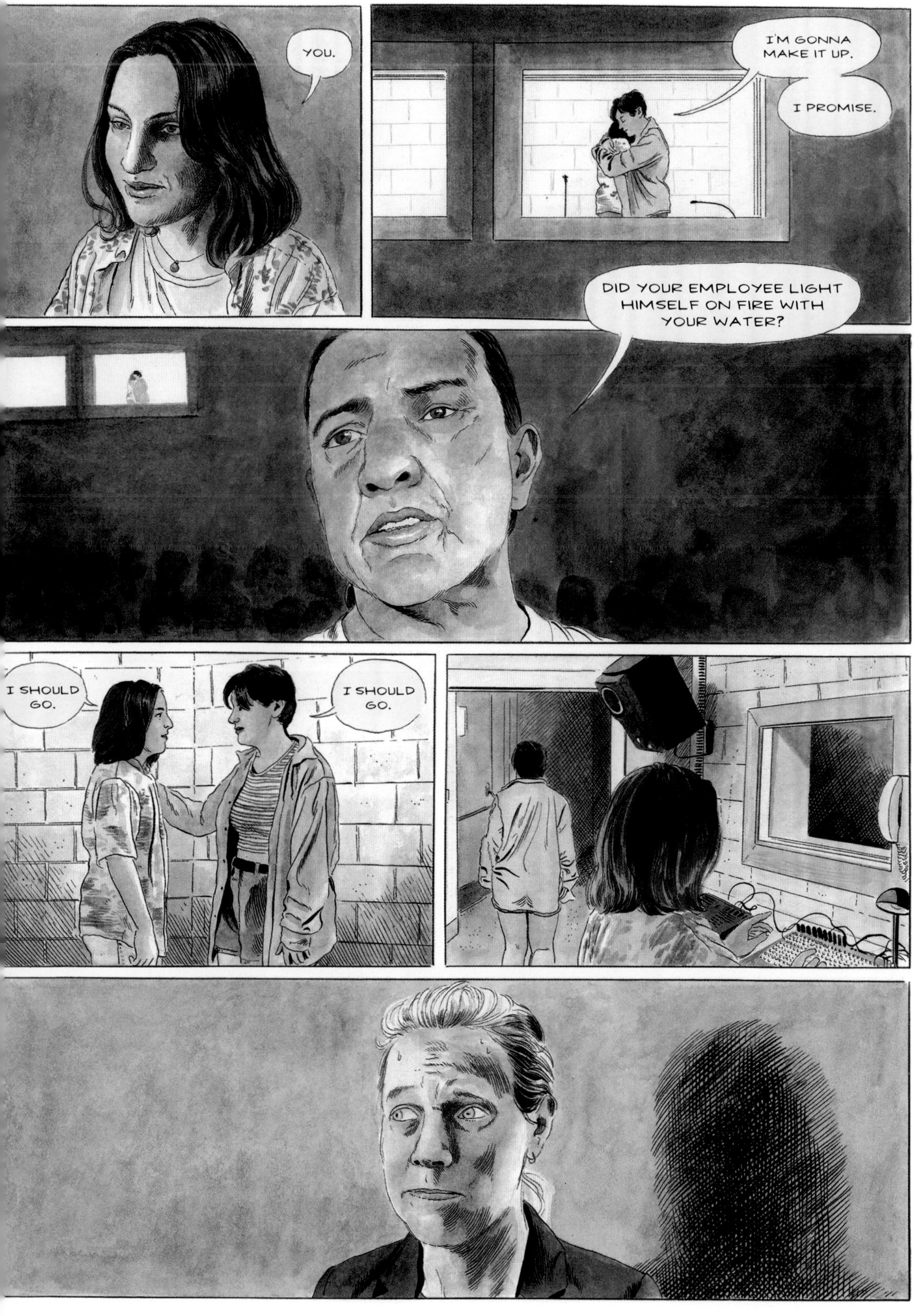
YOU.
I'M GONNA MAKE IT UP.
I PROMISE.
DID YOUR EMPLOYEE LIGHT HIMSELF ON FIRE WITH YOUR WATER?
I SHOULD GO.
I SHOULD GO.

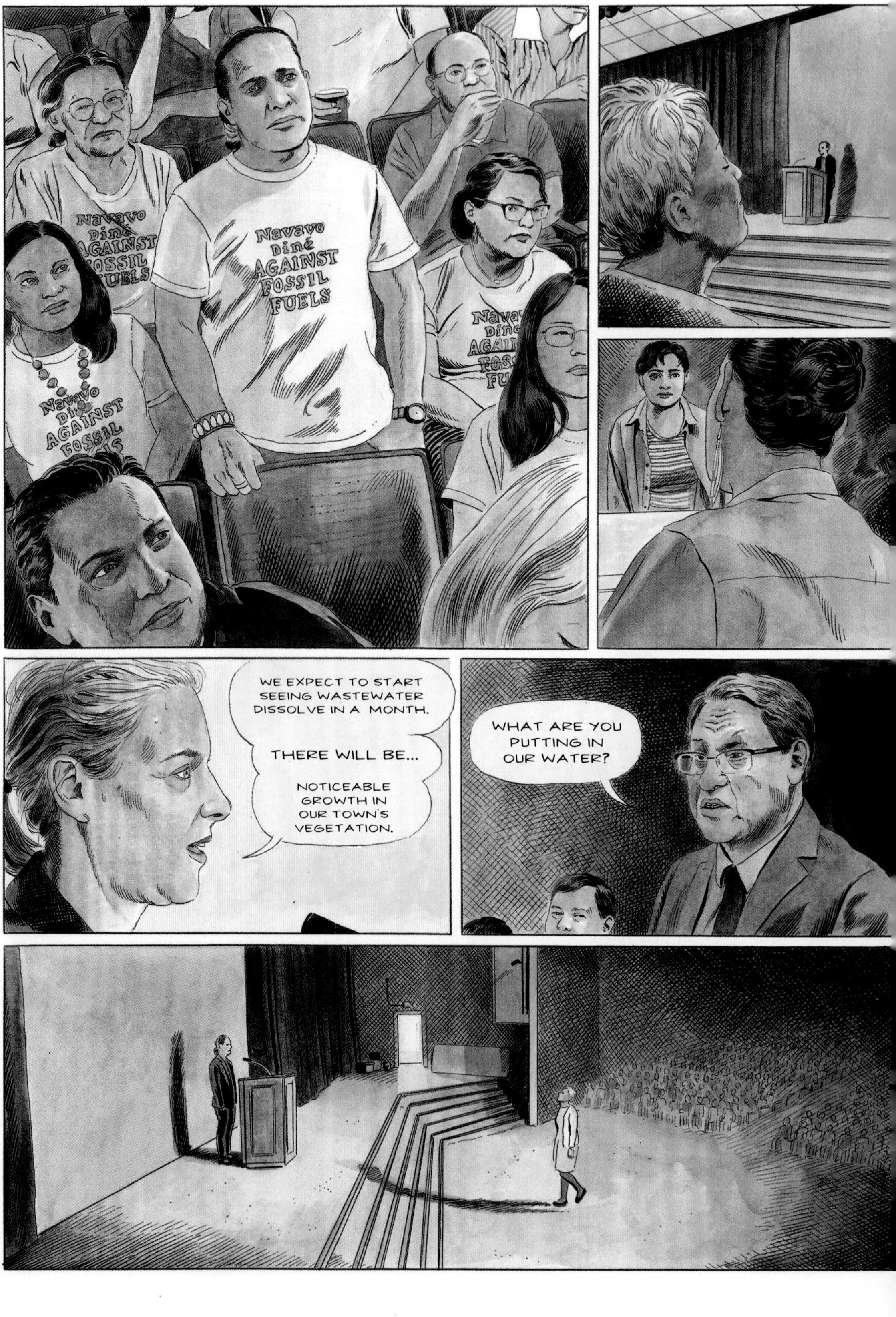
Navavo Diné AGAINST FOSSIL FUELS
WE EXPECT TO START SEEING WASTEWATER DISSOLVE IN A MONTH.
THERE WILL BE...
NOTICEABLE GROWTH IN OUR TOWN'S VEGETATION.
WHAT ARE YOU PUTTING IN OUR WATER?

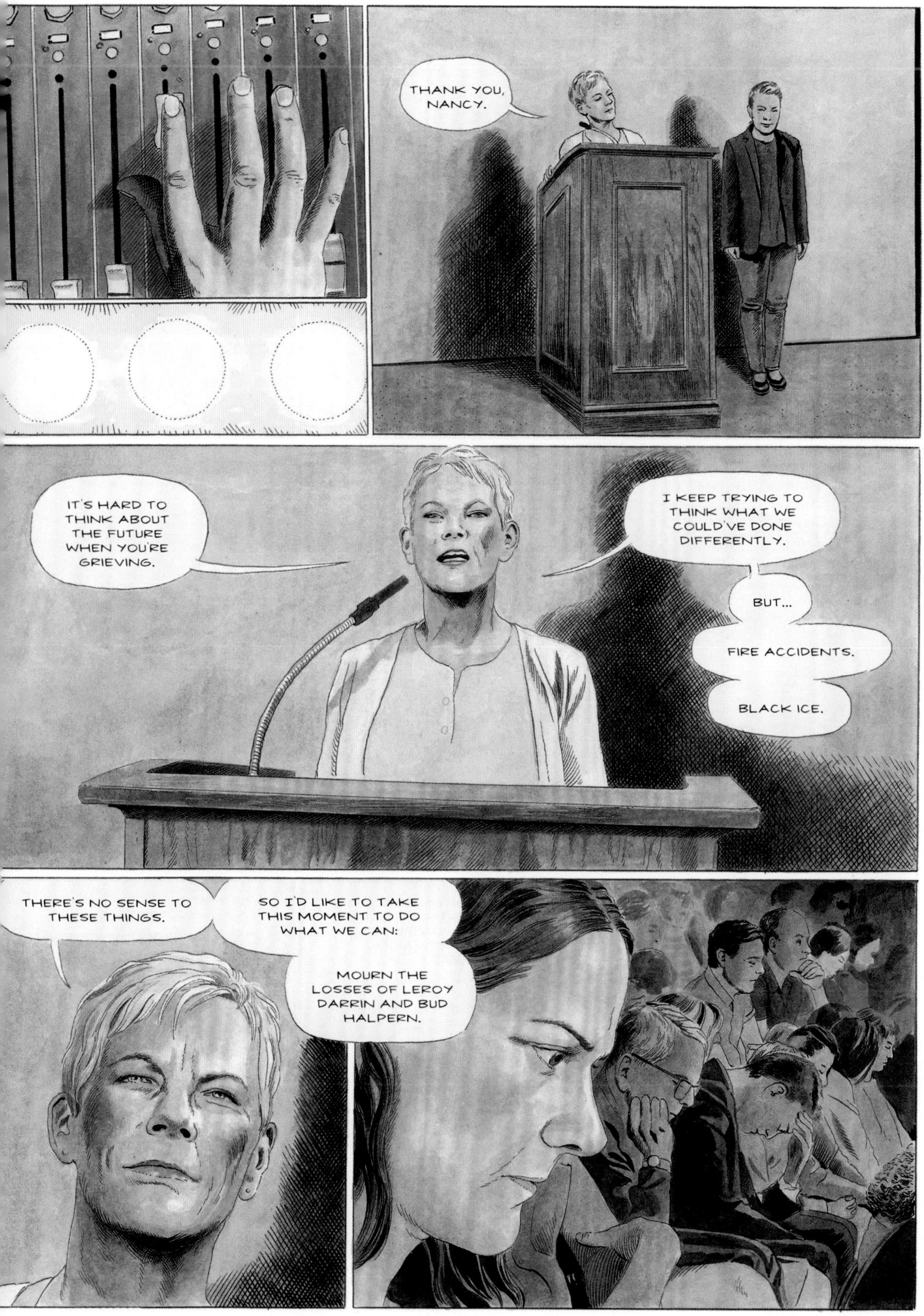
THANK YOU, NANCY.
IT'S HARD TO THINK ABOUT THE FUTURE WHEN YOU'RE GRIEVING.
I KEEP TRYING TO THINK WHAT WE COULD'VE DONE DIFFERENTLY.
BUT...
FIRE ACCIDENTS.
BLACK ICE.
THERE'S NO SENSE TO THESE THINGS.
SO I'D LIKE TO TAKE THIS MOMENT TO DO WHAT WE CAN:
MOURN THE LOSSES OF LEROY DARRIN AND BUD HALPERN.

THEIR GIFTS TO OUR COMMUNITY WERE IMMEASURABLE.

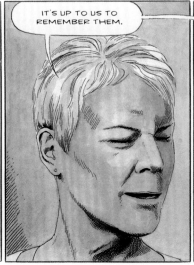

IT'S UP TO US TO REMEMBER THEM.

MY FATHER AND I-- GOD REST HIS SOUL. HE LOVED YOUR TOWN.

HE SAID 'ITS BEAUTY COULD LIGHT THE REST OF THE COUNTRY.'

THAT'S NOT A METAPHOR-- OUR SHALES AND DRILLS CAN BARELY KEEP UP WITH YOU.

BUT ALL THE WATER IT TAKES TO MAKE ENERGY HERE.

TO TAKE IT AWAY FROM YOU WHEN YOU'VE SUFFERED MORE DROUGHTS THAN ANY TOWN IN THE SOUTHWEST.

WITH NANCY DENTON'S SOLVENT, YOU'RE TAKING PART IN THE LARGEST ACHIEVEMENT IN WATER CONSERVATION *EVER*.

WE ARE REBALANCING THE ECOSYSTEM.

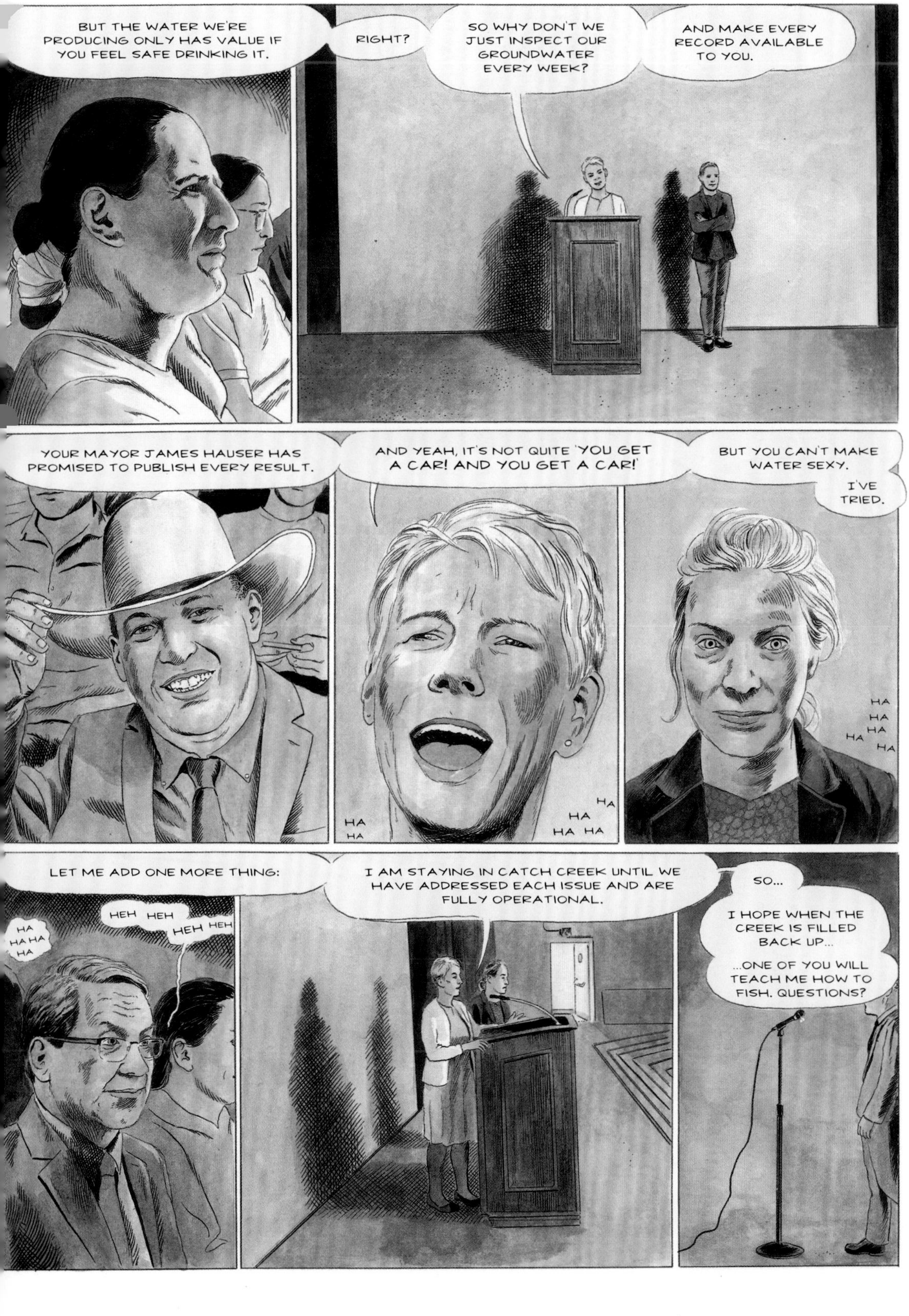
BUT THE WATER WE'RE PRODUCING ONLY HAS VALUE IF YOU FEEL SAFE DRINKING IT.
RIGHT?
SO WHY DON'T WE JUST INSPECT OUR GROUNDWATER EVERY WEEK?
AND MAKE EVERY RECORD AVAILABLE TO YOU.
YOUR MAYOR JAMES HAUSER HAS PROMISED TO PUBLISH EVERY RESULT.
AND YEAH, IT'S NOT QUITE 'YOU GET A CAR! AND YOU GET A CAR!'
HA HA
HA HA HA HA
BUT YOU CAN'T MAKE WATER SEXY.
I'VE TRIED.
HA HA HA HA HA
LET ME ADD ONE MORE THING:
HA HA HA HA
HEH HEH HEH HEH
I AM STAYING IN CATCH CREEK UNTIL WE HAVE ADDRESSED EACH ISSUE AND ARE FULLY OPERATIONAL.
SO...
I HOPE WHEN THE CREEK IS FILLED BACK UP...
...ONE OF YOU WILL TEACH ME HOW TO FISH. QUESTIONS?

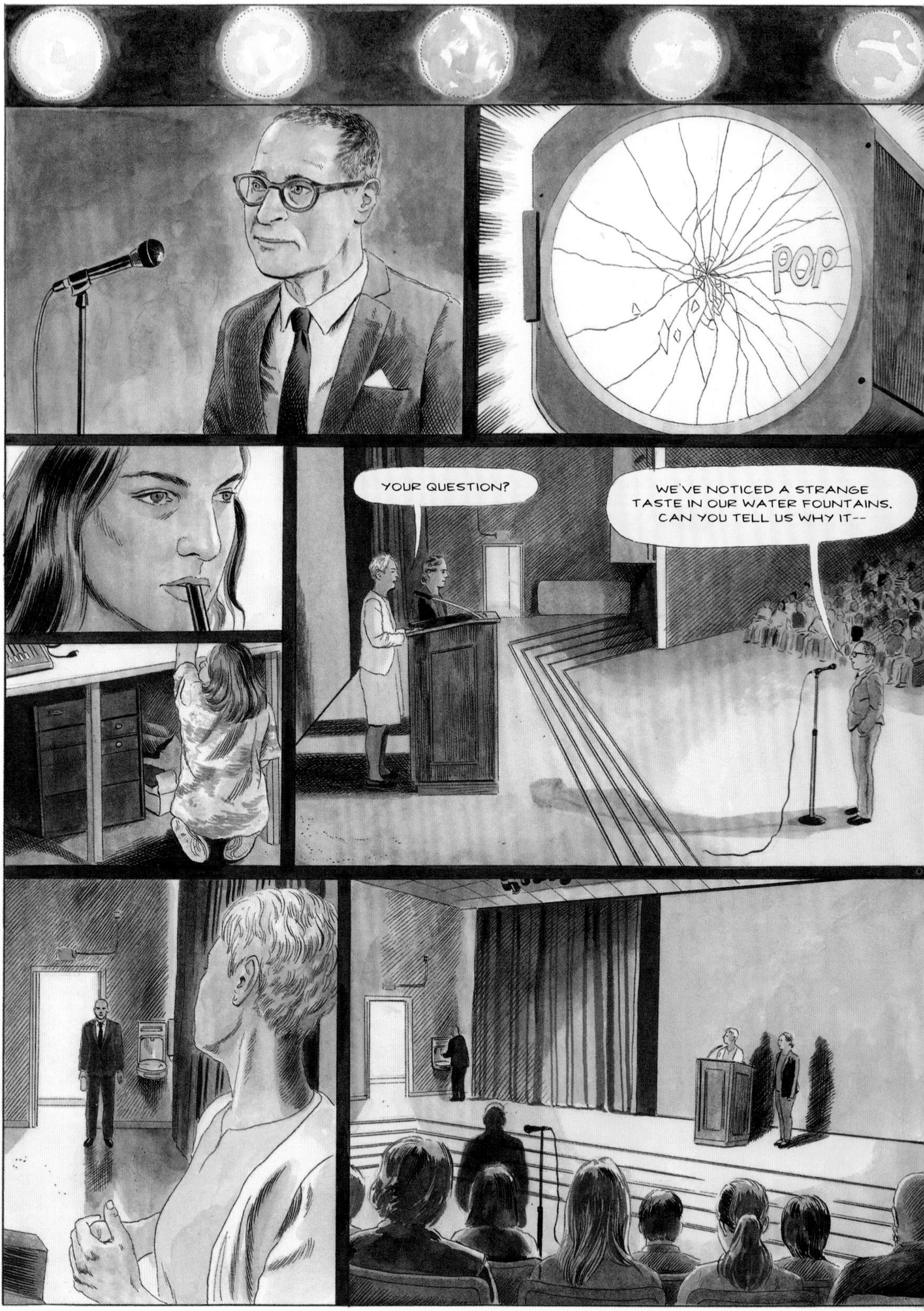
POP
YOUR QUESTION?
WE'VE NOTICED A STRANGE TASTE IN OUR WATER FOUNTAINS. CAN YOU TELL US WHY IT--

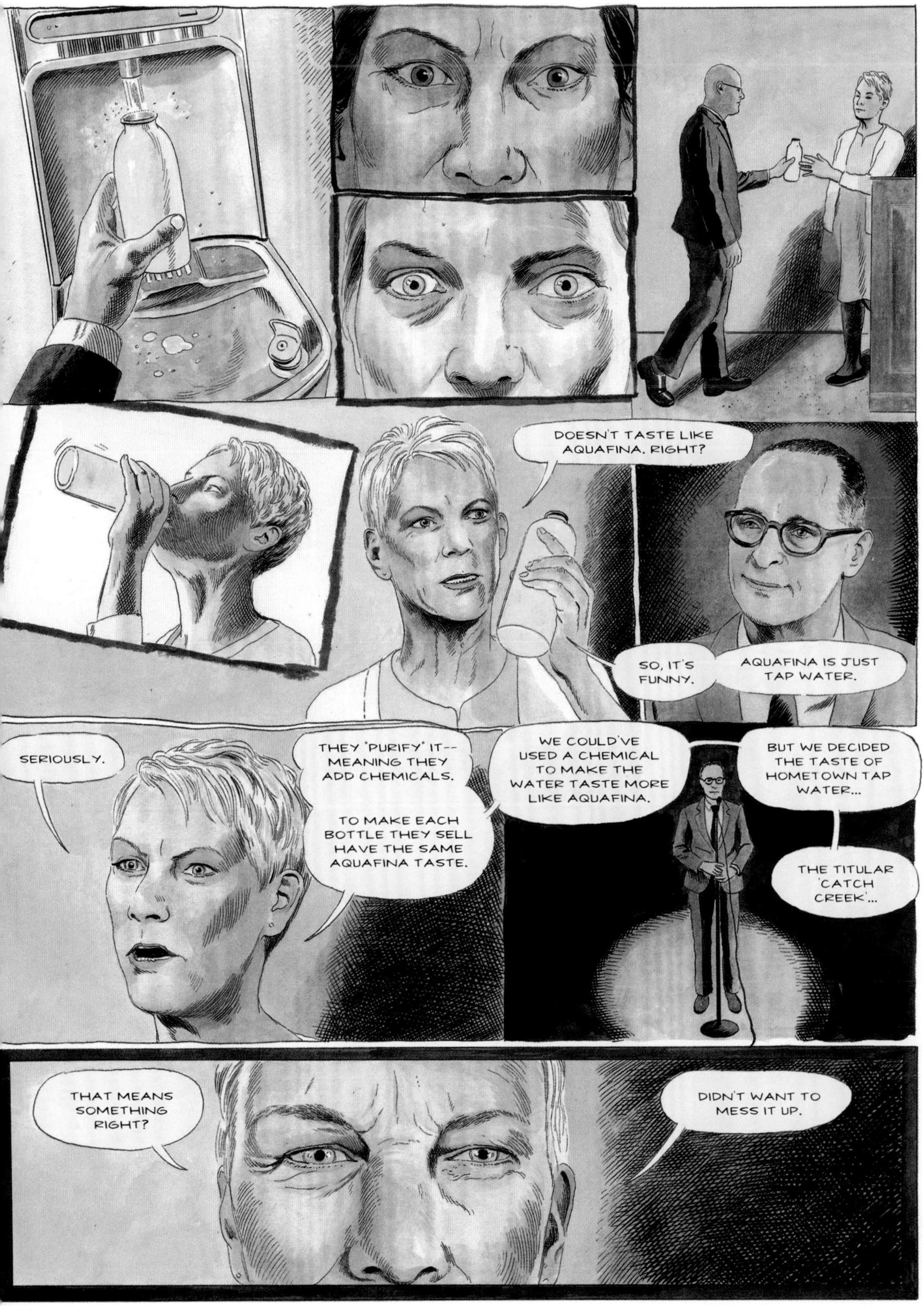

DOESN'T TASTE LIKE AQUAFINA. RIGHT?
SO, IT'S FUNNY.
AQUAFINA IS JUST TAP WATER.
SERIOUSLY.
THEY "PURIFY" IT-- MEANING THEY ADD CHEMICALS.
TO MAKE EACH BOTTLE THEY SELL HAVE THE SAME AQUAFINA TASTE.
WE COULD'VE USED A CHEMICAL TO MAKE THE WATER TASTE MORE LIKE AQUAFINA.
BUT WE DECIDED THE TASTE OF HOMETOWN TAP WATER...
THE TITULAR 'CATCH CREEK'...
THAT MEANS SOMETHING RIGHT?
DIDN'T WANT TO MESS IT UP.

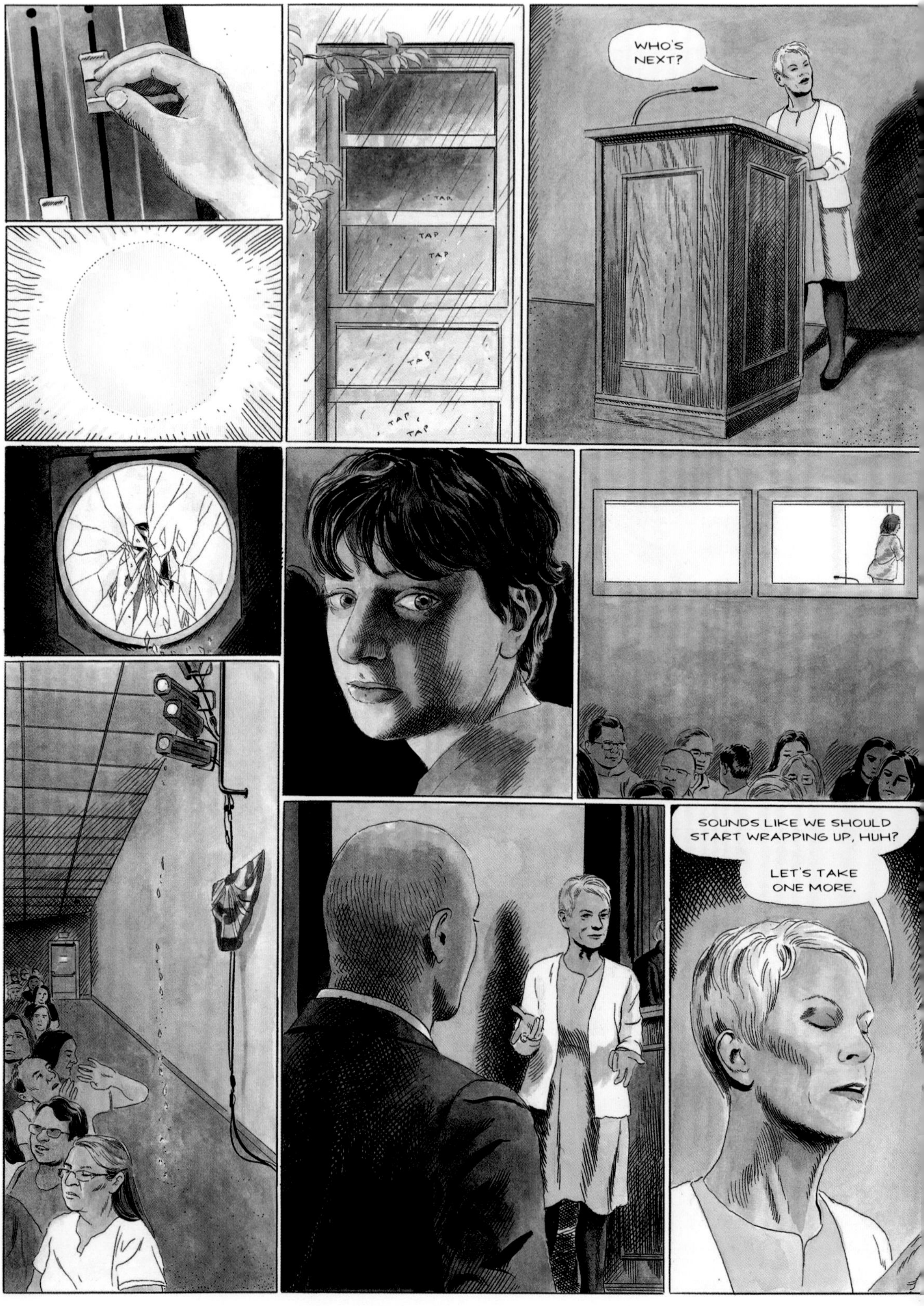
TAP
TAP
TAP
TAP
TAP
TAP
WHO'S NEXT?
SOUNDS LIKE WE SHOULD START WRAPPING UP, HUH?
LET'S TAKE ONE MORE.

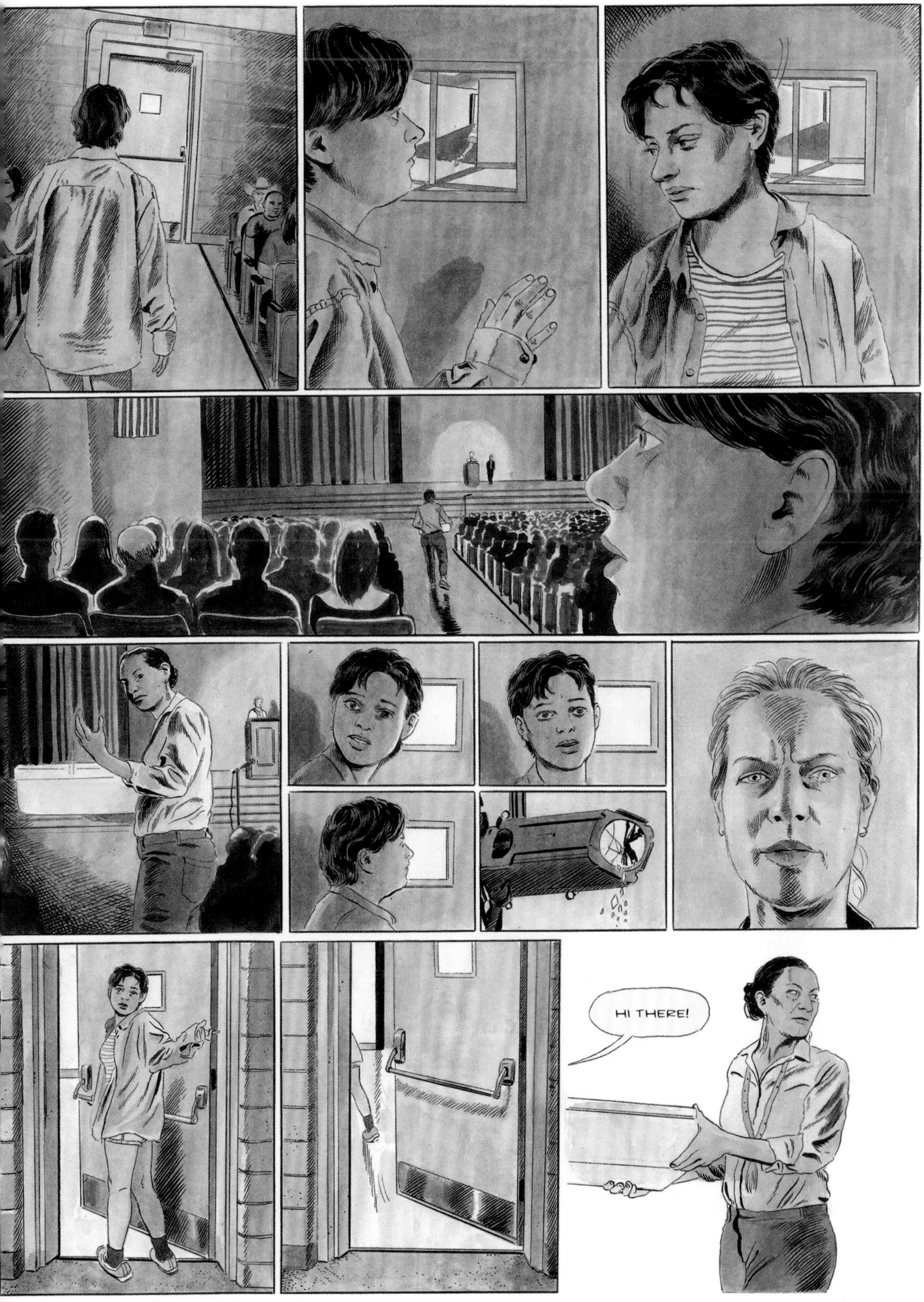
HI THERE!

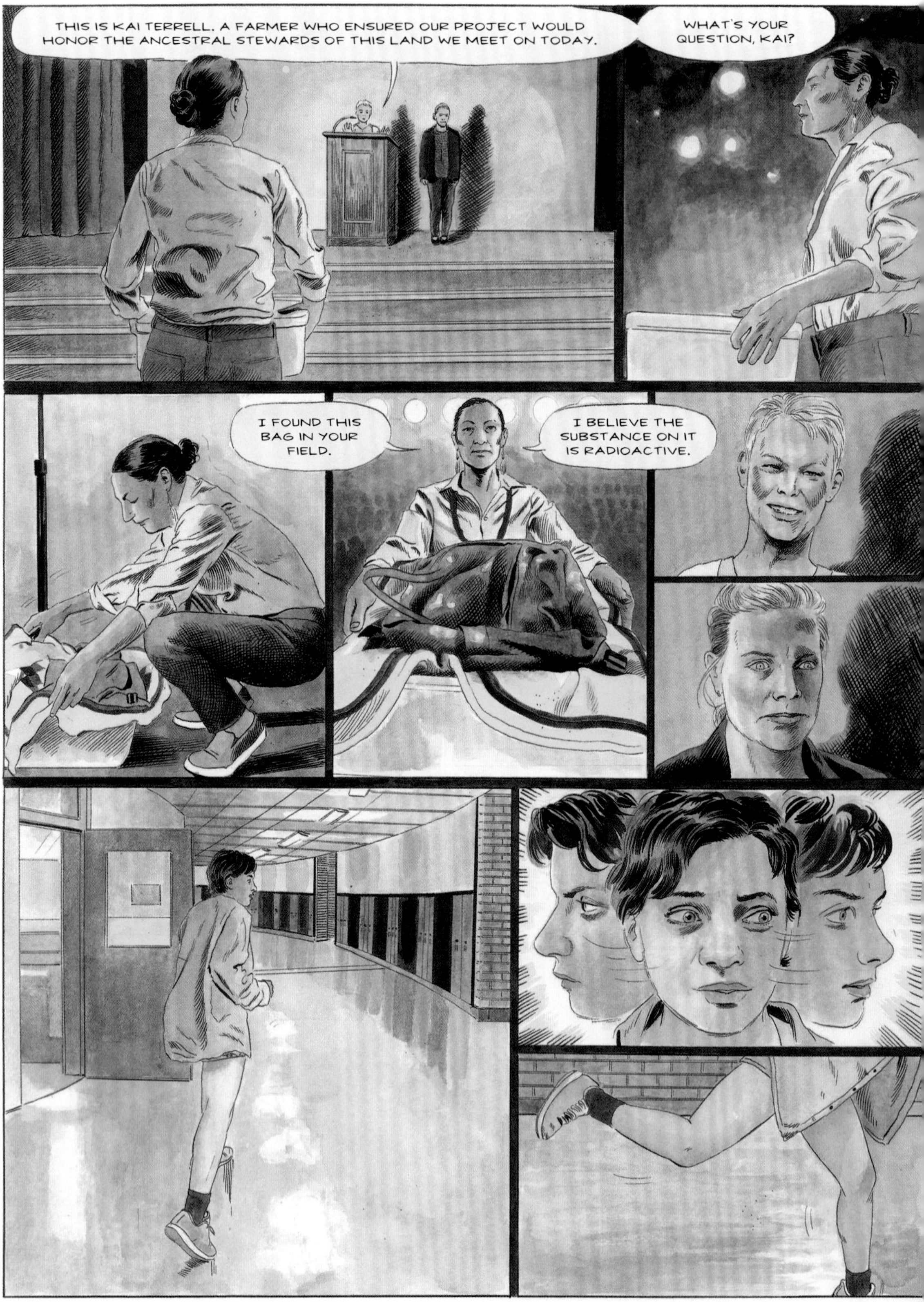
THIS IS KAI TERRELL. A FARMER WHO ENSURED OUR PROJECT WOULD HONOR THE ANCESTRAL STEWARDS OF THIS LAND WE MEET ON TODAY.
WHAT'S YOUR QUESTION, KAI?
I FOUND THIS BAG IN YOUR FIELD.
I BELIEVE THE SUBSTANCE ON IT IS RADIOACTIVE.

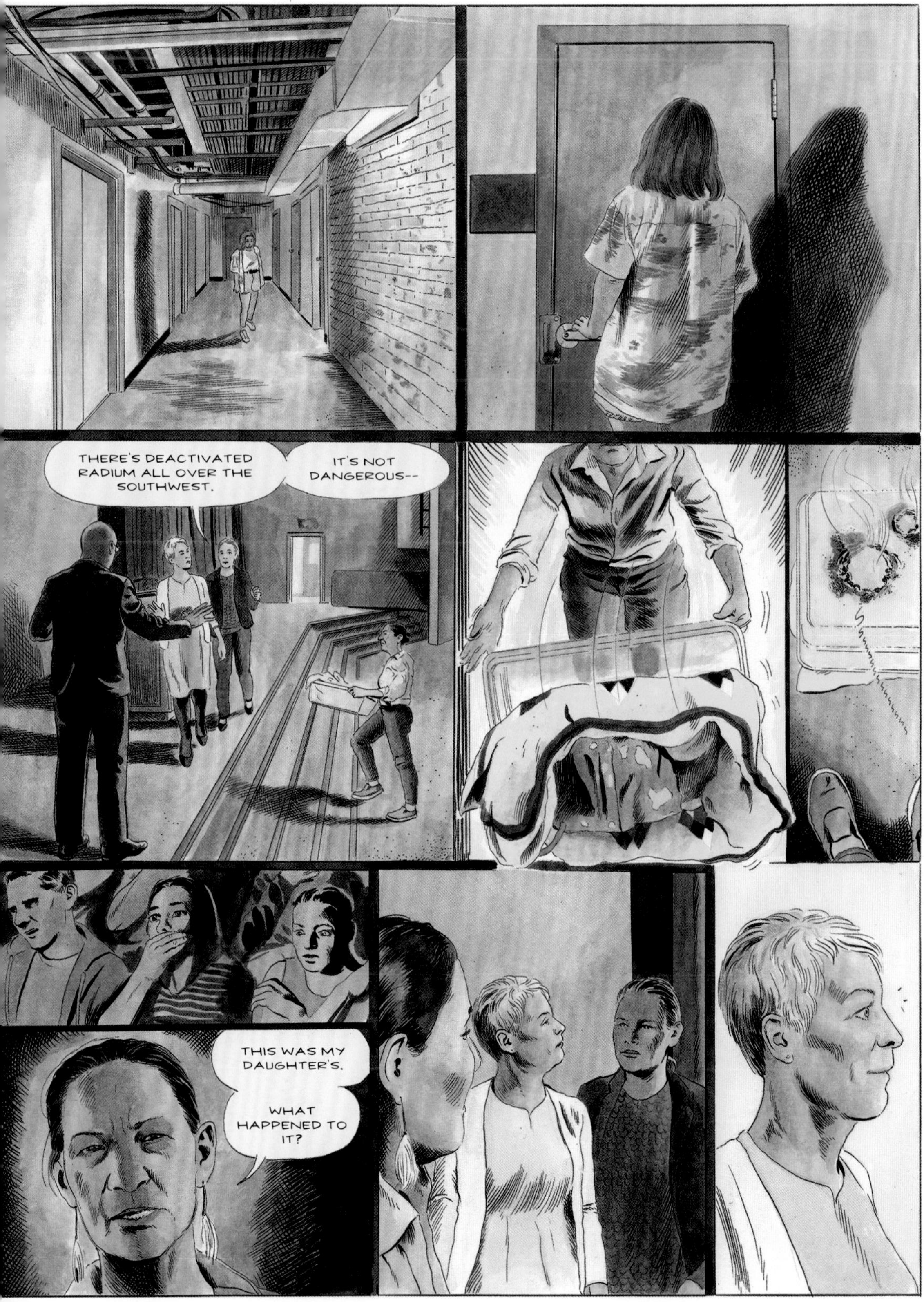
THERE'S DEACTIVATED RADIUM ALL OVER THE SOUTHWEST.
IT'S NOT DANGEROUS--
THIS WAS MY DAUGHTER'S.
WHAT HAPPENED TO IT?

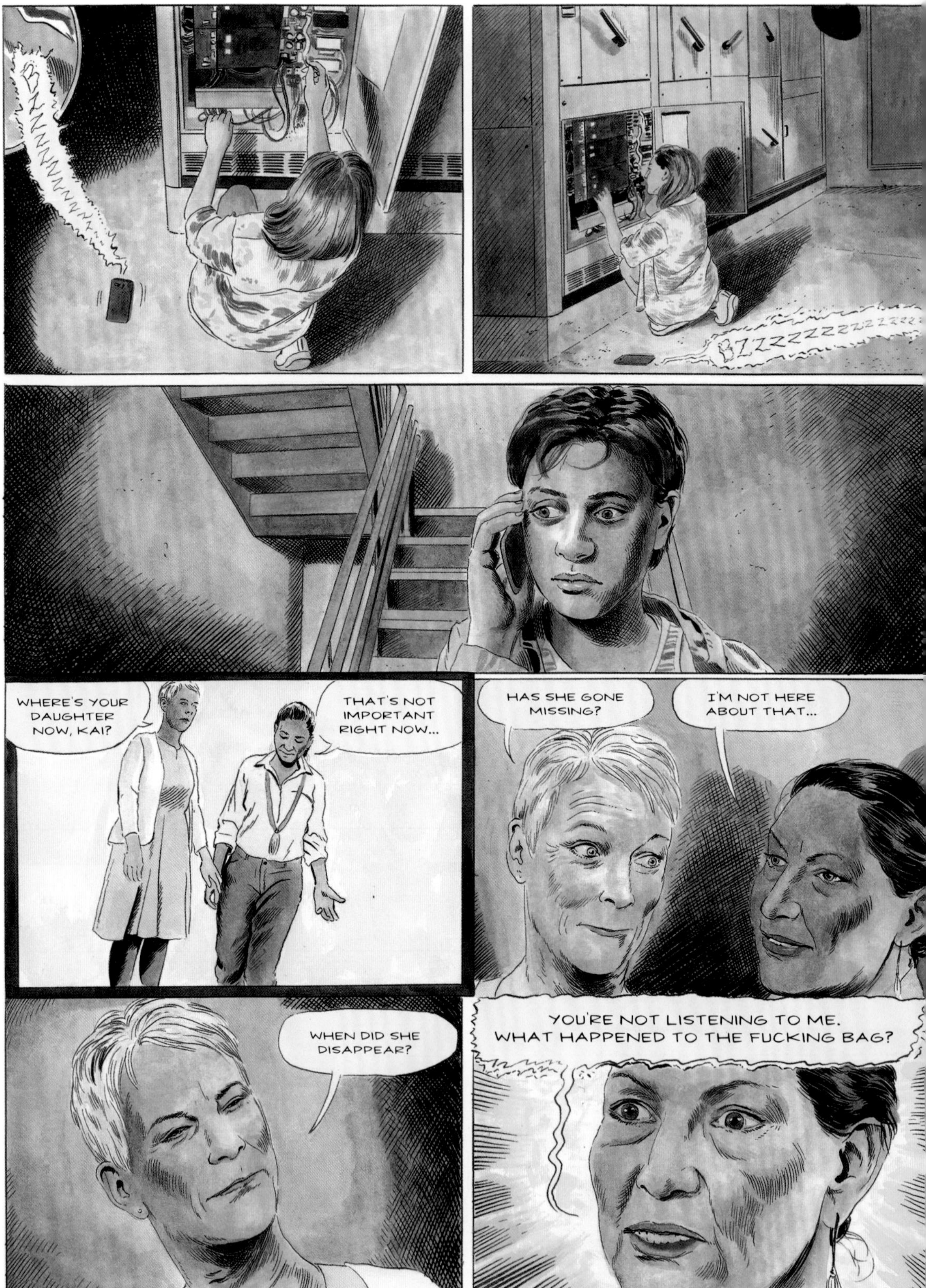
BZZZZZZZZZZZ
BZZZZZZZZZZZZZZ
WHERE'S YOUR DAUGHTER NOW, KAI?
THAT'S NOT IMPORTANT RIGHT NOW...
HAS SHE GONE MISSING?
I'M NOT HERE ABOUT THAT...
WHEN DID SHE DISAPPEAR?
YOU'RE NOT LISTENING TO ME. WHAT HAPPENED TO THE FUCKING BAG?

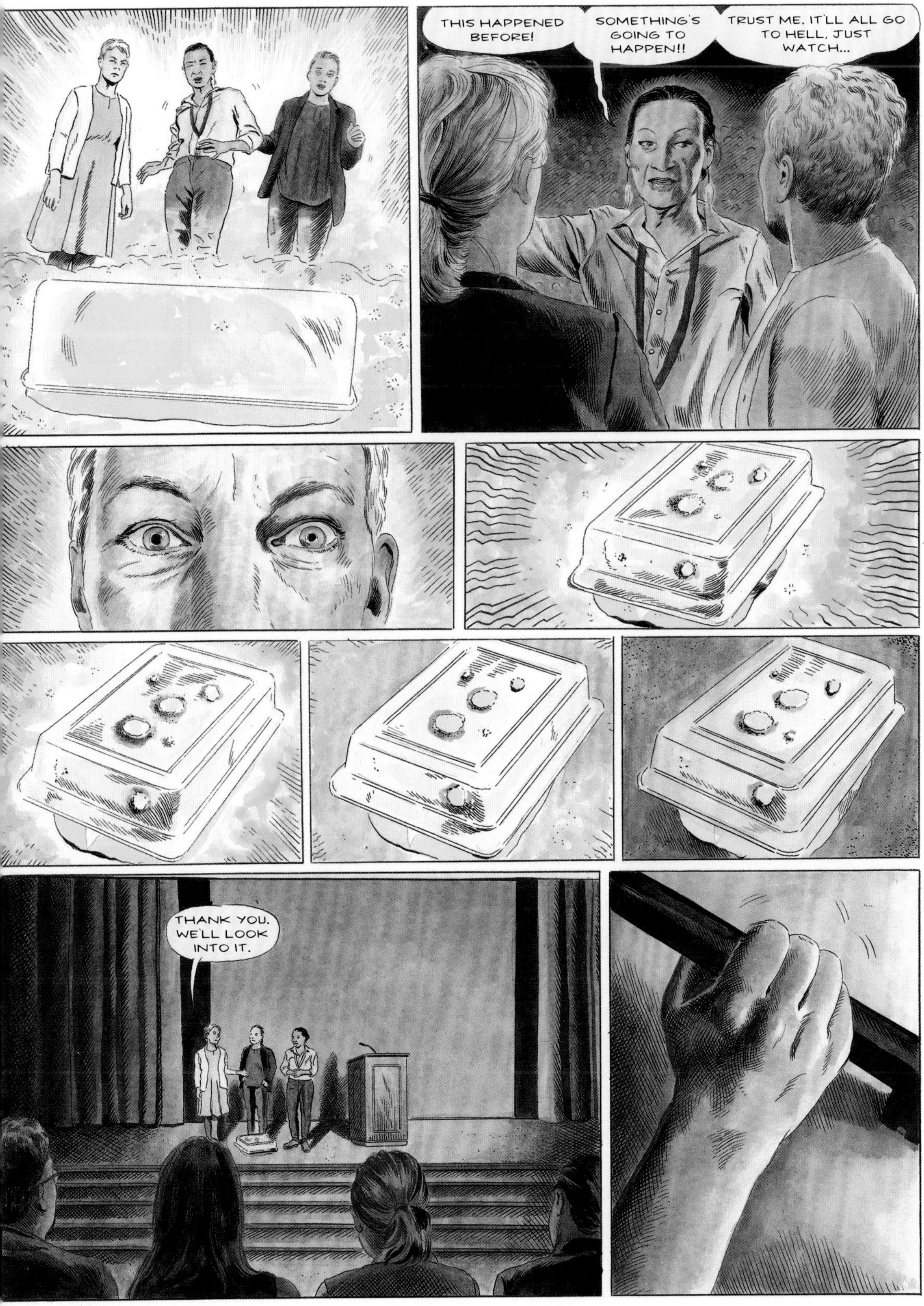
THIS HAPPENED BEFORE!
SOMETHING'S GOING TO HAPPEN!!
TRUST ME. IT'LL ALL GO TO HELL, JUST WATCH...
THANK YOU. WE'LL LOOK INTO IT.

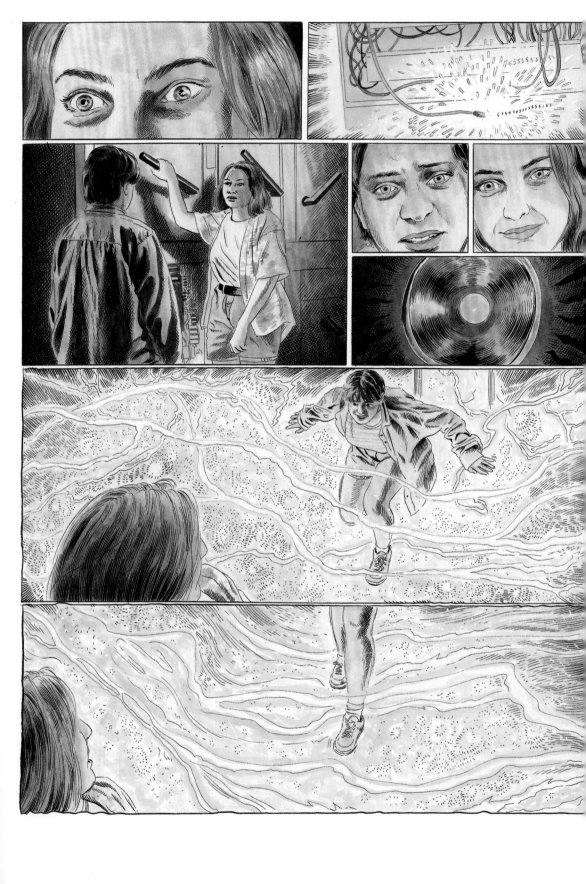

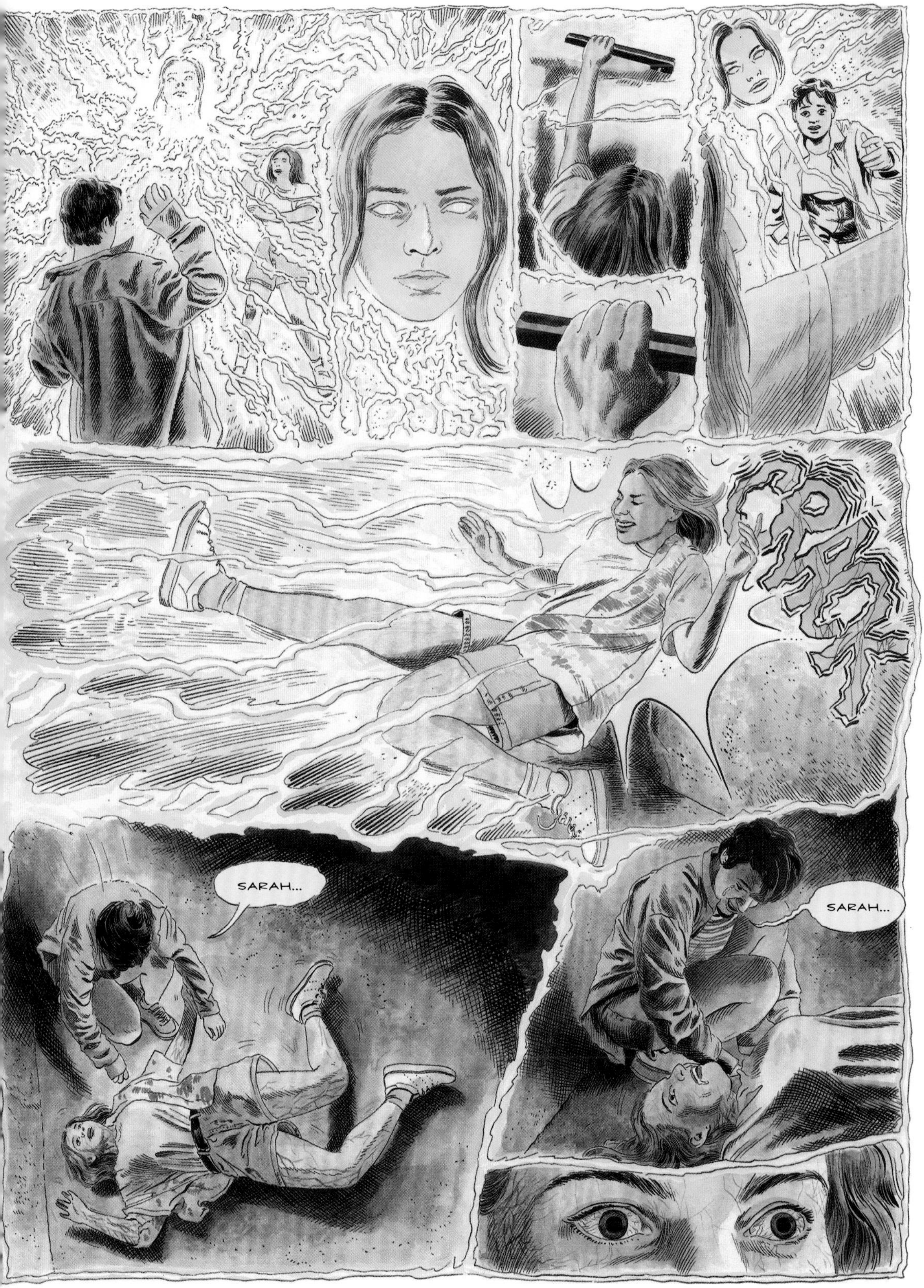
SARAH...
SARAH...

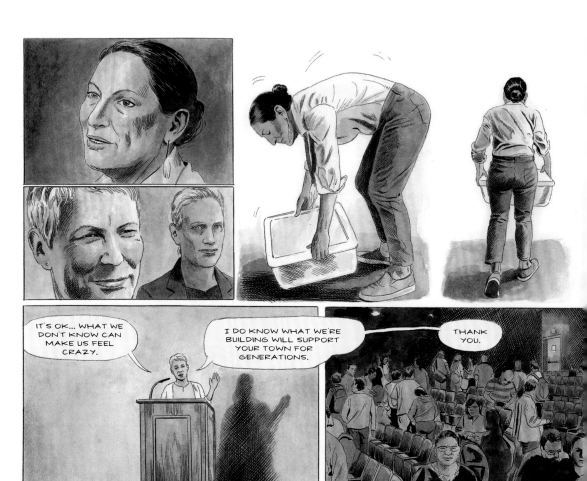

IT'S OK... WHAT WE DON'T KNOW CAN MAKE US FEEL CRAZY.

I DO KNOW WHAT WE'RE BUILDING WILL SUPPORT YOUR TOWN FOR GENERATIONS.

THANK YOU.

CLAP CLAP CLAP CLAP CLAP CLAP

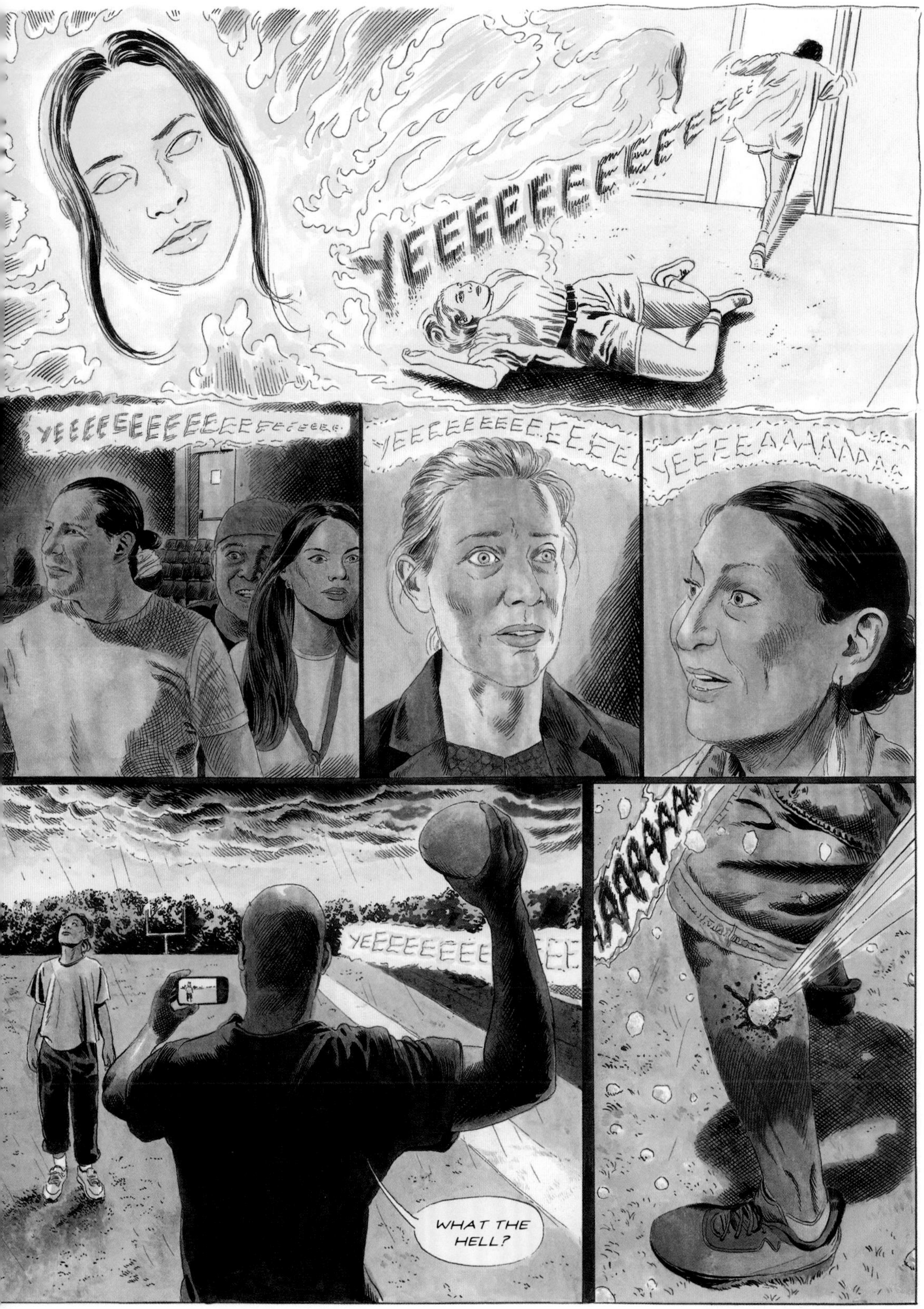
YEEEEEEEEEEEEEEEE
YEEEEEEEEEEEEEEEEEEEE
YEEEEEEEEEEEEEEE
YEEEEAAAAAAAA
YEEEEEEEEE
WHAT THE HELL?
AAAAAAA

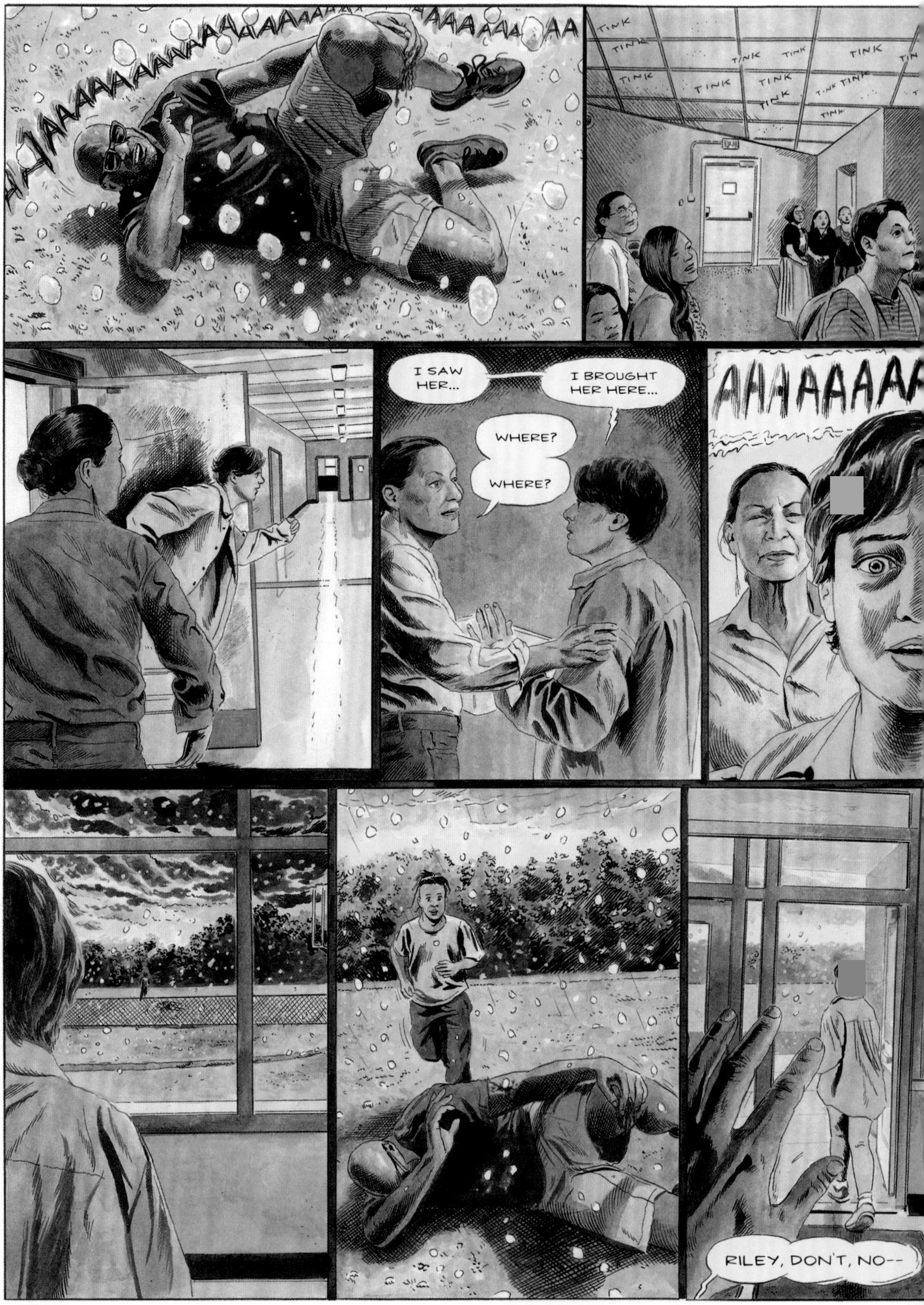
HAAAAAAAAAAAAAAAAAAAAAAAAAAAAAAAAA
TINK TINK TINK TINK TINK TINK TINK TINK TINK TINK TINK
I SAW HER...
I BROUGHT HER HERE...
WHERE?
WHERE?
AAAAAAA
RILEY, DON'T, NO--

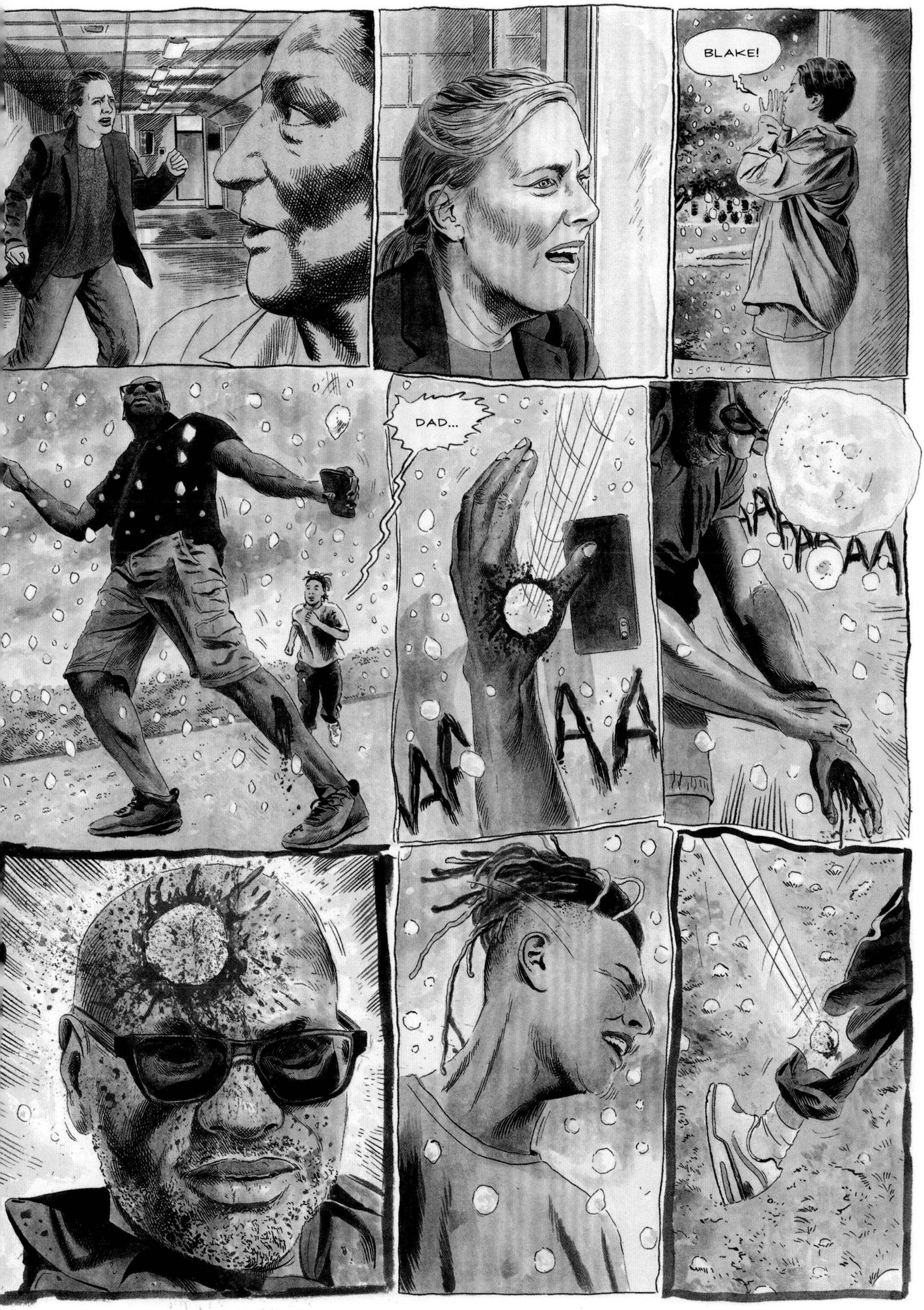
BLAKE!
DAD...

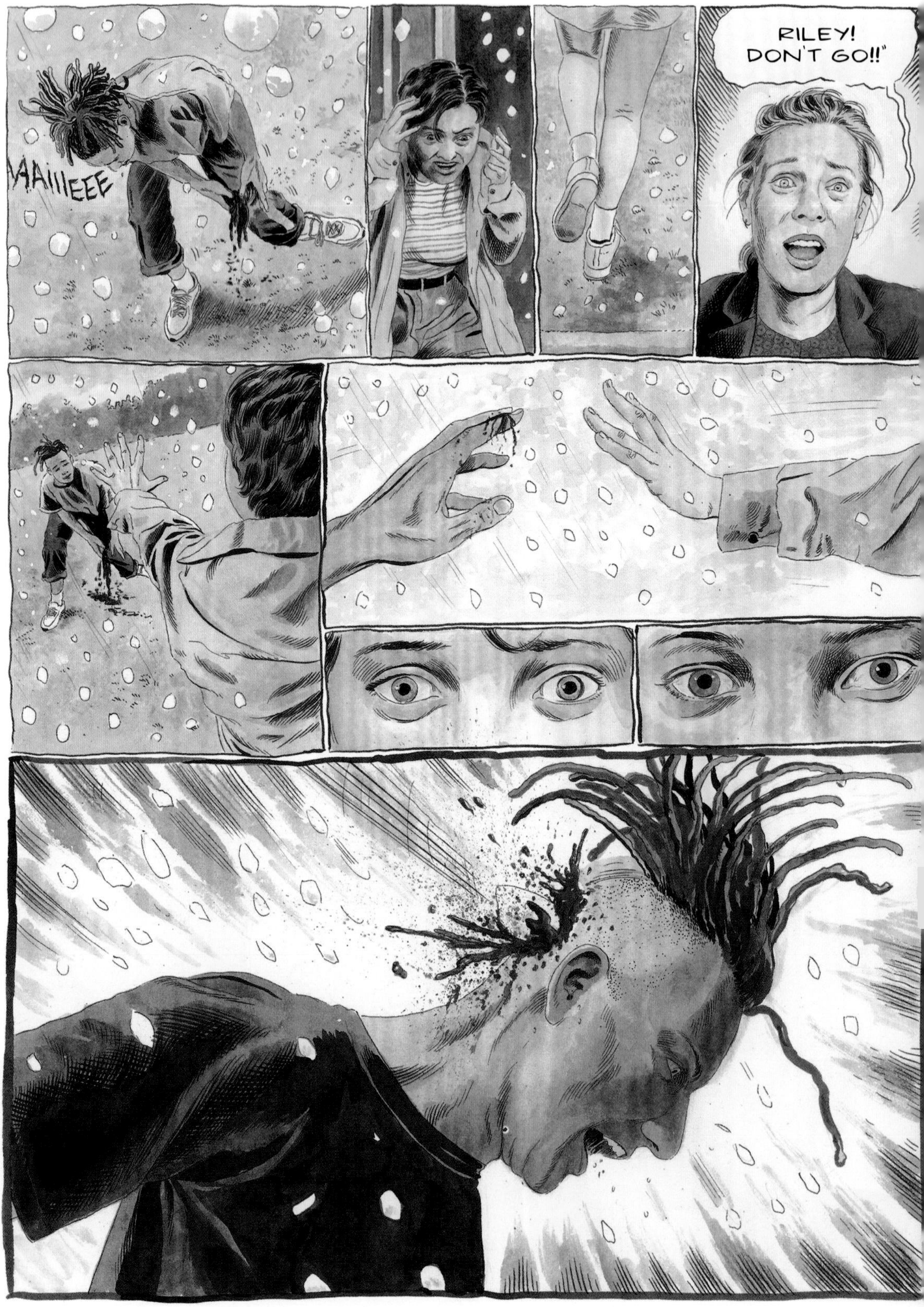
AAIIIEEE
RILEY!
DON'T GO!!"

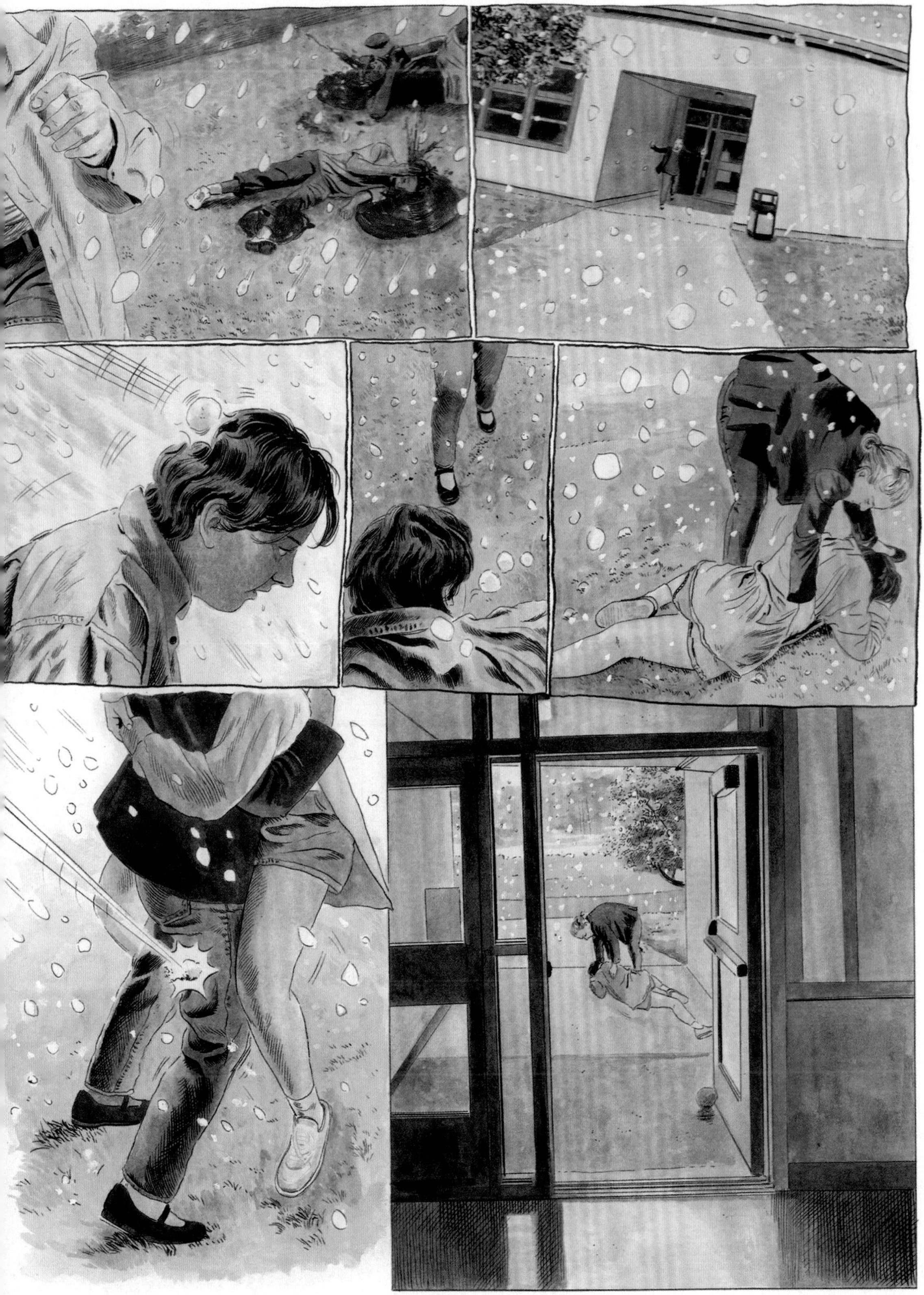

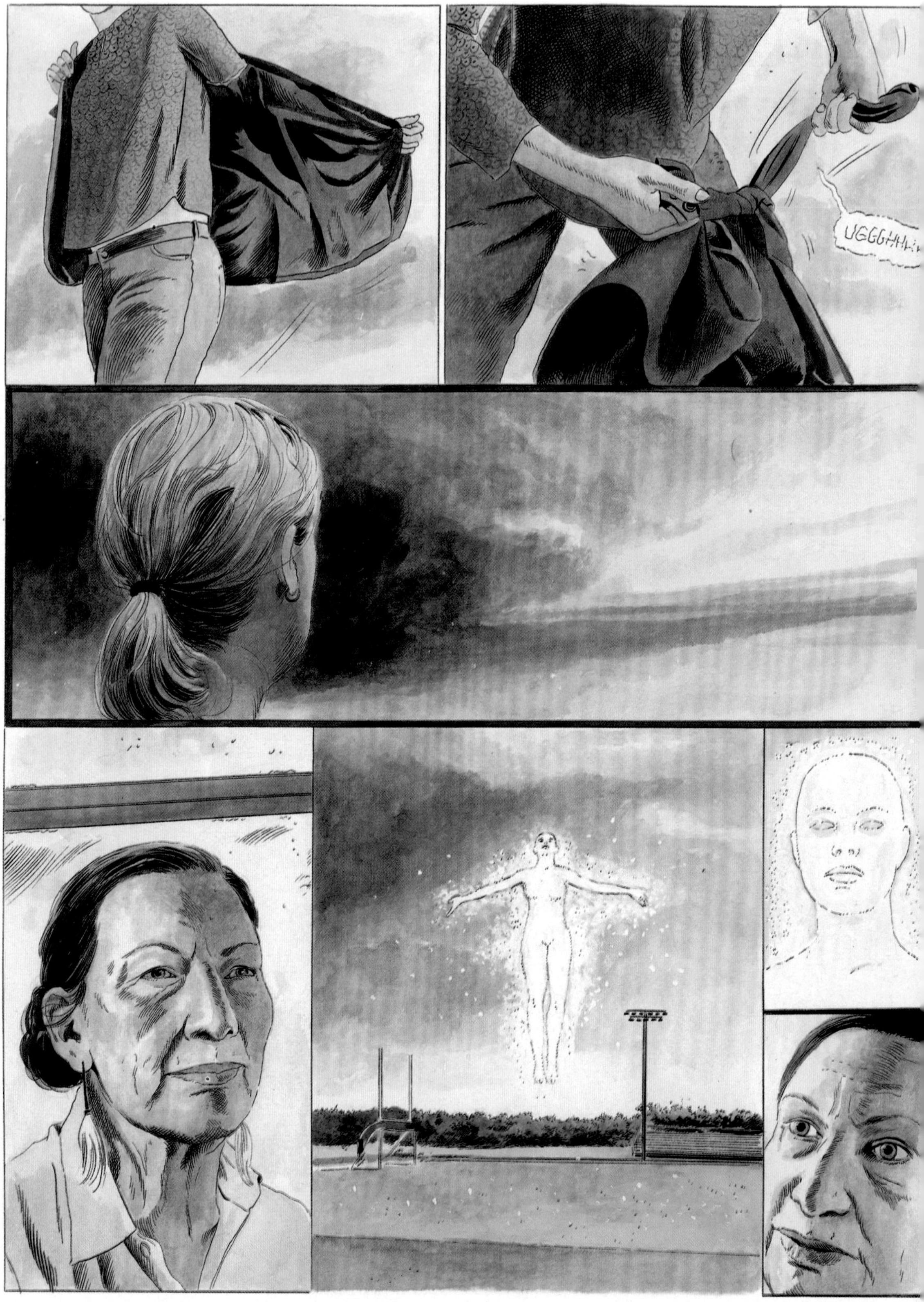
UGGGHH

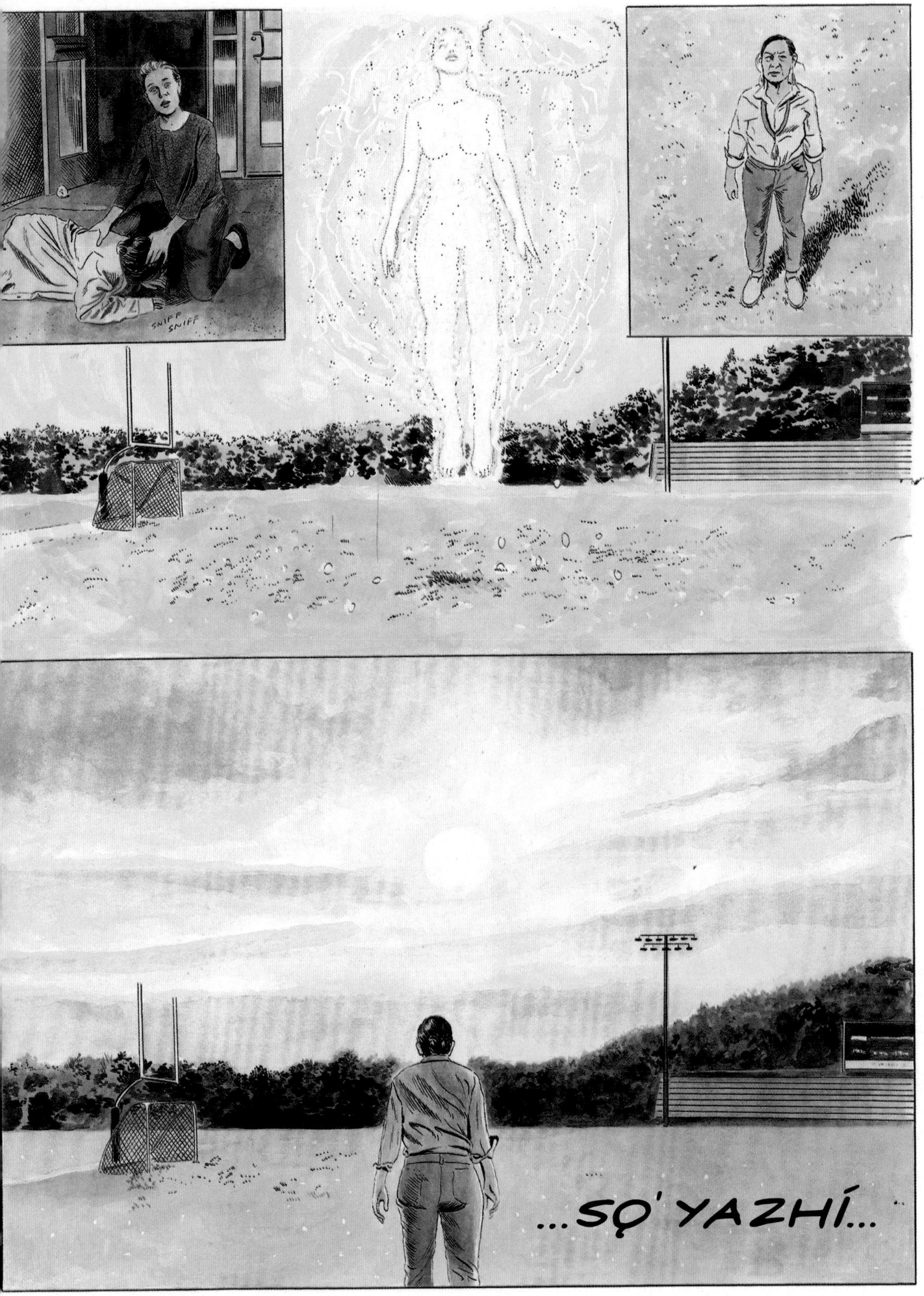
SNIFF
SNIFF
...SǪ' YAZHÍ...

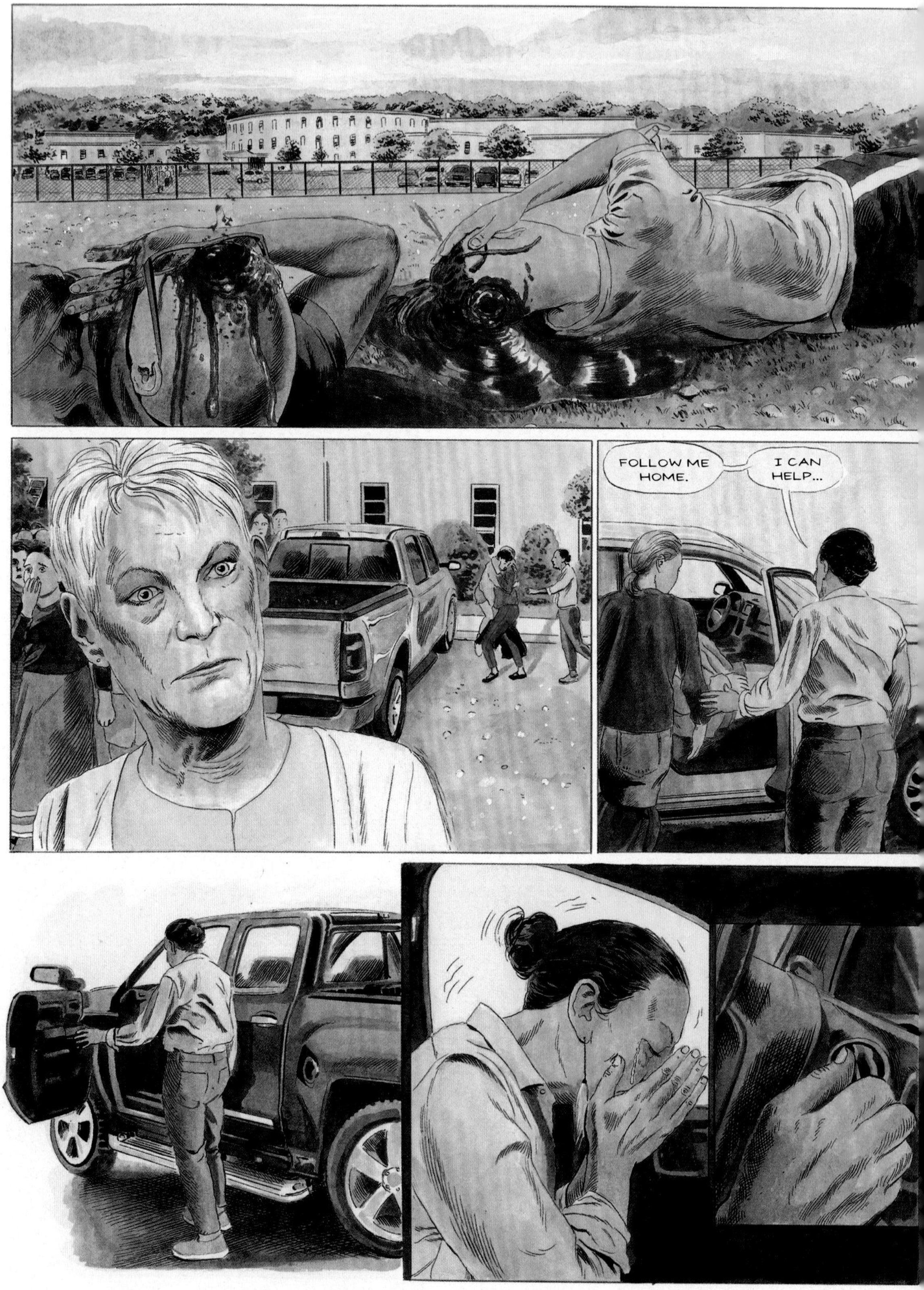
FOLLOW ME HOME.
I CAN HELP...

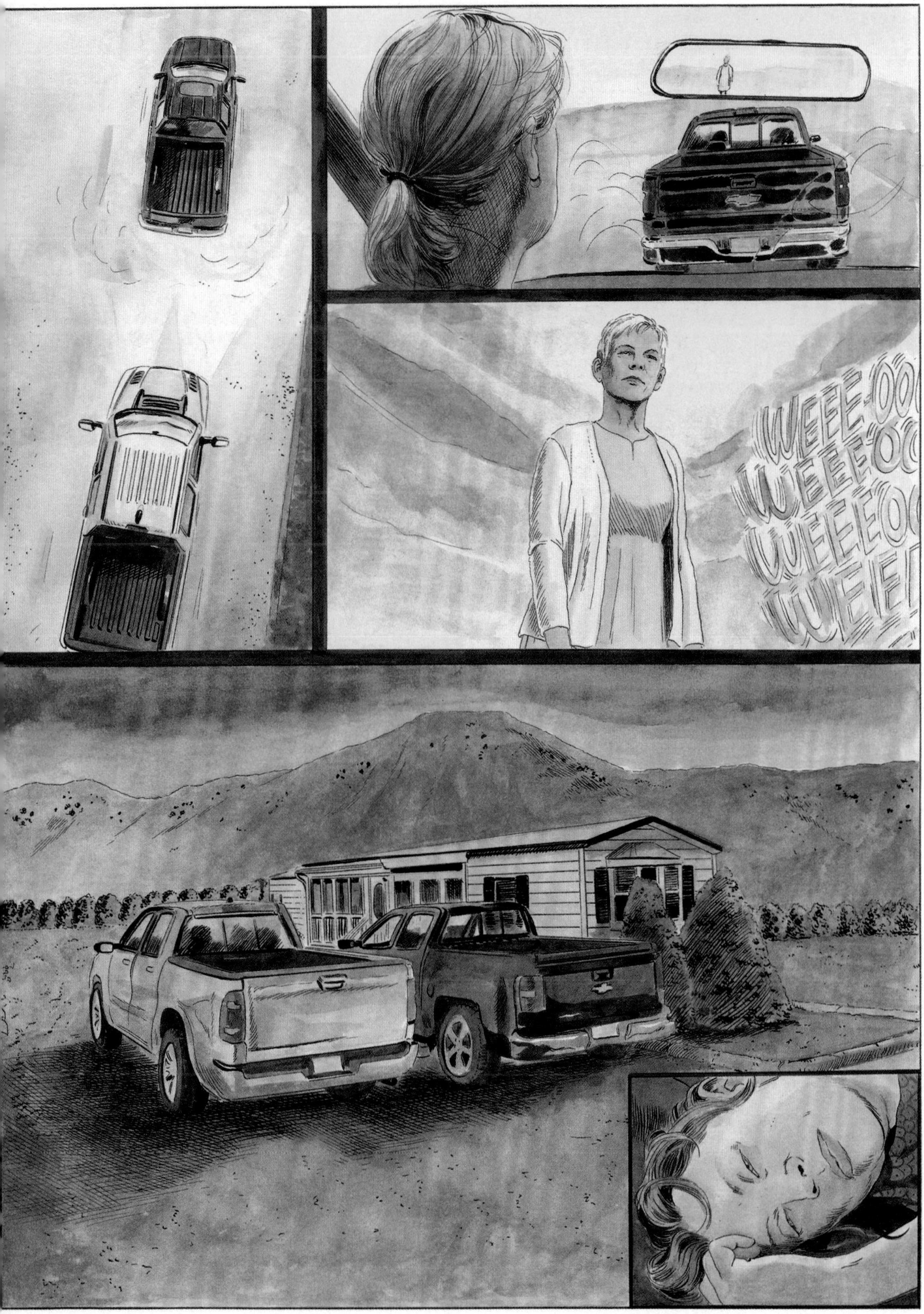
WEEE-OO
WEEEOO
WEEEOO
WEEE

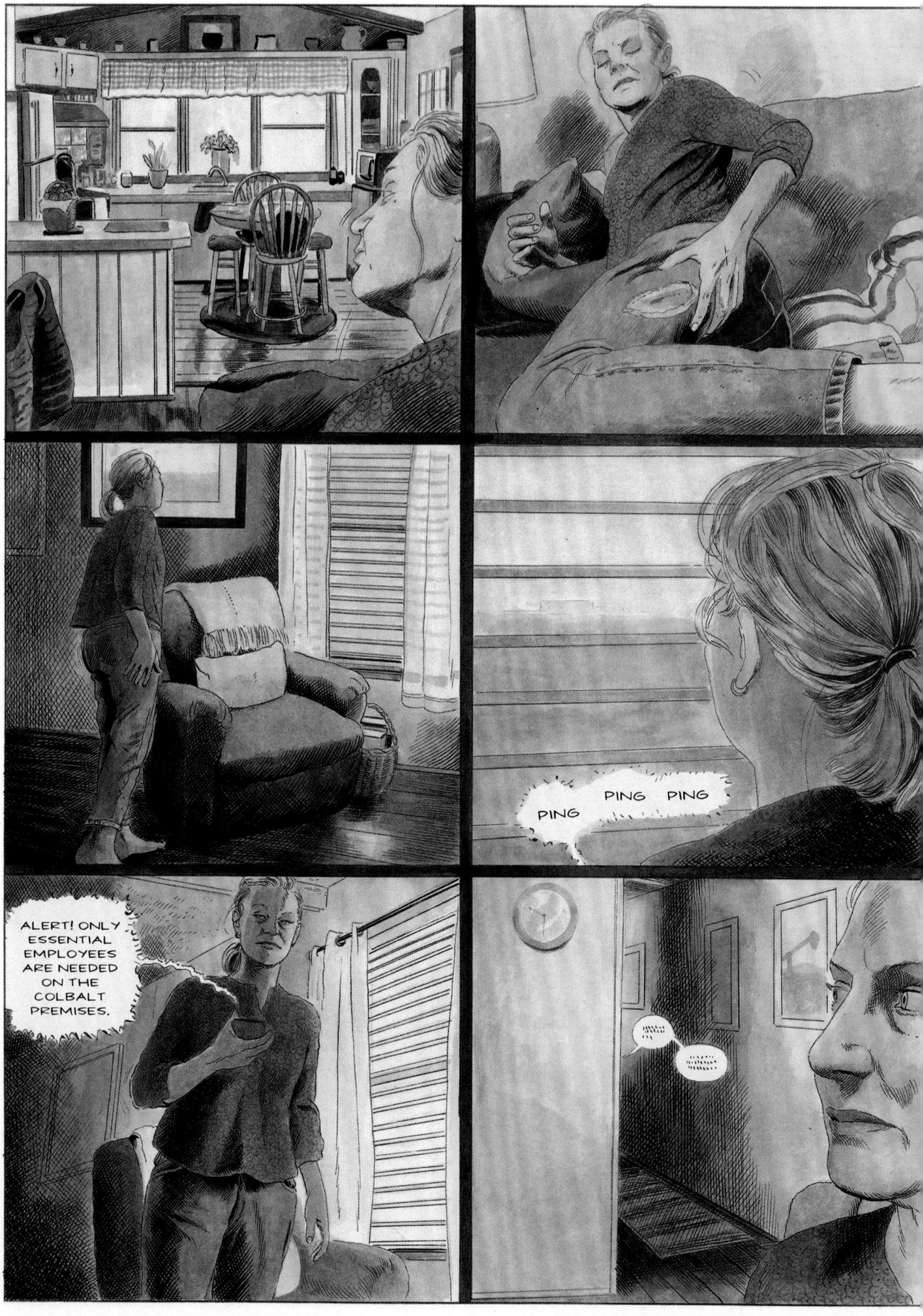
PING PING PING
ALERT! ONLY ESSENTIAL EMPLOYEES ARE NEEDED ON THE COLBALT PREMISES.

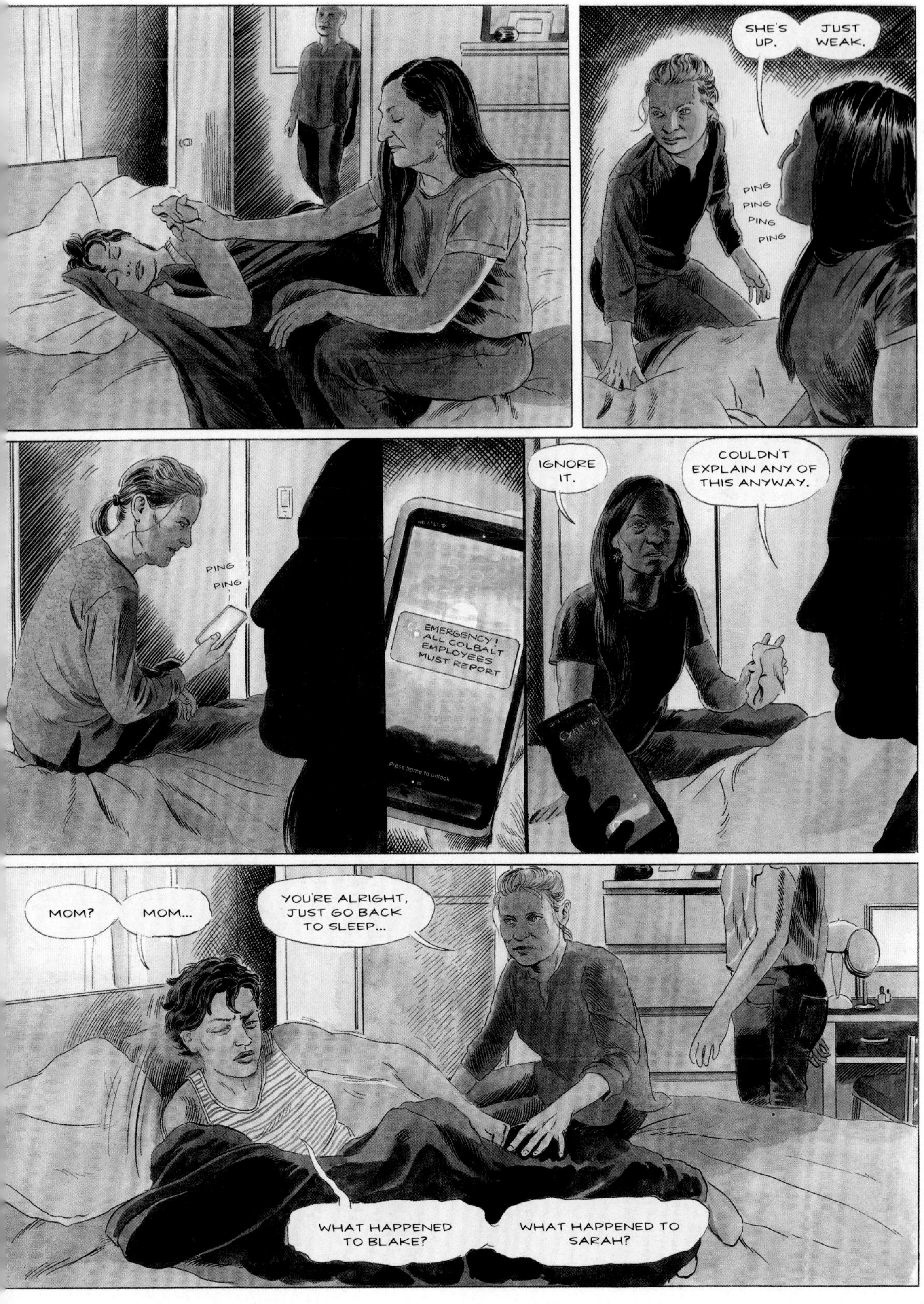

SHE'S UP.
JUST WEAK.
PING
PING
PING
PING
PING
PING
EMERGENCY! ALL COLBALT EMPLOYEES MUST REPORT
Press home to unlock
IGNORE IT.
COULDN'T EXPLAIN ANY OF THIS ANYWAY.
MOM?
MOM...
YOU'RE ALRIGHT, JUST GO BACK TO SLEEP...
WHAT HAPPENED TO BLAKE?
WHAT HAPPENED TO SARAH?

CYNTHIA? I WAS JUST ABOUT TO GO IN...

SORRY FOR SHOWING UP UNANNOUNCED.

AND FOR MY EARLIER BEHAVIOR...

SOMETIMES MY DAD'S FIGHT OR FLIGHT INSTINCTS DON'T WORK OUT.

WHAT DO YOU WANT?

TO MAYBE QUELL SOME OF MY FEARS.

THAT WAS NOVA, RIGHT?

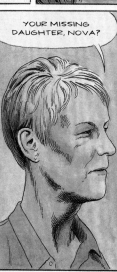

YOUR MISSING DAUGHTER, NOVA?

SHE SAID SǪ' YAZHÍ.

HAVE YOU SEEN ANYTHING LIKE THAT BEFORE? WHAT'S HAPPENED TO HER?

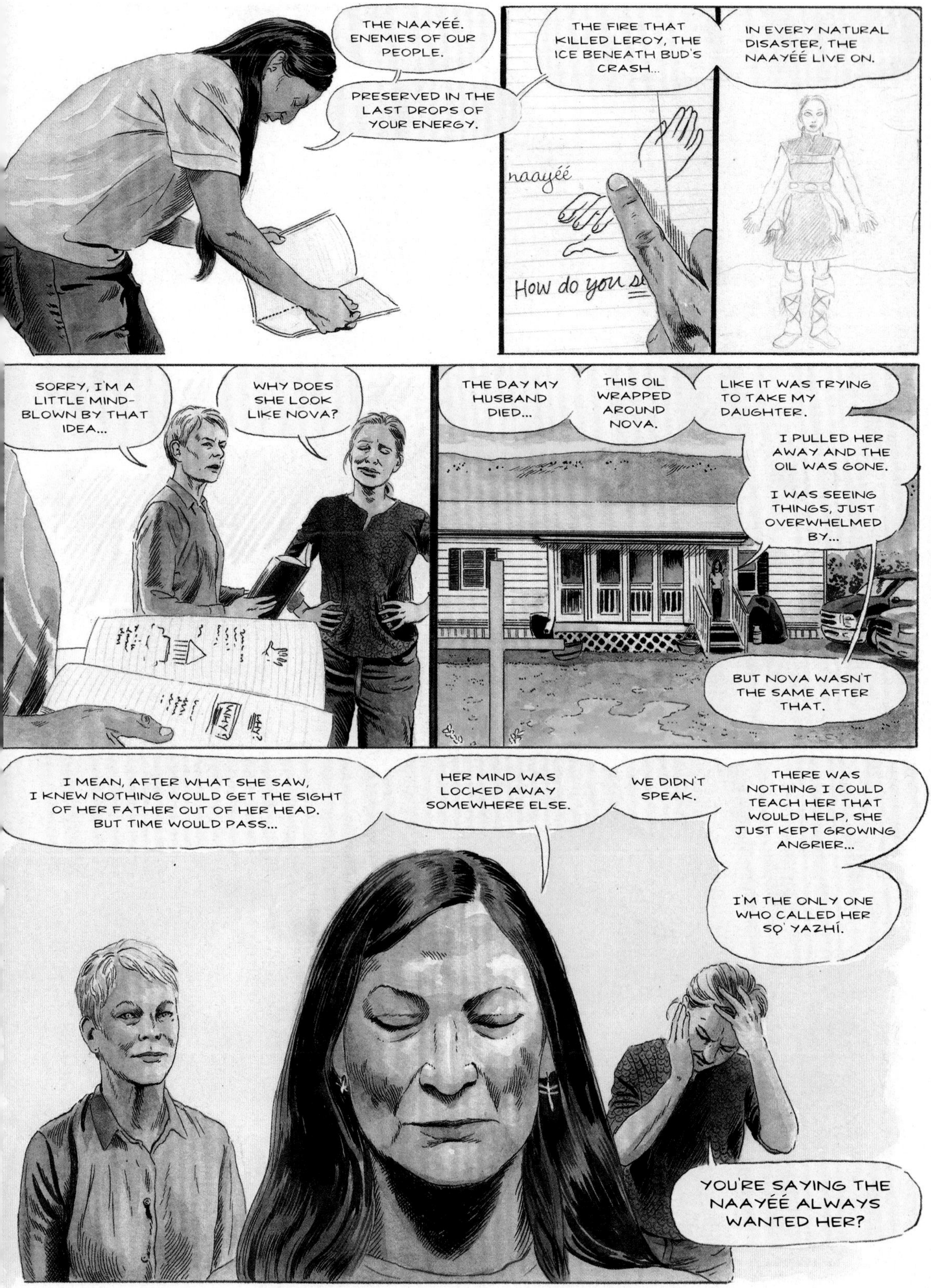

THE NAAYÉÉ. ENEMIES OF OUR PEOPLE.
PRESERVED IN THE LAST DROPS OF YOUR ENERGY.
THE FIRE THAT KILLED LEROY, THE ICE BENEATH BUD'S CRASH...
naayéé
How do you
IN EVERY NATURAL DISASTER, THE NAAYÉÉ LIVE ON.
SORRY, I'M A LITTLE MIND-BLOWN BY THAT IDEA...
WHY DOES SHE LOOK LIKE NOVA?
THE DAY MY HUSBAND DIED...
THIS OIL WRAPPED AROUND NOVA.
LIKE IT WAS TRYING TO TAKE MY DAUGHTER.
I PULLED HER AWAY AND THE OIL WAS GONE.
I WAS SEEING THINGS, JUST OVERWHELMED BY...
BUT NOVA WASN'T THE SAME AFTER THAT.
I MEAN, AFTER WHAT SHE SAW, I KNEW NOTHING WOULD GET THE SIGHT OF HER FATHER OUT OF HER HEAD. BUT TIME WOULD PASS...
HER MIND WAS LOCKED AWAY SOMEWHERE ELSE.
WE DIDN'T SPEAK.
THERE WAS NOTHING I COULD TEACH HER THAT WOULD HELP, SHE JUST KEPT GROWING ANGRIER...
I'M THE ONLY ONE WHO CALLED HER SǪ' YAZHÍ.
YOU'RE SAYING THE NAAYÉÉ ALWAYS WANTED HER?

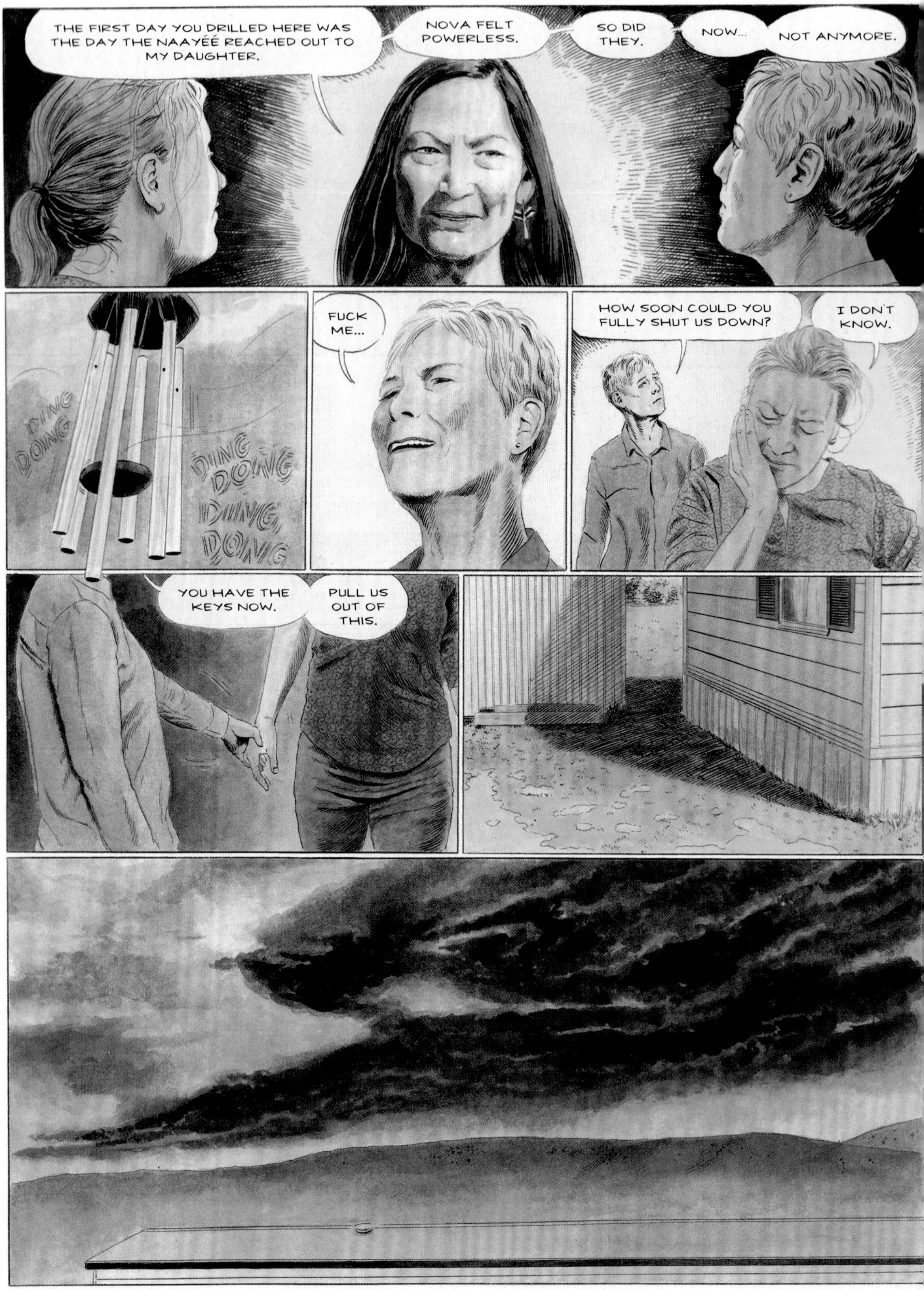
THE FIRST DAY YOU DRILLED HERE WAS THE DAY THE NAAYÉÉ REACHED OUT TO MY DAUGHTER.
NOVA FELT POWERLESS.
SO DID THEY.
NOW...
NOT ANYMORE.
DING DONG
DING DONG
DING DONG
FUCK ME...
HOW SOON COULD YOU FULLY SHUT US DOWN?
I DON'T KNOW.
YOU HAVE THE KEYS NOW.
PULL US OUT OF THIS.

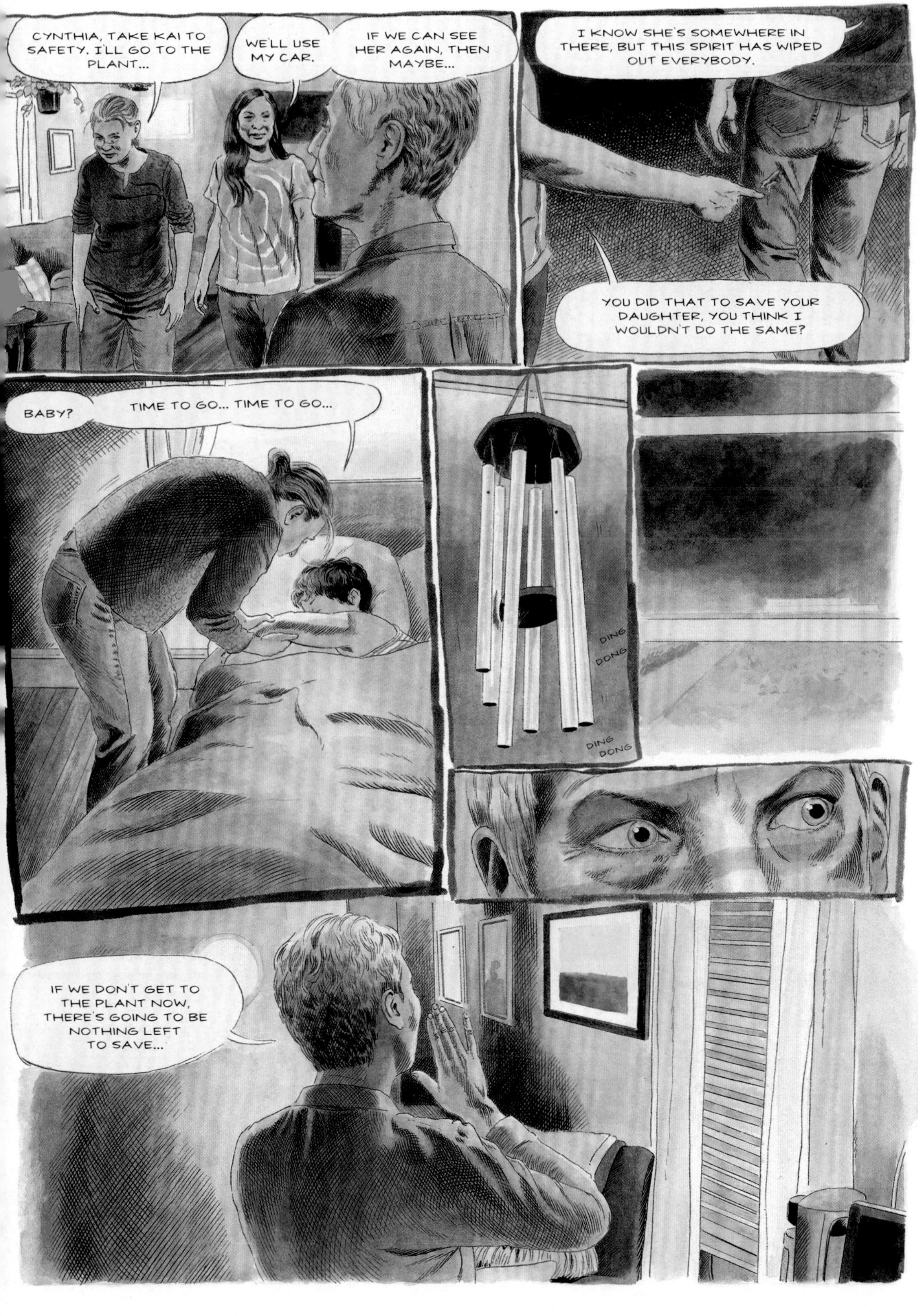
CYNTHIA, TAKE KAI TO SAFETY. I'LL GO TO THE PLANT...
WE'LL USE MY CAR.
IF WE CAN SEE HER AGAIN, THEN MAYBE...
I KNOW SHE'S SOMEWHERE IN THERE, BUT THIS SPIRIT HAS WIPED OUT EVERYBODY.
YOU DID THAT TO SAVE YOUR DAUGHTER, YOU THINK I WOULDN'T DO THE SAME?
BABY?
TIME TO GO... TIME TO GO...
DING
DONG
DING
DONG
IF WE DON'T GET TO THE PLANT NOW, THERE'S GOING TO BE NOTHING LEFT TO SAVE...

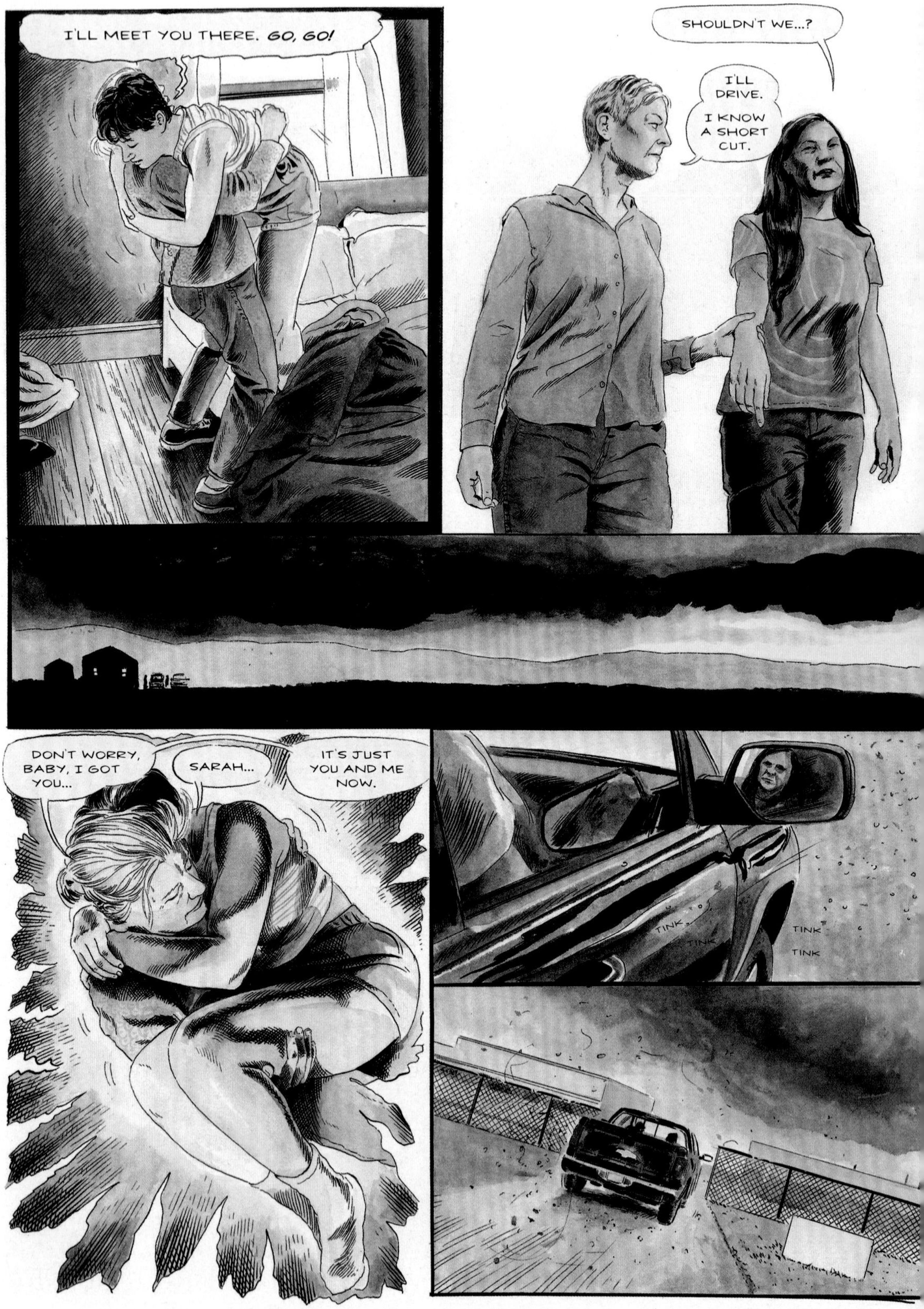
I'LL MEET YOU THERE. *GO, GO!*
SHOULDN'T WE...?
I'LL DRIVE.
I KNOW A SHORT CUT.
DON'T WORRY, BABY, I GOT YOU...
SARAH...
IT'S JUST YOU AND ME NOW.
TINK
TINK
TINK
TINK

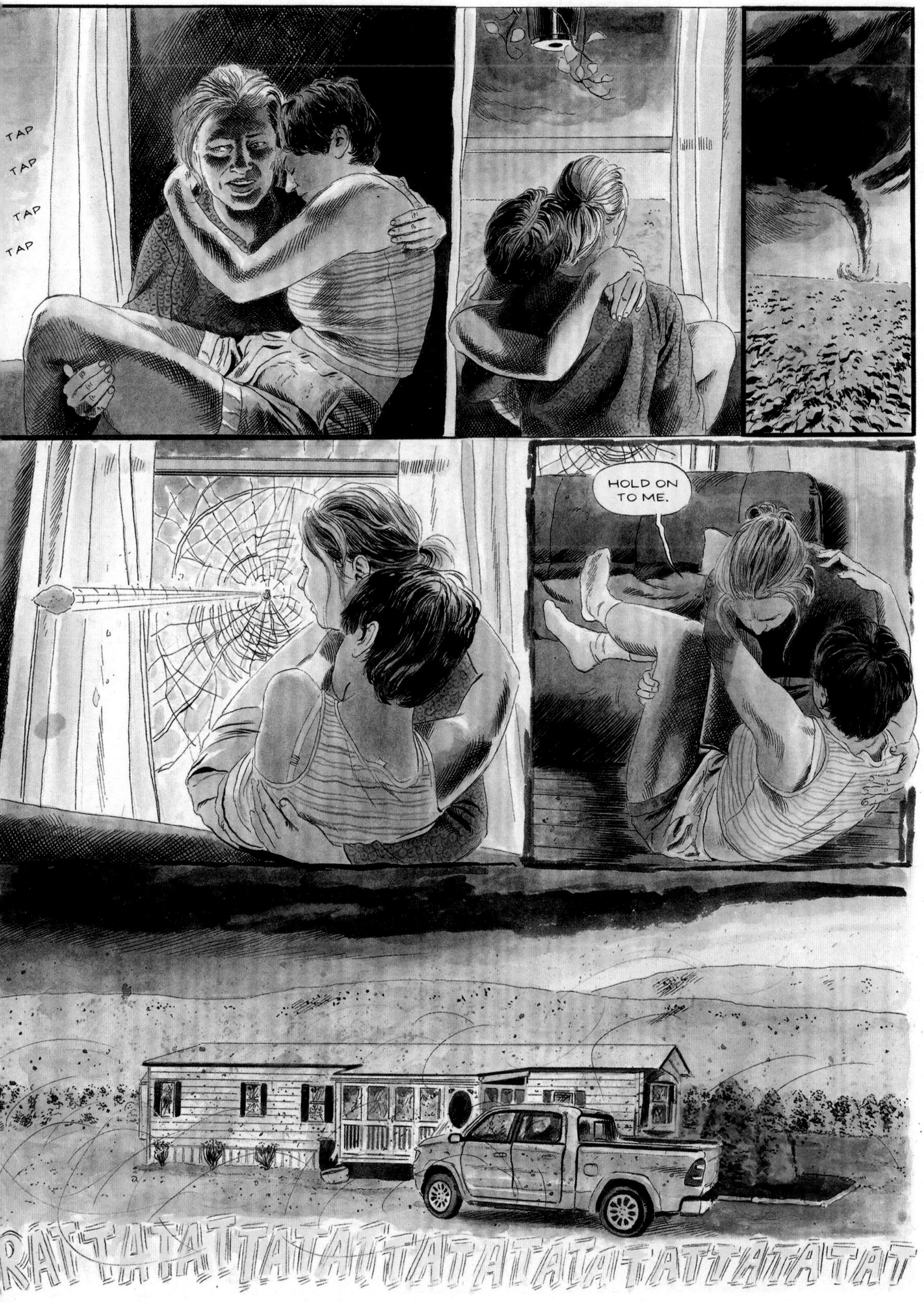
TAP
TAP
TAP
TAP
HOLD ON TO ME.
RATTATATTATATTATATATATATTATTATATAT

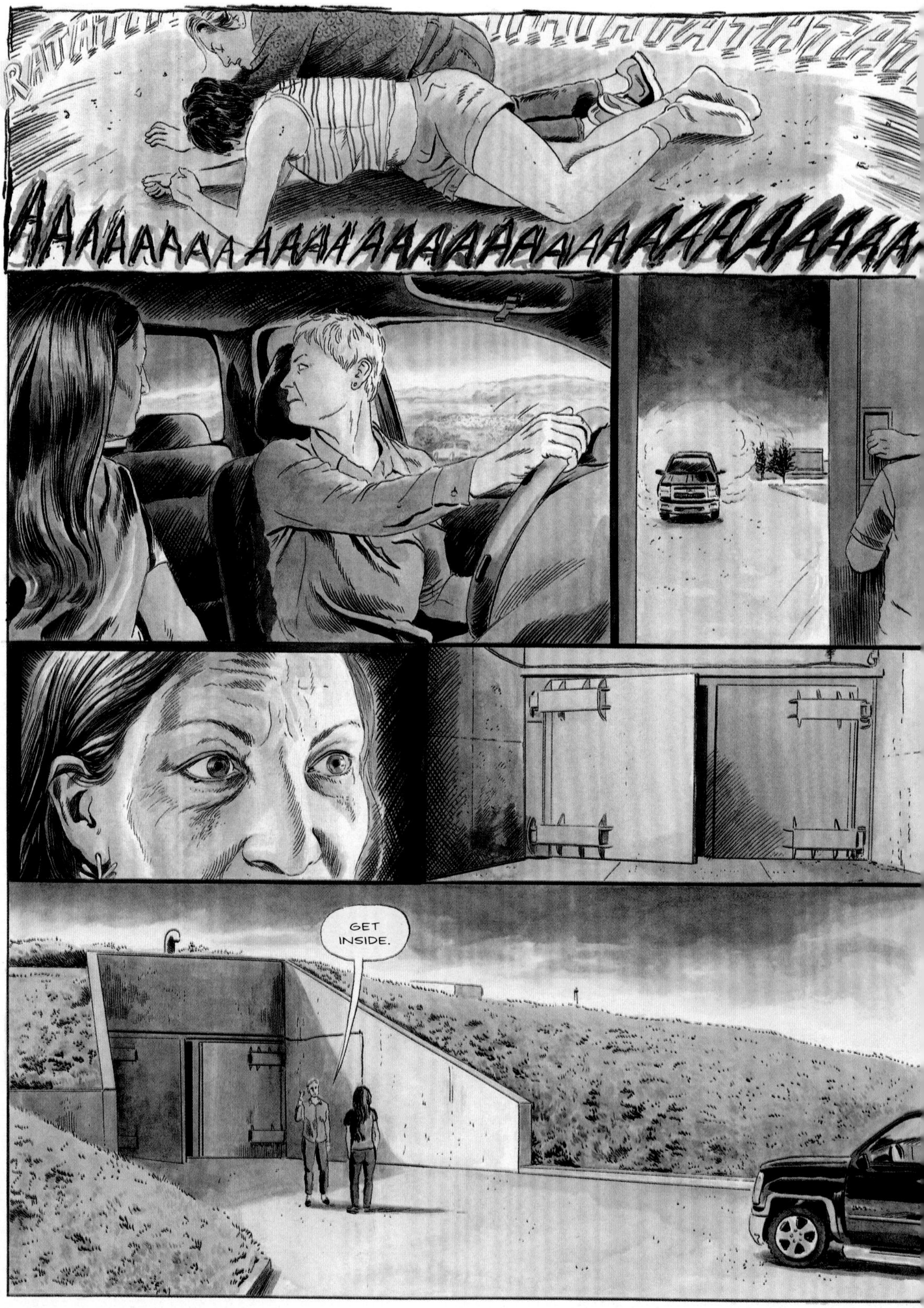
RATATAT
AAAAAAAAAAAAAAAAAAAAAAAAAAAAAA
GET INSIDE.

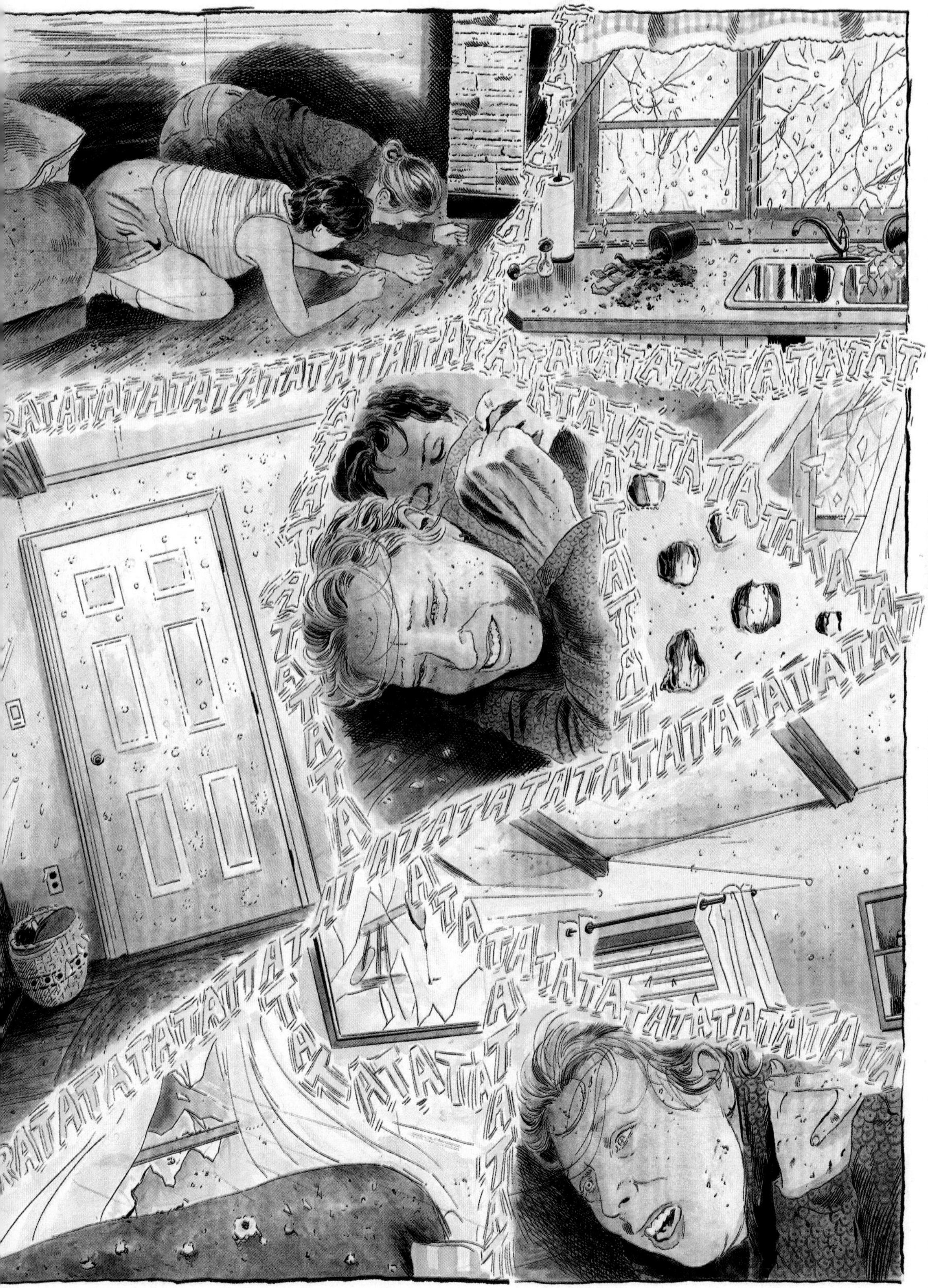

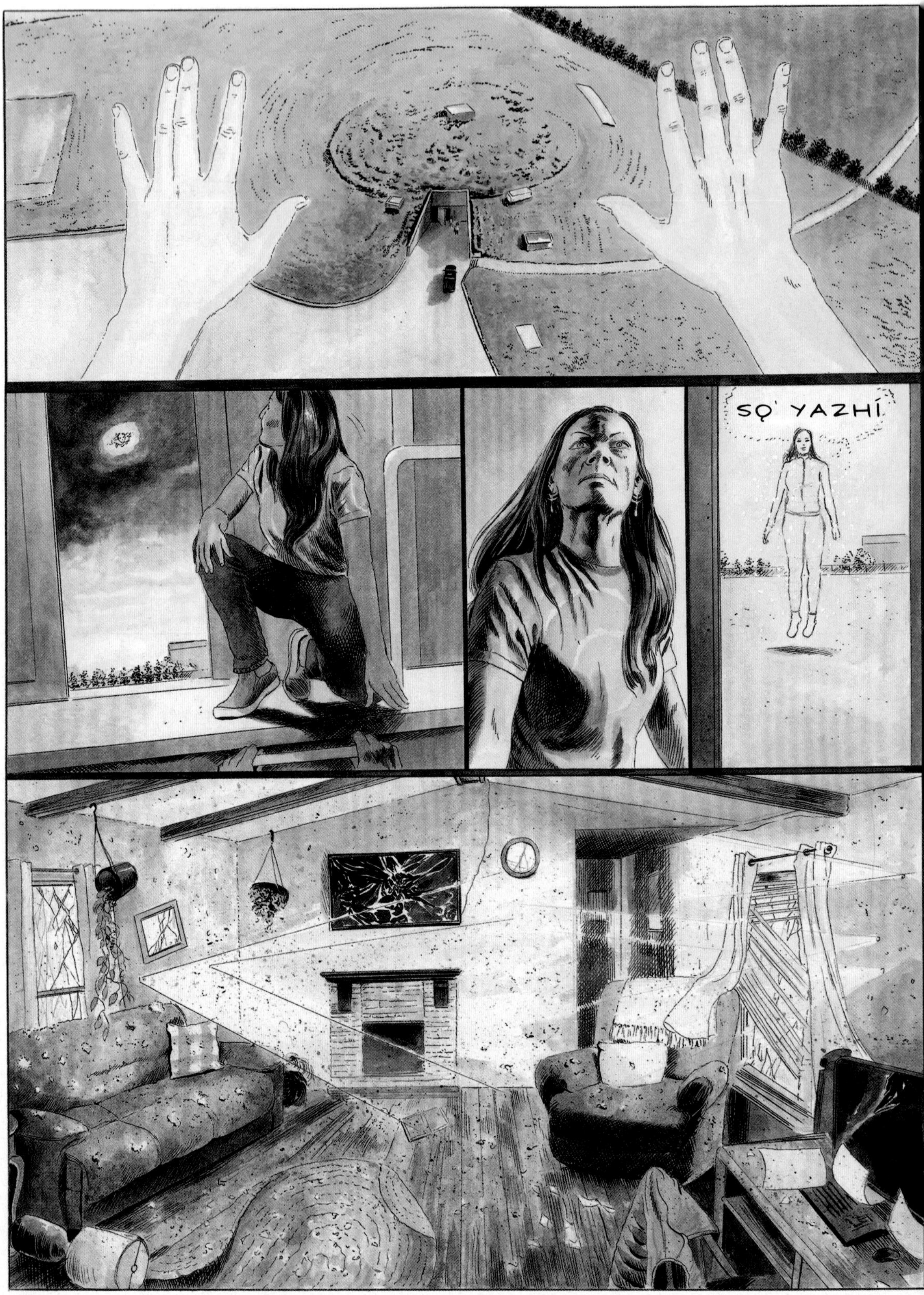
SǪ' YAZHÍ

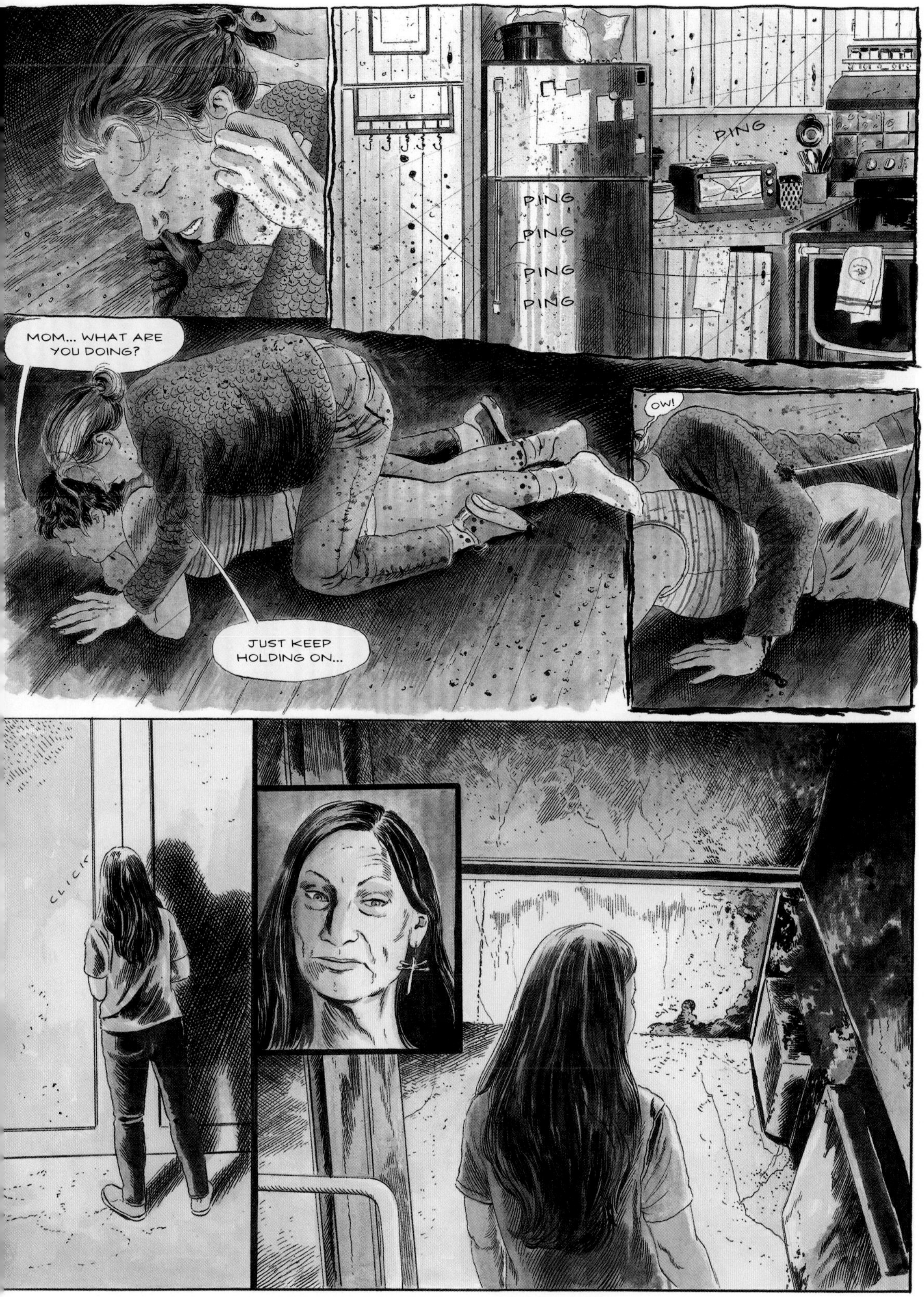
PING
PING
PING
PING
PING
MOM... WHAT ARE YOU DOING?
JUST KEEP HOLDING ON...
OW!
CLICK

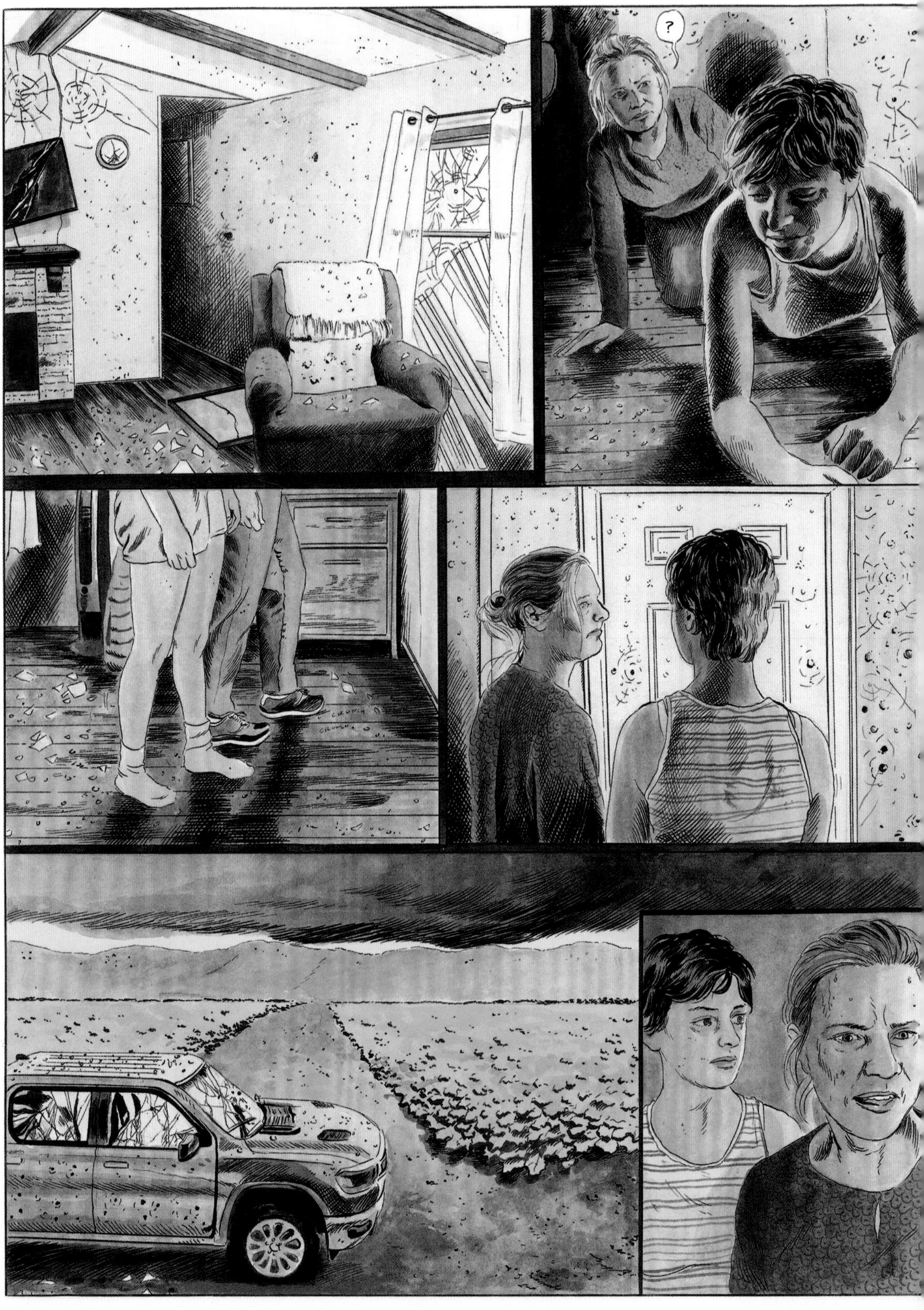
?
CRUNCH
CRUNCH

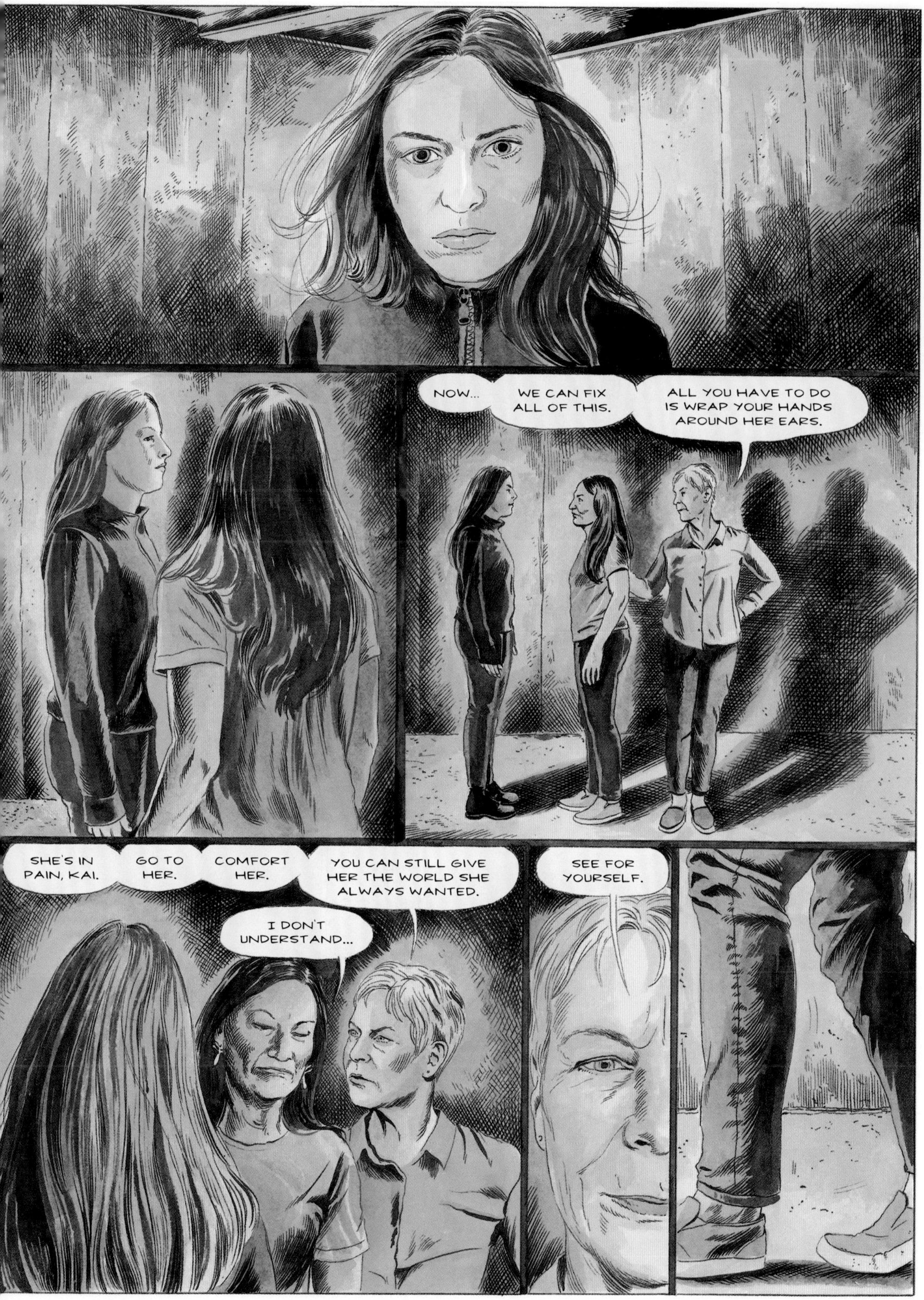
NOW...
WE CAN FIX ALL OF THIS.
ALL YOU HAVE TO DO IS WRAP YOUR HANDS AROUND HER EARS.
SHE'S IN PAIN, KAI.
GO TO HER.
COMFORT HER.
YOU CAN STILL GIVE HER THE WORLD SHE ALWAYS WANTED.
I DON'T UNDERSTAND...
SEE FOR YOURSELF.

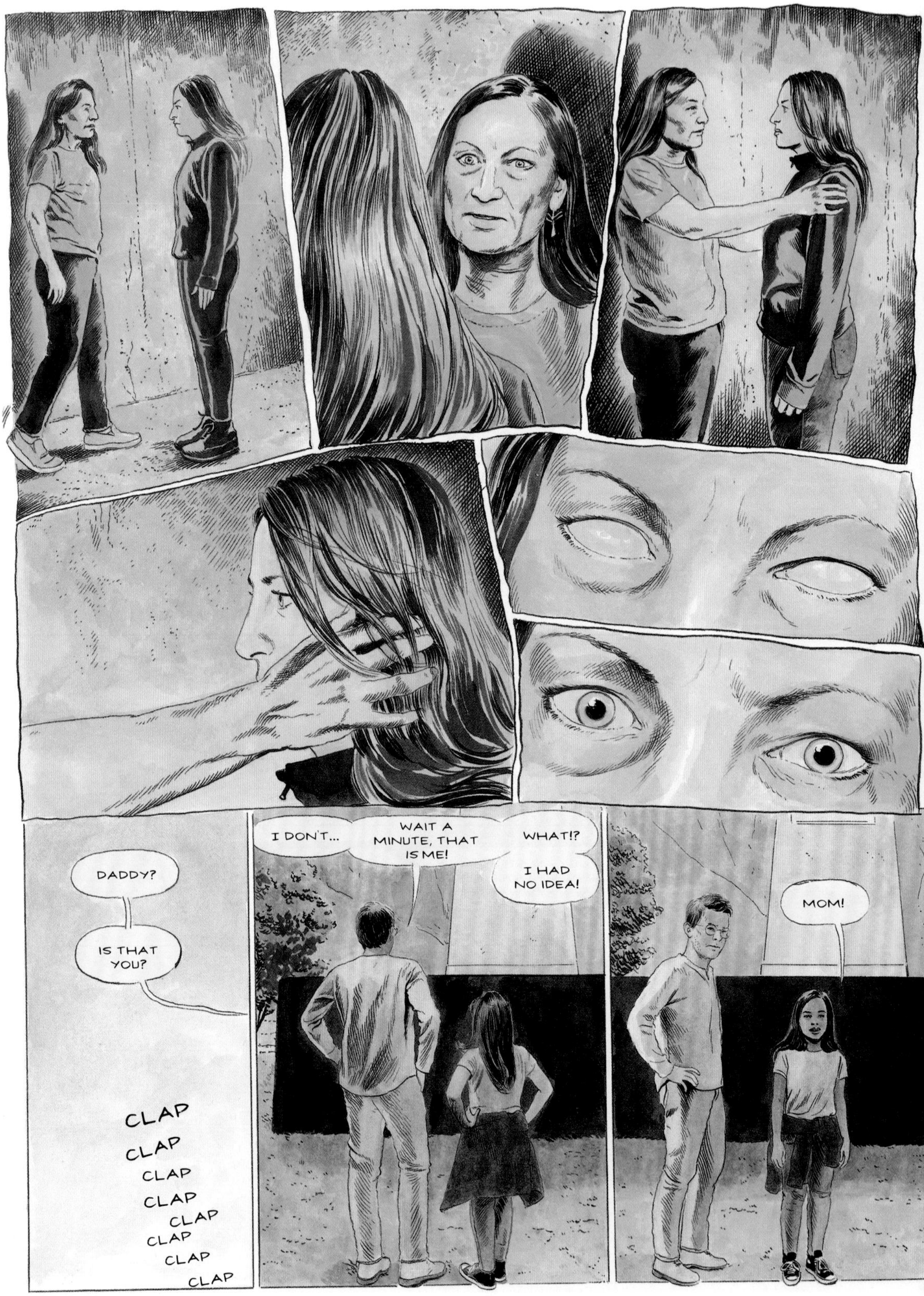
DADDY?
IS THAT YOU?
CLAP CLAP CLAP CLAP CLAP CLAP CLAP CLAP
I DON'T...
WAIT A MINUTE, THAT IS ME!
WHAT!?
I HAD NO IDEA!
MOM!

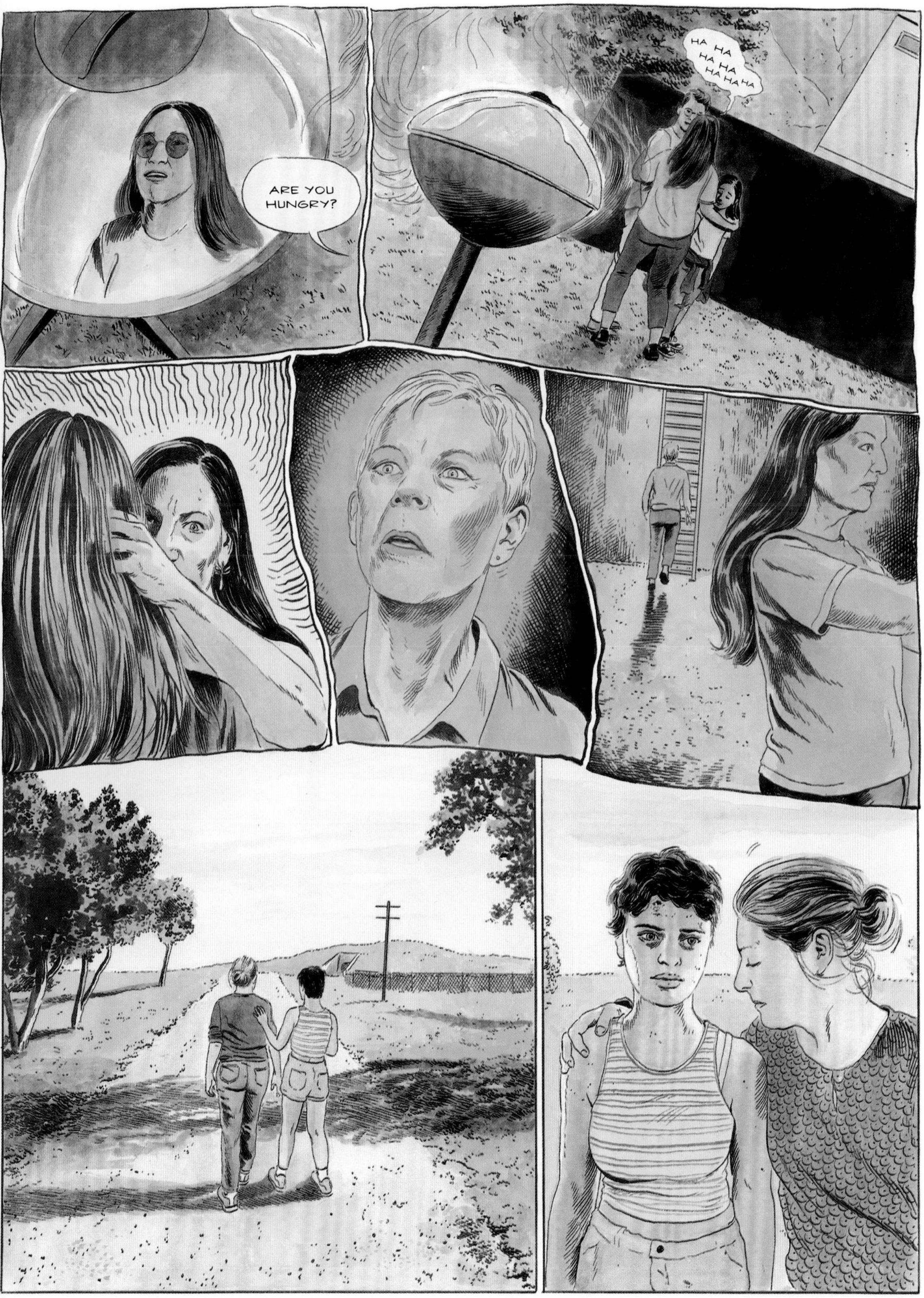
ARE YOU HUNGRY?
HA HA HA HA HA HA HA HA

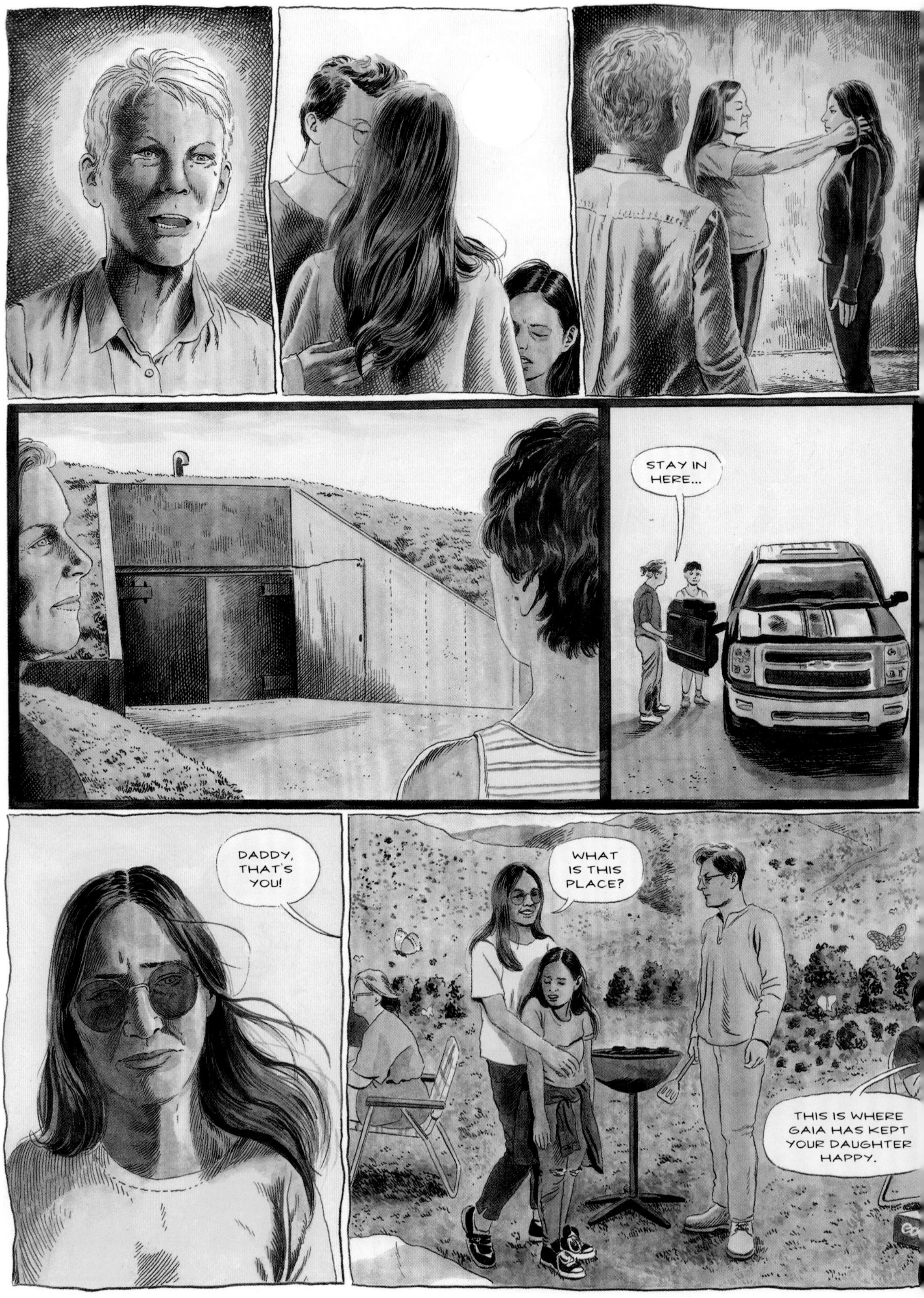
STAY IN HERE...
DADDY, THAT'S YOU!
WHAT IS THIS PLACE?
THIS IS WHERE GAIA HAS KEPT YOUR DAUGHTER HAPPY.

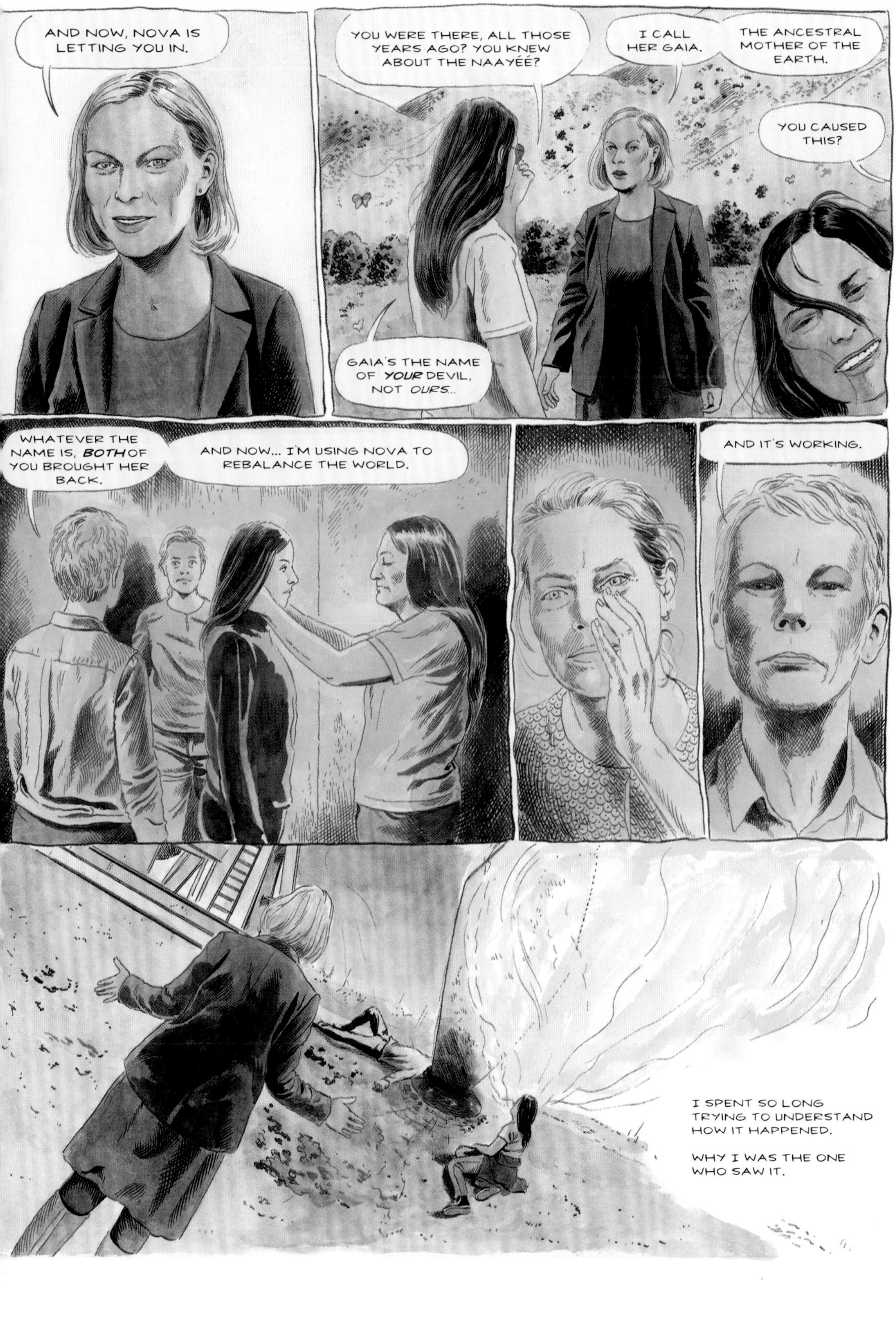
AND NOW, NOVA IS LETTING YOU IN.
YOU WERE THERE, ALL THOSE YEARS AGO? YOU KNEW ABOUT THE NAAYÉÉ?
I CALL HER GAIA.
THE ANCESTRAL MOTHER OF THE EARTH.
YOU CAUSED THIS?
GAIA'S THE NAME OF *YOUR* DEVIL, NOT *OURS*..
WHATEVER THE NAME IS, *BOTH* OF YOU BROUGHT HER BACK.
AND NOW... I'M USING NOVA TO REBALANCE THE WORLD.
AND IT'S WORKING.
I SPENT SO LONG TRYING TO UNDERSTAND HOW IT HAPPENED.
WHY I WAS THE ONE WHO SAW IT.

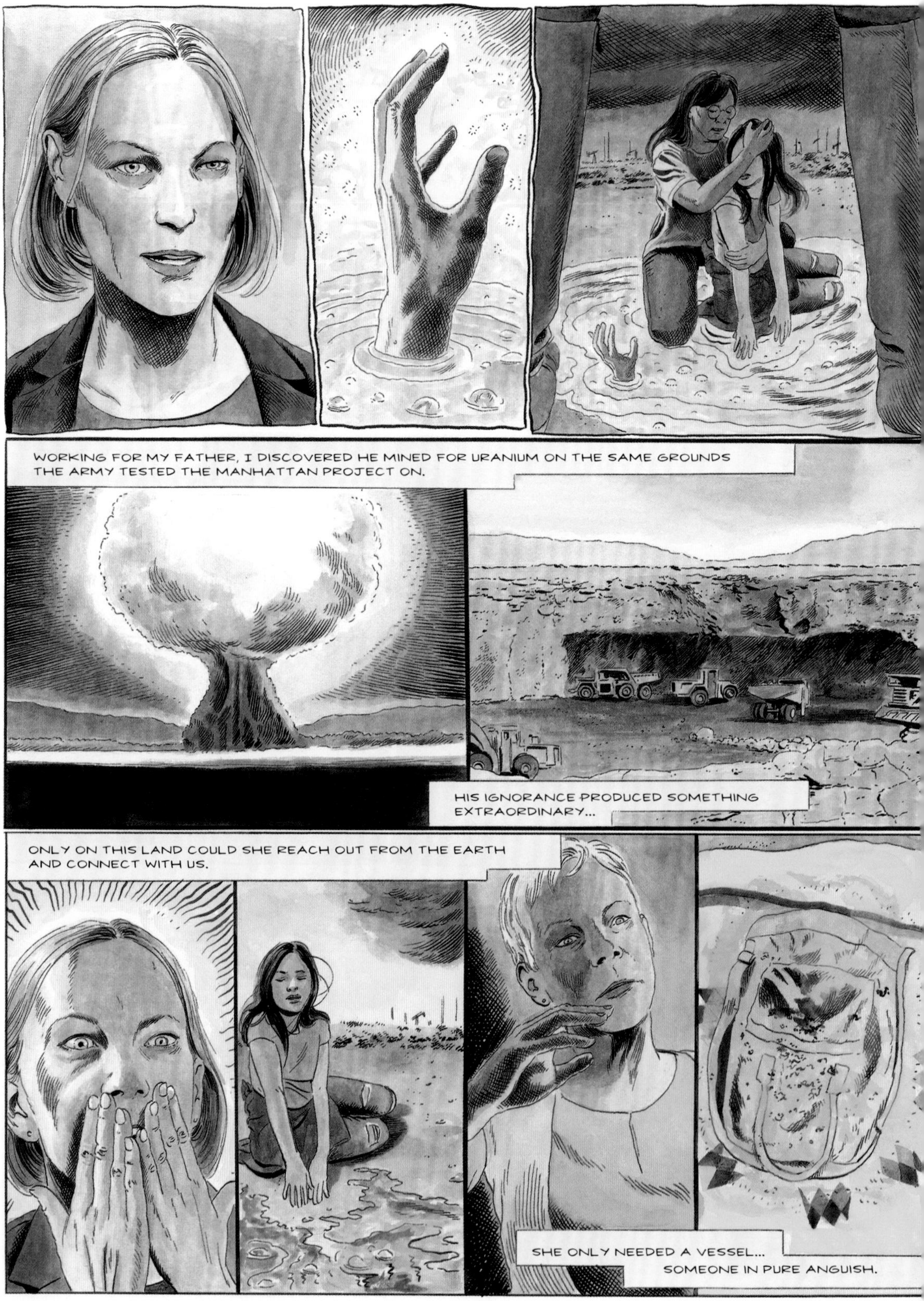
WORKING FOR MY FATHER, I DISCOVERED HE MINED FOR URANIUM ON THE SAME GROUNDS THE ARMY TESTED THE MANHATTAN PROJECT ON.
HIS IGNORANCE PRODUCED SOMETHING EXTRAORDINARY...
ONLY ON THIS LAND COULD SHE REACH OUT FROM THE EARTH AND CONNECT WITH US.
SHE ONLY NEEDED A VESSEL...
SOMEONE IN PURE ANGUISH.

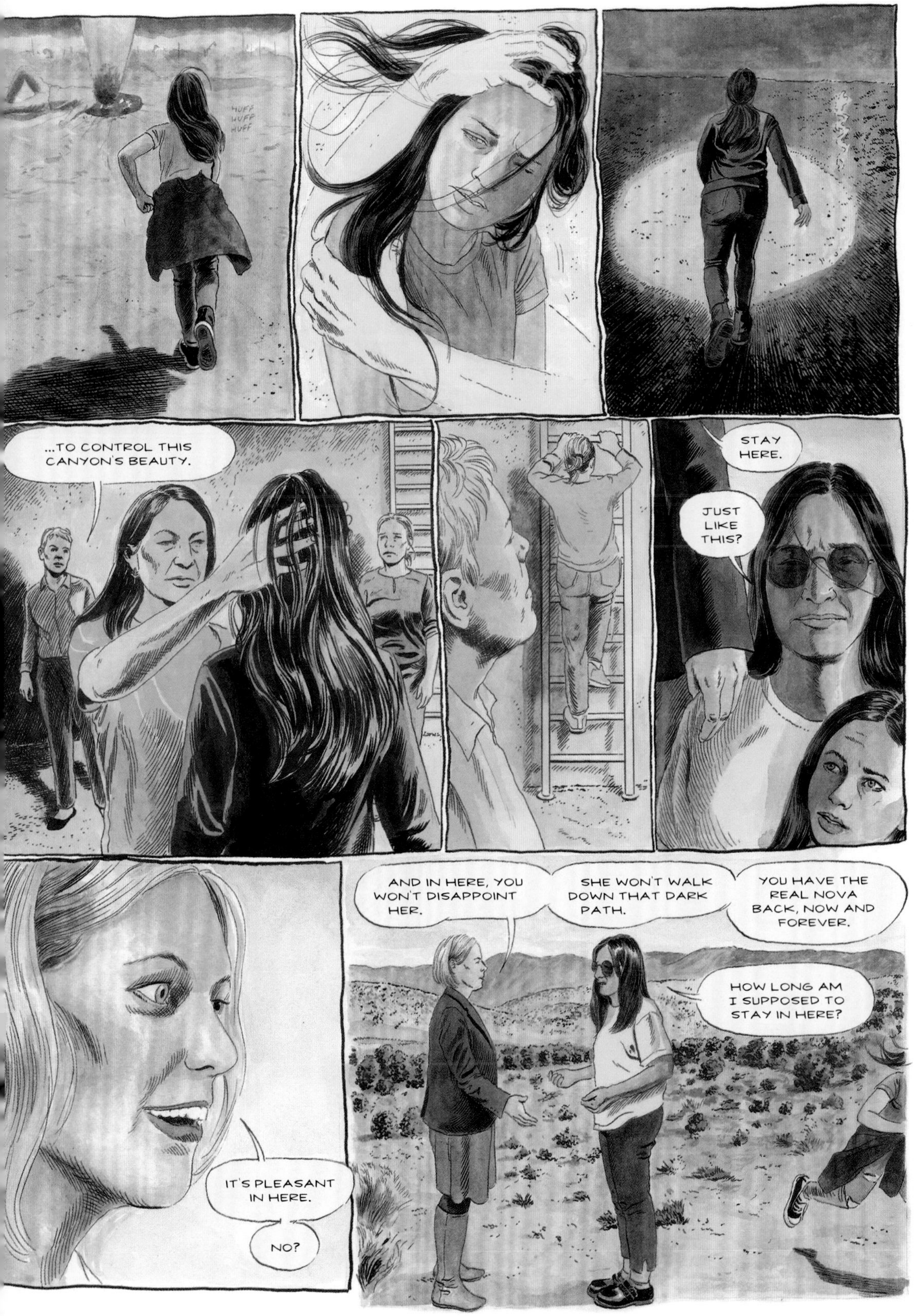
HUFF
HUFF
HUFF
...TO CONTROL THIS CANYON'S BEAUTY.
STAY HERE.
JUST LIKE THIS?
IT'S PLEASANT IN HERE.
NO?
AND IN HERE, YOU WON'T DISAPPOINT HER.
SHE WON'T WALK DOWN THAT DARK PATH.
YOU HAVE THE REAL NOVA BACK, NOW AND FOREVER.
HOW LONG AM I SUPPOSED TO STAY IN HERE?

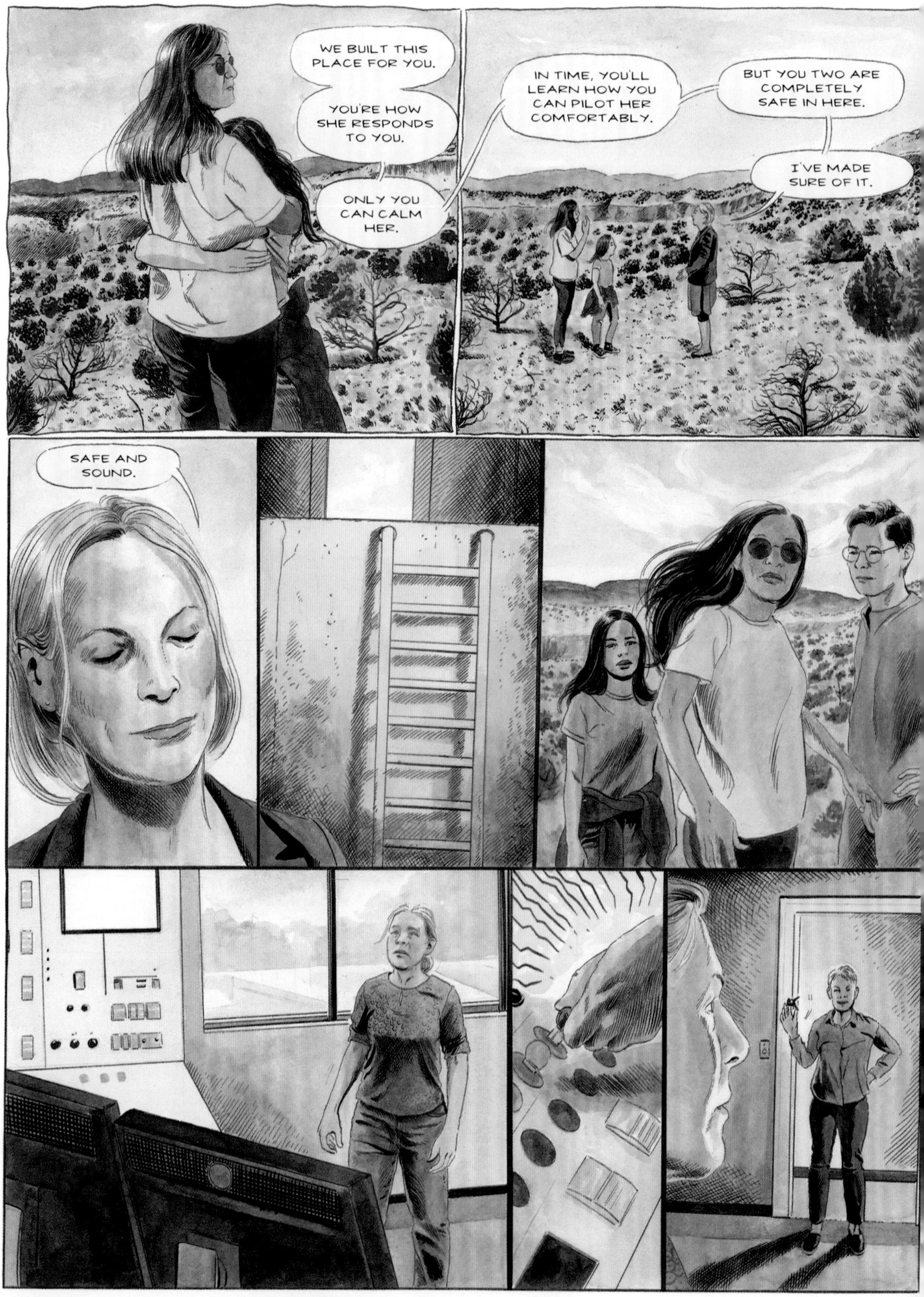
WE BUILT THIS PLACE FOR YOU.
YOU'RE HOW SHE RESPONDS TO YOU.
ONLY YOU CAN CALM HER.
IN TIME, YOU'LL LEARN HOW YOU CAN PILOT HER COMFORTABLY.
BUT YOU TWO ARE COMPLETELY SAFE IN HERE.
I'VE MADE SURE OF IT.
SAFE AND SOUND.

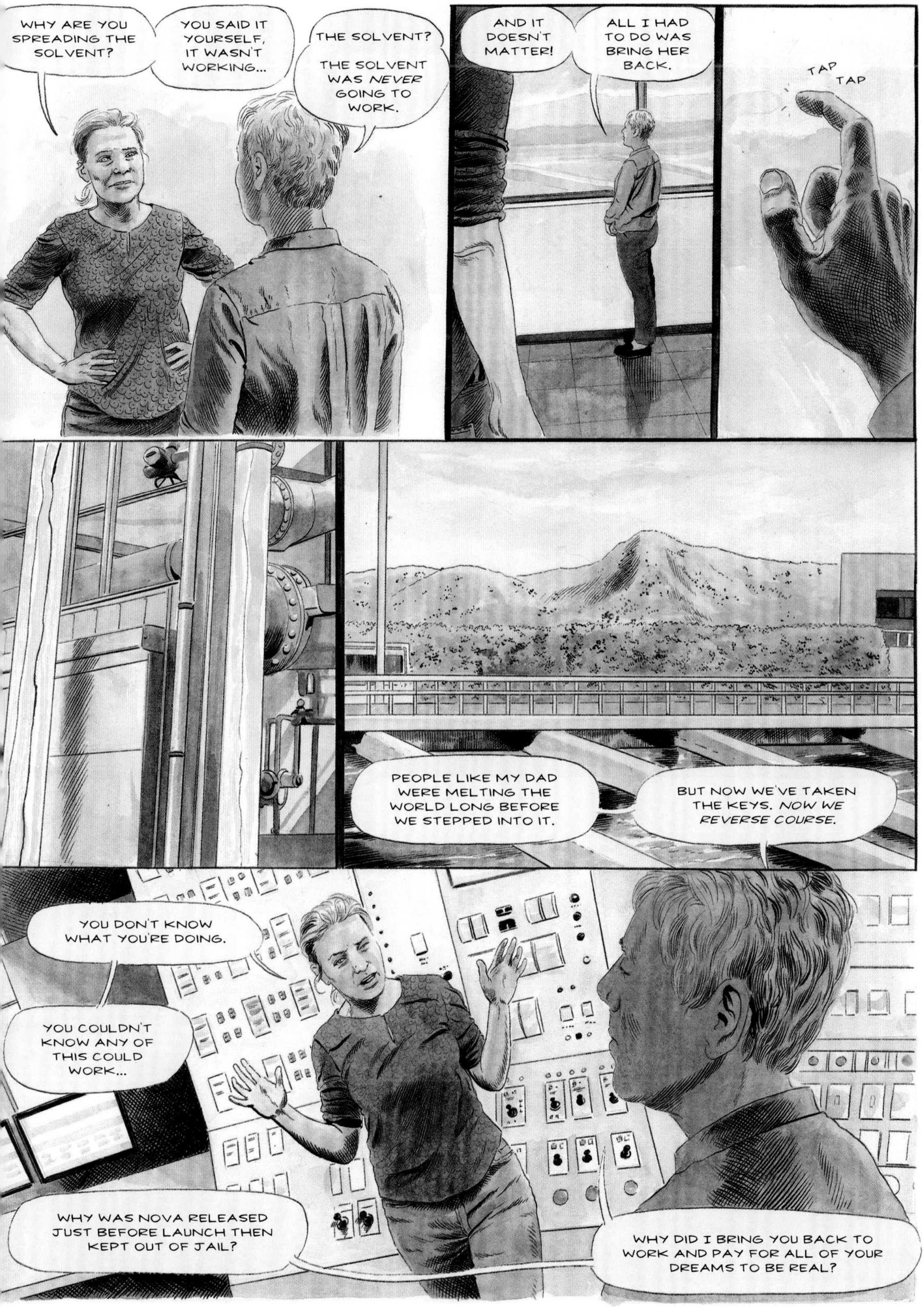
WHY ARE YOU SPREADING THE SOLVENT?
YOU SAID IT YOURSELF, IT WASN'T WORKING...
THE SOLVENT?
THE SOLVENT WAS *NEVER* GOING TO WORK.
AND IT DOESN'T MATTER!
ALL I HAD TO DO WAS BRING HER BACK.
TAP TAP
PEOPLE LIKE MY DAD WERE MELTING THE WORLD LONG BEFORE WE STEPPED INTO IT.
BUT NOW WE'VE TAKEN THE KEYS. *NOW WE REVERSE COURSE.*
YOU DON'T KNOW WHAT YOU'RE DOING.
YOU COULDN'T KNOW ANY OF THIS COULD WORK...
WHY WAS NOVA RELEASED JUST BEFORE LAUNCH THEN KEPT OUT OF JAIL?
WHY DID I BRING YOU BACK TO WORK AND PAY FOR ALL OF YOUR DREAMS TO BE REAL?

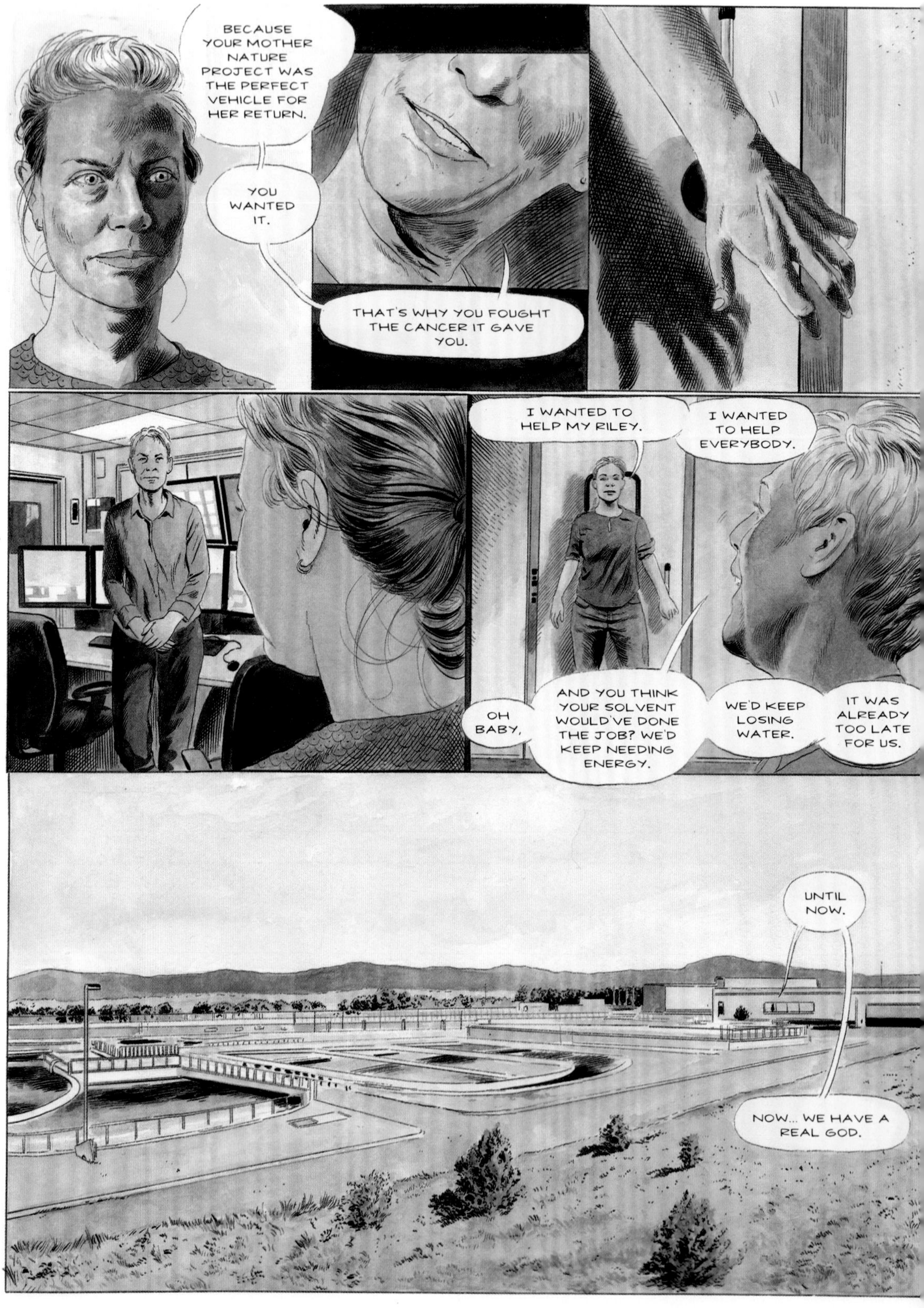
BECAUSE YOUR MOTHER NATURE PROJECT WAS THE PERFECT VEHICLE FOR HER RETURN.
YOU WANTED IT.
THAT'S WHY YOU FOUGHT THE CANCER IT GAVE YOU.
I WANTED TO HELP MY RILEY.
I WANTED TO HELP EVERYBODY.
OH BABY,
AND YOU THINK YOUR SOLVENT WOULD'VE DONE THE JOB? WE'D KEEP NEEDING ENERGY.
WE'D KEEP LOSING WATER.
IT WAS ALREADY TOO LATE FOR US.
UNTIL NOW.
NOW... WE HAVE A REAL GOD.

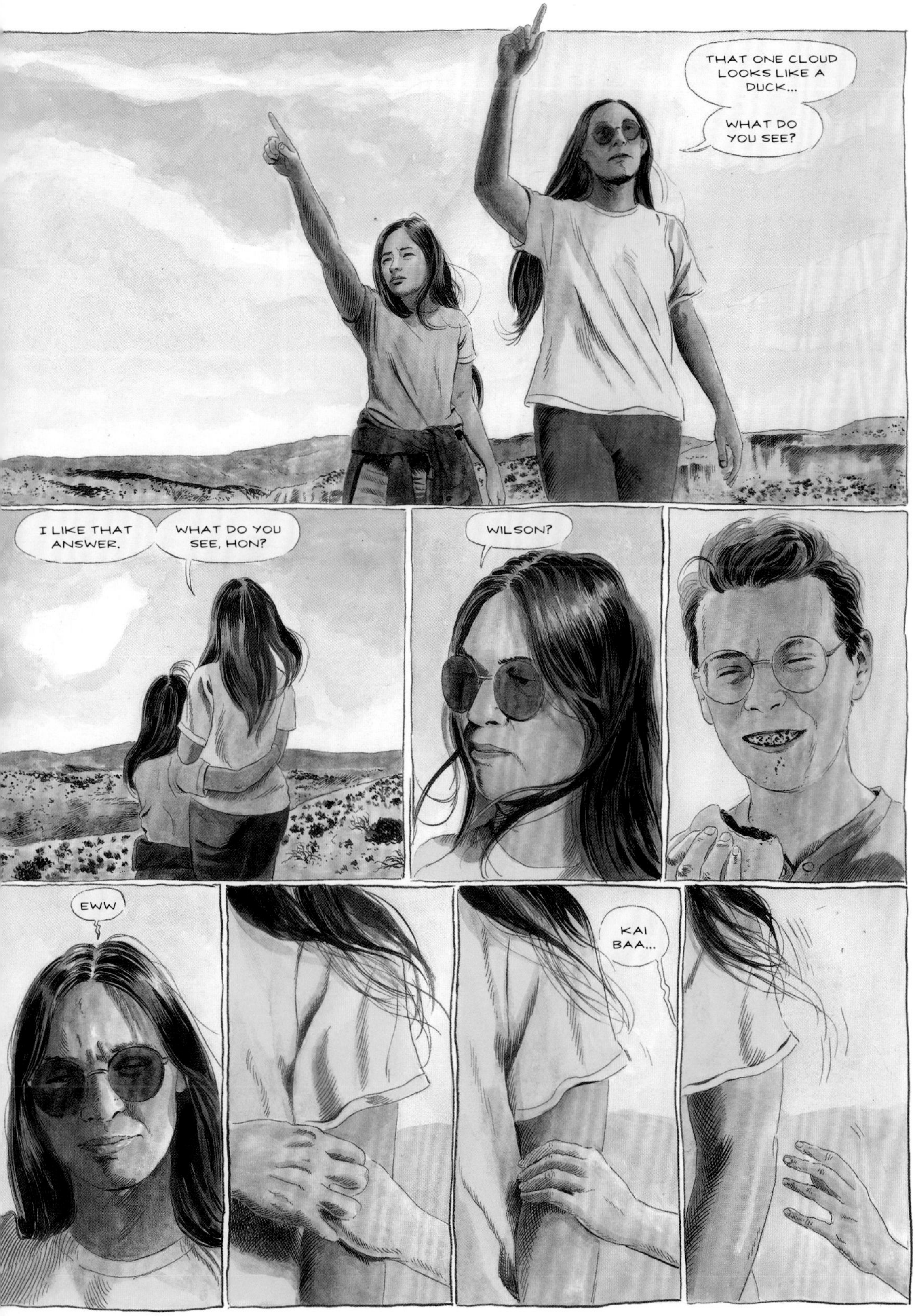

THAT ONE CLOUD LOOKS LIKE A DUCK...
WHAT DO YOU SEE?
I LIKE THAT ANSWER.
WHAT DO YOU SEE, HON?
WILSON?
EWW
KAI BAA...

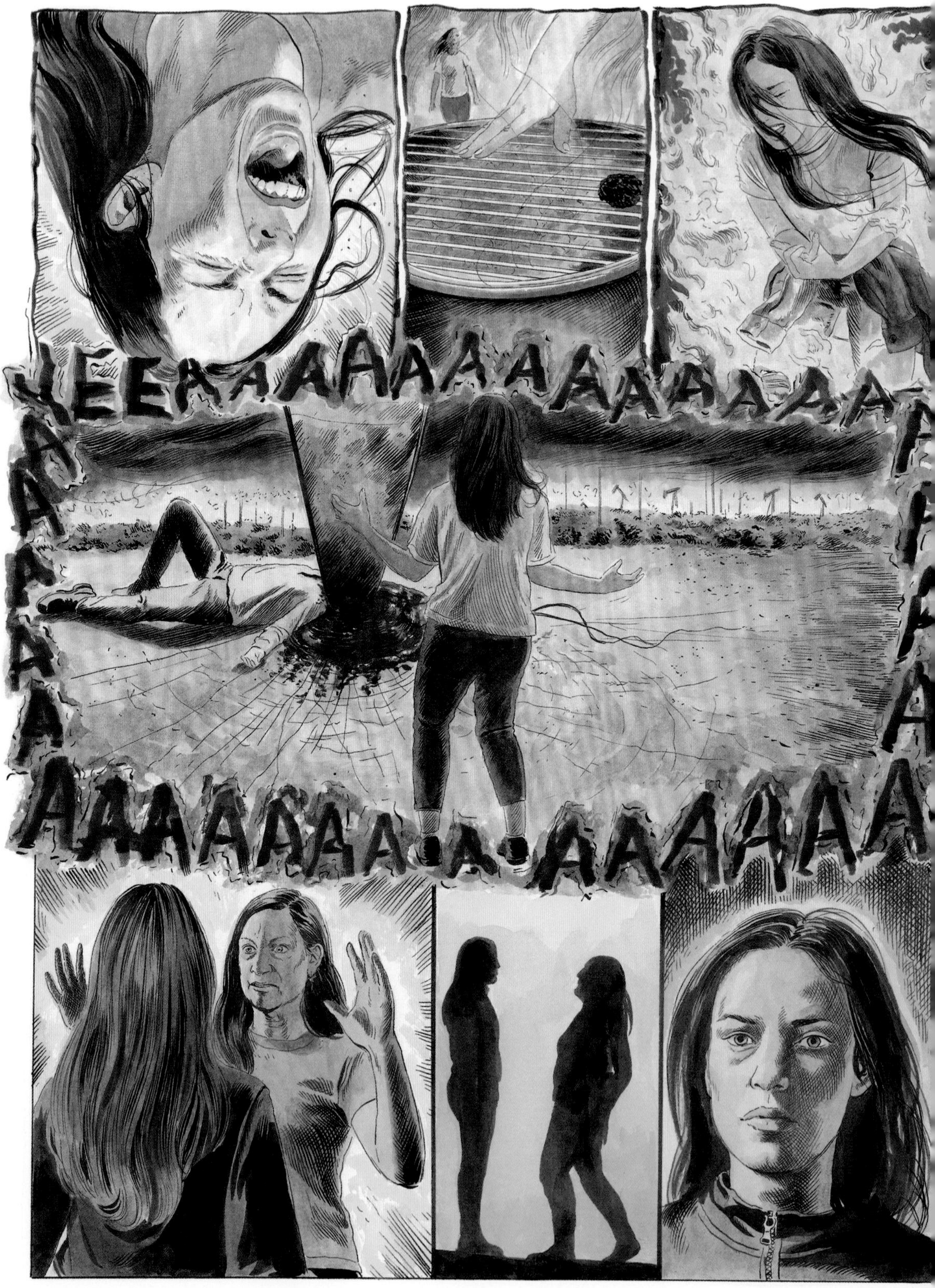
HEEAAAAAAAAAAAAAAAAAAAAAAAAAAAAAAAAAAAAAAA

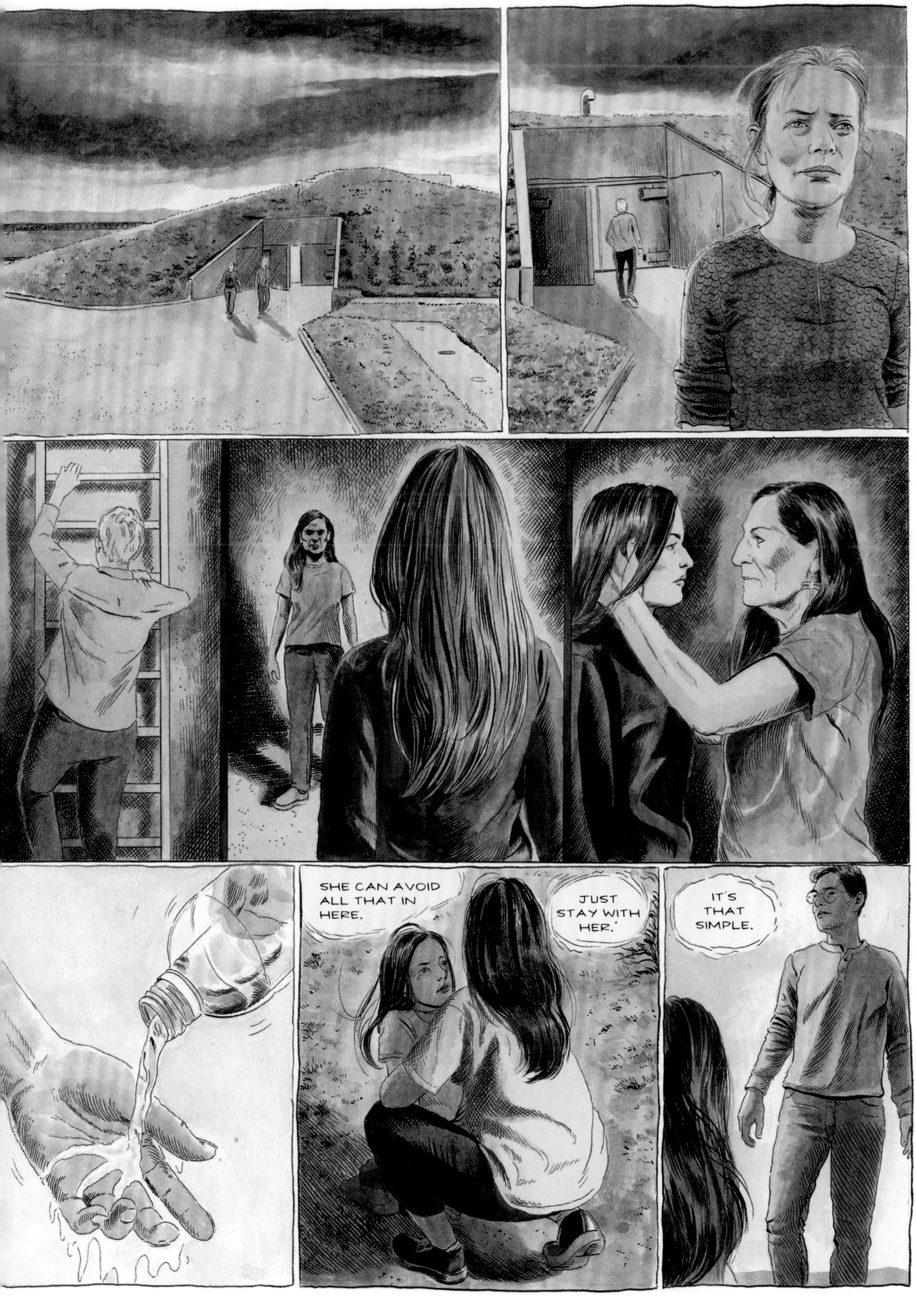
SHE CAN AVOID ALL THAT IN HERE.
JUST STAY WITH HER.
IT'S THAT SIMPLE.

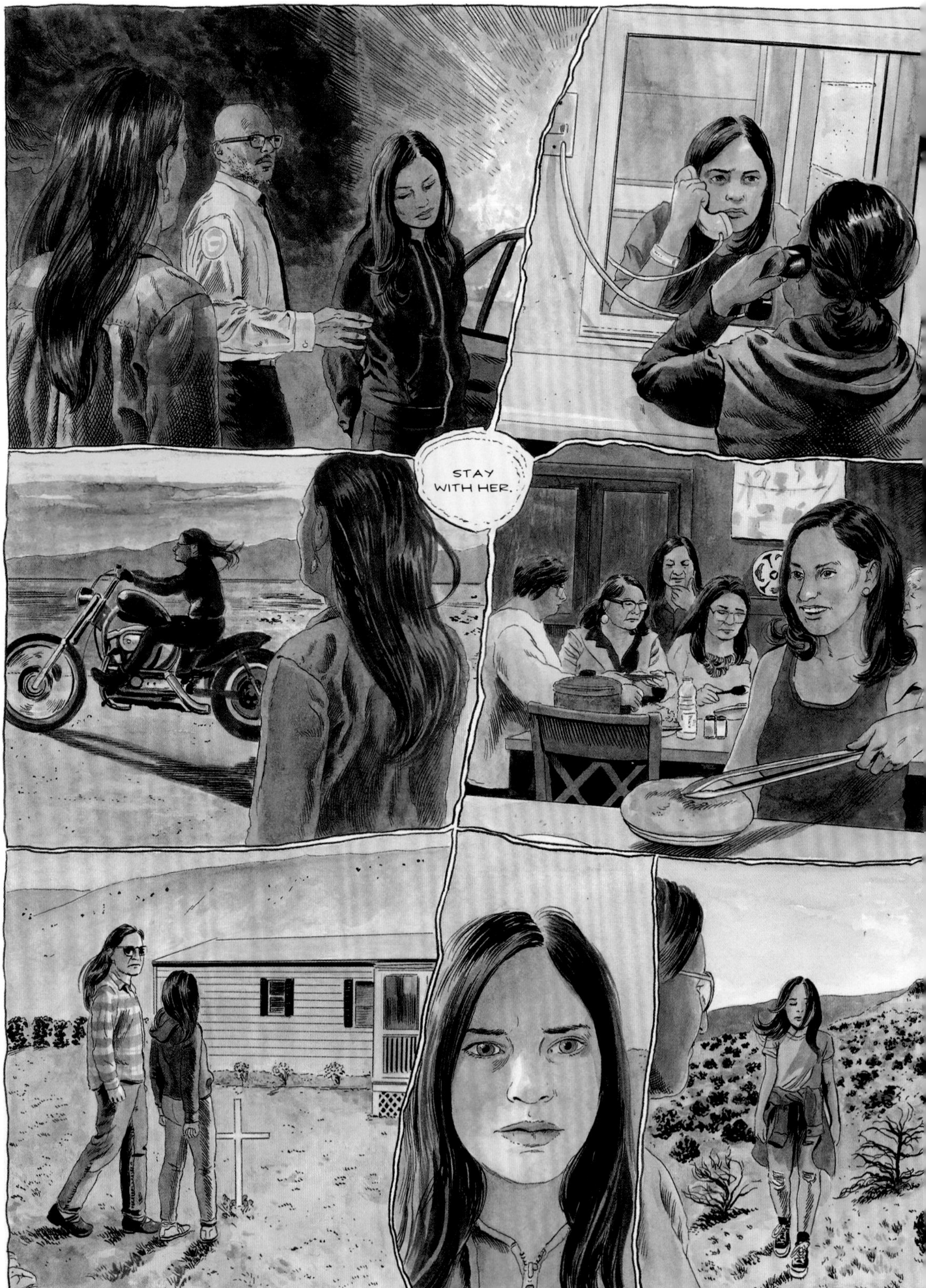
STAY WITH HER.

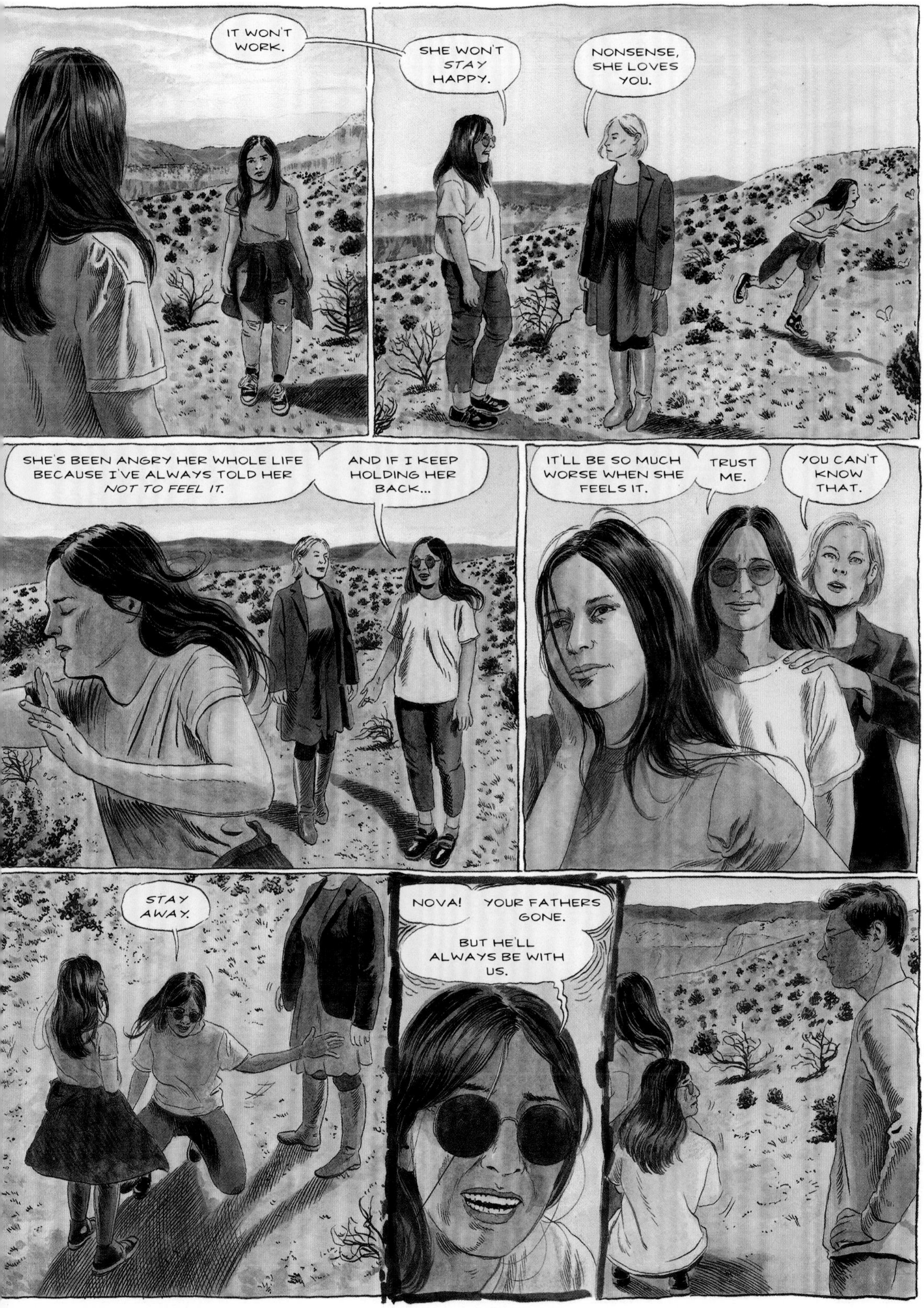
IT WON'T WORK.
SHE WON'T *STAY* HAPPY.
NONSENSE, SHE LOVES YOU.
SHE'S BEEN ANGRY HER WHOLE LIFE BECAUSE I'VE ALWAYS TOLD HER *NOT TO FEEL IT.*
AND IF I KEEP HOLDING HER BACK...
IT'LL BE SO MUCH WORSE WHEN SHE FEELS IT.
TRUST ME.
YOU CAN'T KNOW THAT.
STAY AWAY.
NOVA! YOUR FATHERS GONE.
BUT HE'LL ALWAYS BE WITH US.

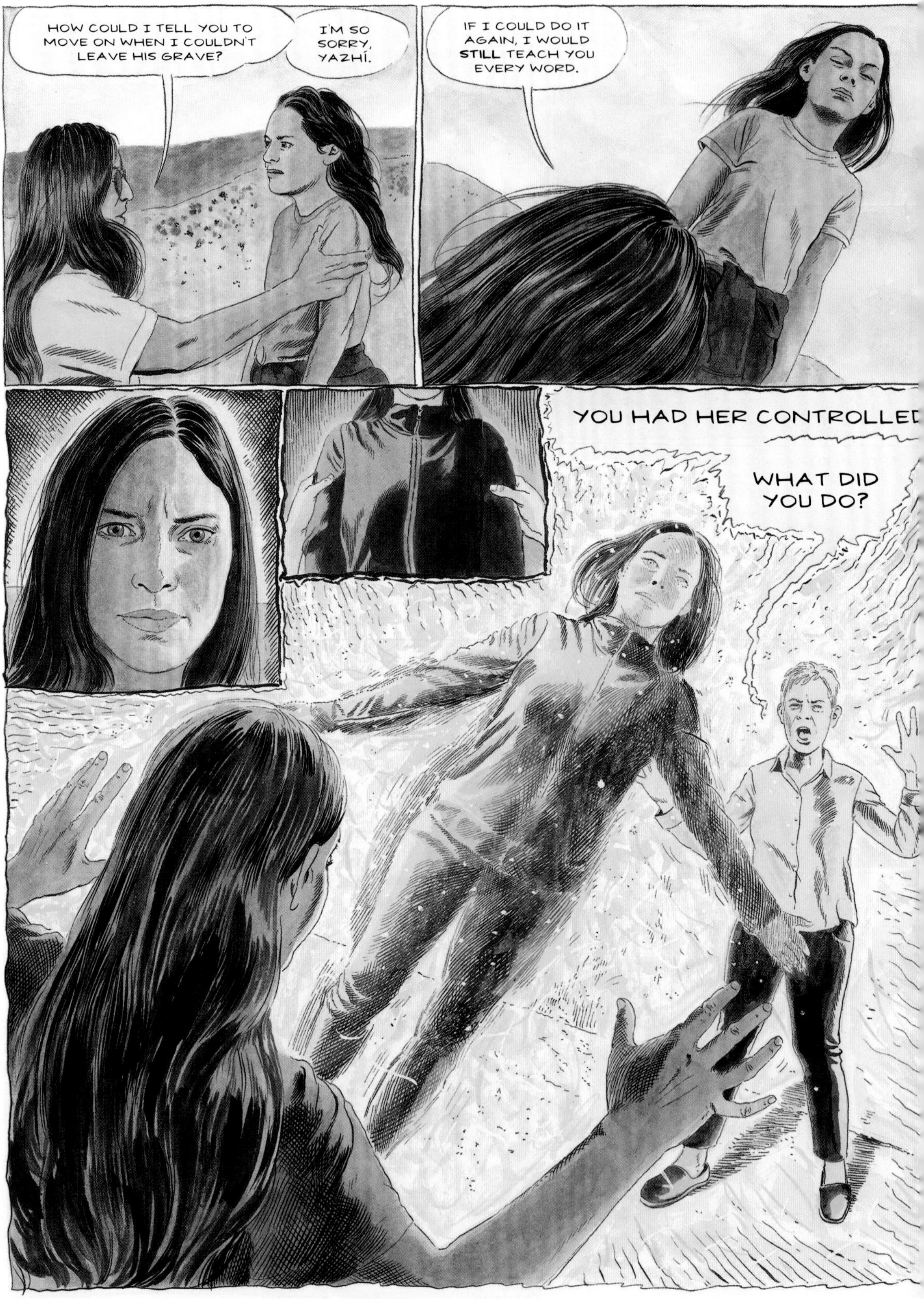
HOW COULD I TELL YOU TO MOVE ON WHEN I COULDN'T LEAVE HIS GRAVE?
I'M SO SORRY, YAZHÍ.
IF I COULD DO IT AGAIN, I WOULD STILL TEACH YOU EVERY WORD.
YOU HAD HER CONTROLLED
WHAT DID YOU DO?

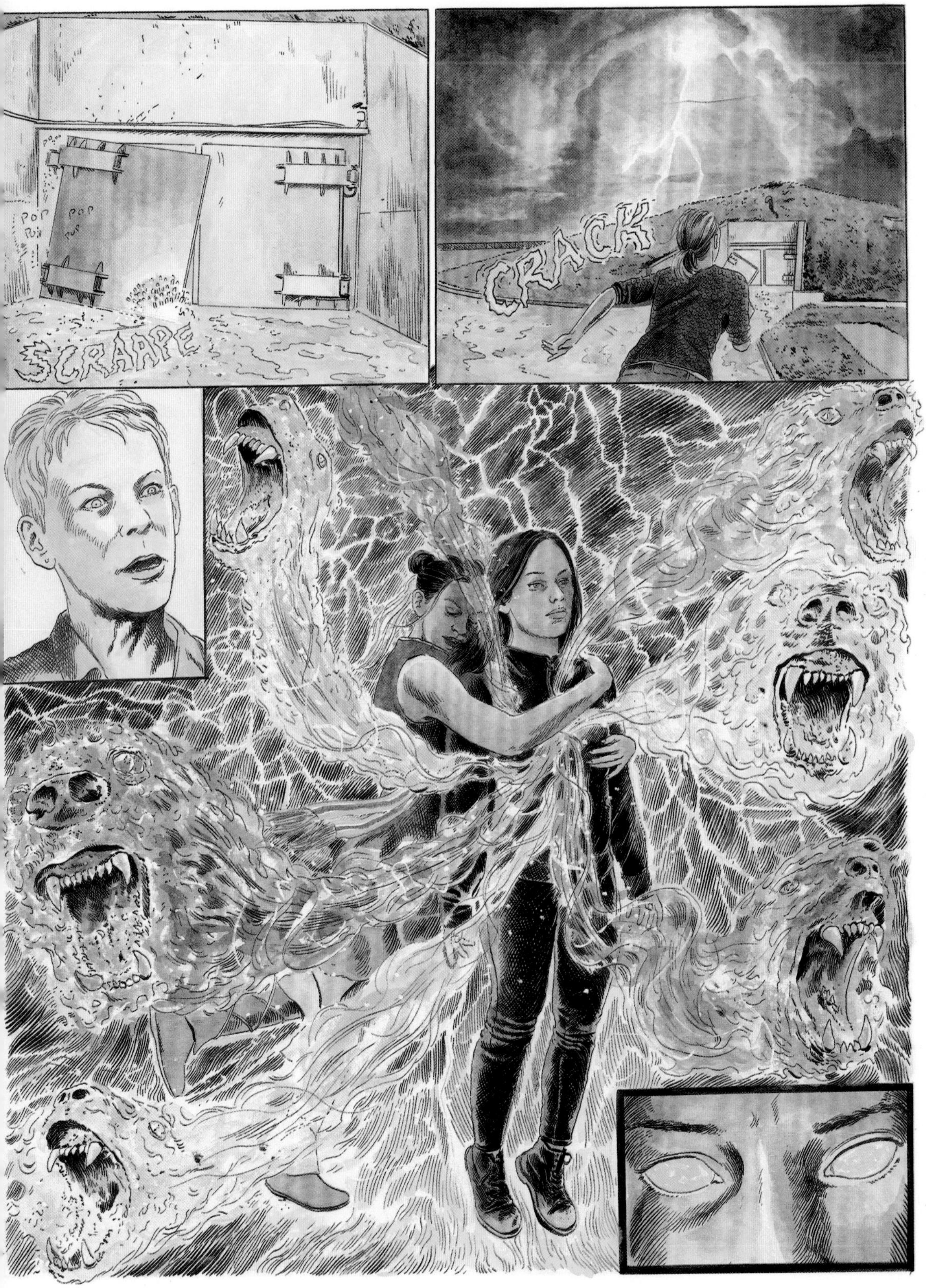
POP
POP
POP
POP
SCRAPE
CRACK

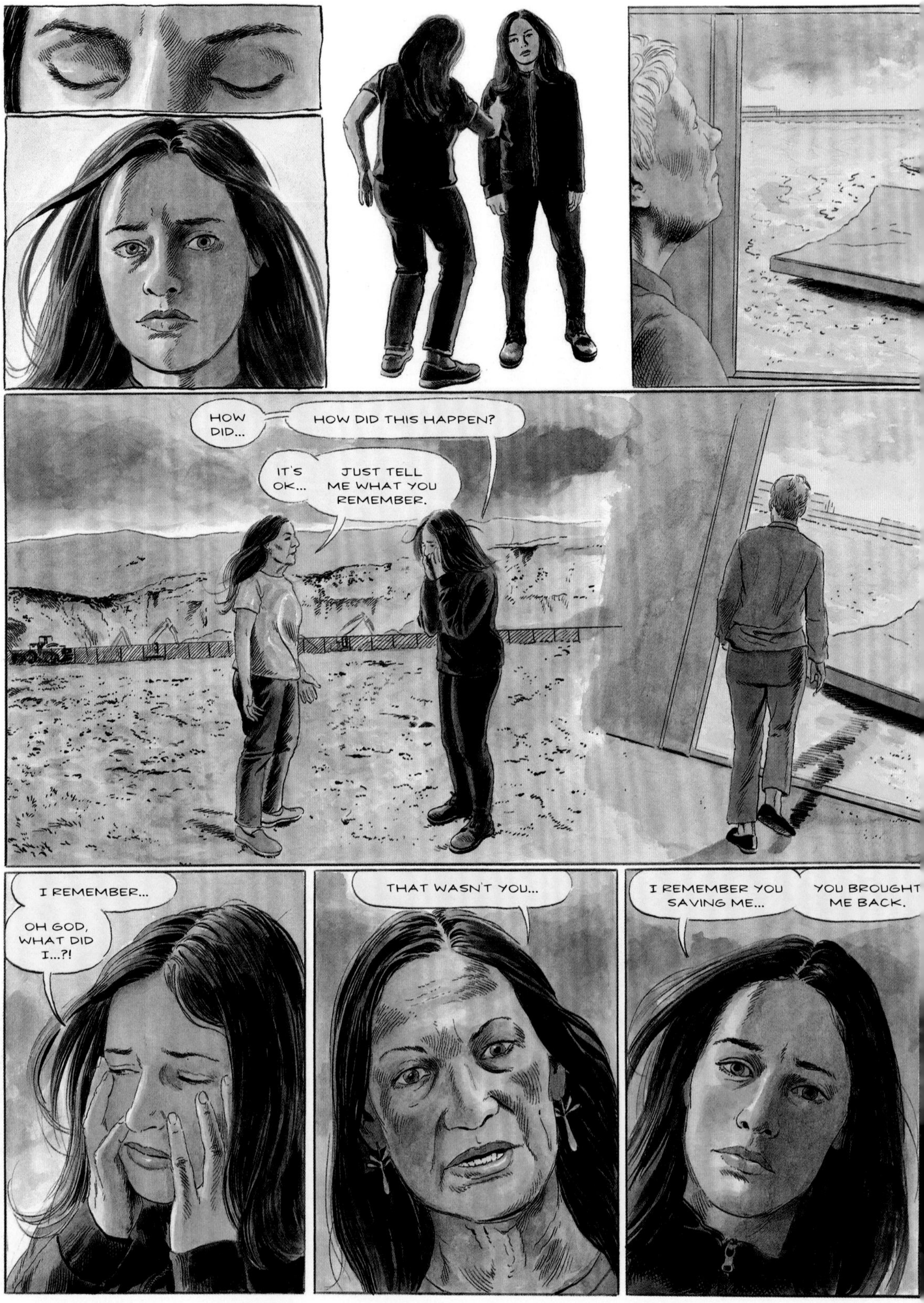
HOW DID...
HOW DID THIS HAPPEN?
IT'S OK...
JUST TELL ME WHAT YOU REMEMBER.
I REMEMBER...
OH GOD, WHAT DID I...?!
THAT WASN'T YOU...
I REMEMBER YOU SAVING ME...
YOU BROUGHT ME BACK.

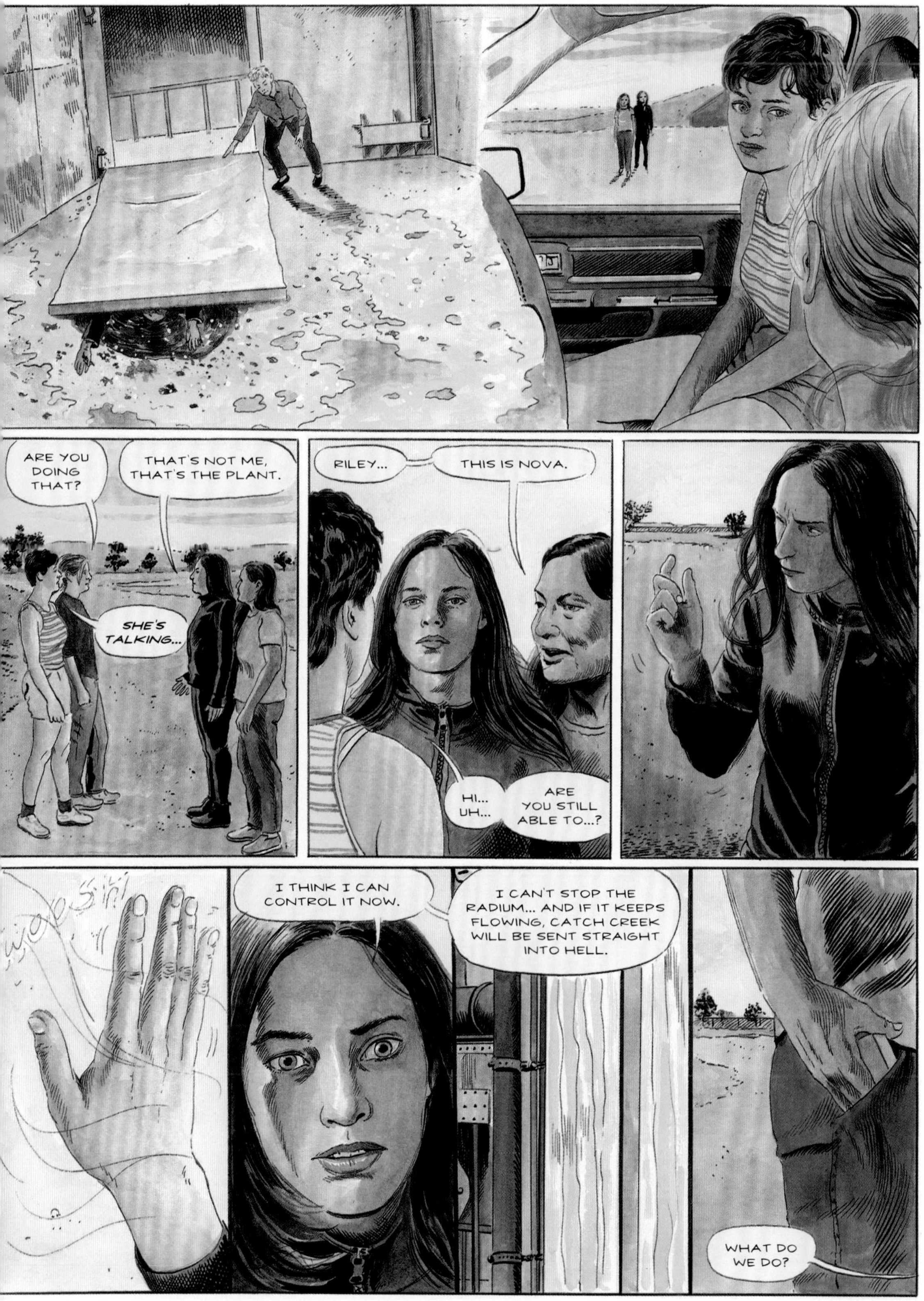
ARE YOU DOING THAT?
THAT'S NOT ME, THAT'S THE PLANT.
SHE'S TALKING...
RILEY...
THIS IS NOVA.
HI... UH...
ARE YOU STILL ABLE TO...?
I THINK I CAN CONTROL IT NOW.
I CAN'T STOP THE RADIUM... AND IF IT KEEPS FLOWING, CATCH CREEK WILL BE SENT STRAIGHT INTO HELL.
WHAT DO WE DO?

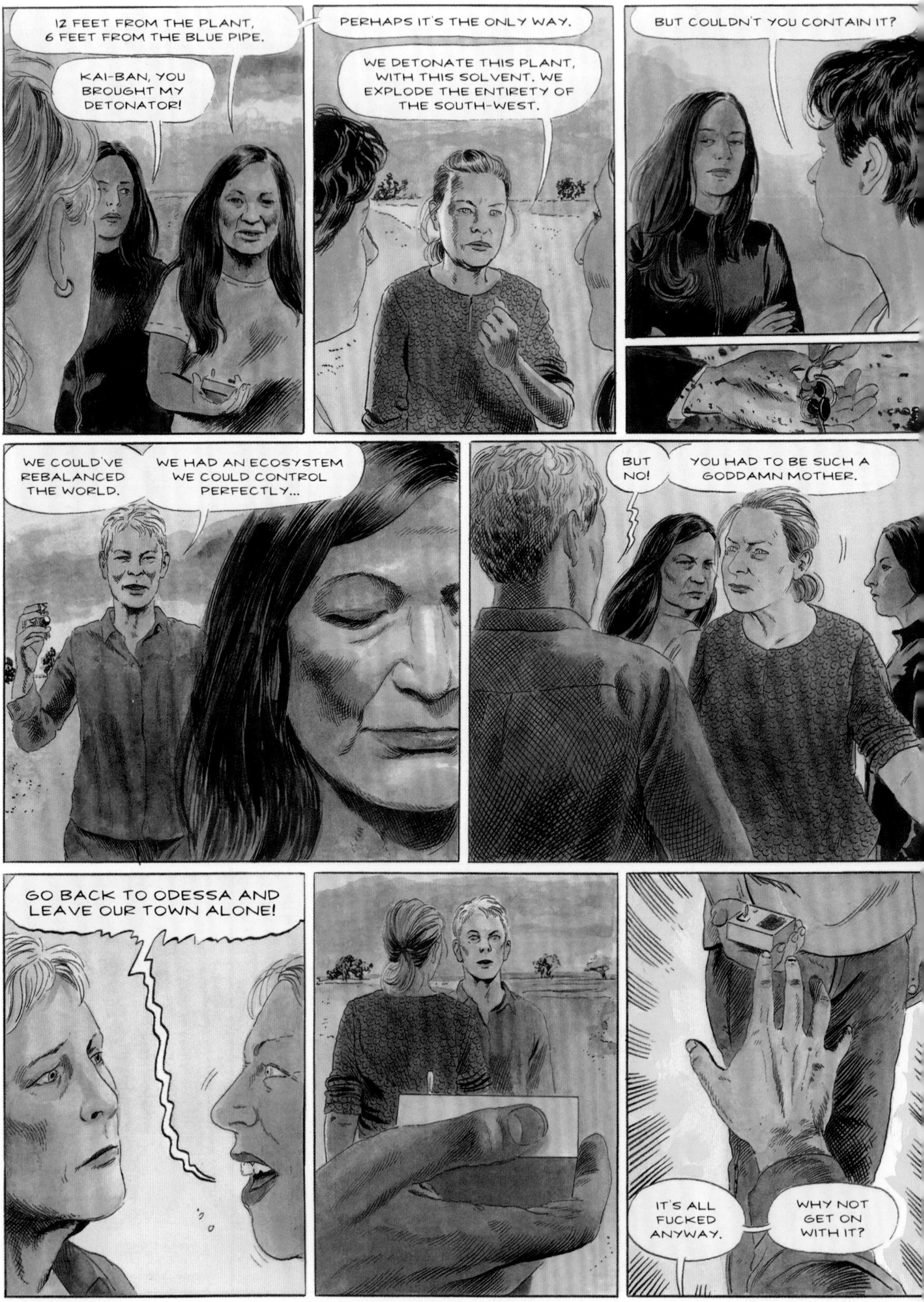
12 FEET FROM THE PLANT, 6 FEET FROM THE BLUE PIPE.
KAI-BAN, YOU BROUGHT MY DETONATOR!
PERHAPS IT'S THE ONLY WAY.
WE DETONATE THIS PLANT, WITH THIS SOLVENT. WE EXPLODE THE ENTIRETY OF THE SOUTH-WEST.
BUT COULDN'T YOU CONTAIN IT?
WE COULD'VE REBALANCED THE WORLD.
WE HAD AN ECOSYSTEM WE COULD CONTROL PERFECTLY...
BUT NO!
YOU HAD TO BE SUCH A GODDAMN MOTHER.
GO BACK TO ODESSA AND LEAVE OUR TOWN ALONE!
IT'S ALL FUCKED ANYWAY.
WHY NOT GET ON WITH IT?

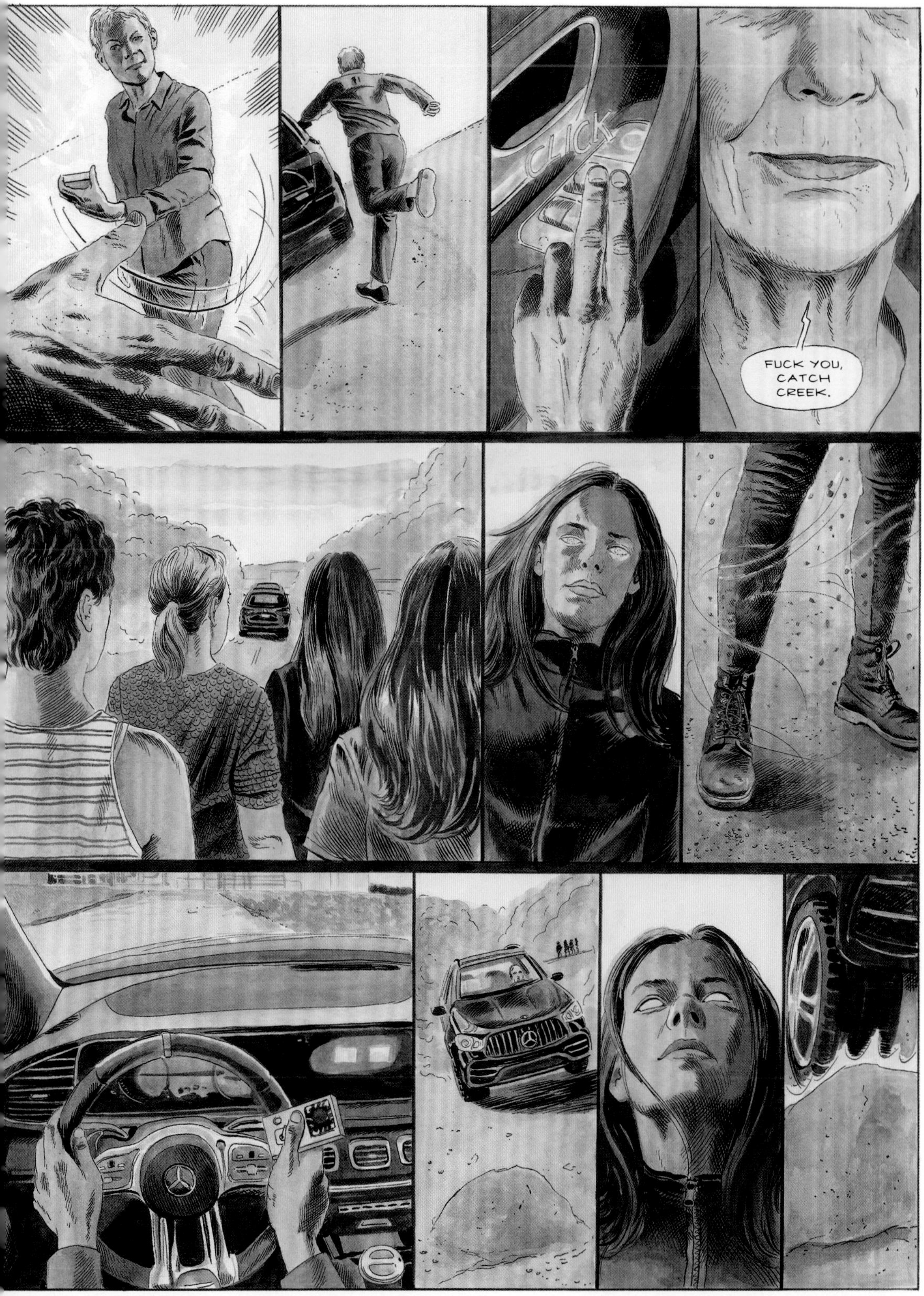
CLICK
FUCK YOU, CATCH CREEK.

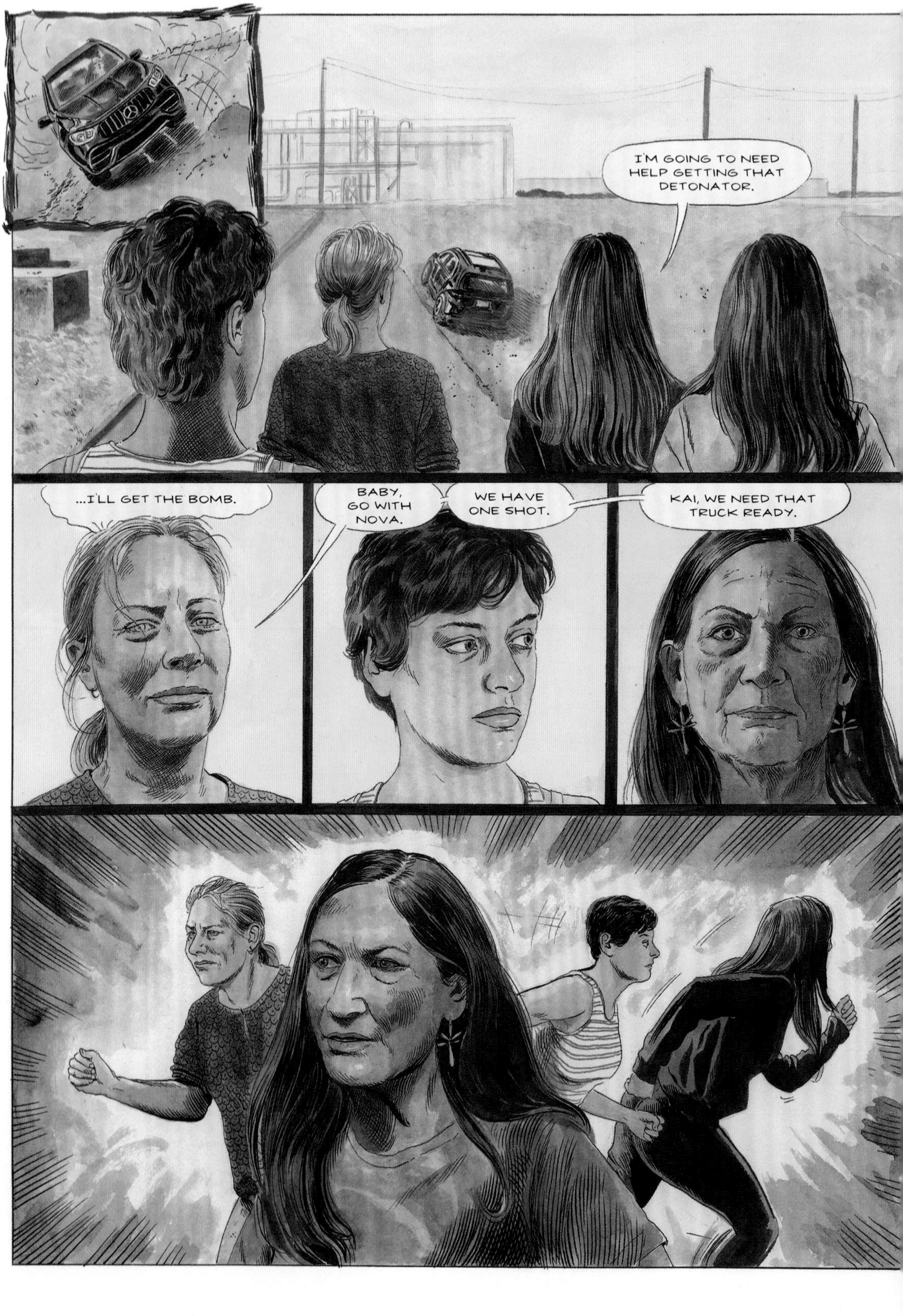
I'M GOING TO NEED HELP GETTING THAT DETONATOR.
...I'LL GET THE BOMB.
BABY, GO WITH NOVA.
WE HAVE ONE SHOT.
KAI, WE NEED THAT TRUCK READY.

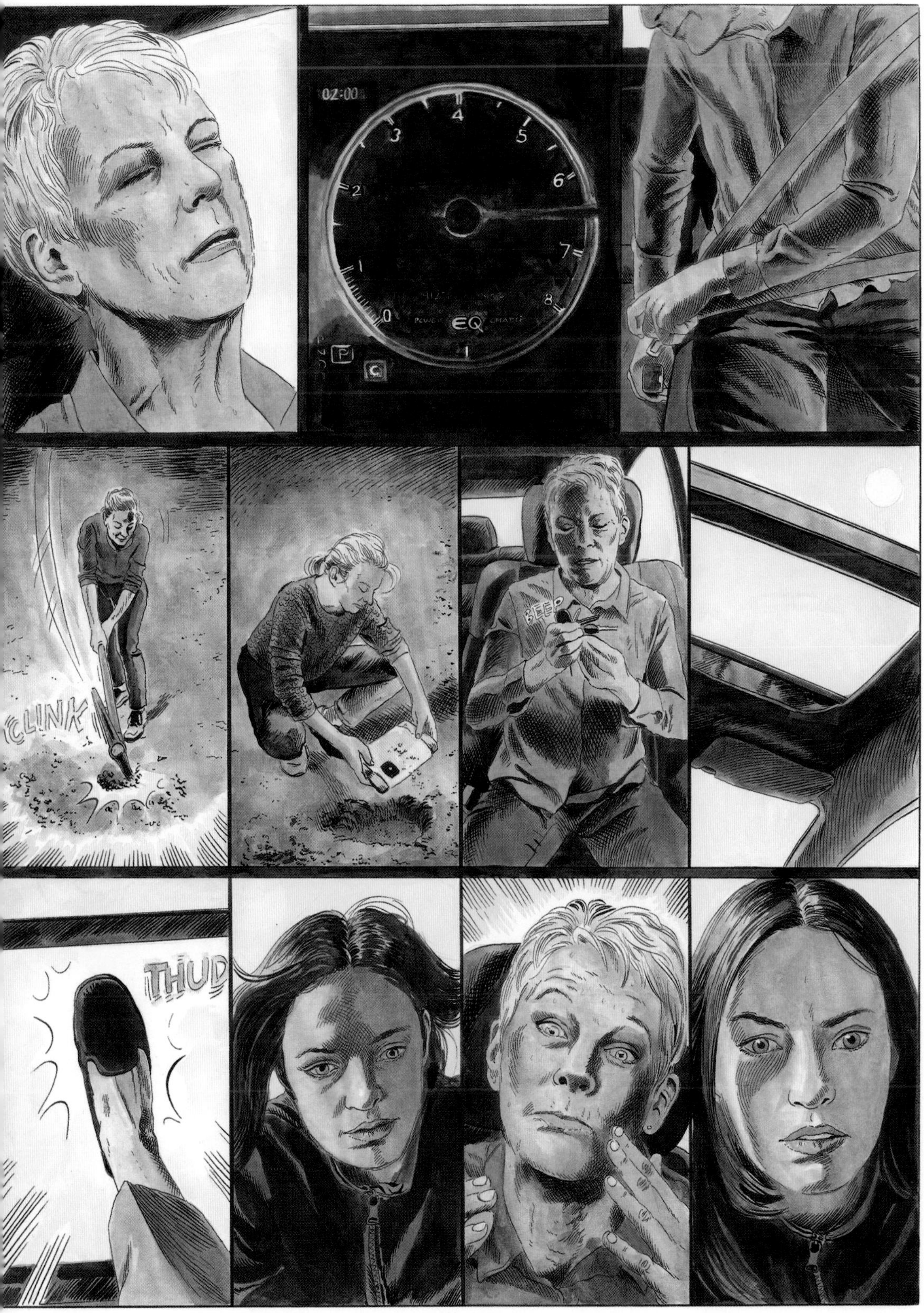
02:00
CLINK
BEEP
THUD

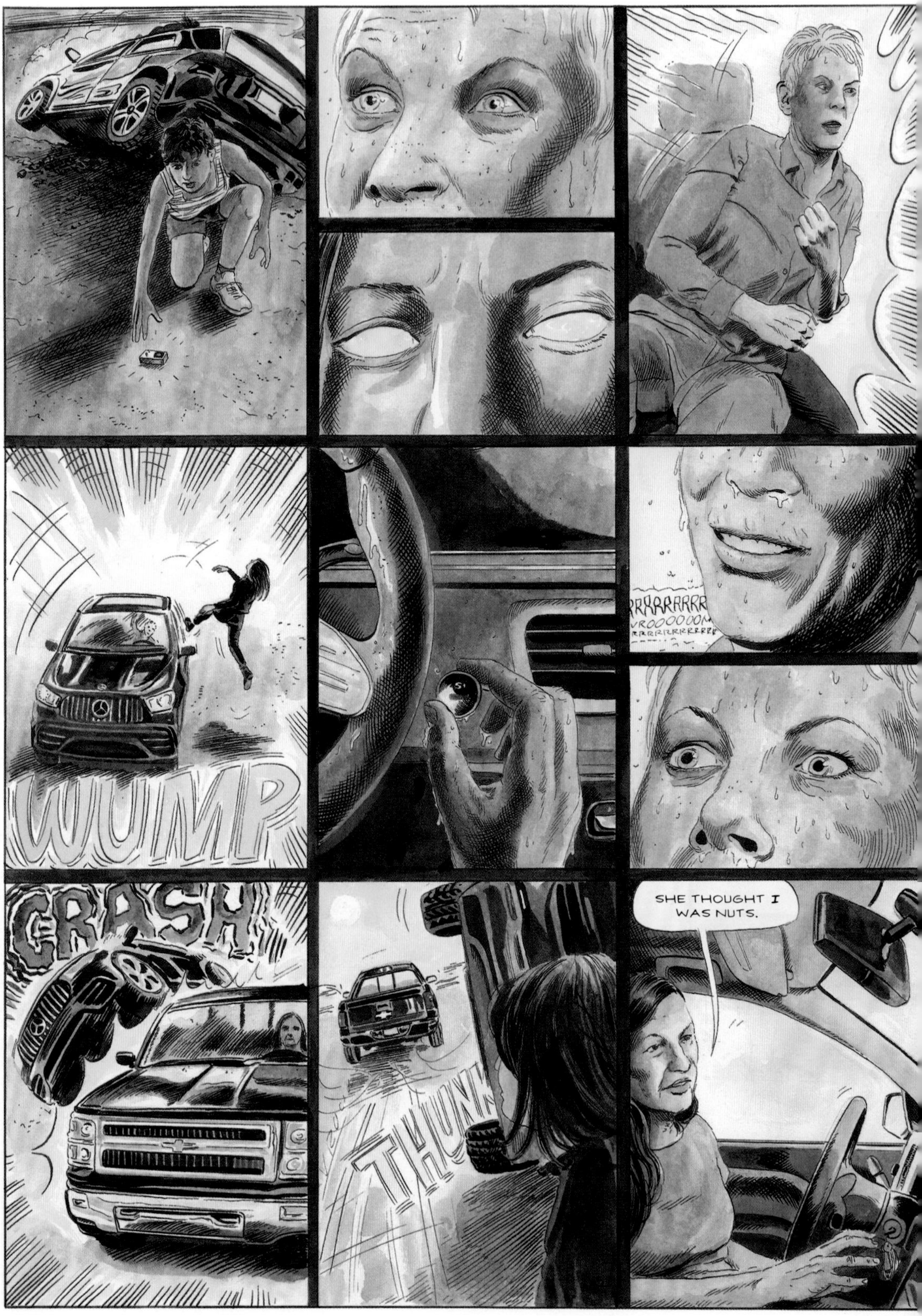
WUMP
RRRRRRRRR
VROOOOOOM
RRRRRRRRRRRRR
CRASH
THUNK
SHE THOUGHT I WAS NUTS.

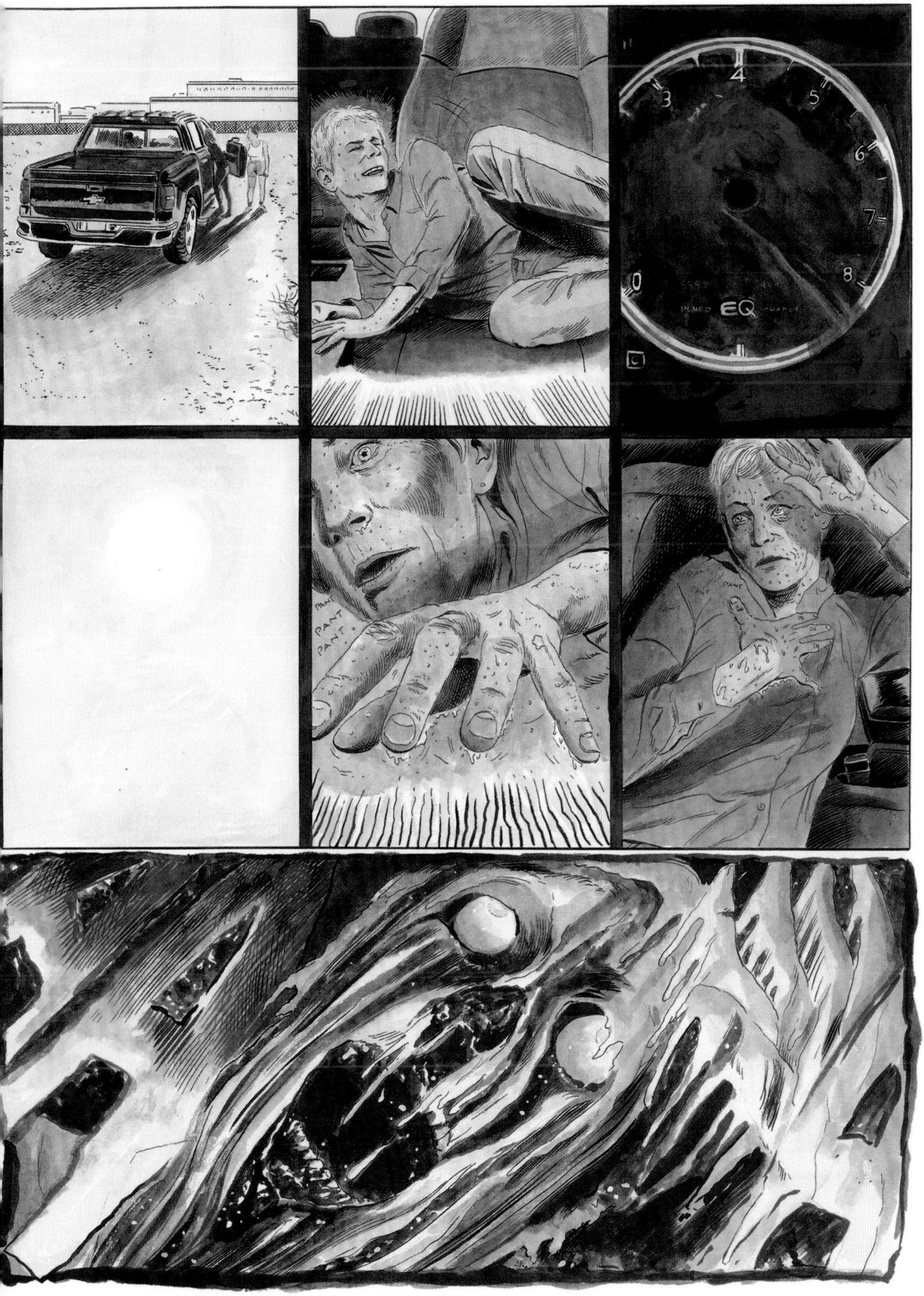
EQ
PANT
PANT
PANT
PANT
PANT
PANT

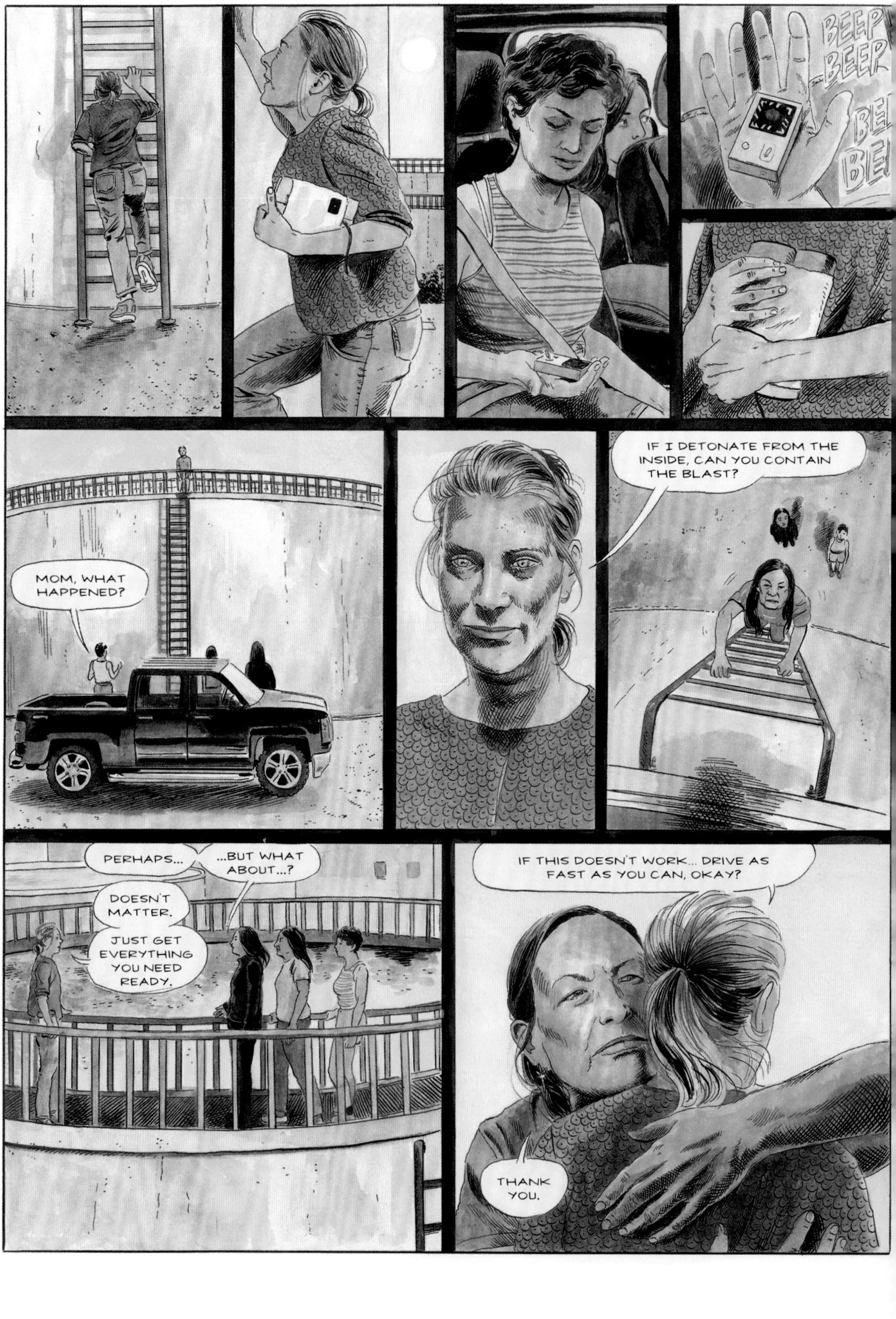
BEEP
BEEP
BE
BE
MOM, WHAT HAPPENED?
IF I DETONATE FROM THE INSIDE, CAN YOU CONTAIN THE BLAST?
PERHAPS...
...BUT WHAT ABOUT...?
DOESN'T MATTER.
JUST GET EVERYTHING YOU NEED READY.
IF THIS DOESN'T WORK... DRIVE AS FAST AS YOU CAN, OKAY?
THANK YOU.

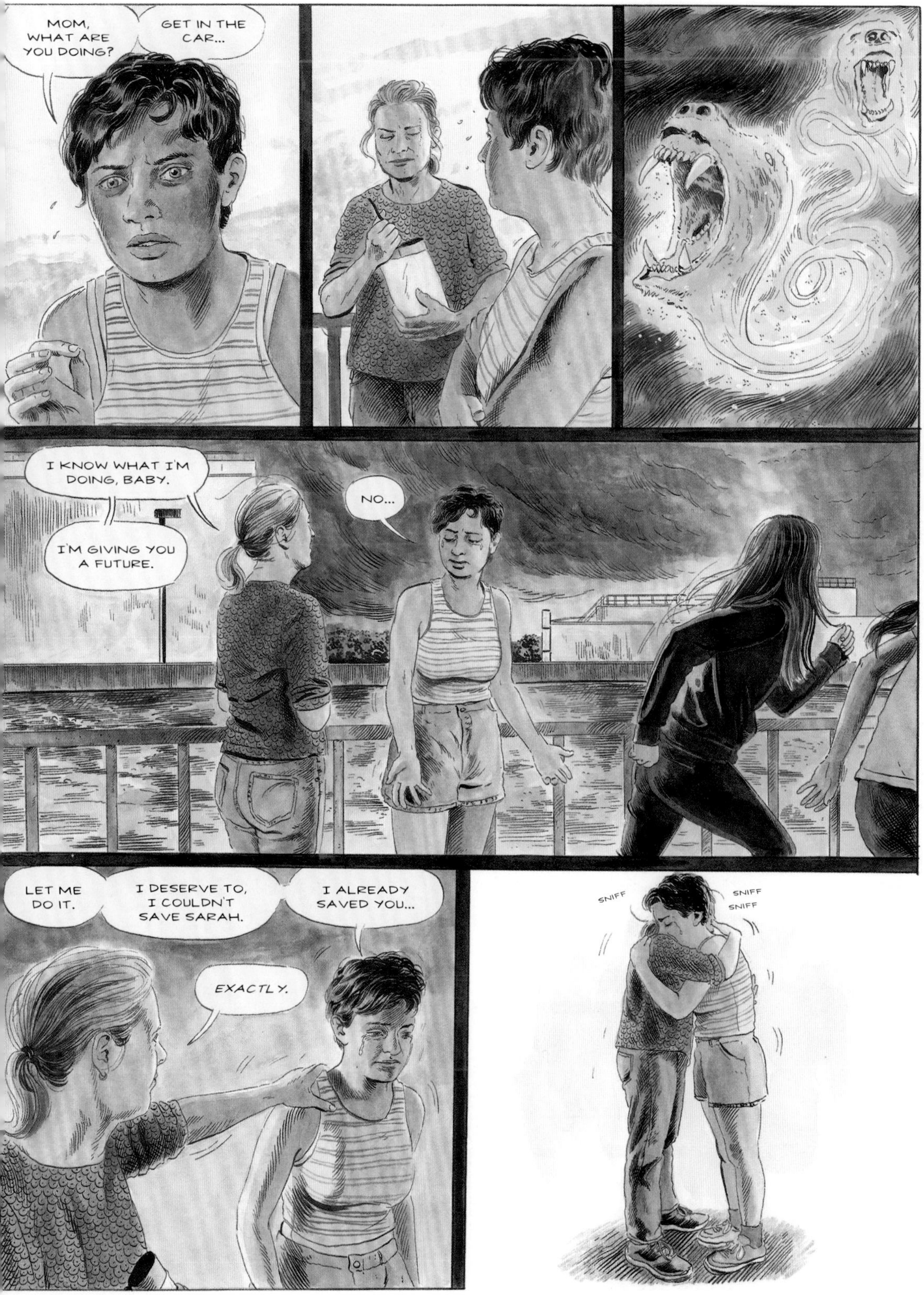
MOM, WHAT ARE YOU DOING?
GET IN THE CAR...
I KNOW WHAT I'M DOING, BABY.
I'M GIVING YOU A FUTURE.
NO...
LET ME DO IT.
I DESERVE TO, I COULDN'T SAVE SARAH.
I ALREADY SAVED YOU...
EXACTLY.
SNIFF
SNIFF
SNIFF

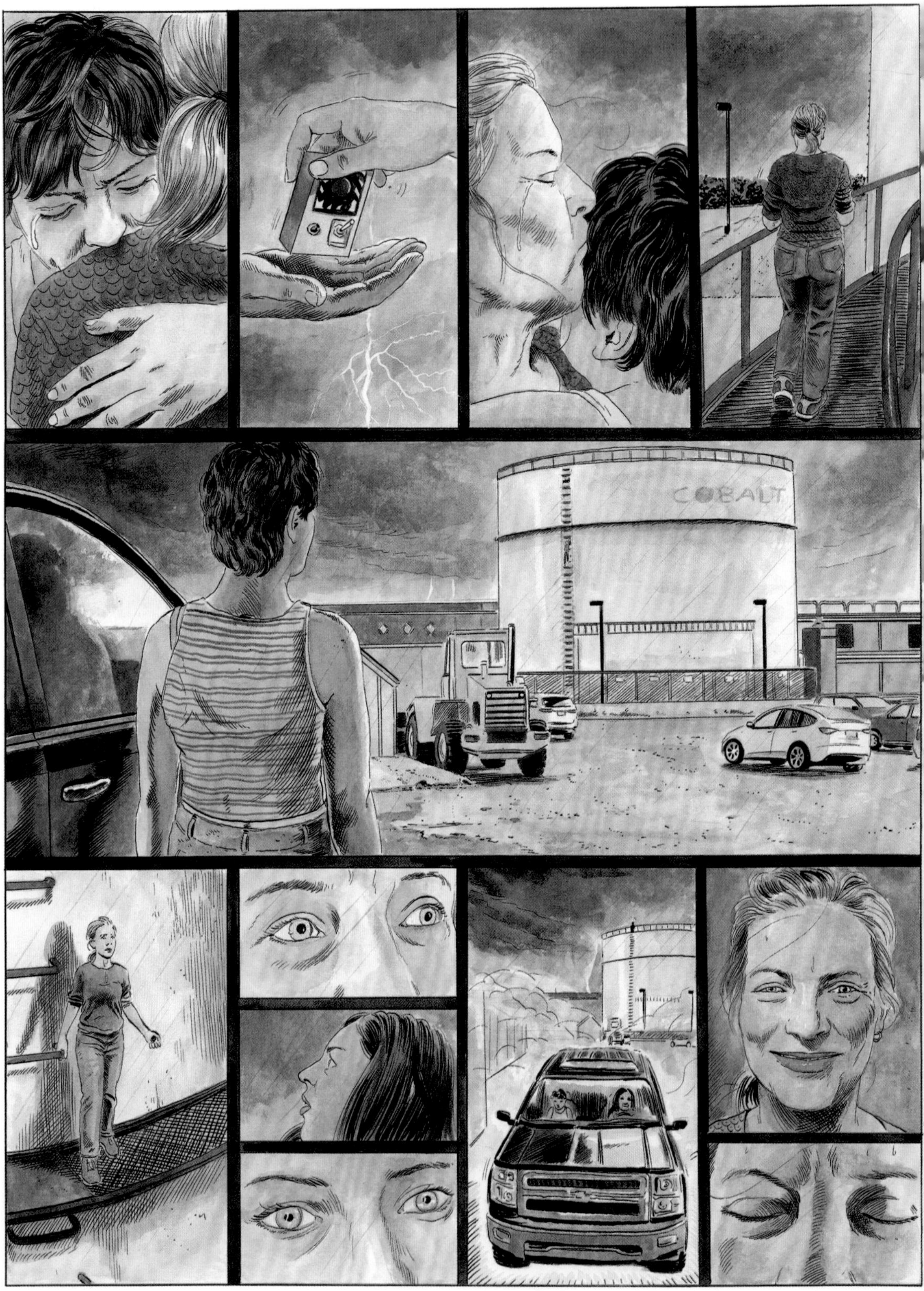
COBALT

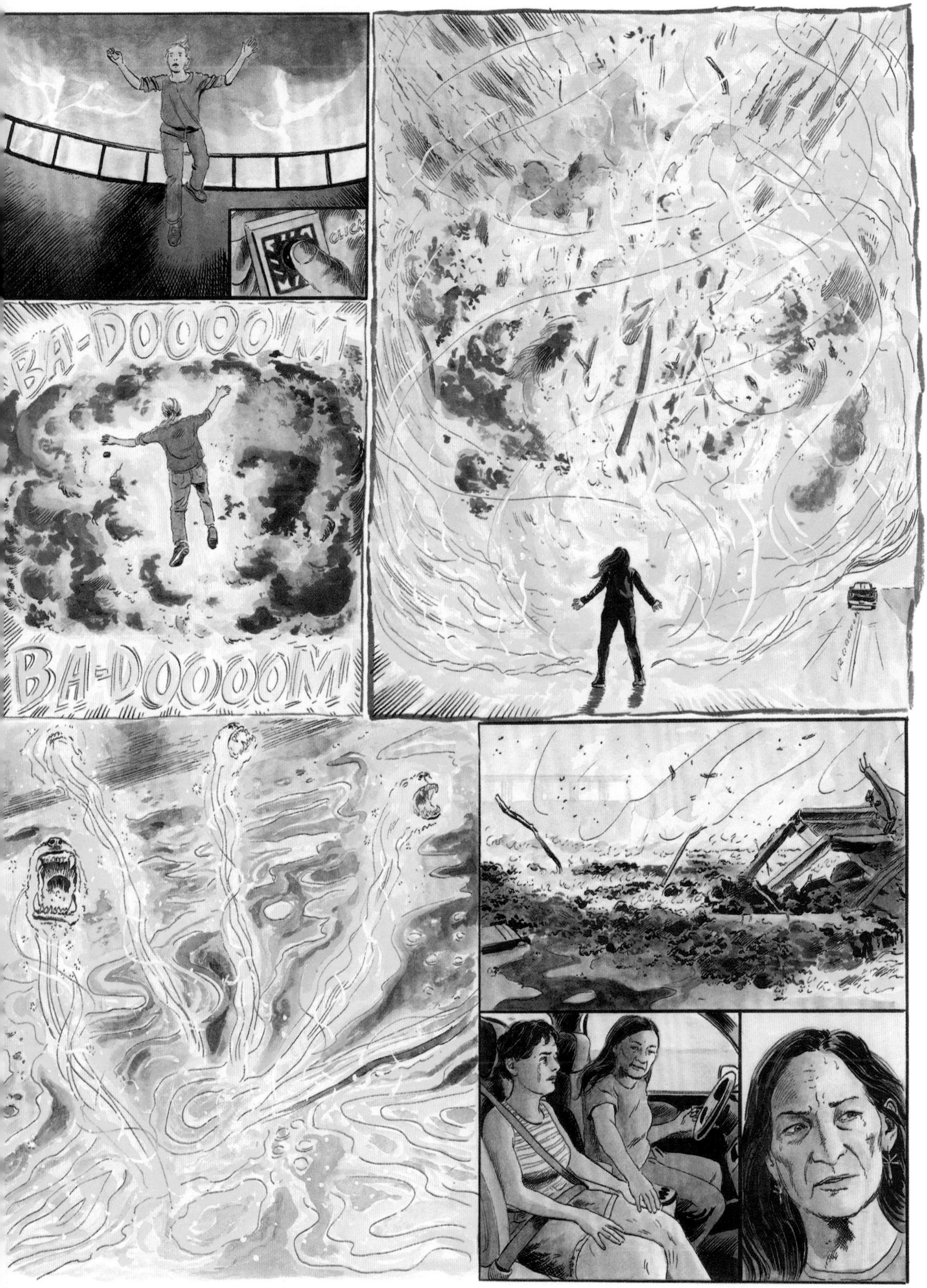

CLICK
BA-DOOOOM
BA-DOOOOM
VROOOOM

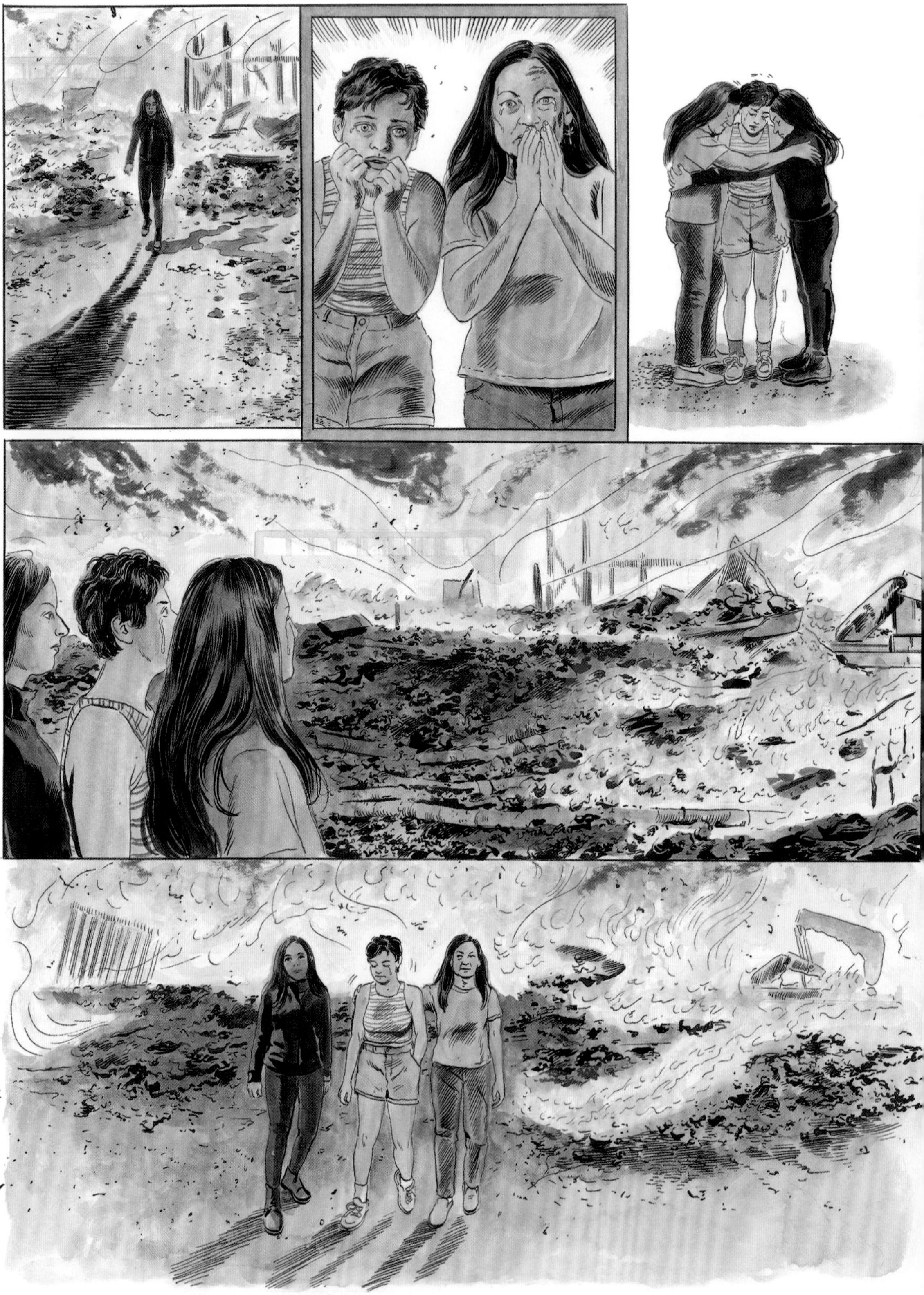

THE END

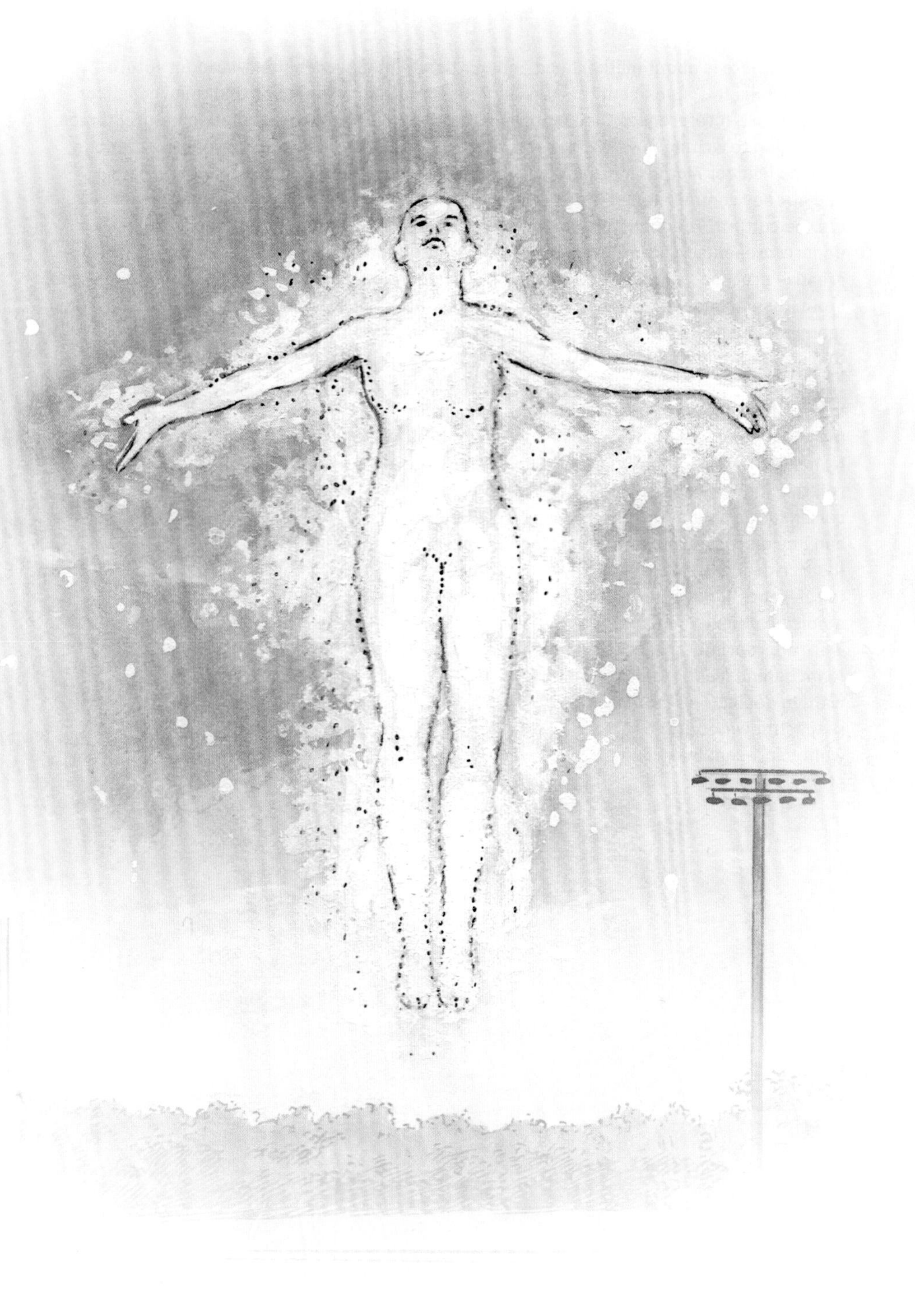

AFTERWORD

Yá'át'ééh reader,

Mother Nature is about motherhood and our desire to leave a better world for future generations. It is also about the natural forces that we have abused and repurposed for our comfort. It references Diné culture in its depictions of those retaliating natural forces. In addition to writing novels that depict my Diné culture, I also do cultural consultations, such as I did for *Mother Nature*. When I joined, I was delighted that Russell and Jamie had already commissioned Diné scholar, Jeremiah Watchman, to guide their depiction of Diné culture. The team of *Mother Nature* reflected their commitment of respect to an underrepresented culture by incorporating multiple members of that culture into the creative process from the very beginning. They demonstrated that it's not difficult to do. As I told Russell and Jamie, inviting cultural consultants as well as diverse creators onto your team isn't just a gesture of respect, it also is an opportunity to discover additional heart in the story.

I, myself, struggled when depicting my own culture in my novel, *Healer of the Water Monster*. Like many Native Nations, there are restrictions and guidelines when referencing our own cultures. For example, certain information and several Diné Holy Beings can't be discussed outside of ceremonial context. It's a critical endeavor when any artist wants to reference Diné culture. I myself interviewed medicine people to ensure that my depictions were appropriate. I feel that the creative team behind *Mother Nature* not only want to depict Diné culture in a respectful way, but they also want to present as strong a story as possible.

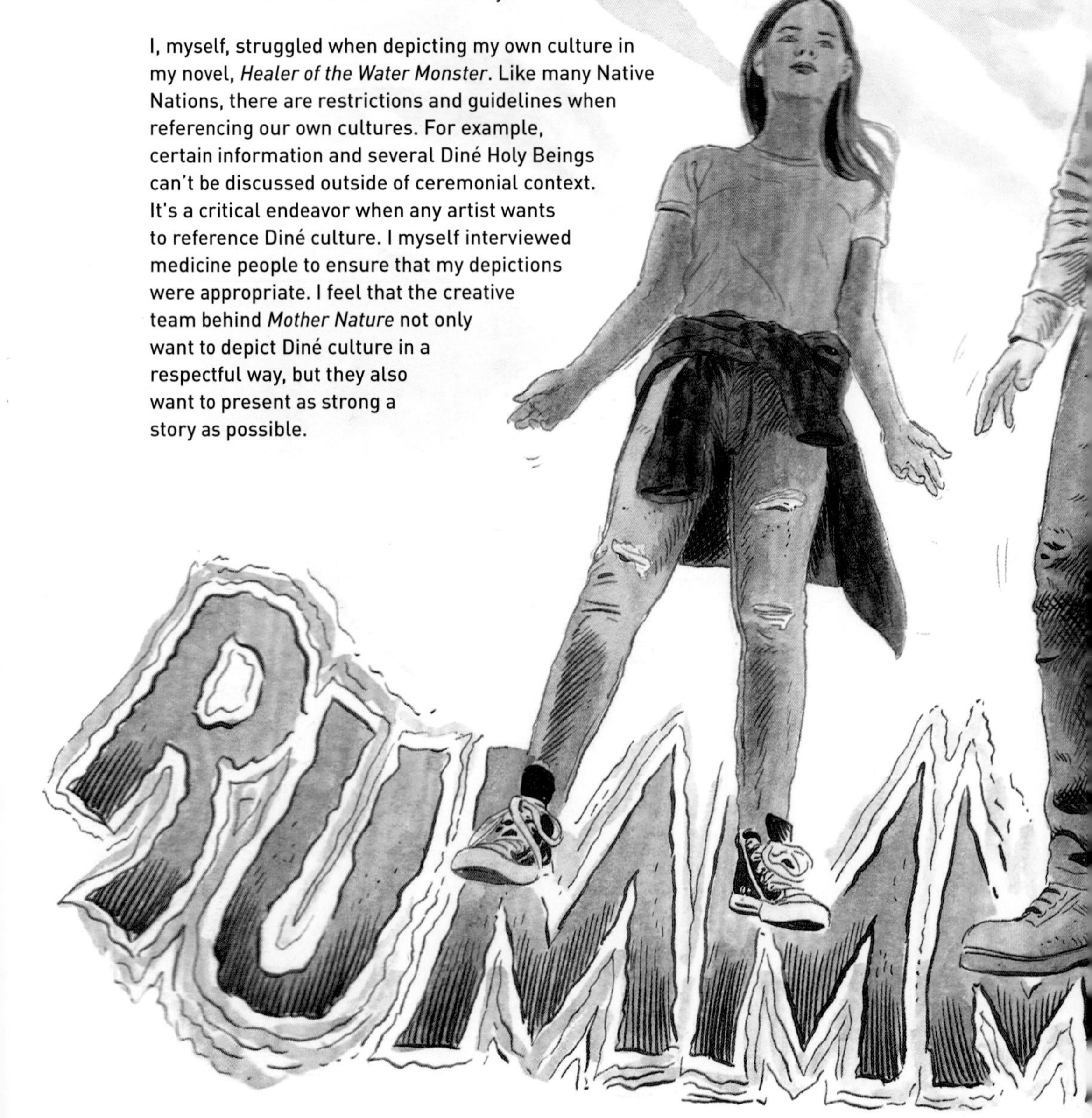

I hope more publishing teams will incorporate diverse creators into their ranks as the team at *Mother Nature* has. From a fellow fan of horror and gruesome deaths, I hope you enjoyed *Mother Nature* as well as the layered themes of motherhood, inheritance, climate change, and the hope for a better future.

'Ahéhee'
Brian Lee Young

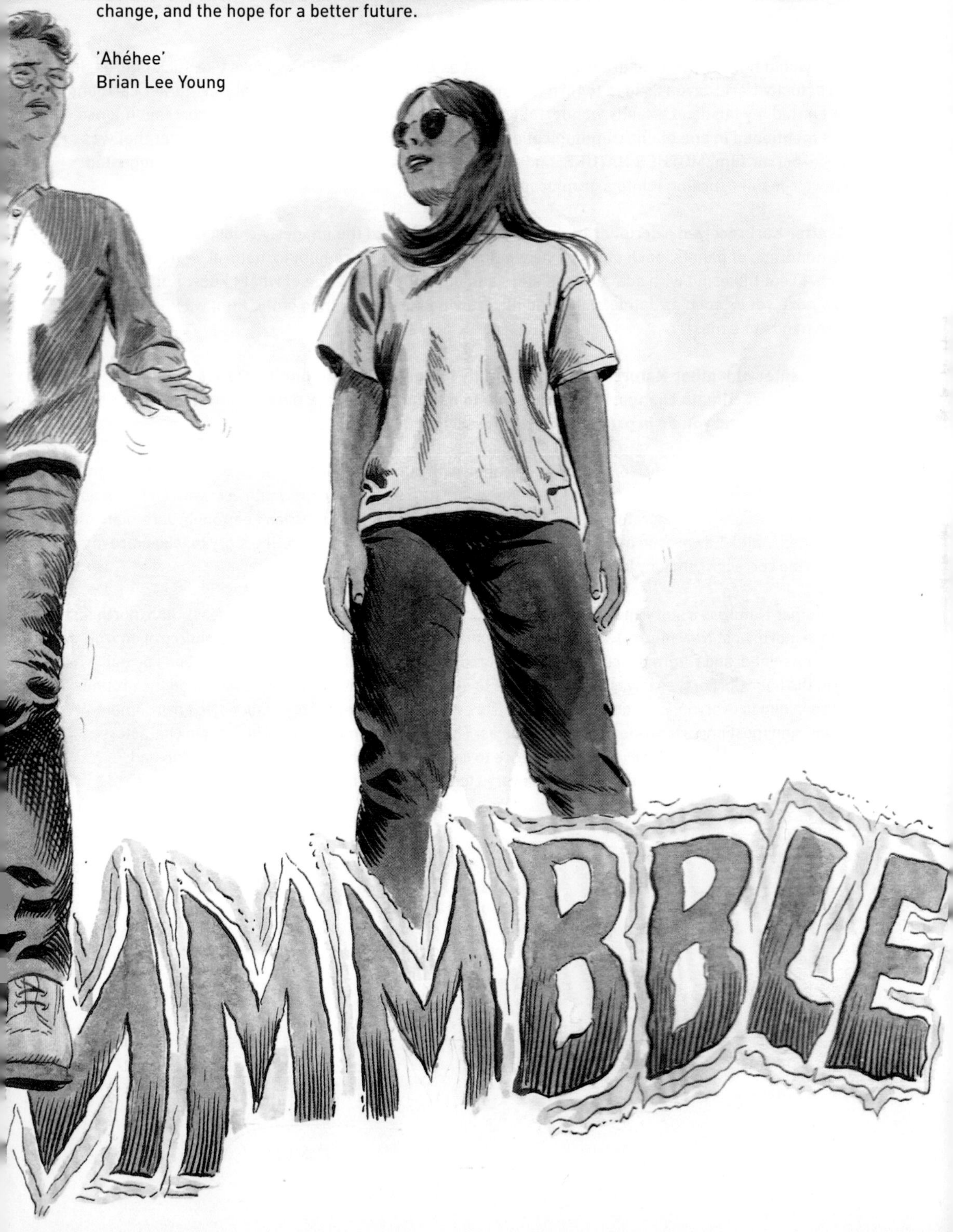
MMMBBLE

BRINGING MOTHER

WITH JAMIE LEE CURTIS AND RUSSELL GOLDMAN

Mother Nature is a graphic novel adapted from a film script. What was the artistic process behind adapting a film script into sequential art form?

JLC: I would never be able to draw a graphic novel as EVERYTHING I draw looks like stick figures. It was actually Karl Stevens's idea to turn it into a graphic novel. I collect original *New Yorker* cartoons and I gifted my husband a really wonderful Karl Stevens cartoon. We then began a correspondence and I mentioned in one of our communications that I had conceived and cowritten a script that was an eco-horror film, MOTHER NATURE, and he wanted to read it, and after reading it, he suggested that we consider turning it into a graphic novel.

RG: After Karl received a script draft, he meticulously adapted the images we described on paper into hundreds of panels, each of which he would give his signature human, natural, watercolor touch. I kept tinkering with adapting the story and dialogue in advance of what I knew Karl would draw next, yet as soon as Jamie and I read his drawings of the opening of the film, we knew we were in the hands of a master.

At the center of Mother Nature is the real fight by Indigenous communities across the United States against climate change. What drove you to making their story part of your narrative, and what research did you do in preparation for the script?

JLC: Russell handled so much of the communication with our Indigenous advisers. When I first thought of the idea for this movie at 19 years old I knew this would be a story set in the southwest with an Indigenous centerpoint. Russell collaborated with our Indigenous advisors including Brian Lee Young, Jeremiah Watchman, Aaluk Edwardson and Dale Deforest to create a lived-in world for the story to take place in as well as the correct mythology for the naayéé. It was crucial we get that right.

RG: Mother Nature is a story specific to the Four Corners (southwest Colorado, southeast Utah, northeast Arizona, northwest New Mexico). It's an amazing part of the world where every major source of energy has been mined, and where the climate and resource crises are acutely felt. Jamie, Karl and I do not live in the Four Corners, so it was our imperative to spend the last five years researching on the ground and speaking to everyone we could, from scientists employed by energy corporations, to environmental groups, and most importantly to Indigenous voices. This is an ensemble story with Navajo characters front and center. We were lucky to have a chance to collaborate with Navajo artists like Brian and Jeremiah. It took years to get this right, and every step was worth it.

NATURE TO LIFE

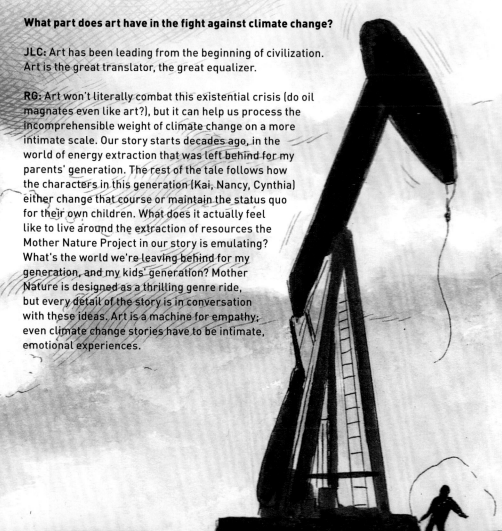

Where do you think the horror of Mother Nature lies?

JLC: I think it's all very scary. Human casualties tug at our heartstrings but the bigger, global, climate challenges tug at our morality. They are not mutually exclusive. It's dangerous. This is a dangerous time.

RG: The devastating effects we see of climate change today were caused by our impact on the environment a generation ago. The true horror to me is what the effects of our present-day impact will be a generation from now.

What part does art have in the fight against climate change?

JLC: Art has been leading from the beginning of civilization. Art is the great translator, the great equalizer.

RG: Art won't literally combat this existential crisis (do oil magnates even like art?), but it can help us process the incomprehensible weight of climate change on a more intimate scale. Our story starts decades ago, in the world of energy extraction that was left behind for my parents' generation. The rest of the tale follows how the characters in this generation (Kai, Nancy, Cynthia) either change that course or maintain the status quo for their own children. What does it actually feel like to live around the extraction of resources the Mother Nature Project in our story is emulating? What's the world we're leaving behind for my generation, and my kids' generation? Mother Nature is designed as a thrilling genre ride, but every detail of the story is in conversation with these ideas. Art is a machine for empathy; even climate change stories have to be intimate, emotional experiences.

COVER PROCESS

The evolution of the *Mother Nature* graphic novel cover image,
from its early beginnings to its final form.

Sketch

First draft

Final Bookstore Edition

Final Direct Market Edition

ART PROCESS

Award-winning artist Karl Stevens' illuminating process of illustrating the interior art pages of the *Mother Nature* graphic novel.

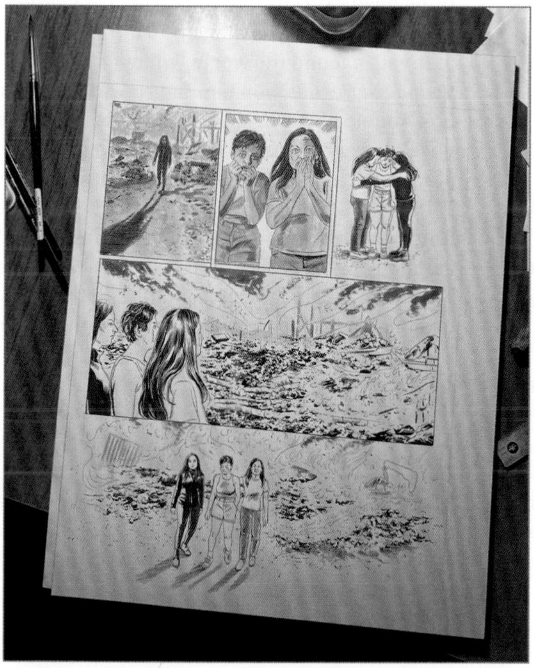

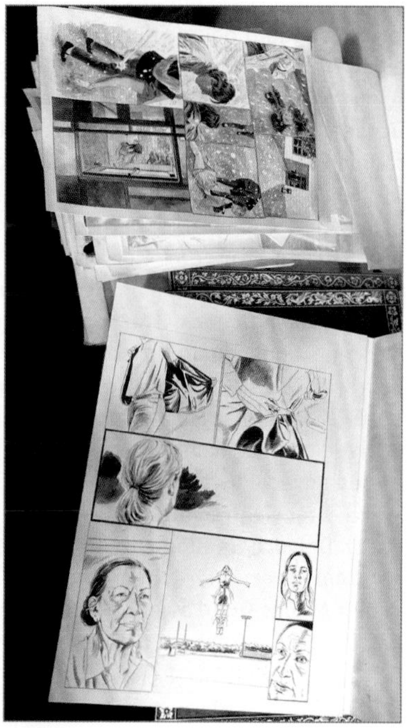

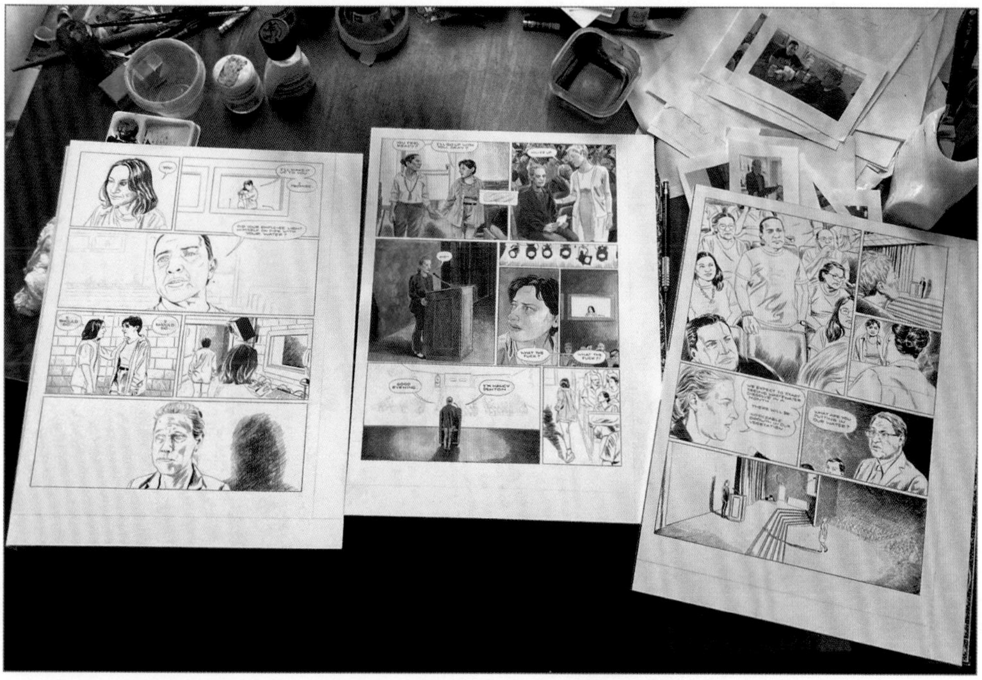

CREATOR BIOGRAPHIES

JAMIE LEE CURTIS is an American film and television actress and writer. Her debut film *Halloween* where she played the role of Laurie Strode established her as the one of the most recognized scream queens in the horror genre. Her subsequent horror films include *The Fog*, *Terror Train*, *Roadgames* and *Halloween II*. Later she excelled in the comedy genre with equal success. Some of her finest comedy films are *Trading Places*, *A Fish Called Wanda* and *True Lies*. Her noted work on television includes series such as *Operation Petticoat*, *Anything But Love*, *NCIS* and *New Girl*. Recently, she played Dean Cathy Munsch, one of the lead roles in the series *Scream Queens*. She has authored many children's books including *When I Was Little: A Four-Year-Old's Memoir of Her Youth* and *Today I Feel Silly and Other Moods That Make My Day* that received critical acclaim. Jamie Lee Curtis has bagged several awards including the Saturn Award, American Comedy Award, and for her role as Deirdre Beaubeirdre in the phenomenon *Everything Everywhere All At Once*, she won the Screen Actors Guild award and the Academy Award for Best Supporting Actress.

RUSSELL GOLDMAN hails from Virginia, USA and studied at Wesleyan University, earning a bachelor's in Film, Cinema & Video Studies. A newcomer to the world of comics, his short films have skyrocketed him to success. *Return to Sender* has played at over 30 different film festivals around the world, while *I Make Good Sounds at Parties* won him the NewFilmmakers Los Angeles award. Needless to say, his films have already garnered the attention of renowned stars such as Emmy-nominated actress Allison Tolman and pop culture icon Jamie Lee Curtis. Goldman now runs Comet Pictures, a production company founded by Curtis based in Los Angeles. Their latest project *Mother Nature* debuted as a graphic novel adapted from the upcoming Comet Pictures/Blumhouse feature film.

KARL STEVENS is a graphic novelist and painter whose comics have appeared regularly in the *New Yorker*, *Village Voice*, and *Boston Phoenix*. Stevens' graphic novels include *Whatever*, *The Lodger*, *Failure*, *The Winner*, and *Penny: A Graphic Memoir*. He lives in Boston with his wife Alex and their cats, Penny and Pepper.

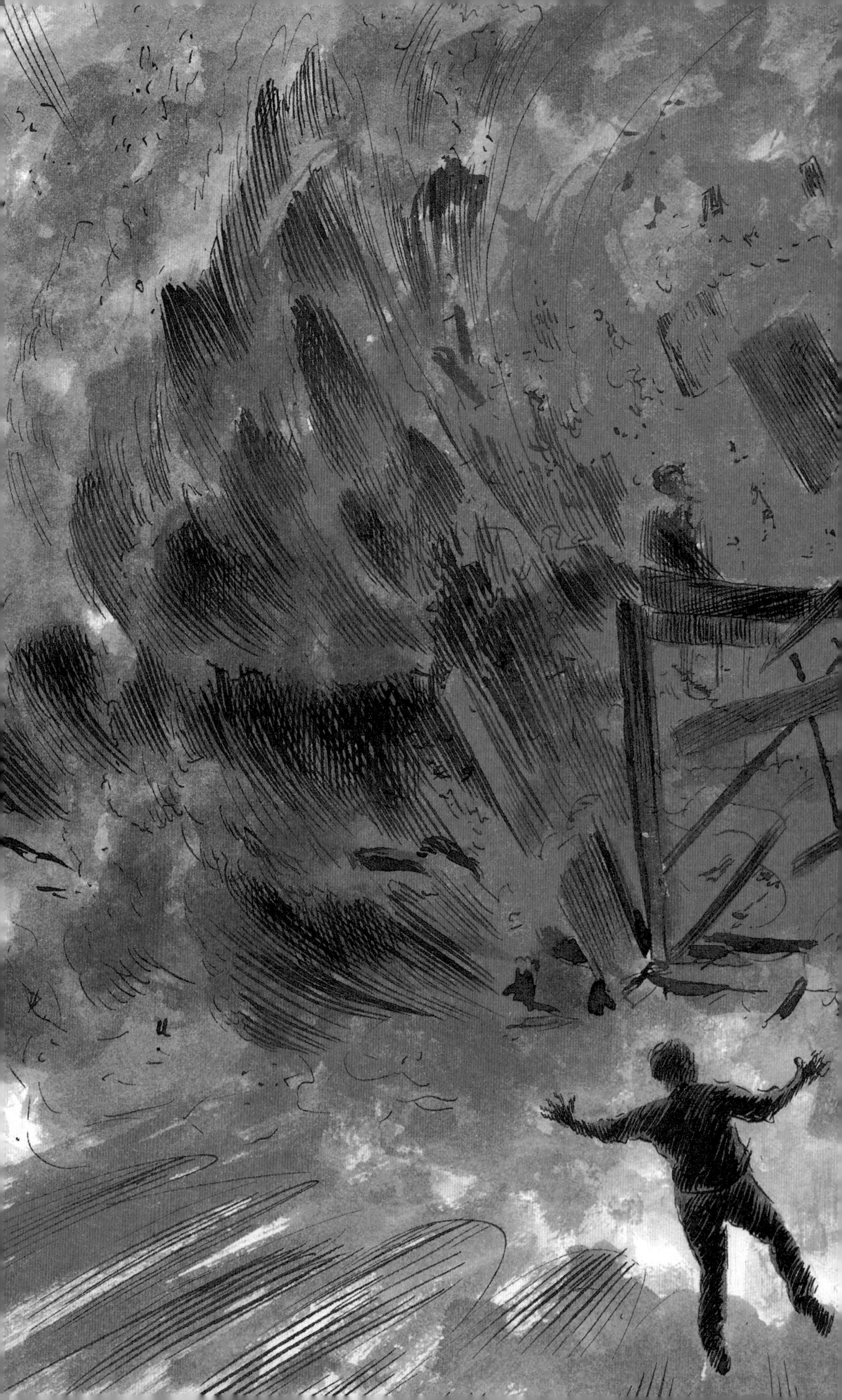